The Queen of Sheba's Gift

Edinburgh Studies in Classical Islamic History and Culture
Series Editor: Carole Hillenbrand

A particular feature of medieval Islamic civilisation was its wide horizons. The Muslims fell heir not only to the Graeco-Roman world of the Mediterranean, but also to that of the ancient Near East, to the empires of Assyria, Babylon and the Persians; and beyond that, they were in frequent contact with India and China to the east and with black Africa to the south. This intellectual openness can be sensed in many interrelated fields of Muslim thought, and it impacted powerfully on trade and on the networks that made it possible. Books in this series reflect this openness and cover a wide range of topics, periods and geographical areas.

Titles in the series include:

Arabian Drugs in Early Medieval Mediterranean Medicine
Zohar Amar and Efraim Lev

Towards a History of Libraries in Yemen
Hassan Ansari and Sabine Schmidtke

The Abbasid Caliphate of Cairo, 1261–1517
Mustafa Banister

The Medieval Western Maghrib
Amira K. Bennison

Christian Monastic Life in Early Islam
Bradley Bowman

Keeping the Peace in Premodern Islam
Malika Dekkiche

Queens, Concubines and Eunuchs in Medieval Islam
Taef El-Azhari

Islamic Political Thought in the Mamluk Period
Mohamad El-Merheb

The Kharijites in Early Islamic Historical Tradition
Hannah-Lena Hagemann

Medieval Damascus
Konrad Hirschler

A Monument to Medieval Syrian Book Culture
Konrad Hirschler

The Popularisation of Sufism in Ayyubid and Mamluk Egypt
Nathan Hofer

Defining Anthropomorphism
Livnat Holtzman

Making Mongol History
Stefan Kamola

Lyrics of Life
Fatemeh Keshavarz

Art, Allegory and The Rise of Shiism In Iran, 1487–1565
Chad Kia

The Administration of Justice in Medieval Egypt
Yaacov Lev

The Queen of Sheba's Gift
Marcus Milwright

Ruling from a Red Canopy
Colin P. Mitchell

Islam, Christianity and the Realms of the Miraculous
Ian Richard Netton

The Poetics of Spiritual Instruction
Austin O'Malley

Sacred Place and Sacred Time in the Medieval Islamic Middle East
Daniella Talmon-Heller

Conquered Populations in Early Islam
Elizabeth Urban

edinburghuniversitypress.com/series/escihc

The Queen of Sheba's Gift

A History of the True Balsam of Matarea

Marcus Milwright

EDINBURGH
University Press

Edinburgh University Press is one of the leading university presses in the UK. We publish academic books and journals in our selected subject areas across the humanities and social sciences, combining cutting-edge scholarship with high editorial and production values to produce academic works of lasting importance. For more information visit our website: edinburghuniversitypress.com

© Marcus Milwright, 2021, 2022

Edinburgh University Press Ltd
The Tun – Holyrood Road
12 (2f) Jackson's Entry
Edinburgh EH8 8PJ

First published in hardback by Edinburgh University Press 2021

Typeset in 11/15 Adobe Garamond by
Servis Filmsetting Ltd, Stockport, Cheshire

A CIP record for this book is available from the British Library

ISBN 978 0 7486 6849 6 (hardback)
ISBN 978 1 3995 0887 2 (paperback)
ISBN 978 0 7486 6850 2 (webready PDF)
ISBN 978 0 7486 6852 6 (epub)

The right of Marcus Milwright to be identified as author of this work has been asserted in accordance with the Copyright, Designs and Patents Act 1988 and the Copyright and Related Rights Regulations 2003 (SI No. 2498).

Contents

List of Figures vi
Permissions x
Acknowledgements xi
Notes for the Reader xiii
Timeline xiv

Introduction 1

1 Travellers' Tales: Experiencing Matarea 22

2 Resins in the Ancient World 53

3 Balsam in Egypt 87

4 The Balsam Tree and Balsam 'Oil' 118

5 Diplomacy and International Trade 153

6 Balsam in Medicine: From Greek to Arabic 182

7 Balsam in Medieval and Early Modern Medicine 210

8 Religious and Royal Dimensions to Balsam 241

9 Conclusion 273

Glossary 285

Bibliography 288

Index 326

Figures

I.1	Bottle of Turlington's Balsam of Life, c. 1880	4
I.2	Albarello drug jar used for 'balsam of the philosophers'	5
1.1	Fruit and flowers of *Calotropis procera*, known as 'Apples of Sodom'	24
1.2	Front cover of Michel-Marie Jullien, *L'Arbre de la Vierge à Matarie*h, fourth edition	27
1.3	Church at Matarea, Egypt, constructed from 1902	28
1.4	Chapel in the gardens of Matarea constructed by the College of Jesuits, Cairo	28
1.5	Sycamore fig in the gardens of Matarea	28
1.6	Woodcut map of Cairo from Sebastian Münster, *Cosmographia*; and detail	30–1
1.7	Illustration of the balsam tree and the walled compound of Matarea from *Tractatus de herbis* manuscript, Salerno, c. 1280–1310	32
1.8	Sketch of a manuscript illustration of the balsam tree and the walled compound of Matarea from a pharmacological manuscript including the *Tractatus de herbis*	32
1.9	Illustration of the chapel and surrounding features of the plantation of Matarea from the travel journal of Bernardino da Gallipoli	34
1.10	Water-lifting device (*sāqiya*) with the obelisk of Heliopolis and in the gardens of Matarea	34
2.1	Map of the sites associated with ancient balsam cultivation and production	54
2.2	Painted relief showing trees carried in baskets	54

2.3	Map of the ancient incense routes in Arabia and the Horn of Africa	56
2.4	View of ancient Petra, Jordan	57
2.5	Installation used in the production of perfumes, 'Ein Boqeq, Israel. After Fischer, Gichon and Tal, *'En Boqeq*	65
2.6	Installation used in the production of perfumes, 'Ein Feshka, Israel. After Dov Porotsky in Hirschfeld, 'The rose and the balsam'	66
2.7	Ceramic juglet wrapped in palm leaves found in the Qumran region	67
2.8	Obverse and reverse faces of a 'Judaea capta' *sesterce* minted by Vespasian in 71 CE	69
2.9	Relief showing the Triumph through Rome of Titus, Arch of Titus, Rome. 71 CE	70
2.10	Inscription panel on the floor mosaic of the synagogue in En-Gedi, Israel	73
2.11	Detail of the floor mosaic in the church of St George, Madaba, Jordan	74
3.1	Stereoscopic photograph of obelisk located at 'Ayn Shams (Heliopolis)	90
3.2	Sheet of papyrus	92
3.3	Map of Cairo and the surrounding areas in the medieval period	94
3.4	Qubba of Yashbak min Mahdi at al-Malaqa bi'l-Matariyya, Cairo	102
3.5	Illustration of Yashbak's palace	103
3.6	View of the Palace of Qawsun, renovated by Amir Yashbak min Mahdi, at al-Malaqa bi'l-Matariyya, Cairo	104
4.1	Balsam tree from the Arabic Dioscorides, dated 1083	127
4.2	Balsam tree being harvested	129
4.3	Balsam tree being harvested. From *Kitāb al-diryāq*	130
4.4	Balsam tree within a walled garden with guards	131
4.5	Balsam tree in the *Book of Simples* of Matthaeus Platearius	132
4.6	Woodcut illustration of a branch from a balsam tree from the 1591 edition of Prosper Alpin, *De balsamo dialogus*	133

4.7	Illustrations of the fruit and wood of the balsam tree from John Gerard, *Herball*	134
4.8	Illustration of the fruit of the balsam tree from John Gerard, *Herball*	134
4.9	Woodcut illustration of a balsam tree from Prosper Alpin, *De plantis Aegypti*	135
4.10	Illustration of a balsam tree from Pierre Pomet, *Histoire générale des drogues*	136
4.11	Illustration of a balsam tree. From Benoît de Maillet, *Description de l'Égypte*	137
4.12	Mecca balsam (*Commiphora opobalsamum*): entire plant	139
5.1	Giorgio Vasari, Lorenzo de' Medici receiving gifts from the ambassador of the Mamluk sultan	159
5.2	Reception of the Venetian ambassadors in Damascus, after 1511	160
5.3	Pilgrim ampulla, Palestine, sixth century. Museo del Duomo, Monza	166
5.4	Metal flask containing Zamzam water	166
6.1	Fragmentary head of Mithradates VI Eupator	193
6.2	Portrait of Emperor Nero from the obverse face of an *aureus*	194
6.3	Dioscorides and student holding a mandrake plant. Arabic Dioscorides	199
7.1	Diagram showing the recipe for pastilles of Hedychroum from *Kitāb al-diryāq*	222
7.2	Diagram showing the theriac of Andromachus. *Kitāb al-diryāq*	223
7.3	Pewter container for theriac, Venice	224
7.4	Theriac stamp, Venice, 1601–80	225
7.5	Drug jars for holding Mithridatium	226
7.6	Glazed albarello for storing theriac, Italy, 1641	227
8.1	Ceramic ampulla with relief images of St Menas and camels. Egypt	242
8.2	Bird-shaped gold ampulla, made in 1661 by Sir Robert Viner and the coronation spoon	254
8.3	Cornice block showing the anointing of a pharaoh, temple of Harendotes, Philae Island, Egypt	255

8.4	Samuel anointing David. Silver plate, 629–30	258
8.5	Samuel anointing David, Theodore Psalter, Constantinople, 1066	259
8.6	Drawing of a detail from an ivory plaque with baptism of Clovis, c. 850	260
9.1	Fifteenth- or sixteenth-century glazed dish set into a vault in the mosque of Nushabad, Iran	280

Permissions

I.3, 7.4 Science Museum, London.
1.1a, b, 3.6 Wikimedia Commons.
1.3 Museums Victoria, Australia.
1.5, 1.10a, 3.1 Library of Congress Prints and Photographs Division.
1.7, 8.5 British Library.
2.1, 2.3 Seyedhamed Yeganehfarzand.
2.5, 2.6, 3.3 Naomi Shields.
2.8, 4.1, 4.4, 5.1, 5.2, 5.3, 6.1, 6.3, 8.1, 8.4 Art Resource, NY.
2.10 Center for Jewish Art, Hebrew University of Jerusalem.
3.4 Victoria & Albert Museum.
4.3, 7.1, 7.2 Bibliothèque Nationale de France.
4.7, 4.8 McPherson Library, University of Victoria.
4.10, 4.11 Syndics of Cambridge University Library.
4.12, 7.3, 7.5, 7.6 Wellcome Collection, London.
5.4 Trustees of the British Museum.
Quotation on pages 121–3 Georg Olms AG-Verlag.

Acknowledgements

This book has developed over an extended period from the mid-1990s to the present. I first came across medieval descriptions of the balsam plantation of Matarea during my doctoral studies in the Oriental Institute in Oxford, and have continued to collect evidence ever since. Other projects have come and gone over more than two decades, but I have always kept in mind the need to create a book-length treatment of balsam. Over the years I have accumulated many scholarly debts, and it is a pleasure to acknowledge them here (with apologies offered to anyone I have inadvertently missed from these lists).

I am deeply grateful to Emilie Savage-Smith for her enthusiastic support of this project, and for sharing her immense knowledge of Islamic medicine. Many others in Oxford also kindly offered their time and expertise, including Jeremy Johns, Julian Raby, James Allan, Robert Thompson, Sebastian Brock, Emmanuel Papoutsakis, Luitgard Mols, Ruba Kana'an, Chase Robinson, Jos van Lent and Martha Repp. I am especially indebted to Evanthia Baboula for her close reading of earlier drafts of chapters and for translating and commenting upon passages of ancient and modern Greek.

I have benefited from insights and information provided by many other scholars, curators and archivists over the last two decades. My thanks to Venetia Porter, Charles Burnett, Adrienne Mayor, Doris Behrens-Abouseif, Fahmida Suleman, Shamma Boyarin, Moshe Fischer, Katia Cytryn-Silverman, Orit Peleg, Domniki Papadimitriou, Ellen Kenney, Iain Higgins, Hélène Cazes, Zahra Kazani and my colleagues in the Department of Art History and Visual Studies and the Program for Medieval Studies in the University of Victoria. None of the people listed above are, of course, responsible for the errors or omissions in this book.

Photographs, maps and diagrams in the book were created by Iona

Hubner, Seyedhamed Yeganehfarzand and Naomi Shields. Mary Milwright read and annotated drafts of several chapters. The anonymous reviewer offered numerous helpful criticisms of an earlier draft of the book. I am grateful also for the guidance and wise advice provided by Nicola Ramsey at Edinburgh University Press and Carole Hillenbrand, the editor of the Edinburgh Studies in Classical Islamic History and Culture series. Parts of the research were supported by a fellowship with the Harold Hyam Wingate Foundation, a Frances A. Yates Scholarship at the Warburg Institute and a Social Sciences and Humanities Research Council Internal Research Grant at the University of Victoria.

This book would not have been possible without the love and support of my family. I dedicate this study to my children, Loukas and Clio.

Notes for the Reader

The transliteration of Arabic follows the conventions employed in the *International Journal of Middle East Studies*. Dotted consonants and long vowels are not, however, included for personal names and toponyms. English spellings are employed for well-known towns and cities (Cairo, Jerusalem, Mecca, Medina and so on). For personal names in Greek I have adopted the forms that most commonly appear in academic publications.

Timeline

1971–1926 BCE: Rule of Senusret I.
1481–1472 BCE: Reign of Hatshepsut as Queen Regent of Egypt.
1353–1336 (or 1351–1334 BCE): Rule of Akhnaten.
971–931 BCE: Approximate dates of the rule of King Solomon.
586 BCE: End of the Jewish monarchy.
336–323 BCE: Rule of Alexander the Great.
140–37 BCE: Hasmonean dynasty.
119–63 BCE: Approximate dates of the rule of Mithradates VI Eupator, king of Pontus.
51–30 BCE: Rule of Cleopatra VII Philopator.
37 BCE–92 CE: Herodian dynasty.
31 BCE: Battle of Actium.
27 BCE–14 CE: Rule of Augustus.
54–68 CE: Rule of Nero.
66: Beginning of the first Jewish Revolt.
69–79: Rule of Vespasian.
70: Destruction of the Temple in Jerusalem.
79–81: Rule of Titus.
106: Roman conquest of the Nabataean empire.
132–6: Bar Kokhba Revolt.
272: Roman conquest of Palmyra.
508: Baptism of the Merovingian king Clovis I (r. 488–511).
618–907: T'ang dynasty of China.
632: Death of the Prophet Muhammad.
640–1: Conquest of Roman Babylon and the foundation of the Arab garrison town of Fustat.

661–750: Umayyad caliphate.
749–1258: Abbasid caliphate.
768–814: Rule of Charles the Great (Charlemagne).
868–905: Tulunid dynasty of Egypt.
871–99: Rule of Alfred the Great, king of Wessex.
935–69: Ikhshidid dynasty of Egypt.
969: Foundation of the Fatimid city of al-Qahira (Cairo). Fatimid rule in Egypt, 969–1171.
1085: Capture of Toledo during the *Reconquista*.
1099: Capture of Jerusalem during the First Crusade.
1171–1250: Ayyubid sultanate in Egypt (in Syria, 1174–1260).
1250–1517: Mamluk sultanate in Egypt (in Syria, 1260–1516).
1291–1327: Rule of Jaime II, king of Aragon.
1310–41. Third reign of the Mamluk sultan al-Nasir Muhammad ibn Qalawun.
1327–36: Rule of Alfonso IV, king of Aragon.
1346–7: First outbreaks of the Black Death in the Middle East and Europe.
1487: Embassy between Sultan Qaytbay (r. 1468–96) and Lorenzo de' Medici (r. 1469–92) of Florence.
1496: Destruction of trees and buildings in the garden of Matarea.
1517: Ottoman conquest of Egypt.
1615: Death of the last balsam tree in Matarea.
1696: Death of the sycamore fig in Matarea.
1761–7: Danish Arabia expedition led by Pehr (Peter) Forsskål.
1798–1801: Napoleonic campaign in Egypt and Syria.
1800: Battle of Heliopolis.
1883: Construction of a chapel in Matarea by College of Jesuits in Cairo.
1906: Death of the second sycamore fig tree in Matarea.

Introduction

In the last days of March 1611 George Sandys (d. 1644) rode to Matarea, about 8 km to the north-east of the Egyptian capital of Cairo. This trip was about midway through a long journey that had begun in Venice in August of the previous year. He sailed to the island of Zakynthos, onward to the Peloponnese and from there via the Greek islands to Troy and Istanbul (Constantinople). The next stage of his journey took him from the capital of the Ottoman empire to the islands of Patmos, Kos and Rhodes, before landing on the Egyptian coast at Alexandria. Like many travellers before him, he was fascinated by the teeming metropolis of Cairo, the Nile river and the antiquities of Egypt. Matarea was another popular stop on the itineraries of European visitors, and was often used as the point of departure for the arduous journey that led through the Sinai to the Holy Land.

What Sandys found when he got to Matarea was a compound contained within a mud-brick wall. The land within owed its fertility to a well, the water of which was drawn to the surface by buffalo and fed into a cistern. From this cistern a channel ran towards a marble basin within a small chapel. This chapel – which the author claims had been 'spitefully defiled' by the Muslims – contained a plaque made of porphyry. The cistern also watered an orchard, within which was an ancient fig tree, the trunk pierced by a hole large enough for a small child to pass through. Sandys saves the greatest attraction of the garden until the end, writing:

> But I abuse my time, and prouoke my Reader. In an inclosure adioyning, they shewed vs a plant of Balme: the whole remainder of that store which this orchard produced: destroyed by the *Turks*, or enuie of the *Iewes*, as by them reported: being transported out of *Iury*, in the daies of *Herod* the

Great, by commandment of *Antonius*, at the suite of *Cleopatra*: but others say, brought hither out of *Arabia Felix*, at the cost of the *Saracen Sultan*.¹

These famous trees were the sole source of the 'oil' of balsam (known in Latin as *opobalsamum* and in Greek as *bálsamon*) and other valued products. Sandys claims an ancient pedigree for these plants, having been brought from the Holy Land in the time of Herod the Great (r. 37–4 or 1 BC), but counters this with the contrary opinion that the trees were actually brought by the sultan from the Yemen (Arabia Felix). Uncertainty concerning the provenance of the balsam trees of Matarea is common in medieval and early modern descriptions of the site. The year 1615, when Sandys' travel journal was first published, also marked the demise of the last balsam tree in the plantation of Matarea.² In fact, the trees had long been in poor health, a problem that can be traced back to the last two decades of the Mamluk sultanate of Egypt and Syria (1250–1517). Repeated attempts by the Ottoman governors of Egypt to restock the plantation failed to produce long-term results and the numbers of trees dwindled. At the beginning of the seventeenth century only a handful remained, a state of affairs wistfully recorded by several travellers. The poor management of the site by the Turkish authorities remained a theme in later writing: for example, Claude Étienne Savary (d. 1788) remarks, 'This precious plant is lost in Egypt, where the Pachas remain too short a time to employ themselves about anything but their own interest . . . At this day it is scarcely in remembrance'.³

In fact, balsam was far from forgotten in European scholarship. The Swiss botanist Prosper Alpin (or Alpinus, d. 1617) penned an entire book on the subject, *De dialogus balsamo*, published in Venice in 1591. The Latin edition was subsequently reprinted in 1615, with a French translation by André Colin (*Histoire du baulme*) appearing four years later.⁴ The *Histoire du baulme* (1619) even contained a versed prologue that praised balsam as an 'ornament of the Levant' and bemoaned its loss to the world. The poem concluded with the sentiment that trees could be brought from the Americas to revive the Egyptian garden.⁵ Interest in balsam continued through the seventeenth and eighteenth centuries.⁶ The botanist and father of modern scientific nomenclature, Carl Linnaeus (d. 1778), commissioned his student, Pehr (or Peter) Forsskål (d. 1763) to travel to Arabia in search of this, and other plants mentioned in the Bible.[7] Forsskål was one of several members of this ill-fated expedition to die in the Yemen, but he recorded the discovery near to the town of Uday of a single example of a tree that he believed was the source of *opobalsamum* (Chapter 4).[8]

If one surveys geographical, historical, pharmacological and medical literature of the Islamic world, it becomes apparent that balsam (Arabic: *balasān*) was held in great regard by members of the literate elite. The Egyptian chronicler Ibn Iyas (d. c. 1523) tells us that in his time, finest *balasān* was traded for its weight in gold.[9] This high price tag reflected its intrinsic rarity and the high demand for balsam of Matarea (known in Arabic as Matariyya) in both the Middle East and Christian Europe. The political value of balsam was also widely understood: from at least the late twelfth century, the gardens of Matarea were under the direct ownership of the sultan of Egypt, who also controlled the supply of the products extracted from the trees (Chapters 3 and 5).

Why did balsam exert such a hold over the imaginations of European and Muslim writers through the medieval period? Certainly, this seems a little strange when one considers that the current usages of the English words 'balsam' and 'balm' hardly bring to mind the sense of wonder and rarity found in medieval literature. Rather, these terms now have the generic meaning of something that will soothe or heal. In the hackneyed vocabulary of modern advertising, balsam and balm appear as part of the titles of shampoos, toilet paper and mild over-the-counter medicines. The practice of applying grandiose labels such as 'balm of Gilead' to cheap commercial medicines can be traced considerably earlier, a memorable instance of this genre being a pamphlet printed in Derby in about 1810 entitled *To the weak, the relaxed and debilitated, Solomon's cordial balm of Gilead is an invaluable restorative*. An earlier medicine, 'Turlington's Balsam of Life', received a royal patent from George II (r. 1727–60) and advertised its curative qualities in a pamphlet printed in London in 1750. The creator of this much praised tonic, Robert Turlington (d. 1767), drew upon the witnessed testimony of those who had experienced its benefits. For the substantial sum of three shillings and sixpence a bottle, purchasers could expect to be relieved of ailments including stomach and back pain, rheumatism, kidney stones, bowel disorders, colic, gout, pleurisy, trembling, whooping cough, high fever and low

Figure I.1 (a) and (b). Bottle of Turlington's Balsam of Life, c. 1880. 7 × 3.4 × 2.1 cm. Captions read: (front face) BY THE KINGS ROYAL PATENT GRANTED (back face) ROB.T. TURLINGTON FOR HIS INVENTED BALSAM OF LIFE. Inscriptions on the sides read: LONDON and JAN[UAR]Y. Collection of the author. Photographs: Iona Hubner.

spirits. Applied to wounds, 'Turlington's Balsam of Life' both healed and disinfected (Fig. I.1a and b).[10]

The understanding of balsam as a sort of panacea occurs in poetry, such as John Donne's (d. 1631) *Twickenham Garden*,[11] as well as in more surprising contexts; for example, in chapter 11 of *The Compleat Angler* Izaak Walton (d. 1683) observes of the tench that it 'carries a natural Balsome in him to cure both himself and others'. The author also asserts that pike refrain from eating or injuring this fish 'because the *Pike* being sick or hurt by any accident, is cured by touching the *Tench*'.[12] For these reasons tench was often more valued in Walton's time for its supposed medicinal qualities than for eating. This notion of the bodies of animals and humans

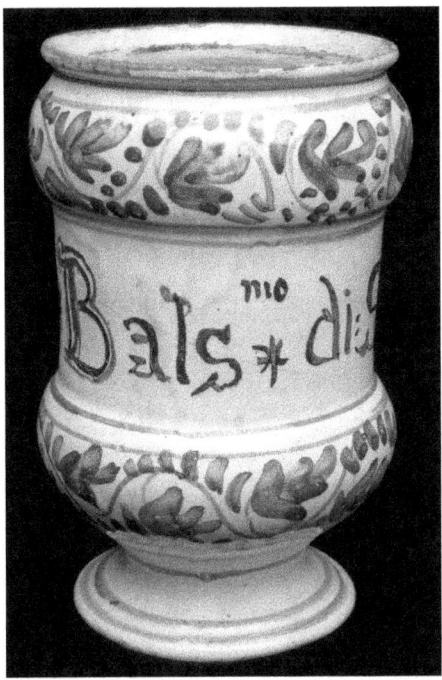

Figure I.2 Albarello drug jar used for 'balsam of the philosophers', from Liguria, eighteenth century. Science Museum, London. Attribution 4.0 International (CC BY 4.0).

containing a natural balsam may draw upon Paracelsian medicine, and particularly the work of Petrus Severinus (Peder Sørenson, d. 1602). In his major work, the *Idea medicinae philosophicae* (1571), there is the claim that 'general cures' operate because they contain a balsam that strengthens the 'natural balsam' of the patient, as well as driving out the disease. The author also develops the idea of vital balsam, containing semina (literally seed, but referring to the component that permits bodies to be generated from spirit), that distinguishes living bodies from dead or inert matter.[13] An anonymous English work, *Philiatros*, published in 1615, directly cites Severinus and his 'Balsome of Nature', and expresses the wish to find a 'Catholique Medecine; that is, such a Medecine as in all cases might furnish that Seede or Balsum, with hability against all sorts of Diseases'.[14] Glazed vessels were also produced in Italy for storing alchemical preparations such as 'balsam of the philosophers', also known as 'balsam of wisdom' and, more prosaically, 'brick oil' (Fig. I.2).[15]

Healing connotations are also a feature of the Arabic word *balasān*; a Jordanian friend informed me that her grandmother would say of her doctor when he came to visit, 'his hands are like the balsam'.[16] In literature as diverse as poetry and church sermons one finds these qualities of balsam employed in similar metaphorical senses.[17] The Spanish Jewish poet Judah al-Harizi (d. 1235) evokes the notion of a 'balm' that would cure love-sickness in his poem the *Tahkemoni*.[18] This theme is also developed by al-Hamdani (d. 945) in his description of the pre-Islamic palace of Ghumdan in Yemen; the sight of this lofty structure is, he claims, like 'pouring balsam on the aching heart'.[19] The scent of balsam could also provide the outward sign of a miraculous intervention; for example, St Gregory of Tours (d. 594) claims that sailors caught in a fierce storm had prayed to St Martin, and had then detected the perfume as the saint calmed the sea.[20]

This book tries to answer the question posed above by presenting an account of the history of the trees of Matarea and of the plantations that existed before the trees were brought to Egypt. The book explores the many texts outlining the uses to which the products of the balsam trees were put in the antique and medieval periods, and the ways in which this knowledge was transferred between authors writing in Greek, Arabic, Latin and a range of other languages. Before embarking on this inquiry, however, it is important to address the fundamental difficulty: how is one to distinguish between the generic or metaphorical employments of the words 'balsam' and 'balm', and the highly valued 'oil' that was harvested from the trees of Matarea? A much fuller answer to this will be presented later, but some preliminary observations can be offered here. First, it is clear from the written sources of the antique and medieval periods that the products from the trees of Matarea commanded far higher prices than any comparable 'balsams' or 'balms' from other localities (Chapter 4). Texts containing recipes for medicines sometimes specify substitutes for the most expensive ingredients, and one can reasonably infer that most pharmacologists and physicians regarded the balsam of Matarea as the product of choice. Second, it was not merely the real, or perceived, qualities of the balsam of Matarea that generated the extraordinary level of demand (and the substantial price). One has to look to a confluence of factors, religious and historical, that led to the formulation of the idea that Matarea was the only 'true' source of balsam in the medieval world. It is in this context that one starts to appreciate the list of famous individuals – among them Mark Antony, Cleopatra, Herod the Great, Solomon, the Queen of Sheba, the Virgin Mary and Christ – whose names are so often linked, directly or indirectly, to this walled garden north-east of Cairo.

That these associations are, to modern eyes at least, as much myth as verifiable historical fact is less important than it might appear at first glance. Travellers and chroniclers of the medieval and early modern periods – even ones as educated and sophisticated as George Sandys and Ibn Iyas – did not evaluate the past in the manner of a contemporary historian. This is not to say that writers before the modern age were incapable of forming astute opinions concerning the veracity of texts or oral traditions,[21] though they certainly lacked the critical editions of primary written sources and the wider scholarly apparatus available to the historian today. Thus, what would now be regarded merely as folk tales often found their way into serious and scholarly tracts bearing on the topography or history of Matarea (Chapter 1). Well-known writers, particularly those of classical antiquity, were often accorded overwhelming credence by European travellers, their observations being repeated verbatim. This is only to state the situation for the most perceptive of writers; for many others 'fact' and 'fiction' were jumbled together and largely indistinguishable. For these reasons the first chapter of this book is devoted not to a conventional historical reconstruction of the gardens of Matarea and its forebears in Palestine, but to the representations of the site in travel writings and Coptic hagiographic literature.

Chapter 2 establishes the history of balsam prior to the creation of the plantation in Matarea. The first part of the chapter reviews the evidence for the collection, distribution and use of aromatic tree resins in the ancient world. This includes well-known substances such as myrrh and frankincense that are still available today. Difficulties arise, however, in the identification of valued resins that are described in Old Testament texts, including the 'balm' (Hebrew: ẓori) of Gilead and another substance known in Hebrew as *bosem*. Greek sources provide more solid evidence for the introduction of balsam into ancient Palestine at least from the fourth century BC. The second section reviews the literary references to balsam cultivation in the period prior to the first Jewish Revolt against the Romans in 66 CE, comparing the claims of Flavius Josephus (who relates that the trees were a gift for King Solomon) with those of botanists and geographers. This part reviews the archaeological evidence for specialised agriculture in the regions of Jericho and En-Gedi. Excavations and surveys have revealed suggestive signs that balsam and other perfumed products were processed in these areas.

The third part of Chapter 2 is concerned with the period from the suppression of the Jewish Revolt through to the end of balsam cultivation in Palestine. Economic factors can be used to explain some acts of Roman territorial expansion, and it appears as if the revenues derived from high-value crops, including balsam, made Palestine a desirable prize. Certainly, Rome was a huge market for aromatic resins and other perfumed products, and after 70 CE the Roman authorities invested heavily in the expansion of the areas given over to balsam trees. There is abundant evidence that the balsam trees were thriving in the second century, with the bulk of the profits held in the hands of the Roman state. The remainder of the chapter looks at the evidence for the decline of the balsam trees of Palestine and the transfer of specimens to Egypt, perhaps in the late fourth or fifth centuries.

The Egyptian phase lasts until the early seventeenth century, and is the subject dealt with in Chapter 3. Arabic geographers note the presence of the trees in the region (known to them as ʿAyn Shams) in the ninth century. Coptic legends associate the event much earlier with the flight of the Holy Family to Egypt (Chapter 1), though this must be understood as an attempt to lend an aura of sanctity to a locality that previously had been most strongly associated with its Pharaonic heritage. The first part of the chapter briefly reviews this ancient history, discussing both the Pharaonic remains at Heliopolis and the textual evidence for religious and scholarly activities at the site. The second part is concerned with the history of Matarea from the Islamic conquest of the seventh century through to the end of the Ayyubid sultanate in 1250. While there are references to the balsam plantations during the Fatimid period in Egypt (969–1171), it seems that it was the Ayyubids (1171–1250) who brought the precious trees under direct state control. This represented a challenge for Coptic patriarchate, and the uneasy relationship is reflected in the construction and demolition of churches at Matarea.

The next part of Chapter 3 is concerned with Matarea during the Mamluk sultanate. This appears to have been the high point in the history of the site, with balsam playing a significant role in Mamluk interactions with other polities and with the representatives of Christian denominations in Europe and the Middle East. Mamluk sultans and high officials attended the annual collection of balsam from the trees, and there is also evidence for investment in agriculture in the region. Political instability in the latter part of the fifteenth century marks the beginning of a long decline that would stretch through the first century of Ottoman rule in Egypt. The period from the Ottoman conquest in 1517 to the death of the last tree in 1615 is surveyed in the final part. While the accounts given by travellers indicate that the numbers of trees continued to dwindle through the sixteenth century, the governors of Egypt remained committed to the maintenance of the plantation, even importing new trees from Arabia. This process of repeated restocking with wild trees from the region of Mecca opens up the possibility that the balsam gathered in the sixteenth and early seventeenth centuries was different from that available in earlier times.

I have already described balsam as an 'oil', but this designation requires further attention. The finest balsam was, in fact, a type of resin (or oleo-resin) gathered by scoring into the bark of the balsam tree. This resin was then subjected to a variety of processes before it was ready for use. These issues are considered in greater detail in Chapter 4. The central issue is the identification of the species of plant found in Matarea, and before that in the plantations of Jericho and En-Gedi. This problem is, of course, made more complex by the fact that no living specimens exist today. Various species of wild tree, most notably *Commiphora gileadensis*, have been suggested as candidates, though it is clear from historical evidence that the balsam of ancient Palestine and medieval Matarea had been selectively grown and possessed qualities quite distinct from its wild counterparts. The first part of the chapter reviews the primary written descriptions of balsam, as well as the visual representations of the plant in mosaics, manuscripts and printed books.

The second part of Chapter 4 turns to botanical and ethnopharmacological research of the nineteenth and twentieth centuries in order to establish the characteristics of *Commiphora opobalsamum*, and of similar plants found in Arabia and the Horn of Africa. The third part is an attempt to reconcile the available evidence about the physical properties of the balsam trees of Palestine and Egypt and their wild forebears. This analysis pays particular attention to the detailed accounts provided by Pliny the Elder, Dioscorides and the thirteenth-century scholar ʿAbd al-Latif al-Baghdadi. The final part draws together the information concerning the collection of balsam from the trees, and of the procedures that were then employed in the creation of the refined balsam 'oil'.

Chapter 5 considers the ways in which the products of the balsam tree were distributed around the ancient and medieval worlds. The rarity of 'true' balsam was one of the factors determining its high cost, though this can also be related to the associations forged between the trees and famous historical figures (Chapter 1). Balsam also enjoyed numerous applications in medicine (Chapters 6 and 7), and religious and royal rituals (Chapter 8). For all of these reasons balsam had an important role to play in diplomatic exchanges and international trade. The first part of the chapter assesses the ways in which balsam was exploited by Muslim rulers from the early ninth to the sixteenth centuries. The second part of the chapter turns to the sphere of trade, tracing the references to the traffic in balsam in the Mediterranean and elsewhere. Balsam is considered in relation to the other high-value commodities transported along land and sea routes in the ancient, medieval and early modern periods. Purchasers of balsam had to be wary of fakes, and scholars such as Dioscorides offer methods to detect fraudulent imitations that were available in marketplaces. The last part of the chapter reviews these methods and identifies the principal plant oils that were used as substitutes, particularly in the preparation of medicaments.

The remaining chapters (6–8) are concerned with the uses to which the products of the balsam tree were put in the ancient and medieval worlds. Chapters 6 and 7 consider the diverse ways in which balsam oil was employed in medicine. This survey encompasses medical and pharmacological writing in Greek from ancient times to the end of late antiquity (seventh century CE), as well as later writings in, to list only the most significant, Syriac, Arabic and Latin. Chapter 6 begins a discussion of the medicinal qualities possessed by tree resins, most notably in the healing of wounds. This part deals with some of the problems in evaluating the claims made in pre-modern medical writings, and contrasts this with modern scientific evaluations of myrrh, and other aromatic tree resins. The main part of the chapter reviews the place of balsam in ancient medicine, from the passing references in the Old Testament to the much fuller presentation found in the corpus of antique Greek medical and pharmacological literature. This evaluation takes in larger issues, most notably the humoral system of medicine and the ways in which balsam was understood as a substance that would encourage heating and drying within the organs of the body.

The third part of Chapter 6 deals briefly with the appearance of balsam in Syriac medical texts of late antiquity. The language of Syriac has additional importance in the history of medicine because of its role in what has come to be known as the 'Translation Movement'. This term refers to the drive, promoted by the Abbasid caliphs of the late eighth and early ninth centuries, to translate Greek scholarship – philosophy, rhetoric, medicine, astronomy, engineering, agronomy and many other branches of science – into Arabic. The fourth part is concerned with the medical writing that came into being during the first phase (late eighth to the tenth century) of the Translation Movement. The aims are to establish the relationships with the practices outlined in earlier Greek writing, and to identify areas of adaptation and innovation.

The first part of Chapter 7 considers the Arabic and Persian medical literature of this later phase. Comments are also made about medical writing in the Byzantine empire in the tenth and eleventh centuries. The second part discusses the translation of the Arabic medical tradition (which by then had fully incorporated earlier works in Greek) in Western Europe, particularly in scholarly centres such as Salerno and Montpellier. Balsam was already known prior to the eleventh century – for example, in the Anglo-Saxon *Leechbook of Bald* – but the translation of fundamental works such as Ibn Sina's (known in Europe as Avicenna; d. 1037) *Qānūn* by Gerard of Cremona (d. 1187) greatly increased knowledge about the applications of this precious oleo-resin. European scholars used these translations and built upon them in subsequent centuries. The last part deals with the creation and sale of compound theriacs, or 'treacles'. These recipes had their origins in ancient antidotes, such as Mithridatium, though they continued to evolve over time, with cities such as Venice producing their own versions.

Tree resins have long been used in a variety of religious and royal rituals. Aromatic resins were burned around the altar of the Jewish Temple, while balsam and other substances were employed in the anointing of the kings of Judaea. Chapter 8 is largely devoted to this question of ritual dimensions, with most attention given to the practices in the Christian Churches, and in the royal dynasties of Western Europe. The first part of the chapter examines connections often made between balsam and the practice of embalming. The second part explores the role played by balsam in liturgy, particularly in the oil of consecration. This oil was made in different ways, with the recipes in some of the eastern Churches being especially involved. Anointment was an important aspect of the investiture of medieval European rulers, and there are numerous references to the inclusion of balsam in these oils. The methods of anointing and the composition of these oils are reviewed in the second part of the chapter.

The previous paragraphs give a summary of the contents, but some further comments are warranted concerning the wider aims of this book. One motivation was simply to relate the story of a single product, illuminating the surprising ways in which this rare commodity was drawn into different aspects of the social and cultural lives of the medieval world. These interactions were not limited to one region, encompassing many polities from the Atlantic coasts of Europe and North Africa to Central Asia and spanning the three major Abrahamic religions. While these factors make it worthwhile to explore the history of the balsam trees and products derived from them, there are also other issues that spring from a detailed consideration of human interactions with a single plant or mineral. This focused approach to a single commodity has been taken in several other published studies, most famously, Redcliffe Salaman's 1949 book, *The History and Social Influence of the Potato*. Other notable examples of this genre in more recent times include Sidney Mintz, *Sweetness and Power: The Place of Sugar in Modern History*; Jenny Balfour-Paul, *Indigo: Egyptian Mummies to Blue Jeans*; Mark Kurlansky, *Salt: A World History*; Iain Gately, *Tobacco: A Cultural History of how an Exotic Plant Seduced Civilization*; and Antony Wild, *Coffee: A Dark History*.[22] Manufactured goods such as silk, paper and blue-and-white porcelain have also received interesting cultural histories.[23]

Potatoes, sugar, tobacco and coffee all draw significance from their ubiquity in modern life. The very fact that they are now rather unremarkable features of human existence across the modern world makes them worthy of scholarly attention. Each one has affected the social and cultural lives of the regions into which they have been introduced at different phases in history.

Their impact has been felt ultimately at all levels of society, regardless of wealth or political power, and it is difficult to imagine the contemporary world without them. This characteristic is, of course, lacking in the story of balsam. Due to its rarity and high cost, balsam remained a commodity appreciated and utilised by a relatively narrow spectrum of society (even if awareness of it was more widespread through popular literature and oral transmission). Furthermore, the trees in Matarea have long since died, denying balsam the chance to shape our contemporary experience, beyond the occasional figure of speech or advertising label. It would be fruitless, therefore, to advance for balsam the claims that might be made for less expensive, but more essential commodities.

The present book takes a different direction, seeking to understand the mechanisms by which a single product comes to be valued and how this value is expressed in social, cultural and intellectual terms (these ideas are addressed further in the Conclusion). All commodities can be said to have intrinsic properties that represent a baseline for the estimation of their value to human society. Foodstuffs can be understood in terms of their calorific content and nutritional qualities, their resistance to decay and a range of other practical considerations. To these can be added subjective criteria, including the perceived qualities of taste and texture, and their relative rarity. Hence, the societal value accorded to a comestible is not merely the sum of its intrinsic properties. Similar points can be made about the organic and non-organic substances that throughout history have been fashioned into clothing, tools, weapons and all other aspects of human material culture. Gold is a good example to explore in the present context, as it shares with balsam the notion of rarity. Gold clearly possesses intrinsic properties in that it does not corrode and is both highly malleable and ductile. The first property means that, unlike most metals, it is commonly found in its pure form rather than bound into a rock matrix, while the second and third allow it to be used economically, either in thin sheets (gold leaf) or as wire. One might also add the metal's distinctive colour and weight (what the Bond villain Auric Goldfinger memorably described as its 'divine heaviness')[24] to its attractive characteristics.

Neither this list of properties nor the rarity of gold on the surface of the Earth fully account for the value attributed to it through history. Ever since they were first extracted, copper and iron have been employed in many more ways, and no past society with access to such metals would countenance the fashioning of tools or weapons from gold. The utilities gold possessed made it attractive primarily for decorative purposes and for the minting of coinage. Hence, it is necessary to consider the ways in which value is generated through the mechanisms of symbolism, ritual and myth. These are all features that are prominent in the story of balsam. It too can be argued to have both intrinsic and culturally constructed properties, though many of these are also found in other aromatic tree resins gathered in regions of the Middle East, East Africa and the Indian Subcontinent (Chapter 4). Balsam cannot necessarily be categorised as the most 'useful' of these substances; for example, prior to the advent of modern medicine myrrh was employed in the treatment of more illnesses. Where balsam differs from its counterparts, however, is in its value, whether this is computed in purely financial terms or according to the range of social-cultural venues in which it operated.

This second factor can be equated with the anthropological concept of 'use value'. This idea has been elaborated in a variety of contexts, but the key point is that value is defined less according to economic criteria and more as a social construct. This approach allows the values associated with material objects to be assessed in relation to societal beliefs and practices. The latter could comprise modes of gift-giving or ceremonial interactions.[25] As a result, two objects might look more or less identical to an outside observer, but be strongly differentiated for members of the society in which they were made. Difference can reside not only in visible characteristics – shape, decoration, colour and so on – but also in perceived properties of the materials used in the construction of objects or rituals associated with the construction process.[26] These points can be illustrated in a contemporary context by the market for collectible books: for example, while a second-hand hardback copy of Ian Fleming's *Goldfinger* can be obtained online for as little as £5, a signed first edition of the same book with its original dust jacket will cost anywhere from 1,800 to 8,000 times as much.[27] For those who wish simply to read the novel there is no meaningful difference between the cheaper and the more expensive volumes, but the aura surrounding both the first appearance of a book in print and the signature of the author are sufficient to stimulate a small group of enthusiasts to pay extravagant sums for the latter.[28] Importantly, high prices in this context are not merely a product of rarity, as there are many equally scarce books by less sought-after authors that can be purchased for considerably more modest amounts. This is not an isolated phenomenon, and elsewhere in the book I have made use of analogies to explicate the values that accrete to balsam over time.

Balsam too had an aura surrounding it in the medieval period. 'True' balsam came only from Matarea, and this site was lent further lustre with its religious and historical associations. The product appears in many different social-cultural contexts, cementing the notion among the literate elite of its unique power and potency. The wealth of primary accounts – in literary genres as diverse as history, geography, poetry, liturgy, travel writing, medicine, botany and pharmacology – offer a rare opportunity to establish the mechanisms by which use value is elaborated over time. This examination is both diachronic and cross-cultural, taking in a broad sweep of time from the fourth century BC to the seventeenth century CE and an extensive geographical region. Notably, there are writers who seek to distinguish between the characteristics of balsam and those resinous materials that apparently exhibited similar qualities (Chapter 4), and there are also accounts detailing how purchasers could detect imitations in the marketplace (Chapter 5). Such analyses – whether or not they are based on verifiable observations – illustrate the ways in which information was circulated in pre-modern cultures.

A central argument of the present book is that the creation of value, at least as it applies to precious and high-cost commodities, is dependent upon the distribution and circulation of information. Quite simply, balsam could not generate its socio-cultural or economic value simply on the basis of its intrinsic properties; the prior or coeval circulation of written or oral testimony is required in order to generate demand.[29] The collecting of information was not, of course, static, but was subject to continual change and adaptation. The challenge, therefore, is to isolate which writers or groups of texts were most influential in this process, and the times when new observations added to the essential core of information (or, indeed, when information was lost). While much of this is specific to balsam, the general dynamics revealed in this study will be of some utility in the study of the distribution and uses of other pre-modern commodities. Distribution patterns have been formulated by archaeologists, anthropologists and economic historians, and these studies can be further augmented by the careful examination of the cultural factors informing the generation of demand and the modes of consumption.[30]

As noted above, the methodology in this book builds on the insights in numerous historical, archaeological and anthropological studies. Lastly, mention should be made of the prior scholarship on balsam itself. While this is, to the best of my knowledge, the first book-length work to track the history of the plants and their products from ancient times to the death of the last tree in the seventeenth century, there are other publications that deal with aspects of this larger subject. The early history of balsam in the plantations of Jericho and En-Gedi has been the subject of excavations, and further important discoveries have been made in Masada and the Qumran caves.[31] In addition, there have been studies making use of textual sources and mosaics of this period (Chapter 2). Scholars have also analysed the writings pertinent to the history of Matarea, drawing out historical facts and mythic detail from Coptic, Arabic and European sources (Chapters 1 and 3). The modern botanical study of balsam can be said to have started with the writings of Prosper Alpin in the late sixteenth century, and detailed accounts of balsam and comparable species appear in a range of botanical works.[32] There are, of course, many other references – some passing and others more extensive – to the place of balsam in areas such as medicine and ritual (Chapters 6–8). There are too many to list here, though they are cited in the notes accompanying the following chapters.

Notes

1. George Sandys, *A Relation of a Journey begun Anno Domini 1610. Four Books containing a Description of the Turkish Empire of Egypt and the Holy Land, and of the remote Parts of Italy, and Lands adioyning*, second edition (London: W. Barrett, 1615. Reprinted in facsimile [The English Experience 554] Amsterdam: Theatrum Orbis Terrarum, 1973), p. 127.
2. Unpublished account of Henry Rantzow, cited in Carsten Niebuhr, *Voyage en Arabie et en d'autres pays* (Amsterdam: S. J. Baalde, 1776–80), I, p. 98.
3. Translated into English as Claude Étienne Savary, *Letters on Egypt* (London: G. G. and J. Robinson, 1786), I, p. 144.
4. Discussed in greater detail in Chapters 4–8.

5. Prosper Alpin, *Histoire du Baulme, ou il est prouvé qve novs avons vraye cognoissance de la plante qui produict le baulme, et par consequent de son fruict, et de son bois: contre l'opinion commune de plusieurs medecins et apoticaires anciens et modernes*, trans. André Colin (Lyon: I. Pillehotte, 1619), pp. 18–19. Colin's poem, entitled 'Elegie sur la traduction et discours du baulme', appears on pp. 15–19. The relevant lines can be translated as: To find again through you its [the tree's] first locations / Led by your sweat / Give back to it the Nile, Egypt, Arabia / Bringing back the balm / And let flow among us this chosen liquor / The ornament of the Levant. / And so may the balm, / If your merit were to take of it, / Having filled you to the bone, / Preserve your fame against the spite of death. / And beset by it [envy] now / You will tame envy and just as the viper / Finds its death in the balm / It [envy] will not be able to do anything against your dear memory / Nor against your support. I am grateful to Martha Repp for this translation.
6. Another author to address this topic in the seventeenth century is Pietro Castelli. See his *Opobalsamum examinatum, defensum, indicatum, absolutum, et laudatum* (Messina: Francisci, 1640) and *Opobalsamum triumphans* (Basle: Peter Perna, 1640). George Wither proposed an alternative to balsam in his *Opobalsamum Anglicanum – an English Balme, lately pressed out of a Shrub, . . .* (London: unknown publisher, 1646).
7. On this expedition, see Niebuhr, *Voyage en Arabie*. Forsskål's botanical study on the region was published posthumously with Carsten Niebuhr as *Flora Aegyptiaco-Arabica. Sive Descriptiones Plantarum quas per Aegyptum Inferiorem et Arabiam Felicem* (Hannover: Mölleri, 1775). An unpublished dissertation on balsam was produced under the supervision of Linnaeus in Uppsala by Wilhelm LeMoine under the title *Opobalsamum declaratum in dissertatione medica* (1764). The manuscript is now in the University of Amsterdam Library.
8. This tree is commonly known as *Commiphora gileadensis*. Forsskål's notes on this discovery have not survived, but Niebuhr offers the following remarks in the introduction to the *Flora Aegyptiaco-Arabica*: 'The second excursion we [Niebuhr and Forsskål] made together, but we followed different roads, and brought back completely different plants which we had collected along our routes. The culmination of the excursion was the discovery of the tree, from which *Opobalsamum* is produced, with the name of which Forsskål more than once had been deceived in Egypt, because now one, now another tree had been passed as the genuine'. Quoted in F. Nigel Hepper and I. Friis, *The Plants of Pehr Forsskal's 'Flora Aegyptiaco-Arabica'. Collected on the Royal Danish Expedition to*

Egypt and the Yemen 1761–63 (Whitstable: Royal Botanical Gardens, Kew in association with the Botanical Museum, Copenhagen, 1994), pp. 15–16 (for further details on the expedition, see pp. 13–19). Forsskål also wrote to Linnaeus from Moccha describing the tree.

9. Abu al-Barakat Muhammad b. Ahmad al-Hanafi Ibn Iyas, *Badā'i' al-zuhūr fī waqa'i' al-duhūr*. Published as Mohammad Mustafa et al., *Die Chronik des Ibn Ijas*, Bibliotheca Islamica 5 (Wiesbaden: Franz Steiner Verlag, 1960–74), IV, p. 149.

10. On the distribution of Turlington's balm, and imitations of the product, see David Watters, 'A Turlington balsam phial from Monserrat, West Indies: Genuine or counterfeit?', *Historical Archaeology* 15.1 (1981): 105–8. Another treatment to bear the name balsam at this time is 'Friar's balsam', a mixture of benzoin, ethanol, aloes and storax, developed by Joshua Ward (d. 1761).

11. The first four lines read, 'Blasted with sighs, and surrounded with tears, / Hither I come to seek the spring, / And at mine eyes, and at mine ears, / Receive such balms as else cure every thing.'

12. Izaak Walton, *The Compleat Angler, 1653–1676*, ed. with introduction by Jonquil Bevan (Oxford: Clarendon Press, 1983), pp. 308–9.

13. Jole Shackelford, *A Philosophical Path for Paracelsian Medicine: The Ideas, Intellectual Context, and Influence of Petrus Severinus (1540/2–1602)* (Copenhagen: Museum Tusculanum Press and University of Copenhagen, 2004), pp. 166–8, 198, et passim. Balsam is discussed in alchemical texts, such as the *Picatrix*. See David Pingree, ed., *Picatrix: The Latin Version of Ghayat al-Hakim*, Studies of the Warburg Institute 39 (London: Warburg Institute, 1986). This text contains numerous references to balsams.

14. Quoted in Shackelford, *A Philosophical Path*, p. 265.

15. This 'balsam' was made by soaking a brick in olive oil and then distilling the brick at a high temperature to create a liquid. This liquid was used in a wide variety of treatments.

16. My thanks to Ruba Kana'an for this information.

17. Some examples employing balsam/balm in a metaphorical sense include: Joseph Hall, *The Balm of Gilead, for the Distressed, both Moral and Divine: Most fit for these wofull times* (London: Thomas Newcomb, 1650); Thomas Walley, *Balm in Gilead to Heal Sion's Wounds, or, a treatise wherein there is a clear discovery of the most prevailing sickness in New England, both in the civil and ecclesiasticall state* (Cambridge, MA: Samuel Green and Marmaduke Johnson, 1669);

Titus Oates, *A Balm presented to these Nations, England and Ireland, to cure the Wounds of the bleeding Protestants, and open the Eyes of the deluded Papists, that are ignorant of the Truth* (n. p.: printed for J. G., c. 1680). See also Elly Truitt, 'The virtues of balm in late Medieval literature', *Early Science and Medicine* 14 (2009): 711–36.

18. Victor Reichert, trans., *The Tahkemoni of Judah al-Ḥarizi* (Jerusalem: Raphael Haim Cohen's Ltd, 1965, reprinted 1973), pp. 339–44.

19. Abu Muhammad al-Hasan b. Ahmad ibn Yaʿqub al-Hamdani, *al-Iklīl*. See Nabih Amin Faris, trans., *The Antiquities of South Arabia, being a Translation from the Arabic with linguistic, geographic, and historic Notes of the eighth Book of al-Hamdānī's al-Iklīl, reconstructed from al-Karmali's Edition and Ms in the Garrett Collection*, Princeton University Library, Princeton Oriental Texts 3 (Princeton, NJ: Princeton University Press, 1938), p. 15.

20. Edward Atchley, *A History of the Use of Incense in Divine Liturgy*, Alcuin Club Editions 13 (London: Alcuin Club, 1909), pp. 108–9.

21. Authors might vary in the degree of credence they gave to information they received during their travels. Gilbert Phelps makes the following assessment of the seventeenth-century traveller William Lithgow: 'Sometimes he is robustly commonsensical, at others his inherent sense of wonder take precedence. On occasions Renaissance scepticism and medieval fondness for marvels exist side by side'. See 'Introduction', in William Lithgow, *The Rare Adventures and Painful Peregrinations of William Lithgow*, ed., Gilbert Phelps (London: Folio Society, 1974), p. 17.

22. Redcliffe Salaman, *The History and Social Influence of the Potato* (Cambridge: Cambridge University Press, 1949); Sidney Mintz, *Sweetness and Power: The Place of Sugar in Modern History* (New York: Viking, 1985); Jenny Balfour-Paul, *Indigo: Egyptian Mummies to Blue Jeans* (London: British Museum, 1998); Mark Kurlansky, *Salt: A World History* (New York: Walker and Co., 2002); Iain Gately, *Tobacco: A Cultural History of how an Exotic Plant Seduced Civilization* (New York: Grove Press, 2003); and Antony Wild, *Coffee: A Dark History* (London: Fourth Estate, 2004).

23. James Watt and Anne Wardwell, eds, *When Silk Was Gold; Central Asian and Chinese Textiles* (New York: Metropolitan Museum of Art, 1997); Jonathan Bloom, *Paper before Print: The History and Impact of Paper in the Islamic World* (New Haven, CT and London: Yale University Press, 2001); John Carswell and Jean McClure Mudge, *Blue and White: Chinese Porcelain and its Impact on the Western World* (Chicago: University of Chicago Press, 1985); John Carswell,

Blue and White: Chinese Porcelain around the World (London: British Museum Press, 2000).

24. The larger part of Goldfinger's monologue reads: 'Mr Bond, all my life I have been in love. I have been in love with gold. I love its colour, its brilliance, its divine heaviness. I love the texture of gold, that soft sliminess that I have learnt to gauge so accurately by touch that I can estimate the fineness of a bar to within one carat. And I love the warm tang it exudes when I melt it down into a true golden syrup. But, above all, Mr Bond, I love the power that gold alone gives to its owner – the magic of controlling energy, exacting labour, fulfilling one's every wish and whim and, when need be, purchasing bodies, minds, even souls'. See Ian Fleming, *Goldfinger* (London: Jonathan Cape, 1959. Reprinted St Albans: Triad/Panther Books, 1978), p. 157.

25. For a discussion of these issues, see Marcel Mauss, *The Gift: The Form and Reason for Exchange in Archaic Societies*, trans. W. D. Halls with a foreword by Mary Douglas (New York and London: W. W. Norton, 1990); Robert Adams, 'Anthropological perspectives on ancient trade', *Current Anthropology* 15 (1974): 239–58; Philip Curtin, *Cross-Cultural Trade in World History*, Studies in Comparative World History (Cambridge: Cambridge University Press, 1984); Arjun Appadurai, 'Introduction: Commodities and the politics of value', in Arjun Appadurai, ed., *The Social Life of Things: Commodities in Cultural Exchange* (Cambridge: Cambridge University Press, 1986), pp. 3–63; Mary Helms, *Ulysses' Sail: An Ethnographic Odyssey of Power, Knowledge and Geographical Distance* (Princeton, NJ: Princeton University Press, 1988). Studies of medieval gift-giving are reviewed in Chapter 5.

26. For example: Berthold Laufer, *Geophagy*, Field Museum of Natural History Publication 280. Anthropological Series 18.2 (Chicago: Field Museum, 1930); Frederick Hasluck, '*Terra Lemnia*', in Frederick Hasluck, *Christianity and Islam under the Sultans*, ed. Margaret Hasluck (Oxford: Oxford University Press, 1929), II, pp. 671–88; Julian Raby, '*Terra Lemnia* and the potteries of the Golden Horn: An antique revival under Ottoman auspices', *Byzantinische Forschungen* 21 (1995): 305–42.

27. These figures were found by searching www.abebooks.com (last consulted: 21 August 2017).

28. On the issue of aura, cf. Walter Benjamin, 'The work of art in the age of its technological reproducibility'. Third edition of the text translated in Howard Eiland and Michael Jennings, eds, *Walter Benjamin: Selected Writing, IV: 1938–1940* (Cambridge, MA: Harvard University Press, 2003), pp. 251–70. Reprinted

in Donald Preziosi, *The Art of Art History: A Critical Anthology. New Edition*, Oxford History of Art (Oxford and New York: Oxford University Press, 2009), pp. 435–42.
29. This argument is first developed in my article, 'Balsam in the Mediaeval Mediterranean: A case study of information and commodity exchange', *Journal of Mediterranean Archaeology* 14.1 (2001): 3–23.
30. For example: Andrew and Susan Sherratt, 'From luxuries to commodities: The nature of Mediterranean Bronze Age trading systems', in Noel Gale, ed., *Bronze Age Trade in the Mediterranean. Papers Presented at the Conference Held at Rewley House, Oxford, in December 1989*, Studies in Mediterranean Archaeology 90 (Jonsered: Paul Åströms Förlag, 1991), pp. 351–86; Roberta Tomber, 'Quantitative approaches to the investigation of long-distance exchange', *Journal of Roman Archaeology* 6 (1993): 142–66; Janet Abu Lughod, *Before European Hegemony: The World System A.D. 1250–1350* (New York and Oxford: Oxford University Press, 1989).
31. These sources are given in the endnotes of Chapter 2.
32. These sources are discussed in greater detail in Chapter 4.

I

Travellers' Tales: Experiencing Matarea

An anonymous early-twelfth-century Latin guide, known as the *Work on Geography*, contains a startling claim about native flora of the Dead Sea (known in the text as the 'Asphalt Lake'). The unnamed author asserts the bitter water cannot long be endured by any creature, and that birds do not fly across the lake. The text continues: 'Islands are in the Lake, on which apples grow, which would be good to eat. But if you pick them they open and are reduced to cinders. They smoke as if they are burning'.[1] About two centuries later Sir John Mandeville claims also to have seen the same fruit. For him the fact that the apples reduced to ashes when cut was 'a token that by the wrath of God the cities and the land were burned and sunk into hell'.[2]

References to the apples of the Dead Sea appear in the works of many other European writers of the medieval period. Travellers to the Holy Land in later centuries often adopted a more critical stance, contrasting what they had read prior to the commencement of their journeys with what they encountered on the ground. The chaplain of the Levant company in Syria, Henry Maundrell (d. 1701), makes the following comments during a visit to the Dead Sea in 1697:

> As for the apples of Sodom, so much talked of, I neither saw nor heard of any hereabouts; nor was there any tree to be seen near the lake from which one might expect such a kind of fruit, which induces me to believe that there may be greater deceit in this fruit than that which is usually reported of it; and that its very being as well as its beauty is a fiction, only kept up, as my Lord Bacon observes many other false notions are, because it serves for a good allusion, and helps the poet to a similitude.[3]

Were these 'apples of Sodom' a fiction, as Maundrell suspected, or did they have some basis in fact? The story has ancient origins, appearing in texts such as the account of the military campaigns of Titus in Judaea in 69–70 CE given by Cornelius Tacitus (d. c. 117).[4] In his description of the plain south of the Dead Sea, Tacitus remarks that it was 'once fertile, they say, and the site of great cities, but afterward struck by lightning and consumed'. He continues:

> Of this event, they declare, traces still remain, for the soil, which is scorched in appearance, has lost its productive power. Everything that grows spontaneously, as well as what is planted by hand, either when the leaf or flower have been developed, or after maturing in the usual form, becomes black and rotten, and crumbles into a kind of dust.[5]

In this case it is the blighted landscape that adversely affects all of the flora unfortunate enough to grow there. Flavius Josephus (d. c. 100 CE) also contributes to the growth of this potent legend, writing that the fruit would dissolve into smoke and ashes in one's hand. He concludes, 'so far are the legends about the land of Sodom borne out by ocular evidence'.[6] It is this ancient pedigree that partly accounts for the longevity of stories about the ash-filled apples. If noted antique writers like Tacitus or Josephus had seen something, and if these claims were also correlated with the recorded observations of other medieval travellers, then such evidence was hard to contradict. To complicate matters further we cannot assume that European pilgrims, merchants and emissaries to the Middle East always visited all the localities they record in their travel accounts. The Dominican monk Burchard of Mount Sion – now regarded as one of the most credible European geographical sources dealing with late-thirteenth-century Palestine – honestly admits that he did not make the journey to the Dead Sea for fear of attacks by local bedouin (he subsequently found this danger to be overstated).[7]

The travels of Sir John Mandeville present another sort of challenge because 'author' is himself a fiction. Composed by an anonymous French writer who had probably never set foot in the Holy Land, the supposed journey of Mandeville was skilfully woven together from existing travel books.[8] While this collation of existing literature reads quite convincingly for Constantinople and the famous sites of the Middle East, the paucity of source material relating to the remainder of Asia led Mandeville's author to put forward wilder claims, including deformed humans and strange religious practices involving cannibalism. A telling indication that this work was once regarded more seriously as a source of geographical and ethnographic data than it is today is that Christopher Columbus included a copy of Mandeville's travels among his reference works during his famous voyage in 1492.[9] For the sixteenth-century Italian miller Menocchio, the book was one of the factors precipitating a spiritual crisis that would lead him to be tried before the Inquisition, and later burned at the stake.[10]

All of this might lead to the conclusion that the 'apples of Sodom' were simply a poetic fiction used to highlight the accursed nature of the region at the southern end of the Dead Sea. The actual answer is more complicated: the region does indeed possess a plant of dogbane family (*Calotropis procera* W. T. Aiton), often known as Apple of Sodom from the Hebrew, *Tapuah Sdom* (Fig. 1.1a and b). Growing to about 4.5 m in height, this bush produces an apple-shaped fruit that is largely hollow, containing only some fibres and a slender seed pod. When struck or squeezed the fruit is liable to explode (sadly without the production of ashes or smoke).[11] The German adventurer Ulrich Seetzen (d. 1811), who, in the early years of the nineteenth century made the dangerous journey around the Dead Sea disguised as a beggar, reports the Arabic name for the plant: *'awshir*. The silk-like threads inside the fruit were collected by the locals to clean the barrels of their rifles and were also made into matches.[12] We can conclude, therefore, that the medieval sources contain elements of truth and fantasy,

 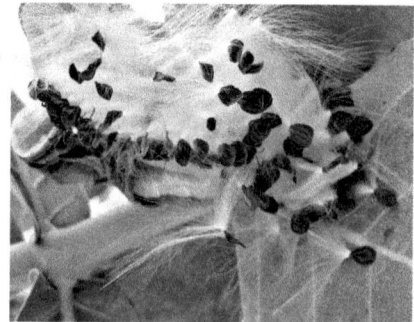

Figure 1.1 (a) Fruit and flowers of *Calotropis procera*, known as 'Apples of Sodom'. Wikimedia Commons, 2007. Photograph: Wilfredo Rodriguez; (b) Opened fruit of *Calotropis procera*. Wikimedia Commons, 2007. Photograph: Viktor Korniyenko.

with the intrinsic character of this hollow fruit amplifying the sterility of the surrounding land.

The accumulated testimony regarding the history of Matarea presents similar difficulties to those posed above. There is certainly no lack of accounts provided by European travellers to Egypt,[13] but the knotty problem is how these texts should be evaluated. Is it possible to pare this mass of descriptions down to a kernel of verifiably accurate historical information? Perhaps even this question is to miss the point, at least if one's goal is to reconstruct the ways in which the site of Matarea and the balsam trees planted there were *perceived* by medieval and early modern readers.

This issue has been addressed by scholars dealing with other periods and regions, particularly in cases where there is evidence for the oral transmission of popular legends.[14] Often carrying fantastical details, these stories might be recorded in variant textual forms. Sometimes these written records were made over extended periods of time, allowing for some evaluation of the ways in which oral tales evolved. A good example of the persistence of stories told by local Egyptian guides is the spurious explanation given for the apparent appearance of a chalice (actually the cup held by the ceremonial cupbearer, or *sāqī*, of the sultan) on the insignia employed by amirs of the Mamluk sultanate. Local guides claimed this to be a representation of the chalice that Louis IX, king of France (r. 1226–70), was required to leave with his captor, the sultan of Egypt, as a guarantee that he would repay the substantial ransom of gold coins when he returned home. This story appears in numerous travellers' accounts from Leonardo Frescobaldi in the 1380s through to the early seventeenth century. Retaining its essential structure in all the versions, specific details of this story were elaborated in later retellings.[15] Such constantly shifting folk tales would now be lost had not Frescobaldi and others included them in the reports of their journeys to Egypt. The same process appears to be at work in the case of Matarea and the balsam plantation, with each travel account providing the reader with a unique condensation of oral and written testimony.

A more conventional historical presentation of Matarea is offered later (Chapter 3), but the remainder of this chapter approaches these travellers' tales from a different perspective by examining the perceptions that were built up in the minds of literate Europeans. Few travellers to Egypt seem to have come to the balsam gardens without having read the accounts of earlier visitors, often also supplemented by a range of antique authors. The appetite for this literary genre was no less voracious among those more sedentary readers who never ventured beyond the borders of the Christian West. In Egypt travellers were also confronted by local stories about the history and religious associations of Matarea. Before trying to tease out the 'true' historical development of the site it is necessary first to immerse oneself in the imaginative worlds of medieval and early modern travellers. The final section of the chapter examines Coptic traditions about Matarea and their role in forming what can be described as the 'spiritual topography' of the site.

Matarea and its Vicinity

The town of Matarea in the early twentieth century still maintained some aspects which would have been familiar to the pilgrims who flocked to the site in earlier times. Although the balsam plants had long ago disappeared, there were still gardens and a small chapel. Near to this chapel was a well and an ancient tree like that seen by George Sandys in 1611. In the vicinity of Matarea was a red stone obelisk – originally one of a pair – and the ruins of an impressive Pharaonic temple of the sun at Heliopolis (from which comes the Arabic name, 'Ayn Shams, or 'Spring of the Sun'). *L'Arbre de la Vierge à Matarieh. Souvenirs du séjour de la Sainte Famille en Égypte,* written by a Catholic father, Michel-Marie Jullien (d. 1911), is a fascinating resource on late-nineteenth- and early-twentieth-century Matarea. Reprinted several times, the fourth edition of this slim book, dating to 1904, announces that it was to be 'sold for the profit of the church under construction' (Fig. 1.2). This imposing neo-Romanesque edifice had been started in 1902 and was designed for pilgrims making their annual trip to Matarea (Fig. 1.3).

Located within the walled compound of the gardens, the other place of worship was less imposing. Although it stood on or near the site of the chapel seen by George Sandys in 1610, the building illustrated by Jullien was only a little older than its sister church, having been constructed in 1883 by the College of Jesuits in Cairo in imitation of the grotto at Lourdes (Fig. 1.4). Just as the chapel was not the one seen by Sandys, the same was also true of the famous sycamore tree (more correctly, as Prosper Alpin was the first to identify in a print publication, a sycamore fig, *Ficus sycomorus* L.).[16] Photographs taken in the late nineteenth century depict a tree of considerable

Figure 1.2 Front cover of Michel-Marie Jullien, *L'Arbre de la Vierge à Matarieh. Souvenirs du séjour de la Sainte Famille en Égypte*, fourth edition (1904). Collection of the author.

antiquity (Fig. 1.5), but Jullien establishes the chronology with greater accuracy. An older tree of the same species had stood in earlier centuries, but one half of the trunk detached in 1656 and the other half fell over in 1694. The sycamore standing in the garden in Jullien's time was only planted in 1672. This venerable tree survived the Napoleonic battle of Heliopolis in 1800 and finally fell down in 1906.[17]

The point to be emphasised here is that the variant experiences of visitors to Matarea were not merely conditioned by what they read before they arrived, but by the precise historical circumstances of their time.[18] This might simply be a case of establishing which buildings were standing when they visited; for example, the chapel in the garden was rebuilt several times (Chapter 3), and also on occasion was taken over for use by Muslims. Another important factor is the degree of access that Europeans enjoyed to the famous balsam plantation through the centuries; the description offered by a traveller who could only glance over the enclosing wall or rely upon hearsay must be

Figure 1.3 Church at Matarea, Egypt, constructed from 1902. Photograph by Captain Edward Arthur McKenna, taken 1914–15. Collection: Museums Victoria (Australia). Donated by Mr J. Willis, c. 1986.

Figure 1.5 Sycamore fig in the gardens of Matarea. Photograph taken between c. 1890 and 1910. Photoglob Company, Zurich. Library of Congress Prints and Photographs Division: LC-DIG-ppmsca-41361.

Figure 1.4 Chapel in the gardens of Matarea constructed by the College of Jesuits, Cairo, in 1883. From Jullien, *L'Arbre de la Vierge*, figure on p. 41.

accorded rather less veracity than one who had enjoyed unfettered access to the wonders located within.

The Pharaonic heritage of Egypt fascinated European travellers. Predictably, the pyramids of Giza ('Joseph's granaries')[19] were the focus of greatest attention, but other sites were mentioned. Ancient Heliopolis (Arabic: 'Ayn Shams) was discussed in relation to the gardens of Matarea. Medieval travellers did not, however, focus on the standing architecture, omitting to mention even the standing obelisk. They chose instead to use Heliopolis as a pagan setting for the visit of the Holy Family. The Venetian statesman Marino Sanudo (d. 1338) claims that the visit of the Virgin and Christ Child to the temple of Heliopolis caused the 365 idols within the building to fall to the floor.[20] Similar themes are developed in Coptic and Ethiopic religious literature (see below). Sanudo's presentation signals the defeat of ancient paganism in the face of the true religion of Christianity, and the theme of miraculous destruction of idols is found elsewhere in European literature.[21] A more contemporary resonance can also be inferred. Medieval Christianity often represented Islam as an idolatrous cult, and Sanudo himself was an enthusiastic proponent of further Crusades against Muslim territories.[22]

During the Mamluk period the road from Cairo to Matarea became a popular location for the construction of mansions for the political elite (Chapter 3).[23] Many authors comment favourably upon these, though Gilbert de Lannoy, writing in 1422, offers a less glowing report: 'On the way to Matarea when the balm grows for the space of two miles in length and one in breadth are houses in ruins and deserted from decay'.[24] Felix Fabri (d. 1502) provides more detail, noting the presence of a palace used by the sultan and a caravanserai for the accommodation of travellers. Another important feature was a bath, big enough for up to 300 men.[25] The balsam plantation itself is represented on sixteenth-century printed maps of Cairo, and can be seen to include a walled compound with small attached buildings and the Pharaonic obelisk located a little to the left (i.e. north) (Fig. 1.6a and b).[26] The map shows trees planted in the vicinity, and the general fertility of the region is alluded to by several travellers.[27] The walls of the plantation enclosed a relatively small area.[28] Estimates range from the vague – Burchard of Mount Sion, for example, claims it to be two bow shots long by a stone's throw wide, while Sanudo talks of it comprising half a *mansus* (the area of land required to

Figure 1.6 (a) Woodcut map of Cairo from Sebastian Münster, *Cosmographia* (Basel: Sebastian Petri, 1575). Entitled *Warhaffte abcontrafehtung der machtigen und vesten Statt Alkair*. Made after original by Matteo Pagani in 1549. Collection of the author.

Figure 1.6 (b) Detail showing Matarea and the surrounding area.

support a family)[29] – to the simply inaccurate.[30] There were, however, those that appear to have been better informed. The Franciscan monk Francesco Suriano (d. after 1481) reports that the balsam trees occupied 450 *braccia* square, which suggests an area of about 300 x 300 m, or nine hectares. This compares to 'Abd al-Latif al-Baghdadi's (d. 1231) calculation of seven *fiddān* (just under three hectares).[31] Fabri estimates the compound contained no more than fifty trees, though the number of healthy specimens was to dwindle dramatically soon after his visit.[32]

Fanciful representations of the walled plantation appear in European manuscript illustrations, suggesting that illustrators did not pay close attention to the information in broadly contemporary travel accounts. For example, the balsam gardens appear in manuscripts of the medieval herbal *Tractatus de herbis*. Aside from the presence of trees and a surrounding wall, these illustrations have little in common (Figs 1.7 and 1.8).[33] Interesting features include the presence of multiple wells with connecting water channels. The plants themselves sometimes have vessels hanging from their branches. The British Library manuscript Egerton 747, produced in Salerno, c. 1280–1310,

Figure 1.7 Illustration of the balsam tree and the walled compound of Matarea (bottom right). From *Tractatus de herbis* manuscript, Salerno, c. 1280–1310. British Library: Egerton ms 747, fol. 12r.

Figure 1.8 Sketch of a manuscript illustration of the balsam tree and the walled compound of Matarea. From a pharmacological manuscript including the *Tractatus de herbis*, written and illustrated by Manfredus de Monte Imperiale, fourteenth century. Bibliothèque Nationale de France, Paris. Ms. Lat. 6823, fol. 25v. Drawing: Marcus Milwright.

carries a caption reading, 'It is found near Babylon (i.e. Cairo), in a field where spring seven sources and if it is transplanted elsewhere it produces neither flowers nor flowing [sap]'.[34]

The *Tractatus* illustrations lack specific details recorded in sixteenth-century woodcuts of Cairo that depict Matarea (Fig. 1.6b). The features that consistently appear in travel accounts are an ancient tree, a chapel dedicated to the Virgin, one or more wells, a cistern or fountain and the balsam plants themselves. An anonymous guide of the thirteenth century creates a narrative to tie these elements together. The author writes that Mary was suffering from great thirst, but could find no water to quench it. She set the infant Jesus on the ground and where his foot hit the soil a spring welled up.[35] Other accounts claim that the Virgin washed the clothes of Christ in the fountains of the site, and that this lent the water a special quality. The fourteenth-century German priest Ludolph von Sudheim offers this version of events, claiming that the water of Matarea was the only source that could sustain the balsam trees.[36] Suriano adds an additional detail, claiming that 'if other water touches them [the balsam trees], they immediately dry up'.[37] Leo Africanus (d. c. 1554) repeats this assertion, though he acknowledges it is based on hearsay.[38] Coptic Marian legends are probably the ultimate source of inspiration for these ideas (see below). The German Dominican monk Johann Wansleben (or Vansleb, d. 1679) also notes that Muslims claimed the water at Matarea had its source at the well of Zamzam in Mecca.[39]

An ancient tree appears in most accounts, though authors disagreed about the precise species: fig, sycamore and other less plausible trees are mentioned.[40] The main area of interest was the fact that the tree contained within it an opening, large enough for a person to enter. Two principal stories appear in the sources. In the first the Holy Family was menaced by malefactors and, in order to shield them from view, the trunk of the tree created within itself a small chamber. In the other version the tree miraculously created a shelter when the Holy Family found themselves without a place to stay for the night. The sanctity of the space encouraged further legends, including the idea that children born illegitimate would be unable to enter the space; the tree would close the aperture in reaction to the presence of such a person.[41] The tree itself appears in an illustration, published in 1596 by the Franciscan father Bernardino Amico (d. 1620). His depiction of the tree shows the trunk bifurcating before reaching the ground (Fig. 1.9). Jullien suggests a distant connection with the veneration of a tree in the ancient Temple of the Sun at Heliopolis.[42] The tree at Matarea continued to be revered in later centuries: the eighteenth-century explorer Carsten Niebuhr observes that: 'This sycomore should seem to have the power of renewing itself: for, of the crowds of superstitious persons who visit it, each usually cuts off, and carries away a piece'.[43]

Bernardino Amico da Gallipoli's illustration shows further components of the site of Matarea, including the walled garden, the chapel and the well.

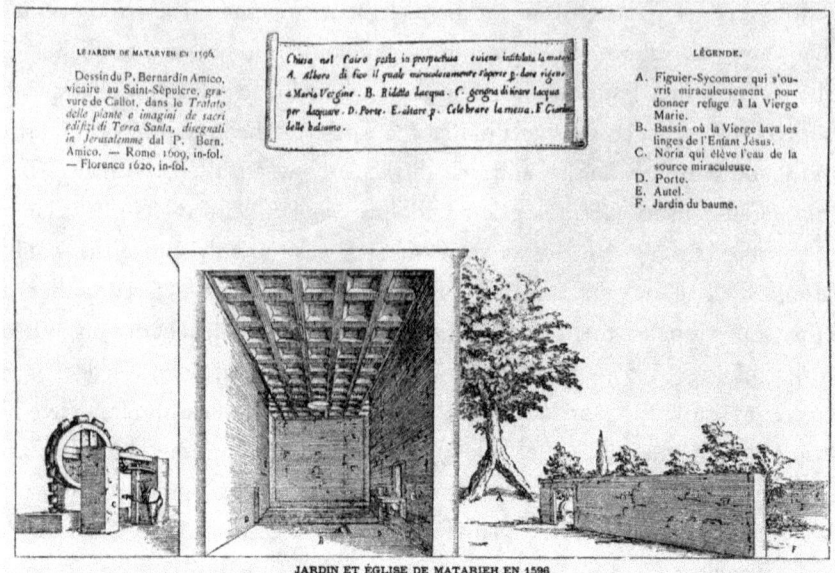

Figure 1.9 Illustration of the chapel and surrounding features of the plantation of Matarea from the travel journal of Bernardino da Gallipoli (1609). Reproduced in Jullien, *L'Arbre de la Vierge*, figure on p. 36.

Figure 1.10 (a) Water-lifting device (*sāqiya*) with the obelisk of Heliopolis in the background. Photograph taken between c. 1890 and 1910. Photoglob Company, Zurich. Library of Congress Prints and Photographs Division: LC-DIG-ppmsca-41360; (b) *Sāqiya* in the gardens of Matarea. From Jullien, *L'Arbre de la Vierge*, figure on p. 11.

The last of these comprises a substantial built structure with a mechanism for drawing water from the ground.[44] Similar water-lifting devices (*sāqiya*) could still be seen in the region in the early twentieth century (Fig. 1.10a and b). Other accounts indicate that oxen were employed to provide the power for this irrigation system. Although some earlier illustrations, such as those in the *Tractatus de herbis*, show multiple wells, the textual sources do not support this idea.[45] Water was channelled both to the balsam trees and into the chapel.[46] It is evident that the chapel changed its appearance, meaning that travellers of different periods were actually describing distinct buildings.

The most extensive information comes from the sixteenth and seventeenth centuries. Jean Palerne (d. 1592) saw the chapel in the 1580s. He recounts that it was a small, brick structure, reached by a set of steps and containing two chambers. In the centre of the main chamber was a recessed pool lined with coloured marble. This pool was supplied with water from the well, and was used for bathing by local Christians and Muslims. The chapel itself had no altar, but possessed a recess lined with scented wood. This area of the building held a porphyry stone said to have been the one on which Christ sat. Lamps were kept lit at all times within the building.[47] Father Amico da Gallipoli provides more information in his account of attempts to renovate the building.[48] There are indications that the chapel was visited periodically by Ottoman governors of Egypt, and some sources claim that the chapel was given over solely to Muslim use.[49] By contrast, Wansleben claims that the place of worship was owned by the Coptic Church, with other Christian denominations being involved in the operation of the building.[50]

Textual descriptions of the balsam trees themselves and the process of harvesting are reviewed later in the book (Chapter 4). Some European travellers, such as Ludolph von Sudheim, offer well-informed accounts of the extraction of balsam that correlate well with descriptions in contemporary Arabic sources. All writers seem to have understood the basic point that scoring into the bark of the tree would release the precious liquid. The idea that this would then drain into cups or other vessels is commonplace, and is a required component of most European manuscript illustrations of Matarea. The placement of the vessels high on the upper branches in some representations betrays a lack of familiarity, however, with the size of the trees and the nature of the process. Most interesting in the present context are the folk tales that came to be associated with the care of the trees. For example, drawing on the testimony of Wilhelm von Boldensele (d. 1338 or 1339), the author of Mandeville's travels writes: 'The balm leaves do not wither; and the branches are cut with a sharp stone, or with a sharp bone, when one wants to prune them. For whoever prunes them with iron corrupts its virtue and nature'.[51] These ideas were well known to medieval European and Arab authors, and can be traced back to writers of the Roman period, including Tacitus, Pliny the Elder and Josephus (Chapter 4).

The second claim relates to the involvement of the Muslim elite of Egypt at the time of the harvesting. For example, Ludolph von Sudheim writes that 'the Soldan of Babylon [i.e. Cairo] is very busy, being himself present in the garden and so carefully does he guard it that no one but he himself can obtain a drop of balsam by any means'.[52] There is support for his assertions, particularly given that the supply of balsam was a sultanic monopoly at least from the early thirteenth century (Chapter 3). The sultan or, in his absence, the keeper of treasury did indeed attend the harvesting of balsam. The third claim found in many medieval travel accounts is that the tending of the trees and the harvesting of the oil had to be done by Christians. Clearly this cannot be attributed to the ancient authors mentioned above, and perhaps has its origins in Coptic traditions. This Christian contribution comprised both the guards entrusted with the protection of the site and the officials designated to collect the balsam and tend the trees.[53] Oliver of Paderborn (d. 1227), a bishop who was present during the capture and occupation of Damietta from 1217 to 1221, elaborates that the garden was run by a Christian who had both Christians and Muslims working for him.[54] Von Sudheim recalls seeing four Germans among the former group, including one who was a renegade.[55] European mercenaries were occasionally employed within the Mamluk military, while others may have entered the sultanate as prisoners-of-war. Pierre Pomet's illustration of the balsam tree (Fig. 4.10) shows a janissary guarding it, perhaps indicating that different practices were in place during the Ottoman period. The latter group is mentioned by several travellers, though Fabri cautions that it was not always possible to distinguish between a Saracen (Muslim) and an eastern Christian.[56] An unnamed pilgrim of the twelfth century writes:

> of old there was no balsam in all the world save in the land of Jerusalem, and that was in Jericho. Afterwards the Egyptians came thither, took away the shrubs into Egypt, and planted them in the city of Babylon [i.e. Old Cairo], which is now the only place where balsam is found. There is nothing

remarkable in these trees, but if they are grown by any save Christians they bear no fruit and will be doomed to barrenness forever.[57]

Evidence in Arabic chronicles of the thirteenth century and later supports the contention that Copts were intimately involved in the care of the trees, though the anonymous pilgrim exaggerates in his claim that the trees could only produce fruit if tended by Christians. The quote is also significant for its attempt to trace the origins of the balsam trees prior to their transportation to Egypt. The author does not address when this occurred, though this issue is considered by others. First, there was a general awareness of the fact that there were earlier plantations of balsam in Palestine (Chapter 2). Jericho is cited above, while the author of Mandeville's travels notes of Dengadda (probably meaning En-Gedi in the Jordan Valley) as the place 'where balm used to grow. But the shrubs were pulled up and taken to be planted in Babylon, and they are still called the vines of Engaddy'.[58] This association was also known to Suriano, who refers to the 'Engaddi Vineyard' in his discussion of Matarea.[59] The circumstances in which the trees were transplanted are mentioned by several medieval writers, with a common claim being that it was instigated by Mark Antony at the urging of Cleopatra. In some accounts the Egyptian queen was motivated to do this out of spite for Herod the Great.[60] The other question to concern medieval writers was the role of the Queen of Sheba. Josephus is the source for the claim that balsam was among the gifts she brought from southern Arabia.[61]

Lastly, the travellers who visited Matarea often alerted their readers to the reasons why balsam was so valued. In the opinion of European visitors, the foremost function of balsam was as a vital component of liturgical oils used in a variety of contexts, including baptism and royal anointing ceremonies (Chapter 8). The idea that the oil could stop the processes of corruption is mentioned by medieval travellers. Ludolph von Sudheim elaborates on this theme. He writes:

> and whatsoever flesh is touched with crude balsam never rots or corrupts, and when it is dripping fresh from the tree, if a drop be placed in a man's hand it will drip through on the other side and pass through his hands. Moreover, if four or five drops of crude balsam be put into a man's eyes, which are going blind through lack of moisture, old age, or any other

infirmity, straightway his eyes will forever remain exactly as they were the instant when the balsam was poured in, getting neither better nor worse; wherefore, in one way it is a perilous venture to try, unless a man despairs of his sight. This fact is clearly shown in the many corpses of great men of old which have been found entirely uncorrupt, because they have been anointed with balsam. Likewise, if the scar of a new wound, when it is beginning to heal, be rubbed round once a day with half a drop of balsam on a pencil, it straightway restores the skin of the wound as it was before, and makes no blemish, as no one can see that there ever was a scar in the place. Moreover, this boiled balsam is an exceeding noble drug, and it is very good for the scars of wounds, as aforesaid; it is especially good when a man falls down from a high place, for then if he takes some of it his whole body, which was broken inside, would be restored and made whole again.[62]

In part, this description draws upon scientific writing of the period. Balsam was indeed employed in the treatment of wounds, and also found extensive applications in ophthalmology (Chapters 6 and 7). What is seen in the account of von Sudheim is an expansion for literary effect. This is not to suggest that his intentions were insincere, but rather to draw a distinction between different genres of writing. Physicians and pharmacologists were interested in the demonstration of specific qualities of plant, animal and mineral products, while the audience of travel literature looked for a balance of information and entertainment (as readers still do today). Balsam becomes more than a simple medicament, shifting into the realm of magic, or, at least, unverifiable claims.

Coptic and Ethiopic Legends about Matarea

European writers ultimately derived a considerable amount of their information from Coptic sources. The extensive discussions of the gardens of Matarea that appear in the writings of the native Christian population of Egypt and their compatriots in the Ethiopic Church have their origins in the New Testament story of the Flight to Egypt. In the Gospel according to Matthew this event occurs directly after the Nativity (2:13–23; the Flight to Egypt does not appear in the other canonical Gospels). On the journey back from Bethlehem to Nazareth Joseph received a vision in a dream:

Now after they had left, an angel of the Lord appeared to Joseph in a dream and said, 'Get up, take the child and his mother, and flee to Egypt, and remain there until I tell you; for Herod is about to search for the child, to destroy him'. Then Joseph got up, took the child and his mother by night, and went to Egypt, and remained there until the death of Herod. This was to fulfil what had been spoken by the Lord through the Prophet, 'Out of Egypt I have called my son'.[63]

Following the death of Herod an angel again appears to Joseph instructing him to return to the 'land of Israel, for those who were seeking the child's life are dead'.[64] Herod the Great, client king of Judaea under Roman overlordship, died in 4 BCE, and Matthew's Gospel does not provide further chronological indications that would allow one to establish the length of the sojourn of the Holy Family in Egypt (if, indeed, it actually occurred).

On this fairly slender scriptural authority was constructed an itinerary of locations at which Joseph, the Virgin Mary and the infant Christ stopped during their time in Egypt.[65] This process of elaborating scripture into longer narratives is well known in all of the Abrahamic traditions. For example, the night journey (*isrā'*) of the Prophet Muhammad is recounted in Qur'an 17:1: 'Glory to Allah who did take His servant for a journey by night from the Sacred Mosque (*masjid al-ḥaram*) to the farthest Mosque (*masjid al-aqṣā*), whose precincts we did bless'. This verse provided the foundations for the evolution of a long narrative that started with the night journey to the 'farthest Mosque' (associated from the beginning of the eighth century with the Aqsa mosque in Jerusalem) and continued with a miraculous heavenly voyage (*miʿrāj*).[66] Each supposed stop on the Egyptian journey of the Holy Family became a site of veneration, usually with an annual celebration where local Christians (and, not infrequently, local Muslims and Jews) would congregate at the site. This type of pilgrimage relates to the ancient Middle Eastern practice of visiting the tombs of saints on the believed date of their birthdays (known by the Arabic term *mawlid*). Again, it is not uncommon for *mawlid*s to be attended by local people of all faiths.[67]

One of the reasons for selecting Matarea as part of the itinerary followed by the Holy Family might be the Biblical associations already existing around this locality. Such associations were also recognised by European travellers (see above), probably drawing upon Old Testament sources, particularly Jeremiah 43:12–13:

> He shall kindle a fire in the temples of the gods of Egypt; and he shall burn them and carry them away captive; and he shall pick clean the land of Egypt, as a shepherd picks his cloak clean of vermin; and he shall depart from there safely. He shall break the obelisks of Heliopolis, which is in the land of Egypt; and the temples of the gods of Egypt shall burn with fire.

The site is called the 'City of the Sun' in Isaiah and 'On' in Genesis.[68] The Old Testament resonances of Heliopolis were surely not lost upon the native Christian population of Egypt during the late antique and early medieval periods. In addition, the coming of Christ to Heliopolis could be seen as the fulfilment of the prophecy in Isaiah: 'the idols of Egypt shall tremble at his presence'.[69]

Coptic texts dealing with the Egyptian itinerary of the Holy Family are often difficult to date with precision; one example assigned a sixth-century date (although some scholars place it in the twelfth century) is the so-called *Arabic Gospel of the Infancy*. Based on a lost Greek prototype, the pertinent passage appears in chapter 24 of the text:

> Hence they turned aside to that sycamore which is now called Matarea, and the Lord Jesus brought forth in Matarea a fountain in which the Lady Mary washed His shirt. And from the sweat of the Lord Jesus which she sprinkled there, balsam was produced in that region.[70]

The capacity of the waters of Matarea to cure illness (in this case leprosy) is mentioned later in the text, as is the miraculous ability of the clothes of Christ to rid a boy of demonic possession. In the recounting of the visit of the Holy Family to Matarea in the *Apocryphal Gospel of Pseudo-Matthew*, believed to date to the eighth or ninth century, a different tree takes centre stage. In this version the Virgin was resting under a date palm and desired to eat some of its fruit. Christ bids the tree to bend down in order to offer the fruit to Mary. He then makes the tree rise up to give them the water concealed beneath its roots. From this location a spring comes forth.[71] Similarities with Qur'an 19:23–6 suggest that this version has its origins in the seventh century or earlier.[72]

A more extensive account appears in the homilies written by an Egyptian monk, Zacharie of Sakha. This work is known in Coptic and Arabic versions. Zacharie resigned his official post in order to enter a monastery, and his ordination was performed by Simon, the forty-second patriarch of the Coptic Church (r. 693–700). The homilies must therefore have been written at some point during Zacharie's time as a monk (reckoned to be about thirty years) in the last years of the seventh and the early eighth century.[73] He deals with the story of Matarea in his homily entitled 'The Coming of Our Lord Jesus Christ to the Land of Egypt with his Mother the Virgin Mary, and Joseph the Carpenter, fiancé of [the latter], and Salome'. According to Zacharie of Sakha, the Holy Family, tired from travelling, were resting under a tree near an unnamed village. Joseph and Salome were asleep while the Virgin held the Christ Child in her arms. The latter had requested to drink, but going to the nearby village the mother and child were refused water. The author continues:

> Our Lady (peace be upon her!) returned and it is said that the Lord brought forth water from under the tree, which was not difficult for Him, as He is called the Son of the Most High, and for Him everything is possible. Yet, later writers disagree about which tree the Lord had made appear, some say it is found in the territory of lower Syria (Syro-Palestine), others affirm it is in the land of Egypt, in the governorate of Sharqiyya, but in fact it is sure, just as it is in the eyes of foreigners, that it is the tree of Matarea that we are speaking of at this time.
>
> Going back to Joseph and Salome now, they were asleep and dreaming when they were awakened by the Virgin Mary. They woke up and saw the source of pure and fresh water, and they were astonished and asked the Virgin how this water had appeared: she indicated the child, and they learned of it as they took the water, as has already been mentioned.
>
> They rose and walked until they were nearly in the territory of Cairo (al-Qahira), in a town called 'Ayn Shams. The old Joseph had in his hand a staff on which he relied, which came from a tree in the land of Jericho (Ariha); the Lord took it and broke it into pieces and planted them in this arid place. He placed his divine hand on the land, and from it sprang excellent water, and He took it with his pure hands and drank, and he watered these

dry pieces of wood, which immediately became green and grew branches with a pleasant fragrance – and this we call balsam. This place is now called Matarea (Matariyya), and the source is called the sacred well.

This balsam grew at Jericho, and they produced an oil (*duhn*) which was employed at the anointing of kings, priests, and the utensils of the Temple. [The balsam of Jericho] lasted until He was returned to power, majesty and sovereignty, removing it from that place [Jericho] and ordering it to grow there [Matarea]. Its oil is employed for the manufacture of Holy Myron (*mīrūn*) that the neophyte receives after his baptism, just after leaving the water, and the grace of the Holy Spirit rest upon the neophyte; [the oil is also used for] anointing the altars, the planks of the altar, and other utensils of the holy shrine.

The Lord blessed this place [Matarea] and said, 'Whoever descends into the sacred well to bathe or drink will be cured of all diseases'. And He blessed the tree saying, 'You will not be annihilated, and not a leaf will fall from you, until God inherits the Earth and all therein'. And there is no doubt, in fact, that the story of the tree is one of the most extraordinary stories, since so many years have passed and the tree remains unchanged: not a leaf falls either in summer, winter, spring or autumn, but it stays there awaiting the visitation of those who want to come there. And whoever comes there engraves his name [on the trees?] and one can enumerate these engraved names. In summary, it (the balsam tree) has become as famous as the sun in broad daylight.[74]

While it is certainly possible that the story given above is substantially as it was set down by Zacharie of Sakha in the late seventh or early eighth century, this dating is rendered somewhat uncertain by one detail. In the Arabic version of the story – at least, as it appears in the printed edition – the settlement of ʿAyn Shams is said to be located in the territory of al-Qahira (Cairo). Since the city of al-Qahira was founded by the Fatimid caliphs in 969, it could not have been known to Zacharie of Sakha. This change reflects the knowledge and experience of an Egyptian scribe copying the Zacharie's homilies at the end of the tenth century or later.

The events at Matarea found their way into compilations of Coptic religious writings (known as *synaxarion*, pl. *synaxaria*), such as an Arabic version usually attributed to Michael of Malij. Unlike Zacharie of Sakha's text, this later version presents the water source as something that already exists. The Holy Family journey from Abu Serga in Old Cairo (i.e. Roman Babylon) and bathe in the waters of Matarea. The text continues:

> This source was sanctified and blessed at this time. This is the origin of the oil of balsam that is used to perform the baptism, the consecration of churches, shrines and sacred vessels; it is actually a beneficial remedy to cure many [diseases], and is given as a present to kings, who greatly esteem it.[75]

There is also evidence for the transmission of this narrative into Ethiopic. For example, the Ethiopic *Synaxarion* (dating to the twelfth or thirteenth century) contains a chapter in which the link between the waters of Matarea and the balsam trees is made more explicit. According to the translation given by Ernest Wallis Budge (d. 1934) this text reads:

> Our Lord took Joseph's staff and broke it into little pieces and planted these pieces in that place, and He dug with his own divine hands a well, and there flowed from it sweet water, which had an exceedingly sweet odour. And our Lord took some of the water in His hand, and watered therewith the pieces of wood which he has planted, and straightaway they took root, and put forth leaves, and an exceedingly sweet perfume was emitted by them, which was sweeter than any other perfume. And these pieces of wood grew and increased, and they called them '*Balsân*'. And the Lord Jesus Christ said unto His mother, the Holy Virgin Mary, 'O my mother, these *balsân*, which I have planted, shall abide here forever, and from them shall be [taken] the oil for Christian baptism, when they baptise in the name of the Father and the Son and the Holy Spirit'.[76]

The Ethiopic *Synaxarion* shares aspects of Zacharie of Sakha's homily and the Copto-Arabic *Synaxarion* probably composed by Michael of Malij, as well as shorter accounts such as the *Arabic Gospel of the Infancy*. It differs from each in matters of detail, however; for example, unlike the Copto-Arabic *Synaxarion* (with which it shares its greatest similarities) the Ethiopic version states that the water source is divinely created and not pre-existing on the site. At the time the Ethiopic *Synaxarion* was being composed, these same stories were starting to appear in the European travel writings surveyed in the previous section. The thirteenth and fourteenth centuries witnessed a considerable growth in interest in the life and personality of the Virgin Mary in Europe, in the Byzantine empire, and among the Christian communities of the Islamic world. One aspect of this phenomenon is the increasing prominence of Mary in paintings and mosaics, but it also had an impact upon literature. Scholars have identified examples of the transmission of Marian legends across the Mediterranean at this time, a process that entailed the translation both of Middle Eastern stories into Latin and of European texts into Arabic.[77]

European travellers surveyed in the first section provide a wealth of complementary information, though they sometimes contradict one another on matters of detail. The inconsistencies and exaggerations apparent in these accounts make them a problematic source for the historical reconstruction of Matarea. Seen in its totality, however, this assemblage of primary sources illustrates well the status of the balsam trees and the related attractions of the site in the minds of educated Christian readers and pilgrims. While a few travellers, such as the fifteenth-century diplomat de Lannoy, exhibit little interest in the balsam plantation, the vast majority felt Matarea to be an essential part of their Egyptian tour. This practice gains momentum in the twelfth century, and it is notable that earlier European travellers to the country such as Bernard the Monk (fl. late ninth century) make no mention of balsam cultivation.[78] It is apparent that visitors to the site commonly came with knowledge drawn from a range of sources, including medical literature, historical texts (such as Josephus) and earlier travel accounts. These sources clearly conditioned expectations in significant ways that partially explain differences between European descriptions of the site and those given by Muslim authors (Chapters 3 and 4). European travellers also appear to have been aware of the local stories concerning the visit of the Holy Family to Matarea. There must also have been strong oral traditions circulating among the Christian communities of Egypt. These spoken narratives may have differed from the surviving written versions. Given that most of the European travellers to the Middle East during the medieval and early modern periods were unable to read Arabic, Coptic or Ethiopic, it is reasonable to assume that much of the information about the miraculous origins of the gardens of Matarea was transmitted to these visitors through intermediaries, such as dragomans.[79]

Notes

1. *Work on Geography*, in John Wilkinson with Joyce Hill and W. F. Ryan, trans., *Jerusalem Pilgrimage, 1099–1185* (London: Hakluyt Society, 1988), p. 185. The author also notes that through the clear water of the Dead Sea one could glimpse 'ancient buildings and ruins'.
2. Iain Higgins, trans. with annotations, *The Book of John Mandeville, with Related Texts* (Indianapolis: Hackett, 2011), p. 61. The destroyed cities referred to here are Sodom, Gomorrah, Admah and Zeboim (Genesis 19:24–5).
3. Henry Maundrell, *The Journey of Henry Maundrell, from Aleppo to Jerusalem, A.D. 1697*, in Thomas Wright, ed., *Early Travels in Palestine* (London: Henry G. Bohn, 1848. Reprinted Mineola, NY: Dover Publications Inc., 2003), pp. 454–5. 'Lord Bacon' is the scholar Francis Bacon, first Viscount of St Albans (d. 1626).
4. Tacitus, *Histories* 5:7.
5. Ibid. 5:7.
6. Josephus, *Jewish War* 4:484–5.
7. Burchard of Mount Sion, *Travels in Palestine, A.D. 1280*, trans. Claude Conder and Aubrey Stewart, Palestine Pilgrim Texts Society 12 (London: Palestine Exploration Fund, 1896), p. 59.
8. Introduction in Higgins, trans., *The Book of John Mandeville*, pp. ix–xix.
9. Miles Davidson, *Columbus Then and Now: A Life Re-examined* (Norman, OK and London: University of Oklahoma Press, 1997), pp. 87–8.
10. Carlo Ginzburg, *Cheese and the Worms: The Cosmos of a Sixteenth-century Miller*, trans. John and Anne Tedeschi (London: Penguin Books, 1992), pp. 41–51, et passim.
11. On this plant, see the entry on *Calotropis procera* (Ait.) Ait.f [family: Asclepiadaceae] in Humphrey Burkill, *Useful Plants of West Tropical Africa*, vol. 1 (Richmond: Royal Botanic Gardens, Kew, 1985). Online entry: https://plants.jstor.org/stable/10.5555/al.ap.upwta.1_478 (last consulted: 22 May 2018).
12. Ulrich Seetzen, *Reisen durch Syrien, Palästina, Phoenicien, die Transjordan-Lander, Arabia Petrae und Unter-Aegypten* (Berlin: G. Reimer, 1854–9), I, p. 422. Also Marcus Milwright, *Fortress of the Raven: Karak in the Middle Islamic Period (1100–1650)*, Islamic History and Civilization 72 (Leiden and Boston: Brill, 2008), pp. 110–11.
13. On medieval and early modern European travellers to Egypt, see Anne Wolff, *How Many Miles to Babylon? Travels and Adventures to Egypt and Beyond, from 1300 to 1640* (Liverpool: Liverpool University Press, 2003).

14. For example, Maximillian Hartmuth, 'Oral tradition and architectural history: A sixteenth-century Ottoman mosque in the Balkans in local memory, textual sources and material evidence', in Daniella Talmon-Heller and Katia Cytryn-Silverman, eds, *Material Evidence and Narrative Sources: Interdisciplinary Studies of the History of the Muslim Middle East*, Islamic History and Civilization, Studies and Texts 108 (Leiden and Boston: Brill, 2015), pp. 341–59. Hartmuth employs ideas developed in Jan Vansina, *Oral Tradition as History* (Madison, WI: University of Wisconsin Press, 1985). See also Robert Dankoff, *An Ottoman Mentality: The World of Evliya Çelebi*, The Ottoman World and its Heritage (Leiden and Boston: Brill, 2004).
15. On this story, see Otto Kurz, 'Mamluk heraldry and the *interpretatio Christiana*', in *Studies in Memory of Gaston Wiet*, ed. Miriam Rosen-Ayalon (Jerusalem: Institute of Asian and African Studies, Hebrew University of Jerusalem, 1977), pp. 297–307. See also Marcus Milwright, 'The cup of the *sāqī*: Origins of an emblem of the Mamluk *khāṣṣakiyya*', *Aram* 9–10 (1997–8): 241–56.
16. Prosper Alpin, *Plantes d'Égypte*, trans. Raymond de Fenoyl, Collection des Voyageurs occidentaux en Égypte 22 (Cairo: Institut Français d'Archéologie Orientale, 1980), pp. 33–6 (= chapter VI, pp. 20–2 in the original edition). See also Georg Schweinfurth, *Arabische Pflanzennamen aus Aegypten, Algerien und Jemen* (Berlin: Dietrich Reimer, 1912), p. 22 (the local name is given as *gimmēs*, as compared to Alpin's rendering of *gjumez*); Stefan Halikowski, 'Meanings behind myths: The multiple manifestations of the tree of the Virgin at Matarea', *Mediterranean Historical Review* 23.2 (2008): 115–17.
17. P. M. Jullien, *L'Arbre de la Vierge à Matarieh. Souvenirs du séjour de la Sainte Famille en Égypte*, fourth edition (Cairo: Imprimerie Nationale, 1904), pp. 30–1; Halikowski, 'Meanings behind myths', p. 115. The venerated remains were taken to the sacristy of the Franciscan church in Cairo in 1656. Jean-Baptiste Kléber, the general responsible for French forces in Egypt during the Napoleonic campaign, apparently carved his name into a branch with the point of his sword.
18. For a critical evaluation of the primary sources on Matarea, see Ugo Zanetti, 'Matarieh, la Sainte Famille et les baumiers', *Analecta Bollandiana* 111 (1993): 21–68. See also Jullien, *L'Arbre de la Vierge à Matarieh*; Halikowski, 'Meanings behind myths'.
19. This claim appears in the writings of Gregory of Tours (d. 594). See his *History of the Franks* I:10. Reproduced in Medieval Sourcebook: http://www.christianiconography.info/gregoryHistoryFranks.htm (last consulted: 22 May 2018).

20. Marino Sanudo, *Part XIV of Book III of Marino Sanuto's Secrets for True Crusaders to Help them Recover the Holy Land, Written in* A.D. *1321*, trans. Eustace Conder and Aubrey Stewart, Palestine Pilgrim Texts Society 12 (London: Palestine Exploration Fund, 1896), p. 58.
21. On European ideas about Muslim 'idolatry', see Norman Daniel, *Islam and the West: The Making of an Image* (Edinburgh: Edinburgh University Press, 1960); Michael Camille, *The Gothic Idol: Ideology and Image-making in Medieval Art* (Cambridge and New York: Cambridge University Press, 1989).
22. On Sanudo's promotion of a new Crusade to the Middle East, see Christopher Tyerman, 'Marino Sanudo Torsello and the lost Crusade: Lobbying in the fourteenth century', *Transactions of the Royal Historical Society*, ser. 5, 32 (1982): 57–73; Catherine Harding and Nancy Micklewright, 'Mamluks and Venetians: An intercultural perspective on fourteenth-century material culture in the Mediterranean', *Revue Art Canadienne/Canadian Art Review* 24.2 (1997): 48–9.
23. Doris Behrens-Abouseif, 'The northeastern extension of Cairo under the Mamluks', *Annales Islamologiques* 17 (1981): 157–89.
24. John Webb, trans., 'A survey of Egypt and Syria, undertaken in the year 1422, by Sir Gilbert de Lannoy, Knt. translated from a manuscript in the Bodleian Library at Oxford, with an introductory dissertation, and notes of illustration and reference to the Crusades', *Archaeologia* 21 (1827): 379–80.
25. Felix Fabri, *Evagatorium in Terrae Sanctae, Arabiae et Egypti Peregrinationem*, ed. Konrad Hassler (Stuttgart: Societatis Litterariæ Stuttgardiensis, 1843–9), III, p. 8. Translated in French as *Voyage en Égypte de Félix Fabri, 1483*, trans. Gisèle Hurseaux, Collection des voyageurs occidentaux en Égypte 14 (Cairo: Institut Français d'Archéologie du Caire, 1975), I, pp. 377–8.
26. On this representation of the city, see Viktoria Meinecke-Berg, 'Eine Stadtansicht des mamlukischen Kairo aus dem 16. Jahrhundert', *Mitteilungen des Deutschen Archäologischen Instituts, Abteilung Kairo* 32 (1976): 113–32, pls 33–9.
27. For example, Jean Palerne, *Voyage en Égypte de Jean Palerne, forésien, 1581*, Collection des Voyageurs occidentaux en Égypte 2 (Cairo: Institut Français d'Archéologie Orientale du Caire, 1971), p. 97 (he lists palm, colocassia, carob, sycamore, fig, orange and herbs). See also Arabic sources reviewed in Chapter 3.
28. Travellers give different accounts of the perimeter wall and the degree of access to the site enjoyed by visitors. For example, Leo Africanus remarks: 'The garden is enuironed with a strong wall, whereinto no man may enter without the speciall favour and licence of the gouernor'. See Johannes Leo Africanus (born al-Hasan b. Muhammad al-Wazzan), *The History and Description of Africa and*

the Notable Things Therein Contained, trans. John Pory with notes by Robert Brown (London: Hakluyt Society, 1896), III, p. 879.

29. Burchard of Mount Sion, *Travels in Palestine*, p. 62; Marino Sanudo, *Secrets for True Crusaders*, p. 59. Ludolph von Sudheim claims that the walled compound is 'half a stone's throw across'. See *Ludolph von Suchem's Description of the Holy Land and the Way thither in the Year A.D. 1350*, trans. Aubrey Stewart, Palestine Pilgrim Texts Society 12 (London: Palestine Exploration Fund, 1895), p. 68.

30. For example, William Lithgow (d. c. 1645) claims that the wall was 'six miles in compass and daily guarded by the Turks'. See his *Rare Adventures*, p. 163.

31. Francesco Suriano, *Treatise on the Holy Land*, trans. Theophilus Bellorini and Eugene Hoade (Jerusalem: Franciscan Press, 1949), p. 195; 'Abd al-Latif al-Baghdadi, *The Eastern Key: Kitāb al-Ifādah wa'l-i'tibār of 'Abd al-Laṭīf al-Baghdādī*, trans. Kamal Zand Kamal et al. (London: Allen and Unwin, 1965), pp. 40 (Arabic), 41 (English).

32. Fabri, *Evagatorium in Terrae Sanctae*, III, p. 13. Translated in French as *Voyage en Égypte de Félix Fabri*, I, p. 387.

33. On the *Tractatis de herbis*, see Minta Collins, *Medieval Herbals: The illustrative Traditions*, The British Library Studies in Medieval Culture (London, Toronto and Buffalo, NY: The British Library and University of Toronto Press, 2000), pp. 239–65.

34. Circa babillonia[m] rep[er]it[ur] in quoda[m] campio[n] i[n] quo su[n]t septe[m] fontes. Si aute[m] alias trasfertur nec flores nec fluctus faceret. The translation is given by Collins in *A Medieval Herbal. A Facsimile of British Library Egerton ms. 747*, introduction by Minta Collins and list of plants by Sandra Raphael (London: British Library, 2003), p. 18.

35. John Bernard, trans., *Guide-book to Palestine (circa A.D. 1350)*, Palestine Pilgrim Texts Society 6, no. 3 (London: Palestine Exploration Fund, 1894), p. 32 (no. 170).

36. Ludolph von Sudheim, *Description of the Holy Land*, p. 70. Also Bernard, trans., *Guide-Book to Palestine*, p. 32; Burchard of Mount Sion, *Travels in Palestine*, p. 62; Sanudo, *Secrets for True Crusaders*, p. 59.

37. Suriano, *Treatise on the Holy Land*, p. 195.

38. Leo Africanus, *The History and Description of Africa*, III, p. 879. He writes: 'and this tree (they say) would utterly wither and decay; if the water of the fountains should chance be deminished'.

39. Johann Wansleben (Vansleb), *The Present State of Egypt: or, A New Relation of a*

Late Voyage into the Kingdom, Performed in the Years 1672 and 1673 (London: John Starkey, 1678. Reprinted Westmead: Gregg International Publishers, 1972), p. 140.

40. For example: Sanudo, *Secrets for True Crusaders*, pp. 58–9 (fig tree); Bernardino Amico da Gallipoli, *L'Église de la Matarea*, reprinted in Carla Burri and Nadine Sauneron, trans., *Voyages en Égypte des années 1597–1601. Bernardino Amico da Gallipoli, Aquilante Rocchetta, Henri Castela*, Collection des Voyageurs occidentaux en Égypte 11 (Cairo: Institut Français d'Archéologie Orientale, 1974), pp. 5–6 [18–19] (fig tree); Wansleben, *The Present State of Egypt*, p. 141 (sycamore tree); Suriano, *Treatise on the Holy Land*, p. 195 (according to the translation, a cactus-like tree). See also Halikowski, 'Meanings behind myths', pp. 115–17.

41. For example, see Aquilante Rocchetta, *Voyage en Égypte d'Aquilante Rocchetta, mai–août 1599*, reprinted in Carla Burri and Nadine Sauneron, trans., *Voyages en Égypte des années 1597–1601. Bernardino Amico da Gallipoli, Aquilante Rocchetta, Henri Castela*, Collection des Voyageurs occidentaux en Égypte 11 (Cairo: Institut Français d'Archéologie Orientale, 1974), pp. 47–9 [316–17]. See also Jullien, *L'Arbre de la Vierge à Matarieh*, pp. 27–8; Halikowski, 'Meanings behind myths', p. 115.

42. Eugène Lefébure, 'L'arbre sacré d'Héliopolis', *Sphinx: Revue critique* 5 (1902): 1–22, 65–88; Victor Loret, 'Carnet de notes égyptologique. 2: L'arbre de la Vierge à Materiéh', *Sphinx: Revue critique* 6 (1903): 99–103; Jullien, *L'Arbre de la Vierge à Matarieh*, p. 28.

43. Carsten Niebuhr, *Travels through Arabia and other Countries in the East*, trans. Robert Heron (Edinburgh: R. Morison and Son, 1792), I, p. 65.

44. A similar structure is illustrated in Jullien, *L'Arbre de la Vierge à Matarieh*, photographs on pp. 11, 18.

45. For example, see the illustration of Matarea in *Tractatus de herbis* manuscript, c. 1340. Bibliothèque Nationale de France, Paris: Ms lat. 6823, fol. 25v.

46. On these features, see Bernard, trans., *Guide-book to Palestine*, p. 32; Sanudo, *Secrets for True Crusaders*, p. 59; Leo Africanus, *History and Description of Africa*, III, p. 879; Suriano, *Treatise on the Holy Land*, p. 195; Amico da Gallipoli, *L'Église de la Matarea*, C on the diagram in Burri and Sauneron, trans., *Bernardino Amico da Gallipoli*; Palerne, *Voyage en Égypte*, p. 96; Wansleben, *The Present State of Egypt*, p. 139.

47. Palerne, *Voyage en Égypte*, pp. 96–7.

48. Amico da Gallipoli, *L'Église de la Matarea*.

49. See sources surveyed in Chapter 3.

50. Wansleben, *The Present State of Egypt*, p. 139; Savary, *Letters on Egypt*, I, p. 144; Jullien, *L'Arbre de la Vierge*, pp. 38–9.
51. Higgins, trans., *The Book of John Mandeville*, p. 31.
52. Ludolph von Sudheim, *Description of the Holy Land*, p. 68.
53. For example, Burchard of Mount Sion, *Travels in Palestine*, p. 62; Sanudo, *Secrets for True Crusaders*, p. 31; Ludolph von Sudheim, *Description of the Holy Land*, p. 70.
54. John Gavignan, trans., *Christian Society and the Crusades. Sources in Translation Including the Capture of Damietta by Oliver of Paderborn*, ed. with introduction by Edward Peters (Philadelphia: University of Pennsylvania Press, 1971), pp. 117–18 (chapter 60).
55. Ludolph von Sudheim, *Description of the Holy Land*, pp. 70–1.
56. Fabri, *Evagatorium in Terrae Sanctae*, III, p. 15; Fabri, *Voyage en Égypte*, p. 391.
57. Titus Tobler et al., trans., *Anonymous Pilgrims I–VIII*, Palestine Pilgrims Texts Society 4 (London: Palestine Exploration Fund, 1894). See V, pp. 34–5.
58. Higgins, trans., *The Book of John Mandeville*, p. 61. Cf. Song 1:14; Jerome, letter 108. Translated in John Wilkinson, *Jerusalem Pilgrims before the Crusades* (Warminster: Aris and Phillips, 2002), p. 50. This is discussed in greater detail in Chapter 2.
59. Suriano, *Treatise on the Holy Land*, p. 195.
60. For examples of these claims, see Burchard of Mount Sion, *Travels in Palestine*, p. 62; Sanudo, *Secrets for True Crusaders*, p. 31; Fabri, *Evagatorium in Terrae Sanctae*, III, pp. 13–14; Fabri, *Voyage en Égypte*, pp. 388–90; George Sandys, *A Relation of a Journey*, p. 127.
61. Josephus, *Jewish Antiquities* 8:174.
62. Ludolph von Sudheim, *Description of the Holy Land*, pp. 69–70.
63. Matthew 2:13–15. The quoted passage comes from Hosea 11:1.
64. Matthew 2:19–20.
65. Otto Meinardus, *The Holy Family in Egypt* (Cairo: American University in Cairo Press, 1963. Reprinted 1986).
66. On the *mi'rāj*, see Brooke Vuckovic, *Heavenly Journeys, Earthly Concerns: the Legacy of the Mi'raj in the Formation of Islam*, Religion, History and Culture 5 (New York: Routledge, 2005); Ronald Buckley, *The Night Journey and Ascension in Islam: The Reception of Religious Narrative in Sunnī, Shī'ī and Western Culture*, Library of Middle Eastern History 36 (New York and London: I. B. Tauris, 2013).
67. On these rituals, see Tawfiq Canaan, *Mohammaden Saints and Sanctuaries in Palestine*, Luzac's Oriental Religions Series 5 (London: Luzac and Co., 1927);

Nicholaas Biegman, *Egypt: Moulids, Saints, Sufis* (The Hague and London: Gary Schwarz/SDU and Kegan Paul International Ltd, 1990), pp. 13–71. See also Christopher Taylor, *In the Vicinity of the Righteous: Ziyāra and the Veneration of Saints in Late Medieval Egypt*, Islamic History and Civilization, Studies and Texts 22 (Leiden and Boston: Brill, 1998).

68. Isaiah 19:18. It is described as one of the five Egyptian cities that 'speak the language of Canaan and swear allegiance to the Lord of hosts'. Genesis 41:45.
69. Isaiah 19:1.
70. Translated in Zanetti, 'Matarieh', p. 24; Meinardus, *The Holy Family in Egypt*, pp. 36–7.
71. Translated in Meinardus, *The Holy Family in Egypt*, p. 36.
72. In the Qur'anic version Mary (Maryam) also sits under a palm and partakes of the fruit and the water beneath the tree. Q 19:23–6: And the pains of childbirth drove her to the trunk of a palm-tree: She cried [in her anguish]: 'Ah! Would that I had died before this! Would that I had been a thing forgotten and out of sight!' / But [a voice] cried to her from beneath [the palm-tree]: 'Grieve not! For thy Lord hath provided a rivulet beneath thee; / 'Shake toward thyself the trunk of the palm-tree: It will let fall fresh ripe dates upon thee / 'So eat and drink and cool [thine] eye. And if thou dost see any man, say, 'I have vowed to fast to [God] Most Gracious, and this day I will enter into no talk with any human being'. According to the translation of Yusuf 'Ali.
73. Zanetti, 'Matarieh', p. 25. Also Georg Graf, *Geschichte der christlichen arabischen Literatur* (Vatican: Bibliotheca Apostolica Vaticana, 1944–53), I, pp. 228–30.
74. Adapted from the French translation in Zanetti, 'Matarieh', pp. 26–7. This has been correlated with the Arabic edition: Zacharie of Sakha in Jirjis Hunayn, ed., *Kitāb mayāmir wa-'ajā'ib al-sayyida al-'adhrā' Maryam* (Cairo: Matba'at al-Hilal, 1902), pp. 51–2.
75. Translated in Zanetti, 'Matarieh', p. 29.
76. Ernest Wallis Budge, trans., *The Book of the Saints of the Ethiopian Church. A Translation of the Ethiopic* Synaxarium, *Made from Manuscripts Oriental 660 and 661 in the British Library* (Cambridge: Cambridge University Press, 1928), III, p. 924. Also translated in Meinardus, *The Holy Family in Egypt*, p. 36.
77. On the transmission of texts and images, see Dan Baraz, 'Copto-Arabic collections of Western Marian legends: The reception of a Western text in the East', in Tito Orlandi and David Johnson, eds, *Acts of the Eighth International Congress of Coptic Studies, Washington, 12–15 August 1992* (Rome: C.I.M., 1993), II, pp. 23–32; Dan Baraz, 'The incarnated icon of Saidnaya goes West:

A re-examination of the motif in the light of new manuscript evidence', *Le Muséon* 108 (1995): 181–91; Krijna Ciggaar, 'Manuscripts as intermediaries: The Crusader states and literary cross-fertilization', in Krijna Ciggaar et al., eds, *East and West in the Crusader States: Context – Contacts – Confrontations*, Orientalia Lovaniensia Analecta 75 (Leuven: Peeters, 1996), pp. 131–51.

78. Bernard the Monk (or Bernard the Wise), *A Journey to the Holy Places and Babylon* in Wilkinson, *Jerusalem Pilgrims before the Crusades*, p. 142 (chapters 7 and 8).
79. On the roles performed by dragomans, see Robert Irwin, *For Lust of Knowing: The Orientalists and their Enemies* (London: Penguin Books, 2007), pp. 110–11.

2

Resins in the Ancient World

While the travellers' accounts present fascinating insights into the beliefs concerning Matarea, texts of this nature are difficult to evaluate as historical documents. Travellers, even those who visited the site a few years apart, may contradict one another, and many make seemingly outlandish connections with famous historical figures in their discussions of the balsam garden. Coptic and Ethiopic legends present similar challenges of interpretation. Chapters 2 and 3 outline a more conventional historical narrative. As many of the travellers discussed in Chapter 1 were aware, Matarea was not the first place where balsam had been cultivated. This chapter discusses the textual and archaeological evidence for the plantations located around the Dead Sea and in the Jordan Valley, with a particular emphasis on the chronology of their foundation, their renovation under the Romans, their ultimate demise and the probable date of the transportation of balsam trees to Egypt (Fig. 2.1). Before dealing with these issues, it is necessary to place balsam into the wider context of the collection and distribution of aromatic tree resins in the ancient world.

Resins in Antiquity

A series of painted reliefs in the temple at Deir al-Bahri near Thebes records the events of an expedition sent in about 1500 BCE by Hatshepsut, the Egyptian queen (r. 1481–1472 BCE), to the land identified in the inscriptions as 'Pwenet', and often known in scholarly literature as 'Punt'. The expeditionary force travelled by land and sea to Punt. They enslaved some of the inhabitants and brought back with them many valuable items (some represented in the frescoes and others in the accompanying inscriptions) including gold, ivory, ebony, animals and animal skins. One of the most precious

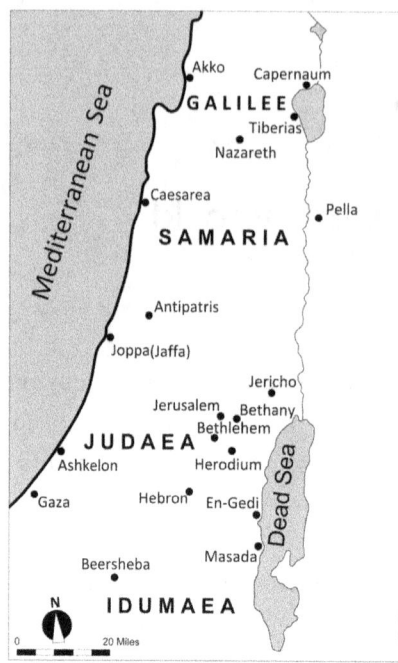

Figure 2.1 Map of the sites associated with ancient balsam cultivation and production. Drawn by Seyedhamed Yeganehfarzand.

elements of the cargo was a group of small trees. It can clearly be seen from the paintings that these were transported with their roots and soil held within baskets or tubs (Fig. 2.2). The legend below this scene lists the precious items being carried aboard the ship. First among them is ' *'ntyw* and *'ntyw* trees'. Another painting later in the series depicts *'ntyw* being offered to the god Amon with Queen Hatshepsut in attendance. The inscription indicates that the queen herself was wearing this substance on her limbs as a fragrant ointment, and elsewhere there is a reference to trees having been taken and set into the ground in Egypt.[1]

There are records of journeys from Egypt to Punt dating as early as 2800 BCE, though Queen Hatshepsut's expedition is the first to make explicit mention of trees and their perfumed products. The location of Punt remains uncertain. Scholars no longer favour southern Arabia, with a plausible suggestion being that Punt, if it ever represented a clearly defined geographical area,

Figure 2.2 Painted relief showing trees carried in baskets. Temple of Deir al-Bahari, near Thebes, fifteenth century BCE. After Hepper, 'An ancient expedition'. Drawing: Marcus Milwright.

should be identified with the Horn of Africa.[2] The other problematic issue is the isolation of the species of tree that the Egyptians called *'ntyw*. It was certainly a tree from which aromatic substances could be manufactured, and it was not the only type of incense that the queen's expedition brought back from Punt (two others are named as *ihmut* and *sntr*). It will probably never be certain what *'ntyw* was, though it seems likely to have been a form of either myrrh (the finest type being a resin from *Commiphora myrrha* [Nees] Engl.) or frankincense (referring principally to resins gathered from plants of the genus *Boswellia*, particularly *Boswellia sacra* Flueck). Nigel Groom speculates that if Punt corresponds to Eritrea, then the Egyptian *'ntyw* was probably gathered from one of the indigenous local species, such as *Commiphora erythraea* Engl. or *Boswellia papyrifera* (Delile ex Caill.) Hochst.[3] Egyptians of the second millennium BCE also employed resins in medicine. Numerous resins are specified in treatments within a medical text known as the Ebers papyrus, dating to the ninth year of the rule of Amenhotep I (probably 1537 BCE).[4] One of these, known in the text as *senen*, has been identified tentatively as a balsam, perhaps 'balm of Mecca' (on this product, see Chapter 4).[5]

The employment of tree resins in perfumes and medicaments, for embalming and as incense (defined here in the narrow sense of a substance burnt in order to generate aromatic smoke) has ancient origins. It is difficult to pinpoint quite when the organised long-distance trade in resins commenced, and particularly those harvested from trees on the Arabian peninsula and the Horn of Africa (Fig. 2.3). That the trade was well developed by the mid-fifth century BCE is clear from the testimony of Herodotus who lists 'frankincense, myrrh, cassia, cinnamon, and a gum called *ledanon* (labdanum or ladanum)' among the products only found in Arabia.[6] The same author records that the Persian king Darius (r. 521–486 BCE) received an annual consignment of 1,000 talents of frankincense as tribute from the tribes of Arabia.[7] Frankincense (also known as olibanum) and myrrh were employed in the rituals of the ancient Israelites in the seventh century BCE, and there are abundant references to these, and other resins, in the Old Testament (see below and Chapter 8). Groom concludes that the trade in aromatic products from southern Arabia is unlikely to have commenced much before the end of the eighth century BCE.[8] By the fourth century the southern Arabian kingdoms profiting from the lucrative trade in frankincense and myrrh are listed by the botanist Theophrastus (d. c. 287 BCE): Saba, Hadramawt, Qataban and Main.[9]

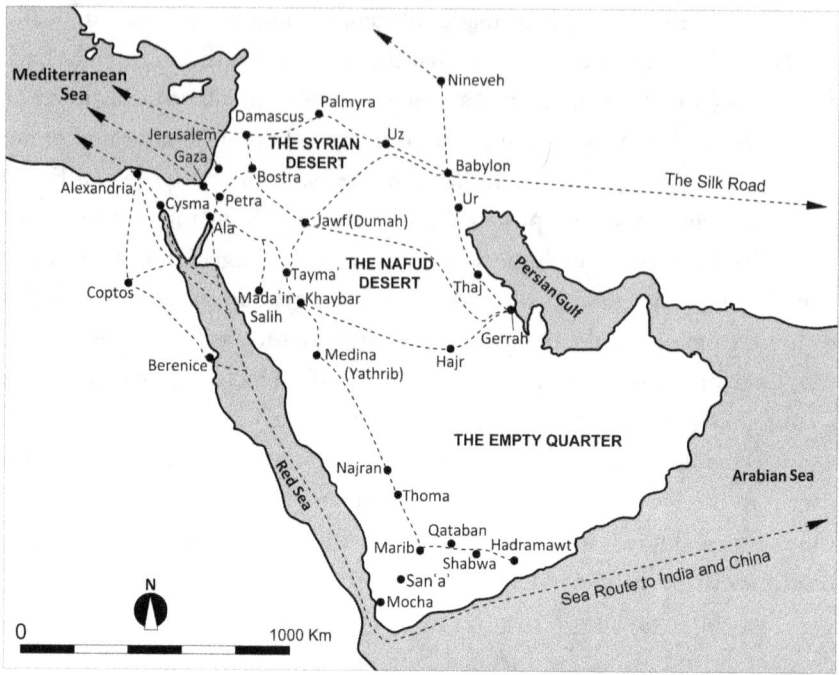

Figure 2.3 Map of the ancient incense routes in Arabia and the Horn of Africa. Drawn by Seyedhamed Yeganehfarzand.

The high point in the international trade in incense (from the Horn of Africa, Arabia and elsewhere in the Middle East) was during the Roman empire, particularly the first and second centuries CE. Pliny the Elder's (Gaius Plinius Secundus, d. 79 CE) *Natural History* is the most extensive source on different types of incense, the places from which they were harvested and the trade routes employed to bring them to Roman lands. The Romans greatly desired these perfumed resins and gums. Not only were these valuable commodities burnt in the pagan religious rituals of the Roman state, but they were also much used in domestic settings. Myrrh, frankincense, balsam and other fragrant products were burnt within houses and were made into perfumes, ointments and medicaments (see also Chapter 8).[10]

Substances like frankincense and myrrh passed through the hands of many middlemen, each extracting his own profit. Dynasties like the Nabataeans (fourth century BCE–106 CE), located in south-eastern Syria, Jordan and the north-west of the Arabian peninsula, based their wealth on

Figure 2.4 View of ancient Petra, Jordan. Photograph: Marcus Milwright.

control of one part of the land route passing from Yemen along the western side of Arabia (the Hijaz), and thence to the ports of southern Palestine. At their height their rule extended as far as the city of Busra (ancient Bostra) in the basalt desert of south-eastern Syria. The wealth generated by this incense trade is well illustrated by the monumental architecture of the Nabatean settlements of Petra (Fig. 2.4) in Jordan and Mada'in Salih in Saudi Arabia.[11] Excavations have also recovered trading entrepôts such as the town of Qaryat al-Faw in the south of modern-day Saudi Arabia, which enjoyed its most active phase between the first century BCE and about the fourth century CE.[12] Incense was also carried by sea routes, and formed part of wider maritime trade that brought raw materials (such as wood, gold and slaves) from East Africa, and manufactured goods (such as printed textiles) and spices from the Indian Subcontinent. This trading network is known from excavations of ancient ports such as Myos Hormos (founded by the Ptolemies in the third century BCE) on the Red Sea coast of Egypt. The most important primary text on this trade is the second-century *Periplus of the Erythraean Sea*. The *Periplus* contains many references to perfumed products, and particularly to myrrh and frankincense.[13]

Old Testament references to frankincense, myrrh and other aromatic resins are significant, though it is often difficult to assign clearly defined chronological parameters for the books in which they appear. Genesis mentions a camel caravan of Ishmaelites from Gilead carrying spices, 'balm' (*zori*) and a substance called in Hebrew *lot* (probably ladanum).[14] Gilead is the region of modern-day Jordan located directly east of the Jordan Valley and Dead Sea depression. Early references to the land of Sheba (i.e. southern Arabia) and the gold and incense it possesses appear in Isaiah, perhaps indicating the presence of a long-distance trade in incense in the early sixth century BCE.[15] The book of Ezekiel, also initially compiled at the time of the Babylonian exile, contains a description of merchants from 'Sheba and Raamah' selling spices, precious stones and gold at the Mediterranean port of Tyre.[16] Jeremiah makes a specific connection between frankincense and Sheba: 'Of what use to me is the frankincense that comes from Sheba, or sweet cane from a distant land? Your burnt offerings are not acceptable, nor are your sacrifices pleasing to me'.[17]

Frequent references are made in the Old Testament to both myrrh and frankincense, usually in the context of perfumes and incense.[18] Myrrh is also mentioned in connection with cosmetics.[19] That they also played important roles in Jewish ritual is indicated by a passage in Exodus.[20] 'Liquid myrrh' (stacte) is employed in the creation of the oil which Moses uses for anointing sacred items (Chapter 8). In the New Testament the medicinal qualities (specifically the alleviation of pain) are implied in the episode recorded in Mark where a cup of wine mixed with myrrh is offered to Christ before his crucifixion.[21] Myrrh and aloes are also mentioned as embalming ingredients brought by Nicodemus to prepare the body of Christ for burial.[22] Myrrh and frankincense are also famously mentioned with gold as the gifts brought by the three Magi to the infant Christ in Bethlehem.[23]

Most interesting in the present context, however, are two other products, known in Hebrew as *zori* and *bosem* (pl. *besamin*), both of which are commonly translated into English as 'balm' though the latter is also understood as 'spice'.[24] As noted above, *zori* is mentioned in Genesis as part of the caravan of Ishmaelites coming from Gilead, indicating that this commodity derived from a plant grown in Gilead (presumably a native species of the region).[25] The word itself may be even older, possibly deriving from the Ugaritic *r-z-w*.[26]

The association with the land of Gilead is made again later in Genesis, while Ezekiel includes ẓori in a list of goods traded by 'Judah and the land of Israel'.[27] Two passages in Jeremiah demonstrate that ẓori was valued for its role in medicine.[28] The first of these reads:

> For the hurt of my people I am hurt, I mourn, and dismay has taken hold of me. Is there no balm (ẓori) in Gilead? Is there no physician there? Why then has the health of my poor people not been restored?

The second passage reads, 'Go up to Gilead, and take balm, O Virgin daughter of Egypt! In vain have you used many medicines; there is no healing for you'. The last line has also been translated as 'no skin shall grow over your wounds', and would fit well with the evidence for tree resins being used in the treatment of wounds and as an antiseptic and an anti-inflammatory (Chapter 6). *Bosem* is probably the root of the Greek *bálsamon*, the Latin *opobalsamum* and the Arabic *balasān*, but has the more generic meaning of 'perfume' in modern Hebrew. Its Old Testament meaning appears to be more circumscribed, as an exotic aromatic spice, probably imported into Israel from another Middle Eastern region.[29] Where the ẓori is characterised as a medicament in the book of Jeremiah, *bosem* seems to have been employed for its fragrant qualities, in perfumes and anointing oils.

Thus, it would appear that these two 'balms' are distinct commodities coming from different sources, ẓori principally from Gilead and *bosem* from some other locality beyond the borders of ancient Israel. It is the former, ẓori or 'balm of Gilead', that has been most frequently equated in medieval and early modern writings with the balsam cultivated in the regions of Jericho and En-Gedi, but there are good reasons to doubt such an identification. That ẓori was some form of tree resin is suggested not just by the testimony of Jeremiah in the Hebrew Bible, but by the fact that the word is translated in the Septuagint (the Greek Bible) as *ritíni* (or *rhetine*). Theophrastus also employs the term *ritíni* (resin) when discussing these products in book 9 of his *Enquiry into Plants*. Although both ẓori and balsam were types of resin, the former appears to have been native to Gilead and the latter an imported species (this issue is discussed in greater detail in Chapter 4). Nigel Groom has suggested that ẓori should probably be identified as the resin of the terebinth tree (*Pistacia palaestina* Boiss.), a native to Syro-Palestine. He speculates further that this may be linked to the 'incense' sent as tribute by the chiefs of 'Retenu' (probably referring to the region of Palestine) following the military campaigns of the Egyptian ruler Thutmosis III (r. c. 1479–1425 BCE).[30]

The Balsam Plantations of Ancient Judaea

Flavius Josephus advances the most ambitious claims regarding the antiquity of the Palestinian balsam trees. As the son of a priest of Jerusalem and a citizen of the Roman empire, he was well placed to document the ancient beliefs of Judaism (*Jewish Antiquities*, written in c. 94 CE) and the events of the Roman suppression of the Jewish Revolt in Palestine between 66 and 70 CE (*The Jewish War*, written in c. 75 CE). In book 8 of *Jewish Antiquities* Josephus relates that the legendary wisdom of King Solomon and the splendour of his palaces attracted the attention of 'the woman who at that time ruled as queen of Egypt and Ethiopia'. Although the author does not name her, it is clear that he is referring to the Queen of Sheba, reputed to have been ruler over the kingdom of south-west Arabia (broadly corresponding to modern-day Yemen). She decided to make the journey to Jerusalem in order to see whether the stories about Solomon were true. Overcome by the reality of the man and his lavish architectural projects, the queen announces, 'let us bless God who has so well loved this country and its inhabitants as to make you their king'. The following passage contains an important reference to the balsam trees:

> And, after she had shown by her words how she felt toward the king, she revealed her feeling more clearly by her gifts, for she gave him twenty talents of gold and an incalculable quantity of spices and precious stones; and they say that we have the root (*ríza*) of *opobálsamon*, which our country still bears, as the result of this woman's gift.[31]

The way Josephus describes the visit of the Queen of Sheba to Solomon follows relatively closely the version in 1 Kings,[32] though he embellishes the Biblical account. In the case of the section quoted above he diverges in two significant points: first in the quantity of gold (1 Kings gives this as 120 talents), and second in the mention of the root of balsam, which Josephus claims was the source of the balsam plantations of ancient Judaea. It seems likely that Josephus was drawing much of his additional information from popular legends circulating among the Jewish communities of the first century CE, though it is unknown how far back one can trace the association of the balsam trees with the visit of the Queen of Sheba. It is also pertinent that 1 Kings employs the term *bosem* for spice, perhaps indicating that in the late first century CE this word was directly associated with balsam. By the time of the compilation of the *Babylonian Talmud* there was evidently some confusion regarding the original meanings of words like *bosem* and *zori*.[33]

Solomon's long rule probably occurred in the mid-tenth century BCE (c. 971–931 BCE). If Josephus' story is to be believed the history of balsam cultivation in Palestine can be placed more than six centuries before the first accurate botanical description of the plant by Theophrastus. There is, however, no independent corroboration for Josephus' claim. Excavations at En-Gedi, one of the major centres for balsam cultivation, provided no signs of activity on the site as early as the tenth century BCE.[34] In addition, the source text for Josephus – 1 Kings – dates after the end of the Jewish monarchy in 586 BCE. It is necessary, therefore, to look elsewhere for evidence concerning the earliest traces of the plant in Palestine. Where Josephus' testimony is useful, though, is in its suggestion that the trees were not native to En-Gedi and Jericho, but were, in fact, brought from Arabia (Chapter 4).

If the *zori* (balm) of Gilead is to be identified as balsam – and this seems rather unlikely – then its appearance in Jeremiah could place evidence for balsam cultivation as early as the late seventh or early sixth century BCE.[35] Of course, the text of this Old Testament book would have experienced numerous later additions and redactions. Also dating to the sixth century BCE (i.e. during the Exilic period) is the book of Ezekiel, containing the reference to the trade in products including balm from 'Judah and the land of Israel'.[36] Again the probability that this text experienced later redactions means that caution is needed when using it as historical evidence. *Bosem* is also referred to in early books such as Exodus and later, post-Exilic works such as the Song of Solomon (fourth–third century BCE).

The discussion of balsam in the *Enquiry into Plants* (9.6) offers greater chronological precision as the birth and death dates of its author, Theophrastus (c. 371–287 BCE) are relatively certain. The botanical aspects of his account of the balsam tree are discussed in greater detail in Chapter 4, but Theophrastus is also a valuable source regarding the early cultivation of the plant. He writes that *bálsamon* 'grows in the valley (*avlōn*) in the vicinity of Syria' (i.e. the geological rift that comprises the Jordan Valley, Dead Sea and Wadi 'Araba) and that the plants are contained within two parks/gardens (*paradeísous*), one about 20 *pléthron* (equivalent to around 1.6 hectares) and the other smaller in size.[37] He does not specify the locations of these plantations, though this can be verified through information in later sources. Significantly, Theophrastus also claims that the balsam tree is unknown in the wild. In other words, those trees in the gardens of the 'valley of Syria' must have diverged from their wild forebears, presumably as the result of selective breeding and intensive cultivation practices, decades or even centuries before the death of Theophrastus.

Diodorus of Sicily, a geographer who was active in the first century BCE, is another source who claims that the balsam trees were unknown in any location other than that of a 'certain valley' near the Dead Sea. According to his description balsam had been cultivated at this location for two centuries prior to the rule of Julius Caesar (r. 48–44 BCE). Diodorus notes that the trees generated a considerable revenue and that balsam was highly valued by physicians. The author does, however, mention the existence of another balsam that grows in Arabia. This Arabian balsam was not greatly valued in commerce and medical practice.[38] The geographer Strabo (d. c. 24 CE) writes that the area of Jericho (Hiericus) has a 'palm grove' (*foinikōn*) some 100 *stadia* (about 18 km) in length. Planted with a variety of fruit trees, the area was intensively irrigated, and also supported many dwellings. In addition, he notes the presence of a palace (*basíleion*) and a 'balsam garden' (*tou balsámon parádeisos*).[39] Pliny claims that there were two balsam plantations, the larger comprising 20 *iugera* (about 5 hectares) and the other being smaller.[40] Josephus calls Jericho 'the nursery of balsam', though he does not provide precise details about the area of the oasis given over to the cultivation of the plant.[41]

The palace mentioned by Strabo can be associated with the Hasmonean (140–37 BCE) and Herodian (37 BCE–92 CE) dynasties, and the palm garden itself was evidently considered to be the preserve of the Jewish kings. Archaeological reconnaissance and excavations in the vicinity of Jericho revealed extensive palatial developments during these two dynastic phases, and it seems probable that considerable attention was paid to the cultivation of balsam in the gardens.[42] Pliny states that the balsam plantations had always been in royal hands (i.e. of the Jewish kings), though he does not elaborate about when this practice originated.⁴³ En-Gedi is another site that has been associated on textual and archaeological grounds with the cultivation of balsam; it may be the location of the second, smaller garden or park mentioned by Theophrastus. Excavations and surveys at En-Gedi indicate that the site was first settled during the seventh century BCE, probably under the rule of Josiah (r. 639–609 BCE), but there is no indication of balsam cultivation at this early date.⁴⁴ John Hyracanus (r. 134–104 BCE) may have established the oasis of En-Gedi as a Hasmonean royal domain and settled farmers in the area.

Roman interest in the lucrative groves of date palm and balsam can be traced to 34 BCE when, according to Josephus, Mark Antony (d. 30 BCE) assigned the agricultural lands of Jericho to Cleopatra (r. 51–30 BCE). These territories had formerly been under the control of Herod I (Herod the Great, r. 37 or 36–4 or 1 BCE), but now he was obliged to lease them from Queen Cleopatra for the considerable sum of 200 talents a year.⁴⁵ It is also possible that the balsam garden had been lost to the Jews in earlier times during the conquests of Alexander the Great (r. 336–323 BCE). This is implied by Pliny, and is not inconsistent with Alexander's imperial ambitions.⁴⁶ Alexander seems to have been interested in spreading his dominion over the lands of southern Arabia (the source of many valuable forms of incense); the planned military campaign was aborted due to his sudden death.

Several medieval sources speculate that the balsam trees were first transplanted to Egypt during the rule of Cleopatra (Chapter 1), though there is no independent support for this idea. The defeat of the fleet of Mark Antony and Cleopatra by Octavian (subsequently Augustus Caesar, r. 27 BCE–14 CE) at the battle of Actium in 31 BCE probably had an impact on the ownership of the balsam gardens of Jericho and En-Gedi, however. The writings of Josephus suggest two possibilities: first, that the lease to Herod was simply continued with the monies paid now to Augustus; and second, that the lands were returned outright to Herod.⁴⁷ Whatever the case, the exile of the Herodian king Archelaus in 6 CE allowed the Romans to take direct control of the balsam gardens. Josephus writes that the property of Archelaus was 'confiscated to the imperial treasury' as part of the process of transforming Judaea into a province of the Roman empire.⁴⁸

A later document found in the 'Cave of Letters' in the Judaean desert offers an insight into the legal status of En-Gedi. The papyrus, which records the acknowledgement of a debt, gives both the date it was written (equivalent to 124 CE) and the location. En-Gedi is defined as 'the village of our Lord the Emperor' (*kóme kiríou Kaísaros*). This unusual formulation is repeated on another undated papyrus. The wording indicates that the village constituted part of the private property (*patrimonium*) of the Roman emperor. Hannah Cotton argues that En-Gedi was probably part of the imperial *patrimonium* from 6 CE, and perhaps as early as 31 BCE.[49] Certainly there were good reasons why the Romans might have sought to gain control of the balsam plantations and the groves of date palms around En-Gedi and Jericho. Balsam was highly valued around the Mediterranean, and the finest *opobalsamum* retailed for extraordinary sums (Chapter 5).

Balsam Processing and Sale: The Archaeological Evidence

Archaeological research in the Dead Sea valley has produced considerable evidence for the processing of fragrant plants for use in perfumes, cosmetics and medicines (Fig. 2.1). To judge by the extent of the enterprise – ranging from substantial processing plants to smaller domestic installations – this represented a lucrative industry for both the state and the inhabitants of the area. Given the paucity of specific references to balsam in the artefacts and documents recovered in excavations (only one vessel and two papyri, all found at Masada, actually mention the product by name),[50] some caution is required in the evaluation of the evidence presented below. In other words, while it seems plausible that the pools, crushing areas and other installations were used solely, or in part, for the processing of balsam there is, as yet, no definitive proof. The abundant textual evidence, both before and after 70 CE, for balsam cultivation in these regions lends credence to the hypotheses advanced by excavators, however. As the archaeological evidence spans the phases of Herodian and Roman-Byzantine rule, it is grouped together in this section.

The Herodian period has revealed evidence for the processing of perfumed plant products. At 'Ein Boqeq, south of Masada, excavations uncovered a substantial two-storey farmhouse with associated industrial structures that are believed to have been used for the production of perfumes (Fig. 2.5). With

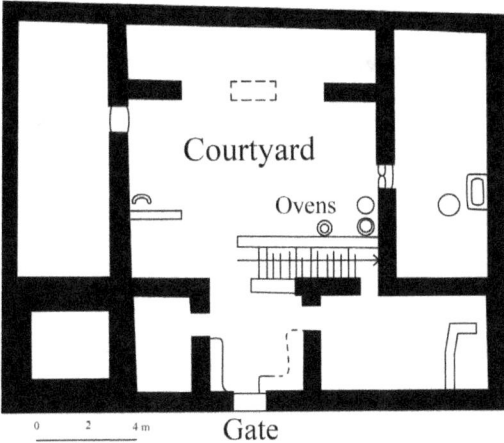

Figure 2.5 Installation used in the production of perfumes, 'Ein Boqeq, Israel. After Fischer, Gichon and Tal, *'En Boqeq* (2000), reproduced in Hirschfeld, 'The rose and the balsam'. Drawing: Naomi Shields.

the living areas on the upper floor, the ground floor and courtyard contained furnaces, soaking pools and grinding stones.[51] Similar evidence was found in the excavation of another processing plant at 'Ein Feshka, south of Khirbat Qumran (Fig. 2.6). In this case the large soaking pool (containing crushing stones) was connected to a channel through which liquid could be transferred into a vat.[52] At Jericho excavations have brought to light the winter palace of the Herodian dynasty. Within this complex are installations that the excavators believed were utilised for the production of date wine. Yizhar Hirschfeld raises the possibility that these installations were also suitable for the manufacture of perfumes. In the light of the textual evidence for the maintenance of royal balsam plantations by the Hasmonean and Herodian kings, the creation of a designated processing area within the palatial complex of Jericho is not improbable.[53]

On the basis of his analysis of the evidence from the Herodian-period site at 'Ein Feshka and the other sites in the Dead Sea region, Hirschfeld suggests that the processing of balsam (in this case *xylobalsamum*) was broken down into four stages. First, the cuttings from the trees were harvested, probably in the early morning to keep them cool. Second, the twigs and branches were crushed in the processing plant, this occurring both outside the pool and within it. Third, the crushed plant matter was soaked in the pool. With

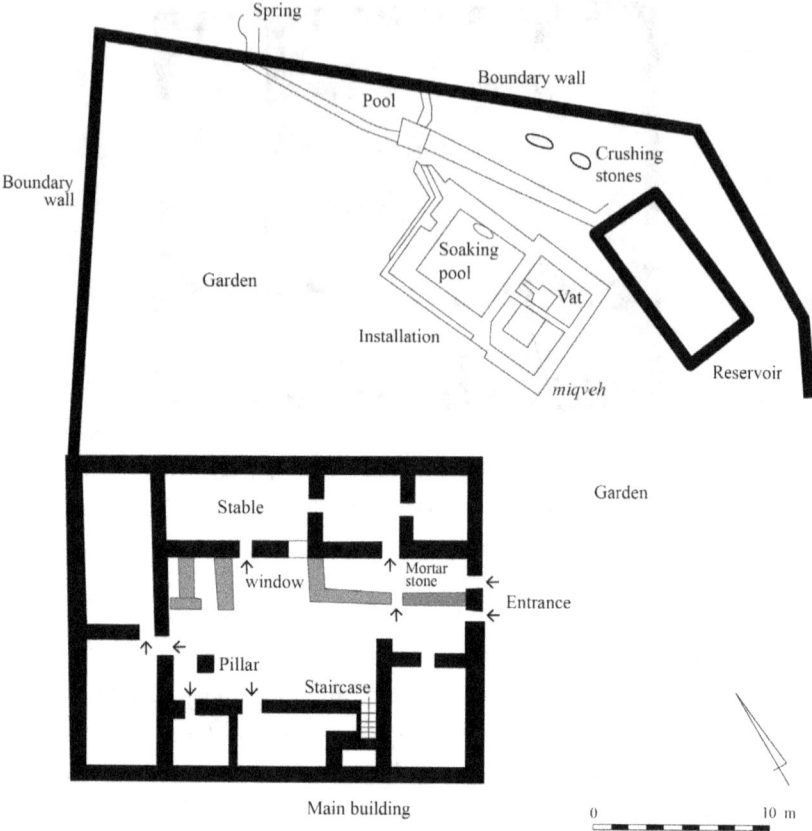

Figure 2.6 Installation used in the production of perfumes, 'Ein Feshka, Israel. After Dov Porotsky in Hirschfeld, 'The rose and the balsam'. Drawing: Naomi Shields.

the evaporation of the water the oleo-resin was drawn out of the cells within the branches, and floated to the surface where it could be skimmed off. In the fourth stage the oleo-resin from the pool was poured into the collecting vat. Hirschfeld notes the absence of furnaces on the site, and he suggests that, after these four stages of processing at 'Ein Feshka, the balsam 'essence' would have been transported to Qumran where there were furnaces to turn the balsam into a finished product for sale in Palestine and elsewhere. In later periods the processing of balsam may have been achieved on a smaller scale. At En-Gedi three houses of the late Roman and early Byzantine periods (i.e. fourth and fifth centuries) were found to contain a small basin leading via a plastered channel into a ceramic jar set into the floor.[54]

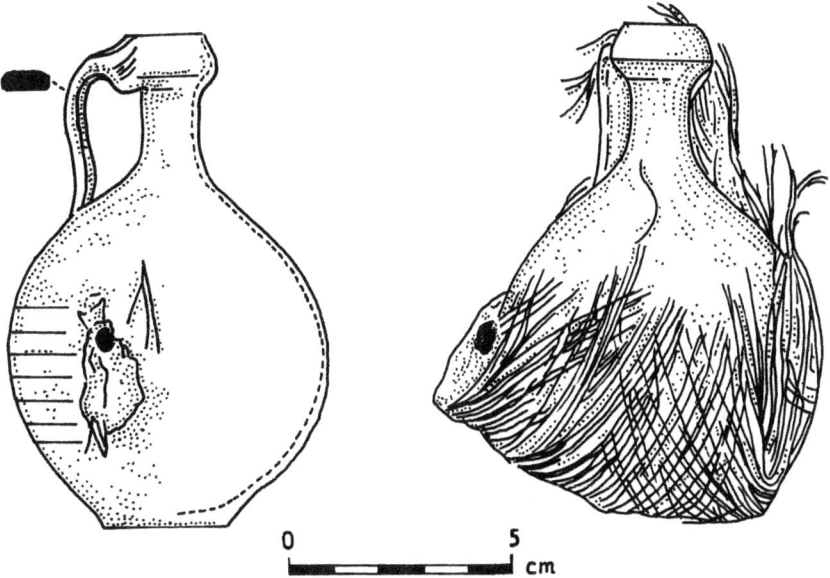

Figure 2.7 Ceramic juglet wrapped in palm leaves found in the Qumran region. After Patrich and Arubas, 'A Juglet', fig. 4. Drawing: Marcus Milwright.

Three other archaeological finds cast a light on the high value attributed to balsam in first-century Palestine. Excavations at the Herodian complex at Masada revealed a ceramic container marked in Aramaic with the words *miz balsama* ('balsam sap'), presumably indicating the commodity it once held. Another, now in the Israel Museum in Jerusalem, is inscribed with the word for balsam in both Hebrew and Aramaic. With a capacity of up to 25 litres, these jars when full would have been precious indeed.[55] More intriguing is a small juglet recovered from one of the caves in the vicinity of Qumran (Fig. 2.7). Encased in palm leaves and still stoppered, the juglet was found with other Herodian era ceramics, and can be dated with relative confidence to the first century CE. Contained within the juglet was about 50 g of a viscous liquid, only slightly oxidised over the course of 1,900 years. Chemical analysis revealed that the liquid was not olive oil, and that it had some affinities with an oil extracted in modern times from date stones. There is no ancient reference to the manufacture of oil from date stones, and the authors of the report speculate that the liquid contained within the vessel is the famous balsam 'oil' of En-Gedi and Jericho.[56]

From the First Jewish Revolt to the Seventh Century CE

Most of the balsam cultivation in the province of Judaea was controlled by the Romans from 6 CE. En-Gedi was principally a private possession of the Roman emperor from this time, and is recorded as such in 124 CE. Prior to the inception of the Jewish Revolt in 66 CE, Jericho contained the larger balsam plantation, but this situation was to change, and by the end of the first century it fades from the written record; En-Gedi is consistently mentioned from this time as the pre-eminent source for balsam. The Jewish Revolt was a turning point in the history of the cultivation of balsam.

Emperor Vespasian (r. 69–79 CE) entrusted the final subjugation of Judaea to his son Titus, a man with proven military experience who would later go on to rule as emperor (r. 79–81 CE). Tacitus states that Titus brought together the three legions already in Judaea (the fifth, tenth and fifteenth), the twelfth legion from Syria, and some parts of the third and eighteenth legions stationed in Alexandria. This was augmented by other troops and cavalry provided by the kings Agrippa, Sohemus and Antiochus, and by a contingent of Arabs.[57] The campaign was marked by bitter fighting and, most notoriously, the destruction of the Herodian Temple. With regard to the precious trees of En-Gedi Pliny records that 'the Jews assaulted and ravaged it just as they ravaged their own life; the Romans warded off the attack, and they battled over the fruit (i.e. the balsam)'.[58] En-Gedi had already suffered significant damage in an earlier phase of the revolt; Josephus records that on Passover of 68 CE a group known as the Sicarii, who had occupied the nearby site of Masada since 66 CE, launched a raid on the village, carrying away supplies and killing many of the women and children.[59] In the same year the Roman army took over the area. Notably, Pliny records that En-Gedi was second only to Jerusalem in quality of its agricultural land and date palms, but that it was now like 'a heap of ashes'.[60]

In the aftermath of the Jewish Revolt, the balsam trees again reverted to the direct control of the Roman state. Pliny writes of balsam that 'it is enslaved now and pays tribute together with its people'.[61] That the people of the region were considered by the emperor to be firmly under his dominion is captured in striking form in a *sesterce* minted by Emperor Vespasian in 71 CE which carried on its obverse a slumped female figure personifying the

Figure 2.8 Obverse and reverse faces of a 'Judaea capta' *sesterce* minted by Vespasian in 71 CE. Israel Museum (IDAM), Jerusalem, Israel. Erich Lessing / Art Resource, NY.

Jewish polity on the left-hand side of a centrally placed date palm (Fig. 2.8). The inscription reads IVDAEA CAPTA ('Judaea conquered'). Following standard Roman practice, the victorious legions paraded through the streets of Rome carrying their battle standards and booty from their campaigns. This commemoration of victory is recorded in visual form on relief panels attached to the Arch of Titus, erected in 81 CE in Rome. Among the objects evidently paraded through the city in 70 CE were the Great Menorah, trumpets and other precious artefacts looted from the Herodian Temple (Fig. 2.9). It is known from written sources that the balsam trees were among the items paraded through Rome, though no trace of them is apparent in the reliefs on the arch. Pauline Donceel-Voûte has suggested they may originally have been present. Roman reliefs could be further adorned with gilded bronze elements, and it is possible that the representations of the trees were once placed in the area behind the Menorah.[62]

The Roman campaign against the Jewish Revolt was partially driven by the revenues generated from such crops as date palm and balsam. Pliny further records that in the five years after the Jewish Revolt the *fiscus* generated 800,000 *sesterces* from the sale of *xylobalsamum*, the cheaper liquid made by boiling the branches and twigs of the balsam trees.[63] Romans made extensive use of incense and perfumes in their everyday lives, and balsam was one of the most valued of these perfumes. Thus, it was in the interests of the state both

Figure 2.9 Relief showing the Triumph through Rome of Titus, Arch of Titus, Rome. 71 CE. Photograph: Marcus Milwright.

to ensure the regular supply of these fragrant commodities and to regulate the prices paid to the major suppliers. The empire sought to bring under their authority the lands controlled by the Nabataean dynasty, completing this task in 106 CE. Another great Arabian trading entrepôt, the Syrian city of Palmyra, caught the attention of the Romans, first under Mark Antony in 41 BCE who organised a raiding party in the hope of seizing some of its riches. By 20 CE Palmyra had been annexed by the Romans, though Emperor Aurelian (r. 270–5) later had to retake it by force from Queen Zenobia (r. 267–c. 273) in 272 CE.

The plantations in En-Gedi were probably in need of restoration as the result of the battles fought in the vicinity, and Pliny indicates that the land planted with balsam trees greatly increased after 70 CE. This probably included the slopes around En-Gedi, as he comments that balsam 'covers hillsides as vineyards do'.[64] Terracing, aqueducts, canals and cisterns have been discovered around En-Gedi. All of these features are dated to the Roman and Byzantine periods, though the initial implementation of water transport and storage infrastructure in the vicinity of Jericho appears to have been the result of Herodian patronage.[65] This sort of major hydraulic engineering around En-Gedi speaks of an active involvement of the Roman state in the revival of the region. Pliny also writes of the cultivation practices used for the balsam trees. The soil was regularly hoed in order to keep it aerated. The trees were nurtured from cuttings (Chapter 4) and then trained in the manner of grapevines. The trees fruited within three years, but from that time the quality of the sap diminished. Hence, trees were usually cut down after about three years.

Mindful that this precious resource might again provoke attempts by the Jews to retake the balsam plantations, or destroy the trees, the Roman authorities garrisoned troops in En-Gedi. The document of 124 CE mentions the centurion of *cohors I milliaria Thracum*, a brigade of troops who may have been billeted there for some time (they are known to have been in Syria until 91 CE). By 128 the troops of *cohors I milliaria Thracum* had been assigned elsewhere.[66] Other potential signs of the Roman official presence at En-Gedi comprised a substantial villa, built on the remains of the Herodian palace, and a bathhouse. Despite its designation as personal property (*patrimonium*) of the emperor, documents from the early second century record the sale and transfer of privately owned agricultural land in En-Gedi. Shimon bar Kokhba probably took control of the balsam plantations of En-Gedi during his revolt against Roman rule (132–6 CE). Papyri of this period indicate that the Jewish leader leased out land in the vicinity.[67] Following the suppression of the Bar Kokhba rebellion, En-Gedi reverted to Roman rule.

The physician Claudius Galen (d. 200 or 217) describes En-Gedi as the location where balsam 'grows most plentifully and most beautifully'.[68] He makes no mention of Jericho as a source of the famous tree.[69] Two third-century references to the balsam of Judaea appear in the Babylonian Talmud. The first (Berachot 43a) divides balsam between that of the emperor and that of Rabbi Judah the Prince.[70] This seems to indicate that the balsam was still owned by the Roman *fiscus*, but with some part of the cultivation (and revenues) being held in private hands. Some lands in En-Gedi were already privately owned in the early second century, and so Rabbi Judah was probably continuing established practices. The second (Shabbat 26a) is a commentary on the conquest by Nebuchadnezzar in the sixth century BCE. Reflecting on the Biblical passage concerning the 'vinedressers and husbandmen' (2 Kings 25:12), Rav Joseph explains that vinedressers are 'the collectors of balsam from Ein Gedi and until Ramtha'. This is likely to reflect the situation of Rav Joseph's own time in the third century rather than during the occupation by the Babylonian king.[71] Notably, this text claims that balsam cultivation from En-Gedi spread as far as Ramtha.

A short description of En-Gedi appears in the *Onomasticon of Biblical Names*, compiled by Eusebius of Caesarea (d. c. 340) in c. 325. He describes it as 'a very large village/settlement (*kóme*) of Jews, lying beside the Dead Sea, from which balsam comes'. Eusebius also mentions the presence of balsam trees nearby at Bela (i.e. Zoar).[72] This testimony dates to the same time as the archaeological evidence uncovered by Hirschfeld at En-Gedi (see above). Perfumes were being processed on a small scale in private houses, perhaps indicating that these activities were no longer under the direct control of the state. From a few decades later comes a reference to the 'balsam vines of En-Gedi' in a letter written by another church father, Jerome (d. 420).[73] His description of 'balsam vines' brings to mind Pliny's account of cultivation practices, though there may also be an allusion to the 'vineyards of En-Gedi' in the Book of Songs.[74]

A fifth-century floor mosaic of a synagogue in En-Gedi (Fig. 2.10) contains an Aramaic inscription with curses on the following:

> He who steals the *zvwtyh* from his fellow, he who reveals the secret of the city (*raza d'karta*) to the non-Jews (Gentiles) – He whose eyes look upon the whole world, He will turn his face upon that man and upon his seed and uproot him from under the heavens. And all the people will answer *amen amen selah*.[75]

Some scholars have linked this 'secret' to the cultivation of balsam. If this is the case, the word *zvwtyh* may refer to palm fibres used to collect the *balsam*, or perhaps to dress the wounds made by scoring into the bark (Chapter 4). Soaked in *opobalsamum*, such fibres would have possessed a commercial value. Assuming that this constituted the most lucrative industry in En-Gedi in the fifth century, one can imagine that the inhabitants would have wished to keep hidden some aspect of the cultivation of the plants or the processing of the 'oil' (as was the case with the balsam plantations of Matarea from the

Figure 2.10 Inscription panel on the floor mosaic of the synagogue in En-Gedi, Israel. Fifth century. Photograph courtesy of the Center for Jewish Art, Hebrew University of Jerusalem.

twelfth century). The processes of balsam cultivation were known in the ancient world as the result of the writings of Pliny, Strabo and Theophrastus, but it may be that this information was not so easily accessible in fifth-century Palestine. Archaeologists have established that the village of En-Gedi was abandoned following a fire in the late sixth century.[76]

A possible piece of related visual evidence comes in the form of a mosaic pavement in the Jordanian town of Madaba. Now housed within the modern church dedicated to St George, this mosaic comprises a map of the Holy Land, dating to the sixth century. In its fragmentary state the map retains sections of Palestine, the lands east of the Jordan river and Dead Sea, the Mediterranean coast of the Sinai and the Nile Delta region of Egypt. The bushes located on either side of the Jordan river have been tentatively identified as representations of balsam trees (Fig. 2.11).[77] This interpretation is supported by the fact that this form of plant is not repeated elsewhere on the mosaic.

Figure 2.11 Detail of the floor mosaic in the church of St George, Madaba, Jordan. Sixth century. Photograph: Marcus Milwright.

Does Madaba map provide documentary evidence for the continuation of the balsam plantations into the sixth century? The mosaicists would have employed earlier maps of the roads of the Roman-Byzantine empire, of which the Peutinger Tablets are the sole surviving example. More pertinent in the present context is the evident reliance on the *Onomasticon* of Eusebius.[78] Is it possible, therefore, that the mosaicists were recording the situation of the fourth century rather than their own times? Egypt may have been the preferred source of balsam in Mediterranean trade when the Madaba mosaic map was constructed. The *Liber Pontificalis*, compiled in the sixth century, records the large quantity of aromatics imported from Egypt for use in the churches of Rome. Among these are nard, cassia, storax and balsam (Chapter 5).[79] Also included in the lists is a famous Egyptian export, papyrus. The *Liber Pontificalis* does not state specifically that the balsam was made in Egypt, however, recording only that this was the country from which it was sent to Italy.

Two written sources have been advanced as evidence for balsam cultivation in Palestine after the Muslim conquests of the early seventh century, but should be treated with some caution. An oft-quoted source on balsam is the account of the pilgrimage of Saint Willibald (d. c. 787) to the Holy Land between 724 and c. 727. Recorded in c. 780 by an amanuensis, a nun from Heidenheim called Hugeburc, the relevant passage (chapter 28) reads:

> Earlier on, when he was in Jerusalem, Bishop Willibald had bought himself some balsam and put it in a flagon. Then he took a cane which was hollow, and put it down inside, filling it with mineral oil. When he had put it inside the flagon, he cut the cane to the same height as the flagon, so that the edges were level with each other. Then he stoppered the flagon. And when they came to Tyre, the citizens arrested them and searched all their baggage in case they were concealing anything, and if they had found anything they would at once have inflicted on them the death penalty. So they held a thorough search of everything, but found nothing apart from this one flagon belonging to Willibald. They opened it, and smelt to find what was inside it. But when they smelt the mineral oil (which was on top, inside the cane) and failed to find what was inside it (underneath the mineral oil, in the flagon), they left them alone.[80]

If one assumes that Willibald had, in fact, managed to procure some *opobalsamum* (or *xylobalsamum*) and not a substitute (Chapter 5), then this account confirms the availability of this rare product in eighth-century Palestine. Importantly, however, Willibald only states where he bought his supply of balsam (Jerusalem) and not its original source. In other words, the balsam could have come from either Palestine or Egypt. According to a written version of Arculf's recollections produced by Adomnán, abbot of the monastery of Iona between 679 and 704, Jericho was a 'ruined city', and between it and the Jordan river were palm groves (2.13). Adomnán makes no mention of balsam, suggesting that neither Jericho nor En-Gedi was producing balsam in the seventh or eighth centuries.[81]

A Chinese text of the ninth century called the *Yu yan tsa tsu* may contain a description of balsam. One section of the text refers to a plant called *a-p'o-ts'an* which is found in the country of Fu-lin (believed to refer to Syria). Certainly, the description given by the author of this text sounds something like balsam:

> The tree is over ten feet high. Its bark is green and white in colour. The blooms are fine, two being opposite each other (biflorate). The flowers resemble those of rape-turnip (*Brassica rapa* L.), being uniformly yellow. The seeds resemble those of the pepper-plant. By chopping the branches, one obtains a juice like oil, that is employed as an ointment, serving as a remedy for ringworm, and is useful for any disease. The oil is held in very high esteem, and its price equals its weight in gold.[82]

It is significant that the renown of Judaean balsam – if that is what is being described – should have spread as far afield as China, but the reliability of the *Yu yan tsa tsu* as a source on specialised agriculture in ninth-century Greater Syria is questionable. The Chinese author was probably relying upon earlier writings, and his observations do not reflect the contemporary realities of balsam cultivation. It is also notable in this context that three eastern Christian writers of this time, Jacob of Edessa (d. 708), George of the Arabs (d. c. 724) and Moses Bar-Kepha (d. 903), only knew of Egypt as the source of balsam.[83] Given that the Syrian Orthodox Church made extensive use of balsam in the preparation of holy oils (Chapter 8), it is likely that these three writers, all of whom served as bishops, would have been well informed about the localities where balsam was cultivated. Some Arabic geographical texts claim that balsam was grown around Zughar at the southern end of the Dead Sea and Jericho, though it is unclear whether these claims have any historical veracity (dates and indigo were clearly the principal export crops of this locality). 'Perfumed plants' (sing. *rīḥān*) were grown in the region of Jericho.[84] A twelfth-century Frankish source says of En-Gedi that it is 'the place where balsam used to grow in great abundance', demonstrating awareness that the plant was no longer cultivated there.[85]

Thus, the written sources and the archaeological evidence suggest that the Palestinian balsam plantations ceased to operate in the seventh century at the latest. Whether this was caused simply by neglect, because Egypt had taken over as the principal supplier of this valued commodity, or for some other reason is unknown. This also leaves one final question: at what point during Roman-Byzantine rule were balsam trees first transferred to Egypt? The first reasonably clear reference to the presence of balsam trees at Matarea is the *Homilies* of Zacharie of Sakha from the late seventh or early eighth century (Chapter 1). Later medieval sources sometimes claim that the trees were moved to Egypt by Cleopatra (Chapter 2), and it is apparent that she was assigned ownership of the lands of Jericho and En-Gedi in 34 BCE. The absence of references to balsam cultivation in such knowledgeable sources as Strabo and Pliny makes it implausible that trees found their way to Egypt at this time, or in the decades up to the suppression of the first Jewish Revolt in 70 CE.

It has been suggested that Vespasian may have chosen to move some balsam trees to Egypt. Certainly, he must have been well acquainted with this valuable resource having spent some days in Jericho and the Dead Sea region in 68 CE.[86] That said, exclusivity had always been one of the factors generating the high price of balsam in Mediterranean markets; the existence of a second source in Egypt would hardly have benefited the emperor's personal treasury (*fiscus*) where the considerable profits from the sale of *opobalsamum* and *xylobalsamum* were sent. It is perhaps significant that Pliny should remark upon the Jews attempting to destroy the balsam trees rather than let them remain under Roman control.[87] Might Vespasian, or one of his immediate successors, have decided to move a stock of plants to Egypt as a safeguard against potential acts of sabotage by the local Jewish population in Palestine? Such speculation enjoys little support in the available written sources. Notably, the first-century CE botanist and pharmacologist Pedanius Dioscorides only knew of Palestine as a source for balsam.[88] Writing in the second century, Claudius Galen also exhibits no awareness of Egyptian balsam cultivation in his numerous references to the plant and the oleo-resins gathered from it.[89]

An anonymous fourteenth-century Arabic manuscript on holy oils (usually known by the French title of *Le livre du chrême*) in the Bibliothèque Nationale in Paris contains a section dealing with Theophilus, who served as patriarch of Alexandria between 385 and 412. In the sixth year of the rule of Theodosius II (r. 408–50) Theophilus performed the baptism of a sick infant. The account continues that, following this good deed, the patriarch received a visitation from an angel who commanded him to go to Jericho, and transport from there balsam trees to the 'place where the Lord had washed himself [i.e. Matarea], prior to his return to the land of Israel, in the company of Mary, Joseph, Salome, and Yusiya (Josias), son of Joseph'.[90] This recounting of events should not be accepted uncritically; written over 900 years after the supposed events, the writer was also unaware that in the fourth century En-Gedi, and not Jericho, was still the principal source of balsam. There is, however, some evidence for the presence of balsam in the vicinity of Alexandria a few decades earlier than the patriarchate of Theophilus. This occurs in a passage in the *Lausiac History* of Palladius of Galatia, bishop of Helenopolis (d. 431). This history of the Desert Fathers had been commissioned by Lausus, chamberlain to the court of Theodosius II, and was written in 419–20. Palladius records his conversations with inhabitants of the monastic community of Nitria, probably located about 65 km south-east of Alexandria, about the founder, an ascetic named Amoun (or Ammon). Palladius writes of Amoun of Nitria that he and his wife agreed on their wedding night to live as celibates, but within the same house. The author continues:

> So he [Amoun] lived with her for eighteen years in the same house, passing his time in the garden and in the balsam grove. For he was a producer of balsam, which is planted out like vines, and involves a great deal of labour in cultivating it and looking after it. He would go home in the evening and after saying prayers would have a meal with her. At night he would have a meal with her. At night he would pray and do the *synaxis*, and the first thing in the morning go out in the garden. Living like this they both came at last to be entirely free from passions, and his prayers came to be very strong and powerful.[91]

Amoun was a contemporary of St Anthony the Great (d. 356), the father of Egyptian monasticism. As Amoun died before St Anthony, and the reference to balsam precedes Amoun's decision to live separately from his wife, one may conclude that balsam was already being grown in Egypt in the second quarter of the fourth century. Quite how and why this should have occurred can only be a matter of speculation. Did the Egyptian church desire to possess a secure source of balsam near to hand or, alternatively, did Amoun cultivate the balsam trees on his own initiative for the benefit of the local community of Nitria? The existing groves at En-Gedi and Zoar may not have been yielding significant quantities of balsam by this time. Whatever the case, it seems likely that Egypt was the major supplier of balsam by the sixth century.

Notes

1. F. Nigel Hepper, 'An ancient expedition to transplant living trees: Exotic gardening by an Egyptian queen', *Journal of the Royal Horticultural Society* 92.10 (1967): 434–8.
2. Ibid. p. 436; Guido Majno, *The Healing Hand: Man and Wound in Antiquity* (Cambridge, MA: Harvard University Press, 1975), pp. 208–9.
3. Nigel Groom, *Frankincense and Myrrh: A Study of the Arabian Incense Trade* (London: Longman, 1981), pp. 25–7; Nigel Groom, 'Trade, incense and perfume', in Ann Gunter, ed., *Caravan Kingdoms: Yemen and the Ancient Incense Route* (Washington, DC: Freer Gallery of Art and Arthur M. Sackler Gallery, 2005), p. 107. For a summary of the main resin-producing plants of the ancient Middle East, see F. Nigel Hepper, 'Trees and shrubs yielding gums and resins in the ancient Near East', *Bulletin on Sumerian Agriculture* 3 (1987): 107–14.
4. Cyril Bryan, trans., *Ancient Egyptian Medicine: The Ebers Papyrus*, introduction by G. Eliot Smith (London: G. Bles, 1930. Reprinted Chicago: Ares Publishers, 1974). This is a translation of an earlier German translation by H. Joachim. See also Zohar Amar, 'Medicinal substances in Eretz-Israel in the times of the Bible, the Mishnah and the Talmud in the light of written sources', in Zohar Amar, *Illness and Healing in Ancient Times* (Haifa: The Reuben and Edith Hecht Museum, University of Haifa, 1996), p. 53.
5. Bendix Ebbell, *The Papyrus Ebers, the Greatest Egyptian Medical Document* (Copenhagen and London: Levin & Munksgaard, 1937), pp. 68, 71–2; Hassan Kamal, *A Dictionary of Pharaonic Medicine* (Cairo: National Publication House, c. 1967), p. 57. *Senen* appears in a lotion for the head and temples (prescription 260) and a range of treatments for the eye (prescriptions 367, 377, 410, 423). On the use of balsam in ancient medicine, see chapter 6.
6. Herodotus, *Histories* 3:107. On early references to the trade in frankincense and myrrh, see Dan Potts, *The Arabian Gulf in Antiquity* (Oxford: Clarendon Press, 1990), I, p. 349; II, pp. 9–10, 149; Juris Zarins, 'Mesopotamia and frankincense, the early evidence', in Alessandra Avanzini, ed., *Profumi d'Arabia: Atti del convegno* (Rome: 'L'erma' di Bretschneider, 1997), pp. 251–72.
7. Herodotus, *Histories* 3:97.
8. Groom, *Frankincense and Myrrh*, pp. 37–54; Groom, 'Trade, incense and perfume', p. 106.
9. Theophrastus, *Enquiry into Plants, and Minor Works on Odours and Weather Signs*, ed. and trans. Arthur Hort, Loeb Classical Library 70, 79, 2 vols

(Cambridge, MA: Harvard University Press, 1916–26, reprinted 2014), 9:4.2. These locations are given as Adramíta, Kitíbaina and Mamáli.

10. Pliny, *Natural History* 12:30–5. On the perfumed substances employed in the ancient Mediterranean and Middle East, see also J. Innes Miller, *The Spice Trade of the Roman World, 29 B.C. to A.D. 641* (Oxford: Clarendon Press, 1969), pp. 100–5; Majno, *The Healing Hand*, pp. 208–11; Ze'ev Safrai, *The Economy of Roman Palestine* (London and New York: Routledge, 1994), pp. 146–55.

11. Judith McKenzie, *The Architecture of Petra* (Oxford: Oxford University Press, 1990); Ehud Netzer, *Nabatäische Architektur* (Munich: Von Zabern, 2003).

12. A. R. Ansary, *Qaryat al-Fau: A Portrait of the Pre-Islamic Civilisation in Saudi Arabia* (Riyadh and New York: University of Riyadh and St Martin's Press, 1992). For a summary of the principal archaeological sites of late antique Arabia, see Derek Kennet, 'On the eve of Islam: Archaeological evidence from Eastern Arabia', *Antiquity* 79 (2005): 107–18.

13. Lionel Casson, ed. and trans., *Periplus Maris Erythrae* (Princeton, NJ: Princeton University Press, 1989), pp. 55, 57, 65, 118–20, 154–6. For more on the incense trade, see Robert Hoyland, *Arabia and the Arabs: From the Bronze Age to the Coming of Islam* (London and New York: Routledge, 2001), pp. 102–12; Groom, 'Trade, incense and perfume'.

14. Genesis 37:25. Ẓori can be transliterated as *tsori*. The following references to the Old and New Testaments are taken from Michael D. Coogan, ed., *The New Oxford Annotated Bible*, third edition, (Oxford: Oxford University Press, 2001).

15. Isaiah 45:2, 6. Given that the book of Isaiah contains a reference to Cyrus the Great, ruler of Iran (c. 600 or 576–530 BCE), this would place the origins of the book in the mid-sixth century (although much of the second half of the text appears to have been the work of another prophetic author known as the 'second Isaiah'). On the history and authorship of the book, see Joseph Blenkinsopp's introductory notes to Isaiah in Coogan, ed., *The New Oxford Annotated Bible*, pp. 974–7.

16. Ezekiel 27:22–4.
17. Jeremiah 6:20.
18. For example, Proverbs 7:17; Song 1:13, 3.6–7.
19. Esther 2:12.
20. Exodus 30:22–38.
21. Mark 15:23.
22. John 19:39.
23. Matthew 2:11.

24. For example, 1 Kings 10:10. On the interpretation of *zori*, see Gideon Hadas, 'The balsam *afarsemon / apharsemon* and Ein Gedi during the Roman-Byzantine period', *Revue Biblique* 114.2 (2007): 163–4. Also, Immanuel and Moses Löw, *Die Flora der Juden* (Vienna and Leipzig: R. Löwit Verlag, 1924–34), I, pp. 299–304; Winifred Walker, *All the Plants of the Bible* (London: Lutterworth Press, 1958), pp. 26–7.
25. Genesis 37:25. Richard Jones, 'Balm', *Anchor Bible Dictionary* (New York: Doubleday, 1992), I, pp. 573–4. The author notes that in the Septuagint *zori* is translated into Greek as *rhētinē*, indicating a resin of pine.
26. Jones, 'Balm'.
27. Genesis 43:11; Ezekiel 27:17.
28. Jeremiah 8:21–2; 46:11. On this, see also Majno, *Healing Hand*, p. 216; Amar, 'Medicinal substances', pp. 55–6; F. Nigel Hepper and Joan Taylor, 'Date palms and opobalsam in the Madaba mosaic map', *Palestine Exploration Quarterly* 136.1 (2004): 40.
29. Jones, 'Balm'; Victor Matthews, 'Perfumes and spices', *Anchor Bible Dictionary* (New York: Doubleday, 1992), V, pp. 226–8; Hadas, 'The balsam *afarsemon*', pp. 166–7, 169–70.
30. Groom, *Frankincense and Myrrh*, p. 29. Other possibilities are that 'balm of Gilead' was the resin harvested from the Aleppo pine (*Pinus halepensis* Miller) or the Phoenician cedar (*Juniperus phoenicea* L.).
31. Josephus, *Jewish Antiquities* 8:174. For references to balsam in antique texts, see Menahem Stern, *Greek and Latin Authors on Jews and Judaism* (Jerusalem: Israel Academy of Sciences and Humanities, 1974), nos 9, 179, 213, 281, 449.
32. 1 Kings 10.1–10.
33. For example, Babylonian Talmud: Kerithoth 6a. Judeo-Christian Research: https://juchre.org/talmud/kerithoth/kerithoth1.htm#6a (last consulted: 21 May 2018). See also comments in Chapter 8.
34. Yizhar Hirschfeld, 'The rose and the balsam: The garden as a source for perfume and medicine', in Michael Conan, ed., *Middle East Garden Traditions: Unity and Diversity. Questions, Methods and Resources in a Multicultural Perspective* (Washington, DC: Dumbarton Oaks Research Library and Collection, 2007), p. 29.
35. Jeremiah 8:21–22; 46:11. The author of Jeremiah himself is believed to have died after 586 BCE. See Mark Biddle's introductory notes to Jeremiah in Coogan, ed., *The New Oxford Annotated Bible*, pp. 1073–4.
36. Ezekiel 27:17.

37. Theophrastus, *Enquiry into Plants* 4:4.14, 9:6.1. See also Safrai, *Economy of Roman Palestine*, pp. 147–8; Joseph Patrich, 'Agricultural development in Antiquity: Improvements in the cultivation and production of balsam', in Jean-Baptiste Humbert et al., eds, *Qumran, the Site of the Dead Sea Scrolls: Archaeological Interpretations and Debates* (Leiden and Boston: Brill, 2006), p. 242.
38. Diodorus Siculus, *Bibliotheca historica* 2:48.9. See also 19:98.1. He mentions (3:46.2) a balsam that was grown in Arabia, perhaps referring to 'balm of Mecca' (see Chapter 4).
39. Strabo, *Geography* 16:2.41.
40. Pliny, *Natural History* 12:111. Another first-century CE source, Pompeius Trogus, gives the cultivated area as 200 *iugera* (about 50 hectares). On this, and other estimates, see Safrai, *Economy of Roman Palestine*, p. 148; Pauline Donceel-Voûte, 'Traces of fragrance along the Dead Sea', *Res Orientales* 11: *Parfums d'Orient* (1998): 93–4, 101–103.
41. Josephus, *Jewish War* 4:469–70. The dimensions he gives for the fertile lands of Jericho are seventy by twenty furlongs (4:468–69). This area was given over to other crops, including date palm, myrobalans, and cypress. Discussed in Samuel Kottek, *Medicine and Hygiene in the Works of Flavius Josephus*, Studies in Ancient Medicine 9 (Leiden and Boston: Brill, 1994), pp. 126–7.
42. Safrai, *Economy of Roman Palestine*, p. 150, figs 34, 35; Patrich, 'Agricultural development in Antiquity', pp. 242–3; Donceel-Voûte, 'Traces of fragrance', pp. 107–8.
43. Pliny, *Natural History* 12:111.
44. Hirschfeld, 'The rose and the balsam', p. 29.
45. Josephus, *Jewish War* 1:361–2; *Jewish Antiquities* 15:96. See also Hannah Cotton, 'Ein Gedi between the two revolts', *Scripta Classica Israelica* 20 (2001): 143–4; Joseph Patrich, 'Agricultural development in Antiquity', p. 243. Ze'ev Safrai cautions that the gift of land to Cleopatra does not necessarily indicate that the land was not, in fact, owned by Herod. See his *Economy of Roman Palestine*, p. 154. On the wider context of the relationship, see Sarah Pearce, 'The Cleopatras and the Jews', *Transactions of the Royal Historical Society* 27 (2017): 29–64 (the assigning of balsam groves to Cleopatra is dealt with on p. 44).
46. Pliny, *Natural History* 12:117. Also Cotton, 'Ein Gedi between the two revolts', p. 143.
47. Josephus, *Jewish War* 1:403; *Jewish Antiquities* 15:296–8. See also comments in Safrai, *Economy of Roman Palestine*, p. 154.
48. Josephus, *Jewish War* 2:111.

49. Cotton, 'Ein Gedi between the two revolts', pp. 139–44.
50. Hirschfeld, 'The rose and the balsam', pp. 31–4, fig. 20; Cotton, 'Ein Gedi between the two revolts', p. 145 n. 26. On balsam cultivation at this location, see also Tommaso Gnoli, 'La production del balsamo nell'oasi di Engaddi (Israele). Su alcuni nuovi documenti dal deserto di giuda', in Alessandra Avanzini, ed., *Profumi d'Arabia: Atti del convegno* (Rome: 'L'erma' di Bretschneider, 1997), pp. 413–29.
51. Safrai, *Economy of Roman Palestine*, p. 150; Hirschfeld, 'The rose and the balsam', p. 34, fig. 22; Donceel-Voûte, 'Traces of fragrance', pp. 112–13.
52. Hirschfeld, 'The rose and the balsam', pp. 34–5, figs 26–8; Donceel-Voûte, 'Traces of fragrance', p. 117. For a critical assessment of the evidence, see Hadas, 'The balsam *afarsemon*', pp. 167–9.
53. Hirschfeld, 'The rose and the balsam', pp. 34–5.
54. Ibid. p. 35, figs 23–4.
55. Ibid. p. 32, fig. 20. On the prices and the monopoly over the supply of balsam, see Hannah Cotton and Werner Eck, 'Ein Staatsmonopol und seine Folgen: Plinius, *Naturalis Historia* 12,123 und der Preis für Balsam', *Rheinisches Museum für Philologie* 140.2 (1997): 153–61.
56. Joseph Patrich and Benny Arubas, 'A juglet containing balsam oil (?) from a cave near Qumran', *Israel Exploration Journal* 39 (1989): 43–59.
57. Tacitus, *Histories* 5:1.
58. Pliny, *Natural History* 12:113
59. Josephus, *Jewish War* 4:402–4.
60. Pliny, *Natural History* 5:15.73.
61. Ibid. 12:111.
62. Hirschfeld, 'The rose and the balsam', p. 35; Donceel-Voûte, 'Traces of fragrance', p. 95.
63. Pliny, *Natural History* 12:118.
64. Ibid. 12:113.
65. Donceel-Voûte, 'Traces of fragrance', pp. 106–8.
66. Cotton, 'Ein Gedi between the two revolts', pp. 146–8.
67. Ibid. pp. 151–2.
68. Galen, *De Antidotis* 1:4. See Karl Kühn, ed., *Claudii Galeni opera omnia, Medicorum graecorum opera quae exstant* (Leipzig: Cnoblochius, 1821–33), XIV, pp. 10–12. Safrai notes that his description may indicate the existence of other sites of cultivation in Palestine. See his *Economy of Roman Palestine*, p. 149.

69. Galen, *De Antidotis* 1:2. See Kühn, ed., *Opera omnia*, XIV, pp. 7–8. Translated in Arthur Brock, trans., *Greek Medicine, Being Extracts Illustrative of Medical Writers from Hippocrates to Galen* (London and Toronto: J. M. Dent and Sons Ltd, 1929), p. 199. He writes: 'From Syria in Palestine also I obtained gum-balsam (*opobalsamum*) in perfect condition. For bitumen cannot be fraudulently adulterated, nor can the fruit of gum-balsam nor the tree-balsam'. The last two must be *carpobalsamum* and *xylobalsamum*.
70. Babylonian Talmud: Berachot 43a. Sefaria.org: https://www.sefaria.org/Berakhot.43a?lang=bi (last consulted: 21 May 2018); Babylonian Talmud: Shabbat 26a. Sefaria.org: https://www.sefaria.org/Shabbat.26a?lang=bi (last consulted: 21 May 2018). Also Safrai, *Economy of Roman Palestine*, p. 149.
71. Safrai, *Economy of Roman Palestine*, p. 149.
72. Eusebius, *Onomasticon* nos 193 (Zoar), 428 (En-Gedi). See also Safrai, *Economy of Roman Palestine*, p. 149.
73. Jerome, letter 108. Translated in Wilkinson, *Jerusalem Pilgrims before the Crusades*, p. 50. Composed in 404, the letter itself (no. 108) is an obituary notice for a nun called Paula, whom Jerome had accompanied to the Holy Land in 385. Paula does not appear to have visited En-Gedi in person, but rather meditated upon them from the hills above.
74. Pliny, *Natural History* 12:112–13; Song 1:14. The connection with the Book of Songs is noted in Cotton, 'Ein Gedi between the two revolts', p. 145 n. 27. Jerome would also have been well acquainted with information about balsam, having produced the Latin translation of Eusebius' *Onomasticon*.
75. Lee Levine, 'The inscription in the "En Gedi synagogue"', in Lee Levine, ed., *Ancient Synagogues Revealed* (Jerusalem: Israel Exploration Society, 1981), pp. 140–5; Safrai, *Economy of Roman Palestine*, pp. 149–50; Hirschfeld, 'The rose and the balsam', p. 31, fig. 19; Patrich, 'Agricultural development in Antiquity', p. 244. Levine and Patrich survey the arguments for and against the connection of the 'secret' to the cultivation and processing of balsam.
76. Hirschfeld, 'The rose and the balsam', p. 31; Patrich, 'Agricultural development in Antiquity', p. 244.
77. Hepper and Taylor, 'Date palms and opobalsam', pp. 36–43.
78. On the visual and textual sources of the Madaba mosaic map, see Yoram Tsafrir, 'The maps used by Theodosius: On the pilgrim maps of the Holy Land and Jerusalem in the sixth century C.E.', *Dumbarton Oaks Papers* 40 (1986): 129–45. See also Herbert Donner, *The Mosaic Map of Madaba: An Introductory Guide* (Kampen: Kok Pharos Publishing House, 1992).

79. Louis Duchesne, ed., *Le Liber Pontificalis: Texte, introduction et commentaire* (Paris: E. Thorin, 1886), I, pp. 174, 177–8, 183. Also Atchley, *Use of Incense*, p. 141.
80. Translated in Wilkinson, *Jerusalem Pilgrims before the Crusades*, p. 132 (chapter 28 of the text). See also comments in Linda Voigts, 'Anglo-Saxon plant remedies and the Anglo-Saxons', *Isis* 70 (1979), p. 260; Malcolm Cameron, *Anglo-Saxon Medicine*, Cambridge Studies in Anglo-Saxon England 7 (Cambridge: Cambridge University Press, 1993), pp. 104–105.
81. Translated in Wilkinson, *Jerusalem Pilgrims before the Crusades*, pp. 106–7. The description of Jericho appears in part 13:1 of the text. See, however, the version in Adomnán (Arculf), *The Pilgrimage of Arculfus to the Holy Land (About the Year A.D. 670)*, trans. James MacPherson, Palestine Pilgrims Texts Society 3 (London: Palestine Exploration Society, 1889), p. 78 (discussed in Chapter 4). On Arculf/Adomnán as a primary source, see Robert Hoyland and Sarah Waidler, 'Adomnán's *De Locis Sanctis* and the seventh-century Near East', *English Historical Review* 129.539 (2014): 787–807.
82. Berthold Laufer, *Sino-Iranica: Chinese Contributions to the History of Civilization in Ancient Iran*, Field Museum of Natural History Publication 201. Anthropological Series 15.3 (Chicago: Field Museum, 1919), p. 429.
83. Patricia Crone, *Meccan Trade and the Rise of Islam* (Oxford: Basil Blackwell, 1987), p. 62, n. 66; R. Hugh Connolly and Humphrey Codrington, ed. and trans., *Two Commentaries on the Jacobite Liturgy by George, Bishop of the Arabs and Moses Bār-Kēphā: Together with the Syriac Anaphora of St James and a Document entitled*, The Book of Life (London and Oxford: Williams & Norgate, 1913), p. 21. George was a pupil of Athanasias II and Jacob of Edessa.
84. The sources are collected in Milwright, *Fortress of the Raven*, pp. 120–2.
85. Anonymous text entitled *Work on Geography*, in Wilkinson, trans., *Jerusalem Pilgrimage, 1099–1185*, p. 185. The same point is also made by Rorgo Fretellus of Nazareth. See *Fetellus (circa 1130 A.D.)*, trans. James MacPherson, Palestine Pilgrim Texts Society 5 (London: Palestine Exploration Society, 1892), p. 12.
86. Crone, *Meccan Trade*, p. 62, n. 64 (citing Reinhold Sigismund, *Die Aromata in ihrer Bedeutung für Religion* [Leipzig: C. F. Winter, 1884], p. 15); Cotton, 'Ein Gedi between the two revolts', p. 146; Josephus, *Jewish War* 4:450, 490.
87. Pliny, *Natural History* 12:113.
88. Dioscorides, *Peri ilis iatrikis* 1:19. See *Pedanii Dioscurides Anazarbei* De Materia Medica. *Libre quinque*, ed. Max Wellman (Berlin: Weidmann, 1907). Dioscorides has sometimes been claimed as a source for the presence of balsam

trees in Egypt, but this is perhaps due to a reliance by scholars (myself included in an earlier article, published in 2003) upon dubious translations. For example, John Goodyer's 1655 English translation contains the sentence 'It [balsam] grows only in Judaea and in a certain valley, and in Egypt' (1:18: the reference to Egypt also appears in some sixteenth-century European printed editions of Dioscorides based on late Byzantine manuscript copies). See Robert Gunther, ed., *The Greek Herbal of Dioscorides, Illustrated by a Byzantine, A.D. 512. Englished by John Goodyer, A.D. 1655* (Oxford, 1933. Reprinted New York: Hafner Publication Company, 1959), pp. 18–19.

89. Safrai, *Economy of Roman Palestine*, p. 149. See also comments in Chapter 6 of the present volume.
90. Zanetti, 'Matarieh', p. 41.
91. Palladius, *Lausiac History* 8:8. See Cuthbert Butler, ed., *The Lausiac History of Palladius* (Cambridge: Cambridge University Press, 1898–1904), II, p. 27 (for the complete account, see pp. 26–9). Also Zanetti, 'Matarieh', p. 60.

3

Balsam in Egypt

The early history of the balsam plantations of Matarea remains mysterious, and the historical veracity of the available earliest written material is difficult to evaluate. Much of these data take the form of legendary accounts in Coptic and Ethiopic religious literature (Chapter 1) that are undated, and not infrequently contain interpolations into the 'original' text (each one probably originating as an orally transmitted account). These stories appear first in a written form in the seventh, or possibly the sixth century, and represent one aspect of a larger phenomenon: the establishment of a series of pilgrimage sites associated with the reputed itinerary of the Holy Family during their sojourn in Egypt. In the case of Matarea, the site's proximity to an ancient site (Heliopolis) with distinct Old Testament resonances may have increased the attractiveness of Matarea as a Christian pilgrimage site.

There are independent sources whose chronological parameters can be fixed with greater certainty. For example, the existence of balsam in 'Ayn Shams (the Arabic name often given for the larger area that included Matarea) is confirmed in the works of two early Arabic geographers, the Persian al-Istakhri (fl. mid-tenth century) and Ibn Hawqal (fl. late tenth century), a native of the town of Nisibis in northern Mesopotamia.[1] Both authors discuss the site of 'Ayn Shams in their geographical encyclopedias, giving much the same information. Ibn Hawqal's version reads: 'And in 'Ayn Shams are grown trees called *al-balsām* and taken from it is oil of balsam (*duhn al-balasān*), and it is not known in any place in the world other than here'.[2] This information is also to be found in the geography produced by the Maghribi scholar al-Idrisi in the twelfth century. The Persian traveller Nasir-i Khusraw (d. 1088) gives an account of the extraction of the 'oil' from the balsam trees during his stay in Cairo (Chapter 4).[3]

Given the brevity of al-Istakhri's and Ibn Hawqal's descriptions, there is little else one can draw from them beyond the fact that by the tenth century it was known among Muslim scholars that Matarea/'Ayn Shams was the only supplier of balsam. They give no indication as to who owned the balsam garden itself nor who controlled the distribution of the precious *duhn al-balasān* (i.e. *opobalsamum*) and other related products gathered from the trees. No mention is made by the two Muslim geographers of the associations that were already well established in Coptic writings between the balsam of Matarea and the Holy Family. One can only speculate as to whether this was a conscious omission on the parts of al-Istakhri and Ibn Hawqal, and later by al-Idrisi and Nasir-i Khusraw, or whether these stories had not circulated widely outside of the Christian communities of Egypt and Ethiopia.

It is only in later centuries that the Christian connections with the site of Matarea are specifically mentioned by Arab Muslim geographers and chroniclers. The author of the monumental geographical encyclopedia, *Mu'jam al-buldān*, Yaqut al-Rumi al-Hamawi (d. 1229), notes that a Christian is responsible for extracting the 'oil' from the balsam trees. The wells of Matarea are particularly noted, and Yaqut reports the tradition that Christ had been washed there.[4] This information is picked up by al-Qazwini (d. 1283) in his *Āthār al-bilād wa-akhbār al-'ibād*, completed in 1275–6.[5] These Christian legends also resurface in the works of later writers, such as the Cairene author al-Maqrizi (d. 1442) in his topographic study of his native city, *al-Mawā'iz wa'l-i'tibār fī dhikr al-khitat wa'l-āthār* (usually known simply as the *Khitat*). Citing the '*Kitāb al-sanaksar*' (i.e. the Arabic version of the *Synaxarion*), al-Maqrizi records that Matarea is venerated by Christians. He describes the legends that the well on the site was the one that the Virgin had used to wash the clothes of her son, and that the balsam trees could not be sustained from any other water source (Chapter 1). In another passage he claims that Christians came to Matarea in order to wash from this water source as a means to cure themselves of illness.[6] Ibn al-Wardi's (d. 1457) *Kharīdat al-'ajā'ib wa-farīdat al-gharā'ib* contains a report that the well was the one in which the Christ Child had been washed.[7]

The relatively late emergence in Muslim geographical and topographical literature of these Christian myths is a demonstration of how authors from different linguistic and historiographic traditions can give variant accounts of the same site. This can also be seen if one compares the testimony of Muslim writers with those of European pilgrims who visited Matarea in the medieval and early modern periods. This chapter reconstructs the history of Matarea through the period of Islamic rule. In doing so, it will be necessary to reconcile the sometimes contradictory evidence in the extensive body of primary sources. Preference is generally given to primary texts that can be assigned a relatively accurate date. As far as is possible, assertions in these sources are evaluated in the light of other textual traditions.

The Vicinity of Matarea in Antiquity

The fertile lands surrounding Matarea have long been cultivated, with evidence of human settlement in the region stretching back to pre-dynastic times. The most important ancient settlement in the vicinity was On, better known by its Greek name, Heliopolis ('City of the Sun'). The Egyptian name for the site appears in hieroglyphs as *Iunu*, a name that refers to the many pillars used in the construction. Located east of the Nile and just to the north of the beginning of the Delta, the city was the capital of one of the administrative regions (*nome* or *sepat*) of Lower Egypt. The principal surviving monument from the site is a red granite obelisk (Fig. 3.1), erected during the Twelfth Dynasty by Senusret I (r. 1971–1926 BCE). Among his architectural achievements was the renovation of the temple of Re-Atum in Heliopolis. Originally one of a pair, the surviving obelisk is 20.4 m tall. Built to commemorate the feast for his thirtieth year of rule, the two obelisks stood together until one fell down in 1160.[8]

Aside from a few carved blocks and fragmentary brick city walls, little else remains of the building work of Senusret, and the other pharaohs who lavished their attention on Heliopolis. Much of the destruction can be attributed to quarrying of stone during the Islamic centuries. The Roman authorities also plundered the temples for their obelisks and columns. The principal deity of Heliopolis was Atum, and the main temple was known as Per-Atum ('the House of Atum') or Per-Aat ('the Great House'). It was believed that Atum had created the deities Shu and Tefnut in Heliopolis. Another important belief was that Atum would terminate the world by returning it to water and chaos. A direct association with the sun came with the construction at Heliopolis of a temple dedicated to Aten, the solar disc,

Figure 3.1 Stereoscopic photograph of obelisk located at 'Ayn Shams (Heliopolis), Egypt. American Colony (Jerusalem) Photographic Department, c. 1900–20. Library of Congress Prints and Photographs Division: LC-DIG-matpc-01486.

by the pharaoh Akhnaten (r. 1353–1336 or 1351–1334 BCE). Another cult practised in the city was that of an aspect of the god Ra known as the Mnevis bull. Heliopolis was also the site of a sacred tree, the 'Asht of the sun (*asheta nu ra*)', an interesting precursor of the famous tree of the Virgin located at Matarea (Chapter 1).

Heliopolis came to be known as a centre for learning, and it is frequently mentioned in ancient Greek sources, starting with Herodotus in the fifth century BCE.[9] The scholars of the city specialised in Egyptian history, and there were also noted 'schools' devoted to the study of astronomy and philosophy. The Ptolemies (305–30 BCE) increasingly focused their scholarly patronage on Alexandria to the north, and by the end of the first century BCE Strabo reports that Heliopolis was largely deserted, the only inhabitants being the priests in the temples.[10] By the time of the foundation of the balsam gardens in Matarea the status of Heliopolis as a cultic and scholarly centre can only have been a distant memory. The ruins must still have been impressive at the time of the Arab conquest, however, and a vestige of its original religious role remains in the Arab name for the site, 'Ayn Shams ('Spring of the Sun'). From 341 the eastern side of Lower Egypt including Heliopolis was designated as the administrative region of Augustamnica, an administrative arrangement that lasted to the end of Byzantine rule.

Matarea from the Islamic Conquest to the End of the Ayyubid Dynasty

Amr ibn al-'As (d. 664) led the campaign to conquer the Byzantine province of Egypt. In 641 the garrison in the fortress at Babylon (Old Cairo), the capital of the Byzantine province, surrendered to the Arab forces, and Egypt was brought within the expanding Islamic state. Christians continued to perform vital bureaucratic roles, at least until the administrative reforms of the Umayyad caliph 'Abd al-Malik (r. 685–705). Although they were now classed as *dhimmī* (protected people) with fewer rights than Muslims, and with an obligation to pay the *jizya* (head tax), they still enjoyed freedom of worship. In the late seventh and early eighth centuries, there were some anti-Christian riots and periodic restrictions upon public processions using ceremonial crosses, and on the placement of crosses on the exteriors of churches, but these difficulties were relatively short-lived.[11]

Arabic chronicles give no indication about how the balsam trees of Matarea were regarded by the Muslim administrative elite during the first two centuries of Islamic rule. It is not known who administered the plantation at Matarea or who controlled the distribution and sale of balsam. A comparison can be made between balsam and papyrus, another highly valued product over which Egypt enjoyed a virtual monopoly (Fig. 3.2). The latter was the pre-eminent writing material of the late antique world. Made from the stems of the papyrus plant (*Papyrus cyperus* L.), which was farmed along the banks of the Nile river and in the Delta, this durable writing material was cheaper than parchment and vellum. Egypt dominated the market, exporting rolls of papyrus to all parts of the Byzantine empire, and the polities of Western Europe. This writing material continued to be used for administrative purposes in Merovingian France (mid-fifth century–751) into the early eighth century, and for papal documents as late as the tenth century. Papyrus was also employed extensively by the new Islamic empire, though its use declined significantly in the ninth century as the state bureaucracy and private consumers switched to paper.

Figure 3.2 Sheet of papyrus. Photograph: Iona Hubner.

The evidence from surviving papyri suggests that the conquest of Egypt had no lasting impact on the export of this writing material to Europe. The export trade was briefly curtailed by ʿAbd al-Malik in the 690s, but then continued through the eighth century. Where the finest papyrus rolls had formerly carried a short Greek inscription certifying their authenticity, under ʿAbd al-Malik this was changed to Arabic, and included both the Muslim profession of faith (*basmala*) and the name and title of the caliph. In other words, the Islamic state saw no benefit in the disruption of this lucrative trade to the Christian states of the Mediterranean. The tending of the papyrus plants and the manufacture of the papyrus sheets continued to be done largely by the native Christian population of Egypt.[12] Where papyrus differs crucially from balsam, however, is in its relevance to the new Islamic empire. Where papyrus was vital to the administrative functions of the caliphate (parchment being employed principally for the writing of the Holy Qurʾan), balsam appears to have had a negligible role in Islamic life. While there are references to the employment of incense in the houses and palaces of prosperous Muslims, balsam does not appear to have been a popular substance to burn for this purpose. Neither does balsam occur in descriptions of state-sponsored rituals performed by early Islamic dynasties. For these quasi-religious functions an aromatic paste known as *khalūq* was preferred (Chapter 8).

In this general context it is likely that during the early centuries of Islamic rule the Coptic patriarchate was able to manage the balsam trees of Matarea, though perhaps under the jurisdiction of the Muslim governor of Egypt. The inclusion of 'Ayn Shams in the geographical encyclopedias of al-Istakhri and Ibn Hawqal is a sign that the site and its products were widely known among Islamic scholars. Balsam is also mentioned with relative frequency in Arabic medical literature from the late eighth century onward (Chapters 6 and 7). Little is known about the site itself until the twelfth century, however. The remainder of this section reviews the historical evidence for the site of Matarea and the balsam trees from the last decades of the Fatimid caliphate to the end of the Ayyubid sultanate.

In order to appreciate the history of Matarea through this phase and that of the Mamluk sultanate, it is necessary to consider the wider context of the urban development of Cairo (Fig. 3.3). In the centuries following the establishment of the garrison town (*miṣr*) of Fustat in the seventh century, all of the new urban foundations were placed to the north of the existing city. First came al-'Askar in the eighth century and al-Qata'i' in the ninth century, and then, most important of all, the Fatimid city of al-Qahira (Cairo) in 969. The construction of al-Qahira brought Matarea closer to the developed area of the Egyptian capital. Soon after 969 the lands to the north of Bab al-Futuh and Bab al-Nasr became the subject of Fatimid patronage. Among the earliest developments north of Bab al-Nasr was a large open prayer ground (*muṣallā*) in which the caliph gave the sermon (*khutba*) on feast days. Known as Husayniyya, this later included an important cemetery (associated with the *muṣallā*) and, further to the east, facilities for caravans arriving on the road from the north via Birkat al-Hajj. The lush lands further north were popular hunting grounds for the Fatimid caliphs and the sultans of the Ayyubid and Mamluk dynasties.[13]

Al-Maqrizi records that al-Juyushi Badr al-Jamali (d. 1094), the Armenian general and vizier responsible for rebuilding the walls of al-Qahira

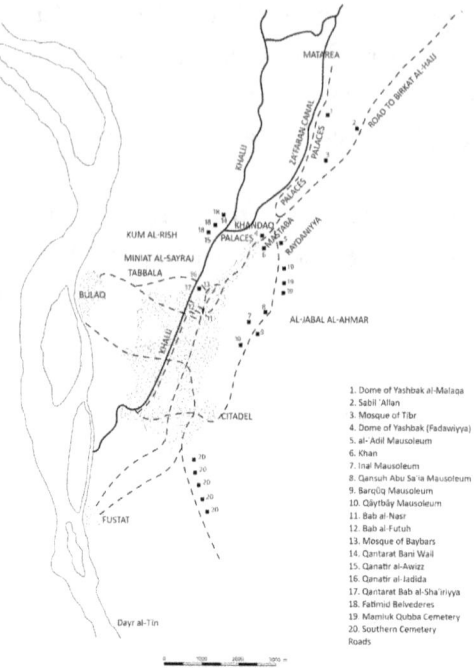

Figure 3.3 Map of Cairo and the surrounding areas in the medieval period, after Behrens-Abouseif, 'Northeastern extension'. Drawn by Naomi Shields.

in the late eleventh century, established gardens between Husayniyya and Miniat Matar (i.e. Matarea). Markets and belvederes (sing. *manzara*) were constructed by his son al-Afdal Shahinshah near to al-Khalij, the great canal running north from Fustat, while the caliph had another *manzara* erected between the gardens of al-Juyushi and Bab al-Futuh. From here the caliph could watch his troops leaving for Syria on the road that led north-east from al-Qahira. The fall of the Fatimid dynasty in 1171 did not interrupt the ongoing development of the areas north of Bab al-Futuh and Bab al-Nasr; al-Maqrizi describes the construction of mosques, hippodromes, caravanserais, markets, belvederes and residential areas in this region.[14]

From the twelfth century there are references to buildings associated with the balsam plantation at Matarea. The *History of the Patriarchs of Alexandria* is a substantial chronicle associated with Severus (or Sawirus) ibn al-Muqaffaʿ (d. 987), but was actually written by numerous authors over an extended period.[15] In the biographies of the patriarchs John V (r. 1131–66) and Mark

III ibn Zurʿa (r. 1166–89), the anonymous continuator records the reconstruction of a church and the subsequent events:

> The Christians had constructed on the remains of an ancient church, a church at Matarea, where one finds the wells of balsam which produce the oil of chrism (myron); they had consecrated it in the name of St George (Mari Jirjis) and celebrated [mass] after having completed the pictures decorating the interior. The Muslims destroyed it and constructed there a mosque (*masjid*).[16]

The short-lived church of St George was built on the site of an older place of Christian worship. It is not stated when this earlier structure was constructed, when it fell into disuse and to which saint it was dedicated. The older church must have been built prior to the twelfth century as it is described explicitly as 'ancient' (*qadīm*). Apparent from this account is the extent to which the survival of Christian religious constructions was subject to the goodwill of the Muslim authorities. While the strict application of Muslim law forbade the erection or renovation of churches and synagogues in conquered territories, there was often room for compromise. For example, in the late tenth century the Copts were permitted to found a monastery south of Matarea in the village of al-Khandaq as a substitute for an earlier monastery that had been razed to make way for a Fatimid palace. The degree of leniency offered by the authorities varied according to precise historical circumstance, the prevailing mood among the Muslim populace, and the interpretations of the law offered by jurists of the different schools of Islamic law.[17] Although the *History of the Patriarchs* offers no exact chronology, it appears as if the construction of the new church of St George, its destruction, and the erection of a mosque took place in relatively quick succession.

Further evidence on this event appears in the work of Abu al-Makarim, a thirteenth-century Coptic author writing in Arabic.[18] Although Abu al-Makarim does not mention the dedication of the church to St George, he provides more information about the historical context. The restoration of the church occurred under the caliphate of al-Zafir (r. 1149–54) 'when ʿAbbas was vizier', in the year 548 H (i.e. 1153–4). The author writes that 'the church was consecrated – and mass was celebrated there – in the name of Our Lady, the pure Virgin Mary'. After a brief outline of the Flight to

Egypt by the Holy Family he continues: 'And when the imam al-Zafir and his brothers were killed, the Muslims of the vicinity (i.e. of Matarea) took possession [of the church] and built there prayer niches (sing. *miḥrāb*), and nothing else. This took place in the month of Rabiʿ I in the year 549 (i.e. 16 May–14 June 1154)'.[19] It is unclear whether the *miḥrābs* were simply placed within the existing church or were meant to be part of a newly constructed mosque or *muṣallā*.

In 1154 the Fatimids lost control of Ascalon, their last port on the Syrian littoral, to the Crusader armies. With this defeat they also relinquished control of the shrine constructed earlier in the twelfth century over the burial place of a skull, believed by the Fatimids to be that of Husayn ibn ʿAli (d. 680).[20] Given these humiliating circumstances one could perhaps view the destruction of the church of Matarea as an act of retribution against a site revered by indigenous Egyptian Christians. According to Abu al-Makarim, however, the pretext for the conversion of the building to Muslim use was that the guardian of the site had rung the bells of the church in the presence of Muslims. This had occurred at the same time as the flight of the vizier ʿAbbas and his son Nasr to Syria following their participation in the assassination of Caliph al-Zafir and his brothers. These events apparently encouraged the 'covetous desires' of the Muslims for this area.[21] The author continues:

> The shaykh Najib al-Dawla ibn al-Muhanna Butrus ibn Mikhaʾil occupied himself, at his own cost, with the construction of a church at Matarea; this was neighbouring [the village of] Qalyub, and he bought a house in the midst of the village, among the dwellings, and it was decided that there would be purified the myron, because the house was close to the balsam [trees]. And it was the patriarch Anba John who constructed with his own hands the sanctuary of this [church], wishing to hasten its consecration in the presence of an assembly of archons (leaders of the lay community); and it was consecrated in the name of Our Lady as we have explained already.[22]

The shaykh mentioned in this passage was also responsible for the restoration of another church dedicated to St George at Qasr al-Mujanni in the region of Qalyub during the caliphate of al-Amir (r. 1101–30).[23] This section of the text is also significant for its reference to the establishment of a house near the balsam trees that would be used for purifying the myron (i.e. chrism;

see Chapter 8). Thus, the officials of the church were free to establish a building near the plantation for the purpose of processing their supplies of *opobalsamum*. This indicates that the Fatimid authorities did not exert direct control over the supply of the 'oil' from the trees. It is less probable that the Coptic Church also owned the trees themselves, but the Fatimids perhaps did not operate a monopoly over the products of the balsam tree as was the case under the Ayyubid and Mamluk sultans. Nasir-i Khusraw, who arrived in Cairo in 1047 and resided in the city for three years, remarks on the collection of balsam in Matarea in his travel journal, the *Safarnāma*.[24] Had this activity been strictly controlled by the Fatimid caliphate one might expect this observant traveller to have commented upon the fact.

Abu al-Makarim also relates an earlier occasion when trees were transplanted from the plantation of Matarea to another site known as the 'garden of camphor (*kāfūr*)'. This occurred in the year 518 H (1124), during the reign of Caliph al-Amir and the vizierate of al-Ma'mun Muhammad ibn Fatik (the latter held this post between 1121 and 1125). The author writes that during the civil war the irrigation of the balsam trees had been neglected. The solution was to move the trees in vases (*qaṣriyya*, perhaps meaning that these vessels were made of copper) to the 'garden of camphor'. While the regular watering of the trees at their new location allowed them to prosper, Abu al-Makarim claims that, having been separated from the venerated wells of Matarea, they lost all of their qualities. Young shoots of balsam were kept in the vicinity of the wells of Matarea, however. The account continues that the vizier promised the sum of a thousand *dīnār*s to the man responsible for the boiling of the balsam oil, Abu al-Hasan ibn Bastiyya, if he could generate a sufficient supply from the cultivation of the trees in the 'garden of camphor'. Predictably, Ibn Bastiyya failed to gather the necessary quantities from the transplanted specimens.[25]

A new phase in the history of the gardens of Matarea was ushered in with the rule of al-Nasir Yusuf ibn Ayyub Salah al-Din (Saladin), first as vizier to the last Fatimid caliph in 1169, and then as the independent ruler of Egypt between 1171 and 1193. Abu al-Makarim observes of the plantation at this time, 'in effect, they (the Ayyubid dynasty) restricted access to this [area] in order to protect the oil and the branches of balsam'.[26] This claim is supported by evidence from later in the Ayyubid period; the *History of the Patriarchs* records that the Coptic patriarch had to obtain the Church's balsam oil from Sultan al-Malik al-ʿAdil (sultan of Egypt, 1200–18).[27] While this desire of the Ayyubids to control the balsam gardens might have been purely an economic matter, external factors – particularly the intensification of the military conflict with the Crusaders – could also have played a part. Establishing a sultanic monopoly over this crucial resource also had propagandist potential in the ongoing struggle with the Franks in the Holy Land.[28]

The geographer Yaqut also mentions the interest of the Ayyubid elite in the balsam trees. He reports that al-Malik al-Kamil had asked his father, al-Malik al-ʿAdil, for permission to cultivate some balsam trees (the date of this event is not mentioned, but it must have been before al-Kamil assumed the sultanate of Egypt in 1218). He continues:

> He (al-Kamil) received them, and, with a firm resolution planted them in land bordering that of the well-known balsam trees (i.e. the existing plantation). He did not succeed in this endeavour and not a drop of oil was purified. He then asked his father to bring an irrigation canal from the wells in question. This project was executed, and [the trees] succeeded and flourished.[29]

Al-Kamil expanded the area of land under cultivation. Abu al-Makarim estimates the size as 12 *fiddān* (a little over 5 hectares), though he provides another estimate of 17 *fiddān* (7 hectares) for the total area covered by the enclosure.[30] Describing the site in the early thirteenth century, ʿAbd al-Latif al-Baghdadi claims that the enclosure comprised only 7 *fiddān*. The cause of this disparity is unclear, though it is possible that ʿAbd al-Latif was referring simply to the area that was devoted to the cultivation of balsam.[31]

Abu al-Makarim provides a brief account of the irrigation of the gardens, presumably reflecting their appearance under Ayyubid administration. He mentions the existence of four *sāqiya* – which could mean either irrigation canals or water-lifting devices – arranged around the four sides of the plantation, and states that each of the wells of Matarea ran out into three channels. He remarks of the irrigation system that 'in the circuit of these channels all the water resembles a single stream which spreads out throughout the garden'.[32] Particular attention is paid to the oldest of the wells, the one which was believed to have been used by the Virgin Mary to wash the clothes of Christ. The author records the celebration of a mass by Anba Mikha'il, bishop of Basta, on the stone of this ancient well, which involved a night vigil on the Sunday of 24 Pachon 901 (i.e. 16 Safar 581/19 May 1185). Attended by many men, women and children, the night vigil was followed by a mass the following day at the Church of Our Lady at Miniat Surad. The celebrant is recorded as being Abu al-Badr, the priest of the village of Bastiyya and the man responsible for making the incisions into the balsam plant and the gathering of the oil.[33] The importance of this event for Abu al-Makarim is that it marks the beginning of the tradition of celebrating a mass over this venerated stone at Matarea.

As noted above, two individuals in charge of harvesting balsam during the twelfth century are named, and both have a connection with the village of Bastiyya. One, Abu al-Badr, is described as being a priest, and the other, Abu al-Hasan ibn Bastiyya, could also have been Christian. *The History of the Patriarchs* relates that a monk from the monastery of Abba Kama was given the task of gathering the annual crop from the balsam trees in 1136–7.[34] Writing in the 1220s Yaqut also states that this task was performed by a Christian. European travellers confirm that this activity remained the preserve of the Copts in later times (Chapter 1). 'Abd al-Latif al-Baghdadi has nothing to say concerning the confessional status of the harvesters of balsam, though he does note that the last stage of cooking the balsam oil was done in secret in the 'owner's store'. The 'owner' in this case is presumably the sultan.[35]

Matarea under the Mamluks

It was under the Mamluks that the areas to the south of Matarea witnessed their greatest phase of urban development. This expansion of Greater Cairo occurred particularly under the Circassian (or Burji) sultans (1389–1517), and resulted in the creation of suburbs of a largely palatial nature along the road that led north from Bab al-Nasr. This road skirted al-Za'faran (Saffron) canal on the way to Matarea (Fig. 3.3). Other monumental structures and a parade ground were placed on either side of the road that led north-east to Birkat al-Hajj, the last stopping point of the annual pilgrimage caravan on the return journey from Mecca and Medina. Many of the European travellers who made the trip from the Egyptian capital to the balsam plantation at Matarea commented upon the ubiquity of palaces along the way. For example, Arnold von Harff (d. 1505) notes the architectural development along the road northward from Bab al-Nasr, finding it to be almost as dense as the intramural area of al-Qahira.[36]

The first suburb to the north was Husayniyya. This area had already attained some importance under the Fatimids and the Ayyubids, and in 1266 the Mamluk sultan Baybars I (r. 1260–77) built a Congregational Mosque on the site of the existing polo ground. Under the third rule of al-Nasir Muhammad ibn Qalawun (r. 1310–41) further improvements were made with the construction of bridges across al-Khalij. The pleasant environment afforded by the waterways and lush landscape made it a popular spot for excursions. While the area west of al-Khalij as far as Raydaniyya was also favoured by Mamluk amirs wanting to build palaces and mosques, it was blighted in the second half of the fourteenth century by a devastating flood and an infestation of termites, as well as by periodic plagues and famines.

To the east and north of Husayniyya was the suburb of Raydaniyya. Encompassing the road to Birkat al-Hajj and the way north to Matarea, this area rose to its greatest economic prominence as the result of changes in the Mamluk economy during the fifteenth century. Most significantly, Sultan Barsbay (r. 1422–37) adopted a policy that required merchants arriving from Syria on their way to the Hijaz to stop in Cairo to pay customs duties. Traders bringing shipments of spice and other valuable commodities from India and further east increasingly shifted their business away from southern Nile towns such as Qus. Instead, much of the traffic diverted to a more northerly Red Sea crossing and the land route to Cairo. Both factors favoured the north-eastern position of Raydaniyya. Birkat al-Hajj possessed a major caravanserai dating to the time of al-Nasir Muhammad ibn Qalawun in the fourteenth century (the sultan also built stables and a hippodrome there), and other structures for accommodating pilgrims were erected by sultans of the Circassian period. The Mamluk elite enjoyed hunting, and an important site in the vicinity of Birkat al-Hajj was the bird feeding ground (*maṭ'am al-ṭayr*) where birds of prey were kept and trained. The *maṭ'am al-ṭayr* was also employed for major ceremonial functions such as the meeting of Mamluk governors when they arrived from Syria. From the time of sultan al-Mu'ayyad Shaykh (r. 1412–21) this site was also utilised for the annual presentation of woollen robes (*libs al-ṣūf*) to the army.[37]

Matarea was also brought into the ambit of the ceremonial processions that took place to the north of Cairo. Saladin had initiated the practice of the ruler being invested outside the city before riding into Cairo itself. Sources recording the investiture of Baybars state that he erected tents in gardens located on the road to Matarea and rode in procession from there through Bab al-Nasr and onward to the citadel. This route continued to be used during the investitures of later Mamluk sultans until the rule of al-Nasir Muhammad ibn Qalawun. The collection of the balsam was also a state-sponsored occasion under the Mamluks, witnessed by the sultan or, in his absence, by the keeper of the royal treasury (*khazindār*). After this ceremony the precious oleo-resin was taken in procession to the sultan's treasury in Cairo.[38]

The amir Yashbak min Mahdi al-Dawadar (d. 1480) was responsible for the most ambitious building programme in the northern suburbs of Cairo. During the rule of Sultan Qaytbay (r. 1468–96) Yashbak assumed several of the highest ranks of state including, as is indicated by his epithet *al-dawādār*, the role of chief secretary to the sultan. Most pertinent in the present context are his constructions south of Matarea on the road leading to Bab al-Nasr. What survives to the present day is a monumental square-planned structure surmounted by a dome pierced with windows around the drum (Fig. 3.4). A similar building known as the Qubbat al-Fadawiyya, also commissioned by Yashbak, is located further to the south at the northern extremity of the old suburb of Husayniyya. The former was built at a site known as al-Malaqa bi'l-Matariyya,[39] and is described by Ibn Iyas as a *qubba* (dome) employed for Friday prayers. Yashbak's patronage in this vicinity also included a *madrasa* (religious school) and palatial buildings with formal gardens. Sultan Qaytbay (r. 1468–96) enjoyed spending time there. It was here that the amirs of Cairo greeted their sultan on his return from pilgrimage. Yashbak's complex was also employed during the state visit of an Ottoman prince in 1481. Qansuh al-Ghawri (r. 1501–16) also made excursions to the *qubba* of Yashbak in the company of his amirs, musicians and dancers.[40]

The road from the walled city of Cairo to Matarea was extensively developed, as is also evident in the map in Münster's *Cosmographia*. The map

Figure 3.4 Qubba of Yashbak min Mahdi at al-Malaqa bi'l-Matariyya, Cairo. Late fifteenth century. Photograph: K. A. C. Creswell, 1916–21. Victoria & Albert Museum 3395-1921. Copyright: Victoria & Albert Museum.

shows the totality of Cairo, including famous monuments in the vicinity of the metropolis (Fig. 1.6a). Represented in the top left sector of the map (Fig. 1.6b) is the route north-east leading to the walled garden of Matarea, and just beyond the single remaining obelisk at ʿAyn Shams (ancient Heliopolis). Although rather schematic, the walls of the plantation are clearly visible, as are some trees within. It is unclear whether the small building inside the southwest corner of the perimeter wall represents the chapel. Moving southward (to the right on the image) from the balsam plantation the artist depicts a series of architectural compounds, including Yashbak's *qubba*. Further south are the substantial extramural suburbs beyond the north wall of Cairo.[41]

Although none of them appears to have been reliably informed as to the identity of the patron, European travellers offer some insights into the original appearance of Yashbak's buildings at al-Malaqa bi'l-Matariyya. Two who saw the buildings during the reign of Qaytbay, De Joos van Ghistele (d. c. 1525)

Figure 3.5 Illustration of Yashbak's palace. From Corneille Le Brun, *Voyage au Levant* (Delft, 1700). After Behrens-Abouseif, 'Northeastern extension', pl. VIII b.

and Felix Fabri, offer descriptions.[42] Van Ghistele praises the extraordinary beauty of the palace, with highly ordered gardens not bettered anywhere in the world. The palace itself was decorated in gold, silver, blue and many other colours, with rare stones set into the floors and walls. Assuming it to be the summer residence of the sultan, Fabri mentions other details such as the presence of painted decoration in some of the rooms and the existence of baths with very large pools. The complex was illustrated in Corneille Le Brun's *Voyage au Levant*, published in Delft in 1700 (Fig. 3.5). By the latter part of the seventeenth century the palace was only a shadow of its former self; the Turkish wanderer Evliya Çelebi (d. after 1683) spent the years 1672–80 in Cairo, and in his time only the main *qāʿa* (palatial hall) and a few other rooms were still standing. Çelebi was unaware of Yashbak's patronage, attributing it instead to Sultan al-Ghawri. The ruins of the building survive through to the present (Fig. 3.6).[43]

This region evidently brought in a valuable agricultural surplus. In administrative terms Matarea constituted a district (*nāḥiya*) within the larger region (*ḥāḍira*) of ʿAyn Shams. According to the geographer al-Dimashqi (d. 1327), ʿAyn Shams was composed of sixty-three villages (sing. *qarya*).[44] The early decades of the fourteenth century were a time of political stability, cultural productivity and intense economic activity. All indications are that the balsam plantations of Matarea were thriving, and the same applied to the surrounding area.[45] The robust self-confidence of the Mamluk state is reflected in the writings of Arab authors; for example, the author and administrator al-ʿUmari (d. 1349) boasts of the sultan's control over a resource greatly desired by Christians (Chapters 5 and 8).[46] Nearly a century later al-Maqrizi repeats al-ʿUmari's assertions verbatim.[47] Although the Mamluk sultanate endured some difficult phases – particularly as the result of the Black Death, the phase of political instability associated with the transition from the Turkic (Bahri) to the Circassian (Burji) sultans in the 1380s, the

Figure 3.6 View of the Palace of Qawsun, renovated by Amir Yashbak min Mahdi, at al-Malaqa bi'l-Matariyya, Cairo. Mid-fourteenth to late fifteenth centuries. Wikimedia Commons: Robert Prazeres.

insurrection against Sultan Faraj (r. 1399–1407) and the invasion of Syria by Timur – the testimony of European travellers suggests that there was continued investment in Matarea, and that the balsam plantation was well tended.

The mismanagement of specialised agriculture during the Circassian Mamluk period has been particularly well documented for the sugar industry. Over taxation and failure to invest in new technology both seem to have damaged this lucrative export crop, and by the end of the fifteenth century many of the sugar mills in Egypt and Greater Syria had ceased to operate.[48] Reports from the late fifteenth century do not indicate that the standards of maintenance of the garden had diminished significantly. From this time we possess some of the most detailed European accounts of Matarea. For example, Fabri found much to admire during his visit in the 1480s, though he reports that there were no more than fifty balsam trees in the garden. His account offers little reason to assume that a catastrophe was soon to occur, however.

Fabri notes that the sultan remained interested in the annual harvest, arriving there each December from Cairo with his court in order to witness the incisions made in the trees to collect the sap.[49] Ibn Iyas reports that in 'earlier times' one of the amirs of the chief treasurer (*khazindār*) was present for the day of oil collection in the Coptic month of Barmahat (April–May), indicating that the practice had ceased by the early sixteenth century.[50] Bernard von Breydenbach (d. 1497) also offers a relatively positive assessment of the state of Matarea during his visit in 1483. Although Francesco Suriano claims that the plantation (he calls it a vineyard) was 'vilely kept', he does mention that, 'when I was in Cairo the sultan had built a beautiful chapel, dedicated to the Blessed Virgin'. The sultan in question must be Qaytbay, though it seems more likely that the chapel was paid for by local Christians.[51]

Neither neglect nor rapacious tax-farming were the primary cause of the greatest damage to the trees. Rather, the origins of their ultimate decline lay in the political instability within the Mamluk regime itself. Following the death of Qaytbay, the last great sultan of the dynasty, in 1496 there were disagreements over the succession. The sultanate passed to Qaytbay's son, who adopted the regnal title of al-Nasir Muhammad (r. 1496–8). Arnold von Harff, who was in Cairo at this time, records the destruction wrought by a rival amir, given in his text as 'Kanszuweh Chamsmiah'. He writes:

> As he fled away he killed all those in the town belonging to the young sultan's party, and withdrew and lay the first night before Cairo in a town called Materya, where balsam is grown in a beautiful garden belonging to the young sultan. They pulled up the little bushes on which the balsam grew, and broke the waterwheels which they used to water the garden and took the oxen which drove the waterwheels, so that they told me, as indeed I saw with my own eyes, that no balsam would grow there for ten years.[52]

It may be that von Harff had gathered his information from German mercenaries who were among the guards of Matarea. The Venetian diarist Marino Sanudo the Younger (d. 1536) and Ibn Iyas confirm the date of this event.[53]

As von Harff feared, the damage was not quickly repaired by the Mamluk elite.[54] Pedro d'Anghiera (Peter Martyr, d. 1526) highlighted the plight of the garden in his embassy to Cairo in 1501, and while this must have brought home to the sultan and his entourage the high status that the balsam of

Matarea enjoyed in Europe, the task of restoring the trees was by no means straightforward.[55] It was a commonplace of medieval writing that 'true' balsam was unique to Matarea, and clear distinctions were drawn by Arab scholars such as Ibn al-Baytar (d. 1248) between *balasān* (from Matarea) and the related, but inferior product from Arabia known as *bashām* (Chapter 4). Where then was the sultan to find replacements for the trees of Matarea? As it turned out, the Egyptian plantation was replenished using specimens located in Arabia. The first unsuccessful attempt to restore the trees probably occurred before the embassy of d'Anghiera because Ibn Iyas writes that:

> In the year 905 (i.e. 1499–1500) the balsam tree became extinct in Egypt. It was one of the remains connected with the story of Jesus, son of Mary – peace be upon them . . . They [the Egyptians] brought the seed of the wild balsam-tree from the Hijaz, planted it in the soil of Matarea and nursed it; but it did not grow and became extinct in the whole of Egypt, as if it had never grown in [the region of] 'Ayn Shams. It was the most venerated tree there, and had never disappeared [before then]. It had existed long before the rise of Islam.[56]

It may be that the new trees were unable to withstand the colder, wetter winter in Cairo. The German botanist Georg Schweinfurth (d. 1925) similarly failed to rear balsam trees (presumably *Commiphora gileadensis*) imported from Arabia in his garden in Cairo. He reports that they perished due to the cold winter nights in the Egyptian capital.[57] The unsuccessful transplantation made shortly before 1499–1500 was not to be the end of the story, however. Sultan al-Ghawri also interested himself in the balsam garden.[58] Describing events of the year 914 (1508–9) Ibn Iyas states of the balsam tree:

> Its husbandry had ceased in the first year of the tenth century (i.e. 901/1495–6). Egypt had been unique among all the lands for its balsam production . . . This essence was customarily extracted during spring, in the Coptic month of Barmahat. When the sultan learned of this lapse in balsam cultivation, he made an inquiry as to its location elsewhere. He pursued this matter until some seeds from wild bushes were brought from the Hijaz. They were planted in the same plots where the crop had previously been sown. Their revival was successful after watering from a well in the vicinity. This was one of al-Ghawri's better acts.[59]

The way this is phrased suggests that there was a second attempt to bring trees from Arabia between 1496 and 1508–9. Given that the first was prior to 905/1499–1500, this second transplantation may have been ordered by al-Ghawri, perhaps in response to the pleas of d'Anghiera. Whatever the case, this practice of bringing seeds or saplings from the Hijaz was continued under the Ottoman governors of Egypt after 1517. Matarea itself may have suffered during the Egyptian campaign of sultan Selim I (r. 1512–20) as one of the key battles between Mamluk and Ottoman troops was fought in the vicinity.[60]

Matarea under Ottoman Rule

The final phase in the history of the balsam of Matarea lasts a little under a century from the execution of the last Mamluk sultan, al-Ashraf Tumanbay II (r. 1516–17), to the death of the last tree in 1615. The sixteenth century represents a low ebb in the writing of Arabic chronicles, particularly following the death of Ibn Iyas, and relatively little can be gathered about balsam from such Middle Eastern source material. During the early Ottoman period Matarea was visited by many European travellers, and it is their accounts that form the largest body of historical evidence. Indeed, the volume of visitors seems not to have declined substantially after 1615 with many of these later European authors providing information about the situation of the site, both as they found it during their visits and as it was in earlier times.

Two issues are worth highlighting in these accounts: first the declining number of healthy balsam trees at Matarea and the periodic interventions of Ottoman governors of Egypt; and second, the changing fate of the chapel and pool at the site. Despite the efforts of Sultan al-Ghawri, the balsam trees never regained the vitality they had enjoyed prior to the destruction of 1496. Pierre Belon (d. 1564) records that at the time of his visit in 1547 there were only nine or ten balsam trees at Matarea.[61] Writing in 1581 Jean Palerne praises the fertility of the land around Matarea – employed for the cultivation of citrus fruits, fig, date palm and carob – but was able to find only two diminutive specimens of balsam. He reports, however, that four or five years before, the pasha (governor) in Cairo had sent to Mecca for several plants. Not long after they all died.[62]

The attempt by the pasha of Egypt – described in European sources as a eunuch named Messinor – to bring plants from the Hijaz is documented in other sources. Antonius González (fl. late seventeenth century) claims that Messinor was in the habit of making frequent visits on Fridays to Matarea to honour the Blessed Virgin. As the result of these visits he became aware of the perilous state of the balsam trees. In 1575 he brought from Mecca forty plants for the Egyptian plantation. González attributes their rapid demise in the following years to the negligence of the gardeners.[63] Given that Lupold von Wedel (d. 1615) claims to have seen no living balsam trees during his visit in 1578, there were probably further expeditions to obtain trees from the Hijaz in later years.[64] Writing in 1599 Aquilante Rocchetta notes that there were considerable quantities of balsam in Mecca and that the 'Grand Turk' (meaning the sultan in Istanbul rather than the pasha in Cairo) would periodically instruct merchants to buy trees and move them to Cairo.[65]

Christophe Harant (d. 1621), who was in Matarea in 1598, observes that the biannual cutting of the branches was still done in the presence of officials and Turkish medics sent by the pasha. The Ottoman authorities placed considerable emphasis upon the maintenance, or revival, of such ceremonies, and balsam continued to feature in diplomatic gifts sent from the Turks to European rulers until the sixteenth century (Chapter 5). Matarea was probably unable to supply the large amounts of balsam that Harant claims, however, and it might be that the sultan's treasury was supplementing their balsam with oleo-resin tapped from Arabian trees.[66] Other 'balsams' from the Middle East and the Americas were also being sold by traders in the Mediterranean during the sixteenth and seventeenth centuries. The last chapter in the history of the balsam trees can be reconstructed from the testimony of European travellers. By the time George Sandys arrived in Egypt in 1610 only one tree remained, and according to Henry Rantzow (d. c. 1630) this lone specimen died following an inundation of the Nile in 1615.[67] Attempts were also made to cultivate balsam in Italy in the late sixteenth century, but the plants did not thrive in this new environment.[68]

Matarea continued to draw European visitors through the remainder of the seventeenth century and into the eighteenth. In part, this can be attributed to the enduring fame of the (now deceased) balsam trees, but it was also due to Matarea's role as a pilgrimage site associated with the Holy Family. Jean Palerne describes a church built of brick that had been converted into a mosque. Samuel Kiechel visited Matarea in 1588 and makes no mention of a mosque, claiming that both Turks and Christians were permitted to enter. Many came to bathe in the pool.[69] In 1597 Father Bernardino Amico da Gallipoli, president and confessor of the Christian traders in Cairo, determined to restore the church at Matarea (Fig. 1.10). Although he was largely unsuccessful in enlisting the financial support of most of the merchants, one, a Florentine called Marsilio Acquisti, was very active in the restoration process. Having completed the restoration he attached a carved inscription onto the building, an act exceeding the permission extended by the pasha. Acquisti was imprisoned, but was later released.[70]

Wansleben visited Egypt in 1672–3. He records that the site of the church had been converted into a Muslim 'oratory' (*maqām*) by Ibrahim, the previous pasha of Egypt. Wansleben found the oratory to be abandoned and with access to it unhindered. The building contained a marble-lined cistern fed with water from the well associated with the Virgin. He admits to reservations concerning the historical veracity of the Coptic legend that the clothes of Christ were washed in the well.[71] The Franciscans of Egypt maintained an interest in the site, disputing with the keepers of the garden over the possession of the famous sycamore fig. Matarea was visited in the eighteenth and nineteenth centuries – Benoît de Maillet (d. 1738), French consul-general in Cairo between 1692 and 1708, is perhaps the last early modern European to devote serious attention to the topography of the site and the legends associated with it – the locality now enjoyed much less prominence in the accounts of European travellers to Egypt.[72] It was only with the efforts of the Jesuit Order in the late nineteenth and early twentieth centuries that the chapel was rebuilt and the gardens renovated (Chapter 1). The town of Matarea continued to thrive, and in the late Ottoman period is one of the few places in the north of Egypt to boast its own guilds.[73]

Notes

1. Ibn Hawqal's text, *Kitāb ṣūrat al-arḍ*, was written first in 967 and reworked in c. 977 and 988, and should be considered as a revision and expansion of al-Istakhri's *Kitāb al-Masālik wa'l-mamālik* (composed around 951). Ibn Hawqal was also extensively travelled, having spent thirty years of his life journeying through Asia and Africa.

2. Muhammad Abu al-Qasim ibn Hawqal, *Viae et regna; descriptio ditionis moslemicae* (*Kitāb ṣūrat al-arḍ*), ed. Michael de Goeje, Bibliotheca geographorum Arabicorum 2 (Leiden: Brill, 1873. Reprinted Brill, 1967 and 2014), p. 106; Abu Ishaq Ibrahim b. Muhammad al-Farisi al-Istakhri, *Viae regnorum; descriptio ditionis Moslemicae* (*Masālik al-mamālik*), ed. Michael de Goeje, Bibliotheca geographorum Arabicorum 1 (Leiden: Brill, 1870. Reprinted Brill, 1967), p. 54. Other mentions of ʿAyn Shams appear in early Arabic geographical texts. See Ahmad b. ʿUmar Abu ʿAli ibn Rusta in *Ibn Rusta's* Kitāb al-aʿlāq al-nafīsa *and* Kitāb al-buldān *by al-Yaʿqūbī*, ed. Michael de Goeje, Bibliotheca geographorum Arabicorum 7 (Leiden: Brill, 1892. Reprinted Brill, 1967), p. 80; Ahmad b. Abi Yaʿqub b. Jaʿfar al-Yaʿqubi in *Ibn Rusta's* Kitāb al-aʿlāq al-nafīsa *and* Kitāb al-buldān *by al-Yaʿqūbī*, ed. Michael de Goeje, Bibliotheca geographorum Arabicorum 7 (Leiden: Brill, 1892. Reprinted Brill, 1967), p. 337; Abu al-Qasim ʿUbayd Allah b. ʿAbdallah ibn Khurdadhbih, *Kitāb al-masālik wa'l-mamālik*, eds Michael de Goeje and Qudamah ibn Jaʿfar, Bibliotheca geographorum Arabicorum 7 (Leiden: Brill, 1889. Reprinted Brill, 1967), pp. 72, 161; Muhammad ibn Ahmad Shams al-Din al-Muqaddasi (or al-Maqdisi), *Descriptio imperii Moslemici* (*Aḥsan al-taqāsim fī maʿrifat al-aqālīm*), ed. Michael de Goeje, Bibliotheca geographorum Arabicorum 3 (Leiden: Brill, 1877. Reprinted Brill, 1967), pp. 55, 194, 200.

3. Abu ʿAbd Allah al-Idrisi, *Opus geographicum, sive 'Liber ad eorum delectationem qui terras peragrare studeant'* (*Kitāb nuzhat al-mushtāq fī dhikr al-amṣār wa'l-aqṭār wa'l-buldān wa'l-juzur wa'l-madā'in*), eds Enrico Cerulli et al., published in 9 parts (Naples and Rome: Istituto Universitario Orientale, 1971–84), p. 326; Abu Muʿin Nasir-i Khusraw, *Nāṣer-e Khosraw's Book of Travels* (Safarnāma), trans. Wheeler Thackston, Persian Heritage Series 36 (New York: Persian Heritage Foundation, 1986), p. 51.

4. Yaqut ibn ʿAbd Allah al-Rumi al-Hamawi, *Jacut's geographische Wörterbuch* (*Kitāb al-muʿjam al-buldān*), ed. Ferdinand Wüstenfeld (Leipzig: Brockhaus, 1866–70), IV, pp. 564–5. Translated in Zanetti, 'Matarieh', pp. 45–6.

5. Zakariya b. Muhammad b. Mahmud al-Qazwini, *Zakarija ben Muhammed ben Mahmud al-Cazwini's Kosmographie* (*Āthār al-bilād wa akhbār al-ʿibād*), ed. Ferdinand Wüstenfeld (Göttingen: Verlag der Dieterichschen Buchhandlung, 1848–9. Reprinted Wiesbaden: Martin Sändig, 1967), I, pp. 139–40.

6. Taqi al-Din Ahmad b. ʿAli al-Maqrizi, *Kitāb al-mawāʿiẓ wa'l-iʿtibār fī dhikr al-khiṭaṭ wa'l-āthār*, ed. Gaston Wiet (Cairo: Institut Français d'Archéologie Orientale du Caire, 1911–27), IV, p. 101.

7. Zanetti, 'Matarieh', p. 45.
8. On the history of the city, see James Allen, 'Heliopolis', in Donald Redford, ed., *The Oxford Dictionary of Ancient Egypt* (Oxford and Cairo: Oxford University Press and American University in Cairo Press, 2001), II, pp. 88–9. For a brief report on recent German-Egyptian excavations in the region, see Anon., 'Excavations this season yield several findings at el Matareya, Cairo': https://www.archaeology.wiki/blog/2019/05/24/excavations-this-season-yield-several-findings-at-el-matareya-cairo/ (last consulted: 13 October 2019).
9. Herodotus, *Histories* 2:3, 8, 59.
10. Strabo, *Geography* 17:1.27–9.
11. For a brief history of the Copts under Islamic rule, see Barbara Watterson, *Coptic Egypt* (Edinburgh: Scottish Academic, 1988), pp. 142–59; Christian Cannuyer, 'Les Coptes, vingt siècles d'histoire chrétienne en Égypte', in Anon., *L'Art copte en Égypte: 2000 ans de christianisme* (Paris: Gallimard and Institut du Monde Arabe, 2000), pp. 26–33. See also Shaun O'Sullivan, 'Coptic conversion and the Islamization of Egypt', *Mamluk Studies Review* 10.2 (2006): 65–79. On the treatment of crosses, see Geoffrey King, 'Islam, iconoclasm and the declaration of doctrine', *Bulletin of the School of Oriental and African Studies* 48 (1985): 267–77.
12. Robert Lopez, 'Mohammed and Charlemagne: A revision', *Speculum* 18.1 (1943): 15, 20–1, 26–8; Jonathan Bloom, *Paper before Print*, pp. 20–2, 27–9.
13. On the urban development of Cairo, see André Raymond, *Cairo*, trans. Willard Wood (Cambridge, MA: Harvard University Press, 2000); Hani Hamza, *The Northern Cemetery of Cairo* (Costa Mesa, CA: Mazda, 2001); Behrens-Abouseif, 'The northeastern extension of Cairo'.
14. Behrens-Abouseif, 'The northeastern extension of Cairo', pp. 160–4.
15. Sawirus ibn al-Muqaffaʿ and continuators, *History of the Patriarchs of the Egyptian Church, Known as the History of the Holy Church*, eds Yassa ʿAbd al-Masih et al., Publications de la Société d'Archéologie Copte. Textes et Documents (Cairo: Société d'Archéologie Copte, 1943–76). Comprises vols II, pt I–IV, pt 2 (Khaël II to Cyril III, Ibn Laqlaq).
16. *History of the Patriarchs*, III, p. 73 (Arabic text: p. 44). Also Zanetti, 'Matarieh', p. 40.
17. On the status of churches and monasteries under Islamic rule, see Arthur Tritton, *The Caliphs and Their Non-Muslim Subjects: A Critical Study of the Covenant of ʿUmar*, Islam and the Muslim World 14 (London: Frank Cass, 1970). On anti-Christian sentiments in Egypt, see Moshe Perlmann, 'Notes on anti-Christian

propaganda in the Mamlūk empire', *Bulletin of the School of Oriental and African Studies* 10 (1942): 552–69.

18. His full name is Abu al-Makarim Saʿdallah ibn Jirjis ibn Masʿud. See Zanetti, 'Matarieh', pp. 32–8, 63–4. On the misidentification as 'Abu Salih, the Armenian', see p. 32. His work was first presented in an edition and translation under the latter name. See *The Churches and Monasteries of Egypt, and Some Neighbouring Countries, Attributed to Abû Ṣâliḥ, the Armenian*, trans. Basil Evetts with notes by Alfred Butler, Anecdota Oxoniensia (Oxford: Oxford University Press, 1894–5). This edition does not contain any information about the churches of Matarea. A more recent English translation is Abu al-Makarim, *History of the Churches and Monasteries in Lower Egypt in thr* [sic] *13th Century*, trans. Mina al-Shamaaʿ and revised by Mrs Elizabeth (Cairo: Institute of Coptic Studies, 1992). For an analysis of Abu al-Makarim's writing, see Mat Immerzeel, 'The renovation of the churches of Cairo on the Fatimid and early Ayyubid periods according to Abu al-Makarim's *Churches and Monasteries of Egypt*', *Eastern Christian Art* 9 (2012–13): 27–52.

19. Translated in Zanetti, 'Matarieh', p. 33; Abu al-Makarim, *History of the Churches*, p. 41.

20. Caroline Williams, 'The cult of the ʿAlid saints in the Fatimid monuments of Cairo. Part I: the mosque of al-Aqmar', *Muqarnas* 1 (1983): 37–52; Daniel de Smet, 'La translation du *raʾs* al-Ḥusayn au Caire fatimide', in Urbain Vermeulen and Daniel de Smet, eds, *Egypt and Syria in the Fatimid, Ayyubid and Mamluk Eras* (Leuven: Peeters, 1998), pp. 29–44; Marcus Milwright, 'Reynald of Châtillon and Red Sea expedition of 1182–1183', in Maya Yazigi and Niall Christie, eds, *Noble Ideals and Bloody Realities: Warfare in the Middle Ages* (Leiden: Brill, 2006), pp. 253–5.

21. Translated in Zanetti, 'Matarieh', p. 33; Abu al-Makarim, *History of the Churches*, p. 42. Abu al-Makarim also writes that these events happened after an armistice had been signed with the 'Franks' (i.e. the European occupants of the Crusader states) comprising an annual payment by the Fatimids of 30,000 *dīnār*s. Quite what armistice is being referred to here has not been established.

22. From translation in Zanetti, 'Matarieh', pp. 33–4. Also Abu al-Makarim, *History of the Churches*, p. 42.

23. Abu al-Makarim, *History of the Churches*, p. 55.

24. Nasir-i Khusraw, *Nāṣer-e Khosraw's Book of Travels*, p. 51.

25. Translated in Zanetti, 'Matarieh', p. 36; Abu al-Makarim, *History of the Churches*, p. 44.

26. Translated in Zanetti, 'Matarieh', p. 37; Abu al-Makarim, *History of the Churches*, p. 45.
27. *History of the Patriarchs* IV.1, p. 151.
28. On the Muslim propagandistic activities of this period, see Yasser Tabbaa, 'Monuments with a message: propagation of *jihad* under Nur al-Din (1146–1174)', in Vladimir Goss and Christine Bornstein, eds, *The Meeting of Two Worlds: Cultural Exchange between East and West during the Period of the Crusades* (Kalamazoo, MI: Medieval Institute Publications, 1986), pp. 223–40; Carole Hillenbrand, *Crusades, Islamic Perspectives* (Edinburgh: Edinburgh University Press, 1999), pp. 310–20, et passim.
29. Yaqut, *Jacut's geographische Wörterbuch*, IV, p. 564. Zanetti, 'Matarieh', p. 46.
30. Translated in Zanetti, 'Matarieh', p. 37. Also Abu al-Makarim, *History of the Churches*, pp. 45–6.
31. 'Abd al-Latif al-Baghdadi, *The Eastern Key*, pp. 40 (Arabic), 41 (English).
32. Translated in Zanetti, 'Matarieh', p. 37. Abu al-Makarim, *History of the Churches*, p. 46.
33. Translated in Zanetti, 'Matarieh', p. 38. Abu al-Makarim, *History of the Churches*, p. 47.
34. *History of the Patriarchs* III, p. 58.
35. Yaqut, *Jacut's geographische Wörterbuch*, IV, p. 564; 'Abd al-Latif, *The Eastern Key*, pp. 41 (Arabic), 43 (English). Also Zanetti, 'Matarieh', pp. 44–6.
36. Arnold von Harff, *The Pilgrimage of Arnold von Harff, Knight from Cologne, through Italy, Syria, Egypt, Arabia, Nubia, Palestine, Turkey, France and Spain, which he Accomplished in the Years 1496 to 1499*, trans. and annotated by Malcolm Letts, Works issued by the Hakluyt Society, second series 94 (London: Hakluyt Society, 1946), pp. 109–10.
37. Behrens-Abouseif, 'The northeastern extension of Cairo', pp. 166–8.
38. 'Abd al-Latif al-Baghdadi, *The Eastern Key*, pp. 42 (Arabic), 43 (English). See also Johannes Schiltberger, *The Bondage and Travels of Johann Schiltberger*, trans. John Buchan Telfer with notes by Filip (Philip) Bruun, Works issued by the Hakluyt Society 58 (London: Hakluyt Society, 1879), pp. 60–1. This is also confirmed by the author of a fourteenth-century Arabic text on chrism/myron. See Louis Villecourt, 'Un manuscrit arabe sur la saint chrême dans l'Église Copte II', *Revue d'Histoire Ecclésiastique* 18 (1922): 5–6.
39. *Malaqa* refers to a low-lying cultivated area regularly flooded by a river.
40. Behrens-Abouseif, 'The northeastern extension of Cairo', pp. 171–2.

41. Meinecke-Berg, 'Eine Stadtansicht des mamlukischen Kairo'; Behrens-Abouseif, 'The northeastern extension of Cairo', pp. 158–9, pl. X. See also Bernard Blanc et al., 'À propos de la carte du Caire de Matheo Pagano', *Annales Islamologiques* 17 (1981): 203–86. For Matarea, see p. 219, pls XV, XVI. See also Sebastian Münster, *Cosmographia* (Basel, 1628. Reprinted Antiqua-Verlag, Lindau 1984), II, pp. 1648–9. Also I, p. 11; II, p. 1652.
42. Discussed in Behrens-Abouseif, 'The northeastern extension of Cairo', pp. 173–4.
43. Ibid. pp. 173–4.
44. Shams al-Din Muhammad b. Abi Talib al-Dimashqi, *Kitāb al-nukhbat al-dahr fī 'ajā'ib al-barr wa'l-bahr*, ed. August Mehren (St Petersburg: Académie Impériale des Sciences, 1864. Reprinted Amsterdam: Meridian, 1964), pp. 42, 229–31.
45. A fourteenth-century document in the Geniza archive (Bodleian library ms Heb. d.66 [cat. 2878]) describes the leasing to a tax farmer the revenues of Matarea by an individual named as *malik al-Umarā'* ('king of the amirs'). See Shlomo Goitein, *A Mediterranean Society: The Jewish Communities of the Arab World as Portrayed in the Documents of the Cairo Geniza. Volume II: The Community* (Berkeley, CA and Los Angeles: University of California Press, 1971, reprinted 1999), pp. 361, 606.
46. Shihab al-Din Abu al-'Abbas Ahmad Fadl Allah al-'Umari, *L'Égypte, la Syrie, le Hiğāz et le Yémen* (*Masālik al-abṣār fī mamālik al-amṣār*), ed. Ayman Sayyid, Textes arabes et études Islamiques 23 (Cairo: Institut Français d'Archéologie Orientale, 1985), p. 68. The full quote is given in Chapter 5.
47. Maqrizi, *Khiṭaṭ*, IV, p. 100.
48. Eliyahu Ashtor, 'Levantine sugar industry in the later Middle Ages: a case of technological decline', *Israel Oriental Studies* 7 (1977): 226–80. Reprinted in Abraham Udovitch, ed., *The Islamic Middle East, 700–1900: Studies in Economic and Social History* (Princeton, NJ: Princeton University Press, 1981), pp. 91–132.
49. Fabri, *Evagatorium*, III, pp. 15–16; Fabri, *Voyage*, I, p. 393. Fabri does, however, identify the wrong month for this visit.
50. Ibn Iyas, *Die Chronik des Ibn Ijās*, IV, p. 149.
51. Bernhard von Breydenbach, *Die Reise ins Heilige Land: Ein Reisebericht aus dem Jahre 1483*, ed. with introduction Elizabeth Geck (Wiesbaden: J. Pressler, 1977), pp. 34–6 (the balsam garden is also represented on the right-hand side of the woodcut showing the panorama of the city of Jerusalem); Suriano, *Treatise*, p. 195.

52. Von Harff, *The Pilgrimage of Arnold von Harff*, pp. 104–5.
53. Marino Sanudo (Sanuto), *I Diarii di Marino Sanuto*, ed. Rinaldo Fulin (Venice: F. Vinsentini, 1897–1903), I, p. 756; Ibn Iyas, *Die Chronik des Ibn Ijās*, IV, p. 149.
54. Doris Behrens-Abouseif points to the fact that balsam is notably absent from a diplomatic gift sent by Sultan al-Zahir Qansawh (r. 1498–1500) to Venice in 1499. See Behrens-Abouseif, *Practicing Diplomacy in the Mamluk Sultanate: Gifts and Material Culture in the Medieval Islamic World* (London: I. B. Tauris, 2014), p. 108.
55. Petrus Martyr de Angleria (Peter Martyr), *Opera: Legatio Babylonica de orbe novo decades octo opus epistolarum*, facsimile of edition of 1516 with an introduction by Erich Woldan (Graz: Akademische Druck, 1966), book 4 (see p. [29] in facsimile).
56. Ibn Iyas, *Die Chronik des Ibn Ijās*, IV, p. 149.
57. Schweinfurth, *Arabische Pflanzennamen*, p. 14.
58. He also included lands around Matarea in his *waqf*. See Khalid Alhazmeh, *Late Mamluk Patronage: Qanṣūh al-Ghūri's Waqf and his Foundations in Cairo*, unpublished doctoral thesis, Ohio State University, 1993, p. 115.
59. Ibn Iyas, *Die Chronik des Ibn Ijās*, IV, p. 149. Also Doris Behrens-Abouseif, 'Gardens in Islamic Egypt', *Der Islam* 69 (1992): 308–9; Carl Petry, *Protectors or Praetorians? The Last Mamluk Sultans and Egypt's Waning as a Great Power* (New York: State University of New York Press, 1994), p. 119.
60. On the last years of the Mamluk sultanate and the transition to Ottoman rule, see Petry, *Protectors or Praetorians?*; Carl Petry, *Twilight of Majesty: The Reigns of the Mamlūk Sultans al-Ashrāf Qāytbāy and Qānṣūh al-Ghawrī in Egypt* (Seattle and London: University of Washington Press, 1993); Peter M. Holt, 'Ottoman Egypt (1517–1798): An account of Arabic historical sources', in Peter M. Holt, *Studies in the History of the Near East* (London: Frank Cass, 1973), pp. 151–60. On the military dimensions, see David Ayalon, *Gunpowder and Firearms in the Mamluk Kingdom* (London: Vallentine, Mitchell, 1956). *Contra* Robert Irwin, 'Gunpowder and firearms in the Mamluk sultanate reconsidered', in Michael Winter and Amelia Levanoni, eds, *The Mamluks in Egyptian and Syrian Politics and Society*, Medieval Mediterranean 51 (Leiden and Boston: Brill, 2004), pp. 117–39.
61. Pierre Belon du Mans, *Voyage en Égypte*, trans. and ed. Serge Sauneron, Collection des Voyageurs occidentaux en Égypte 1 (Cairo: Institut Français d'Archéologie Orientale du Caire, 1970), p. 110b.

62. Palerne, *Voyage en Égypte*, pp. 96–7.
63. Antonius González, *Voyage en Égypte du Père Antonius González, 1665–1666*, trans. and ed. Charles Libois, Collection des Voyageurs occidentaux en Égypte 19 (Cairo: Institut Français d'Archéologie Orientale, 1972), I, p. 62.
64. Lupold von Wedel cited in the notes of Samuel Kiechel in Ursula Castel and Nadine Sauneron, trans., and Serge Sauneron, ed., *Voyages en Égypte pendant les années 1587–1588*, Collection des Voyageurs occidentaux en Égypte 6 (Cairo: Institut Français d'Archéologie Orientale, 1972), p. 89 [365], n. 152. Hans von Lichtenstein claims to have seen two balsam plants during a visit in 1587. See his account in Castel and Sauneron, trans., *Voyages en Égypte pendant les années 1587–1588*, p. 11.
65. Aquilante Rocchetta, 'Voyage en Égypte d'Aquilante Rocchetta, mai–août 1599', in Burri and Sauneron, trans., *Voyages en Égypte des années, 1597–1601*, p. 43 [313].
66. Christophe Harant de Polzic, in Claire and Antoine Brejnik, trans. and ed., *Voyage en Égypte de Christophe Harant de Polzic et Bezdruzic, 1598*, Collection des voyageurs occidentaux en Égypte 5 (Cairo: Institut Français d'Archéologie Orientale, 1972), p. 88.
67. Sandys, *A Relation of a Journey*, p. 127; Unpublished account cited in Niebuhr, *Voyage en Arabie*, I, p. 98. William Lithgow also mentions this tree during his visit in c. 1612–13. See his *The Rare Adventures and Painful Peregrinations*, p. 173 (see also comments in Chapter 4).
68. On the attempts to cultivate balsam in Italy, see Gregorius Abu al-Faraj (Bar Hebraeus), *The Abridged Version of 'The Book of Simple Drugs' of Ahmad ibn Muhammad al-Ghâfiqî by Gregorius Abu'l-Farag (Barhebraeus). Fasc. II: Leter BÂ' and GÎM*, ed. and trans. Max Meyerhof and G. Sobhy, The Egyptian University Faculty of Medicine Publications 4 (Cairo: Government Press, 1937), p. 253 (commentary by Meyerhof and Sobhy for the entry on *balasān*). Prosper Alpin grew a balsam plant from seeds obtained in Cairo, and in about 1600 his pupil Johannes Vesling saw balsam plants in some gardens in Italy.
69. Palerne, *Voyage en Égypte*, pp. 87–8 [364–5]; Samuel Kiechel, in Castel and Sauneron, trans., *Voyages en Égypte pendant les années 1587–1588*, p. 87 [364].
70. Amico da Gallipoli, *L'Église de la Matarea* in Burri and Sauneron, trans., *Bernardino Amico da Gallipoli*, pp. 5–9 [18–20]; Rocchetta in Burri and Sauneron, trans., *Bernardino Amico da Gallipoli*, pp. 43–7 [313–16]. According to the accounts left by da Gallipoli and Aquilante Rocchetta, the Florentine

merchant was able to pay for much of the work on the chapel through the purchase from a Muslim boy of a valuable emerald at a fraction of its true value.
71. Wansleben (Vansleb), *The Present State of Egypt*, pp. 139–40.
72. Benoît de Maillet, *Description de l'Égypte, contenant plusieurs remarques curieuses sur la géographie ancienne et moderne de ce païs, sur ces monumens anciens, sur les moeurs*, ed. Jean-Baptiste Le Mascrier (Paris: L. Genneau and J. Rollin, fils, 1735), pp. 111–12.
73. Gabriel Baer, *Egyptian Guilds in Modern Times*, Oriental Notes and Studies 8 (Jerusalem: The Israel Oriental Society, 1964), pp. 21, 106, 111. At the time of the French occupation of Egypt, the fishermen of Matarea were the only ones allowed to fish on Lake Manzala. Taxes on hunting and fishing in the lake of Matarea were also levied during the Ottoman period. See Stanford Shaw, *The Financial and Administrative Organization and Development of Ottoman Egypt, 1517–1798* (Princeton, NJ: Princeton University Press, 1962), pp. 130, 301, 382, 387, 389, 390.

4

The Balsam Tree and Balsam 'Oil'

Primary written sources surveyed in the previous chapters provide a wealth of information concerning both the balsam trees and the 'oil' and other products gathered from them. The key points can be briefly summarised. There is general agreement among Arab and European writers from the tenth century onwards that the trees of Matarea in Egypt were the only source of 'true' balsam, and that all other comparable products were inferior in quality. This elevated status is confirmed by the high prices paid for the balsam from Matarea (Chapter 5). The balsam trees themselves were transferred to Egypt from the plantations in the regions of En-Gedi and Jericho, possibly as early as the first century CE, but more likely in the fourth or fifth centuries. Theophrastus indicates that balsam was being cultivated in Palestine in the third century BCE. Josephus' claim that the balsam trees were a gift from the Queen of Sheba to King Solomon is not to be taken literally, but it suggests that the plant was known in ancient Judaea some centuries before it was mentioned by Theophrastus.[1]

Theophrastus is explicit that the balsam trees in the plantations were unknown in the wild, and this judgement is echoed by many later authors (Chapter 2). Some Arab writers make a distinction between the 'true' balsam of Matarea (*balasān*) and a cheaper 'oil' from the Hijaz known as *bashām*.[2] The latter was little valued in commercial terms as it possessed neither the fragrant smell nor the medicinal efficacy of *balasān*. *Bashām* is also known as *bishām*, *abū shām* and 'balm/balsam of Mecca', and is also sometimes discussed by European travellers and botanists.[3] 'Balm of Mecca' can be bought today in the markets of Arabia, though this crystalline balm's intrinsic properties do not correlate closely with the descriptions of the wondrous nature of liquid balsam. For example, while the balsam of Matarea was employed as a form of incense, the smell of 'balm of Mecca' when heated has been likened to the aroma of burning India rubber. 'Balm of Mecca' is also said to have a bitter taste, quite unlike the astringent, citric quality of balsam.[4]

Is it possible to reconcile these contradictory data and establish what species of plant was grown in the gardens of Matarea, and before that in Palestine? The last balsam tree in the Egyptian plantation died prior to the evolution of modern botanical nomenclature by Linnaeus, and it is unlikely that this problem will yield a definitive answer. What is remarkable, however, is how many written descriptions and illustrations exist of the balsam trees. These can be compared with recent botanical studies of comparable resin-producing plants, as well as scientific analyses of archaeological finds. These sources are assessed in the present chapter. The last section reviews the primary sources that describe the processes involved in the extraction and processing of the 'oil' of the balsam trees of Palestine and Matarea.

Descriptions and Representations of the Balsam Tree

The earliest description on the balsam tree occurs in *Enquiry into Plants* by Theophrastus. His comments on the plant come in book 9, entitled 'Of the juices of plants, and of the medicinal properties of herbs'. He notes that fragrant 'gums' (*kómmi*) are produced from parts of trees including frankincense, myrrh, balsam (*bálsamon*) and galbanum.[5] Elsewhere in the text he also employs the appellation 'Syrian balsam'. Frankincense, myrrh and balsam should all be harvested 'at the rising of the Dog Star (Sirius) and on the hottest days'.[6] He devotes a chapter of the text to balsam, part of which reads:

> The tree is as tall as a good-sized pomegranate (*Punica granatum* L.) and is much branched; it has a leaf like that of rue (i.e. Common Rue, *Ruta graveolens* L.), but it is pale; and it is evergreen; the fruit is like that of terebinth (*Pistacia palaestina* Boiss.), in size and shape and colour, and this too is very fragrant, indeed more so than the gum.[7]

The highly fragranced gum was harvested by making incisions into the bark with 'bent pieces of iron', and, though the collection continued through the summer, the total volume was small. The larger of the two enclosures (comprising about 1.6 hectares of land) apparently produced about 20.4 litres of balsam, and the smaller only 3.4 litres.[8] The daily quota from one tree was only 'a shell-full', an estimate later echoed by Pliny in his *Natural History*. Theophrastus asserts that the trees need to be constantly irrigated and that they are regularly pruned in order to sell the branches. In this context he observes: 'And the cutting of the boughs seems likewise to be the reason why the trees do not grow tall; for since they are often cut about, they send out branches instead of putting out all their energy in one direction'.[9] In other words, without the continual pruning, the trees would grow to a greater height.

Diodorus Siculus confirms that balsam was only to be found in the area around the Dead Sea in Palestine. He does note, however, the existence of another type of balsam grown in Arabia.[10] Later writers such as Pompeius Trogus (fl. first century BCE), Strabo, Tacitus and Flavius Josephus all agree that the trees were only found in the plantations in Roman Judaea, though none furnishes many additional data concerning the characteristics of the plants themselves.[11] Pliny's *Natural History* is a valuable source on the physical appearance of balsam, and of the properties of the liquids gathered from it. He asserts on several occasions that balsam was known only in Judaea. Pliny writes:

> it bears a much stronger resemblance to the vine (*Vitis vinifera* L.) than to myrtle (i.e Common Myrtle, *Myrtus communis* L.). This recent acquisition by conquest has learned, like the vine, to be reproduced by mallet-shoots, and it covers its declivities just like the vine, which supports its own weight without the aid of stays. When it puts forth branches it is pruned in a similar manner, and it thrives by being raked at the roots, growing with remarkable rapidity, and bearing fruit at the end of three years. The leaf bears a very considerable resemblance to rue, and it is an evergreen.[12]

Pliny's allusion to 'mallet-shoots' is a reference to a practice whereby new shoots springing from a branch of the previous year's growth are cut off and planted with sections of old wood on either side in the form of a mallet (*malleosis*). Balsam never grows above a height of two cubits (one Roman cubit is equal to 0.44 m). Significantly, he identifies three types of balsam: the first with 'thin, hair-like foliage' called *eutheriston*; the second, named *trachy*, with a more rugged appearance and more odoriferous quality than the first; and the third, *eumeces*, that is taller with a 'smooth, even bark'. *Eumeces* is considered by Pliny to be second in quality to *trachy*, with *eutheriston* the least valued of the three.[13] According to *Natural History*, the seeds contain an unctuous liquid the colour of red wine, while the grains are inferior in quality, being 'lighter in weight [than the seeds] and of a greener hue'.[14] In contrast to Theophrastus, Pliny asserts that iron tools are injurious to the plant – this claim is repeated by Tacitus and many later writers – and that incisions into the bark should be made with sharp knives constructed of bone, glass or stone.[15] The 'tears' of balsam are of 'extraordinary sweetness', being like a thick oil and white in colour when collected, but losing their transparency and turning red as the liquid hardens.

The most detailed description of the balsam tree is that written by Pedanios Dioscorides in his *De materia medica*. His written portrait of the plant was known to scholars of the late antique and medieval periods, and is reproduced in many later pharmacological texts written in Greek, Latin, Syriac and Arabic. Given its influential status, Dioscorides' chapter on the balsam tree deserves to be quoted in full:

1.19: *Bálsamon*

1. The size of its tree is the same as that of the turpentine tree or the pyracantha (*Crataegus oxycantha* L.). It has leaves like those of rue only white, longer-lived, more minute and differing from it in roughness, height, and size. It is only found in a certain valley of Judaea. It varies in the [degree of] ruggedness, tallness, and slenderness, and that [part] of the shrub which is thin and hairy, is called *theriston* ['the mown']. It may be because it is easily collected by reason of the slenderness of it.

That which is known as *opobálsamon* is the juice which is gathered by incising the tree with iron scrapers in the Dog days of the summer. So little drops from it every year that no more than six or seven *congii* (or *choes*) of it are collected, and it is sold locally for double its weight in silver.

2. The good juice is that which is fresh, strongly smelling and pure, not inclining to sweetness, [but] dissolving easily, smooth, astringent, and a little biting on the tongue. But it is adulterated in numerous ways. There are some who mix with it ointments, such as turpentine [resin], henna oil (*Lawsonia inermis* L.), mastic oil (*Pistacia lentiscus* L.), lily oil (*Lilium candidum* L.), zuchum oil (*Balanites aegyptiaca* Delile), bitter almond oil

(*metópion*, could also be the resinous juice of all-heal, *Ferula galbaniflua* Boiss. et Buhse), honey, cerate of myrtle, or very thin unguent of henna flowers. However, these things are easily detected through testing. One can let pure balsam drop in a woollen cloth. Then wash it and it comes out clean. The counterfeited substances, however, stain the cloth. Or the pure balsam can be dropped in milk and it does what false substances do not do. If one drops the genuine balsam in milk or water, it disperses smoky and milk-like, but the false kind swims on top like oil, forming little balls together, then spreading out like a star. After a period of time even genuine balsam deteriorates, thickening by itself.

3. But those who believe that if one takes the genuine article and drops it into water, it will sink to the bottom, then rise to the top undissolved are mistaken.

The wood, which is called *xylobálsamon*, is dearest if it is fresh, with thin stalks, yellowish-red, and fragrant and for a while having a smell like *opobálsamon*. Regarding the fruit, which is also highly useful, one should choose the yellow, full, large, heavy, with a biting and burning taste, and smelling something like *opobálsamon*. From Petra there grows a seed, namely from the ground-pine (Saint John's wort, *Hypericum perforatum* L.), a fruit which is counterfeited [for balsam]. This may be recognised because it is larger, emptier, less strong, and tastes like pepper.

4. It is the juice (*opobálsamon*), however, that is the most efficacious, being capable of heating to the greatest extent, and cleaning away the elements that cast a shadow over the pupils of the eyes, and of counteracting uterine chills when applied with cerate of roses. It draws down both the afterbirth and foetuses and it dissipates fits of shivering when rubbed on. It also cleanses the sordid elements of sores. It is both digestive and diuretic when drunk; it is suitable for those suffering from dyspnea, [mixed with] milk for those who have drunk leopard's bane (*Doronicum orientale* Hoffm.), and for those bitten by wild animals. It is compounded with analgesics, with emollients, and with antidotes. In general *opobálsamon* has the most efficacious properties, the fruit ranks second, and the wood is the least efficacious.

5. When drunk, the fruit is suitable for pleurisy, inflammations of the lungs, coughs, for patients suffering from hip disease, for epileptics, for

dizziness, for those suffering from orthopnea, colic, difficult micturition, and for those bitten by wild animals; it is a good thing to use for making a thick smoke from below to treat female problems and boiled down in sitz baths, dilating the cervix and absorbing moisture. As for the wood, it has the same properties as the fruit, but to a lesser degree. When boiled in water and drunk, it is helpful for indigestion, colic, venomous bites, and spasms. It is a diuretic, and with dried iris it is suitable for head injuries; it also reduces epithelial waste. It is mixed also into the astringents of unguents.[16]

The main points of his account agree with Theophrastus, Pliny and other classical authors. He implies that there are different types of balsam tree, though he is less explicit than Pliny in naming specific categories. While both mention the 'hairy' plant known as *theriston* or *eutheriston*, it is curious that this variant is believed by Pliny to produce the least powerful fluid. Pliny's is the fullest ancient description of the gathering of the 'oil' in the 'Dog days' of the summer (c. 3 July–11 August), and it is apparent that only a relatively small amount – six or seven *congii* (equivalent to about 16–19 litres). Judging by the estimates offered by Theophrastus, this figure refers to an entire plantation rather than a single tree.

One of the features of the *De materia medica* of Dioscorides that makes it so useful – both to modern researchers and to the physicians and pharmacists of earlier times – is the care with which he describes the products derived from plants. He outlines the general characteristics of the 'oil', wood and fruit, as well as the ways to test the authenticity of the finest liquid balsam. These were important issues because the high cost (according to Dioscorides, double its weight in silver) naturally encouraged sellers either to substitute it with cheaper substances or adulterate true balsam. Dioscorides mentions one of the commonly employed imitations, the seed of ground-pine brought from Petra in Jordan, as well as the ways in which it differs from the fruit of the balsam tree. His most detailed analysis is reserved for *opobalsamum*. This is characterised by its strong fragrance, lack of sweetness, smoothness and astringency. Tests could be applied to liquids sold as balsam in order to ascertain the presence of other oils (such as turpentine, henna oil and mastic oil). Dioscorides' inclusion of a last and, presumably, commonly employed test – the dropping of balsam into water (or milk) to see if it sinks, rises and then diffuses – alerts the reader to the fact that this method of verification did not work.[17] Small wonder then that one finds Dioscorides' tests for balsam repeated in the works of so many later writers (Chapter 5).

The polymath al-Biruni (d. 1048) devotes considerable attention to balsam (*balasān*) in his *Kitāb al-ṣaydana fī'l-ṭibb*. Although his primary focus is the medical applications of the 'oils' derived from the plant, he summarises what he discovered from earlier sources about the provenance and appearance of the trees. Citing earlier Arabic authorities, he claims that it is known only in 'Ayn Shams (i.e. Matarea) in Egypt, though he concedes later in the chapter that it might grow elsewhere. He writes that 'its structure is like that of *hudud* (*Lycium barbarum* L.)', with leaves that resemble rue but larger, longer and white in colour. On the authority of al-Khutaybi, he asserts that it does not produce seeds, the shoots being planted in the ground in order to propagate new specimens. The seeds that are often ascribed to balsam come, in fact, from an Egyptian plant known as *muharraqa*. Al-Biruni reviews the different scholarly opinions regarding the seeds of balsam but fails to come to a definitive conclusion. His observations about the physical qualities of balsam 'oil' and the ways to test its purity are similar to those of Dioscorides (whose work al-Biruni had evidently read in Arabic translation) and Pliny. The branches of the balsam tree are round in profile and knotted, with 'the layer of oil (*duhn*) present in their surface'.[18]

While al-Biruni had to draw together his description from written sources, the thirteenth-century author 'Abd al-Latif al-Baghdadi was able to observe the balsam trees at first-hand. He describes them as no more than one cubit (*dhirā'* = 0.68 m) in height, with a thin red outer bark and a thicker green inner bark. In common with many other sources, he likens the balsam leaves to those of rue.[19] Another broadly contemporary Middle Eastern writer to claim to have seen the trees for himself is Yaqut al-Hamawi. He writes that balsam resembles henna and pomegranate when they 'begin to bring forth leaves'.[20] Leo Africanus gives a different description, stating that the plant has short stock and leaves that are like those of the vine.[21]

One of the most astute descriptions of the balsam plant was made in the last years of its existence. A Swiss physician and botanist who lived in Egypt between 1581 and 1584, Prosper Alpin wrote extensively on the physical attributes of the balsam tree and on the medical applications of the products derived from the plant.[22] He also succeeded in cultivating his own balsam plant on his return to Italy in 1584. His comments on balsam are contained principally within three publications: *De balsamo dialogus* (1591, and later in French as *Histoire du baulme*), *De medicina Aegyptiorum* (1591) and *De plantis Aegypti* (1592). He offers a concise account of the plant in chapter 14 of *De plantis Aegypti*:

> Balsam is a small tree like a vine. It rises to the height of henna, or privet (*Ligustrum vulgare* L.), or of our laburnum (*Laburnum anagyroides* Medik.). Its leaves are very small, similar to those of rue. They are not, however, as Dioscorides says, paler than these [i.e. rue], but are more like those of the mastic tree; that is to say greenish-white and evergreen. The wood is rich in gum and smooth. It has a reddish exterior. Its branches have the same colour, and are long, straight and thin, adorned with thin leaves rarely arranged without order in [groups of] three, five or seven, a little like those of mastic. The branches are fragrant and loaded with gum; they stick to the fingers when pressed. The flowers are small and white, similar to those of the acacia tree, hung three by three from the branch, and [are] umbellate. They are very fragrant, but the smell disappears very quickly. The yellow seeds, enclosed within follicles of a blackish-red colour, contain a yellow liquid resembling honey. The flavour of these seeds is impossible to describe, though it is a little bitter and slightly pungent; it is said that balsam is similar in shape and size to the fruit of terebinth, with their pointed ends and medial thickness.[23]

He continues with some observations about the liquid gathered by scoring into the bark of the tree. He records that *opobalsamum* is clear, and tends to thicken with age like the juice of the terebinth.[24] The very strong aroma of the liquid when first extracted is noted by Alpin. Indeed, it does not appear from his comments that this smell was agreeable. He writes: 'it smells very strong and special, and it frequently causes headaches, or in some people, nosebleeds. But that smell, at first as acute and violent as *zebet*, fades with time and becomes more pleasant'.[25] By contrast, Pierre Pomet (d. 1699) likens the smell of balsam to lemon.[26] Regarding the colour, Alpin states that the liquid changes from milky white to a green oil, finally turning the colour of honey. Alpin continues with the ways in which to test the authenticity of *opobalsamum*, his information deriving from Dioscorides.[27]

Lastly Alpin makes some important comments about the origins of the balsam trees. He believes that these plants were native neither of Egypt nor Palestine, coming instead from Arabia Felix (i.e. southern Arabia). He points to the fact that Egypt is not mentioned as a source for balsam by the authors of antiquity. For Palestine he notes the claim of Josephus that the trees had been a gift from the Queen of Sheba to Solomon, and, thus, must have come from southern Arabia. Alpin is also mindful of the situation in the late sixteenth century; he recalls the example of the governor of Egypt, the eunuch 'Messinor', bringing trees from Mecca in order to restock the garden (Chapter 3). Alpin observes that the route between Cairo and Mecca was very easy (something of an exaggeration) and well frequented at this time.[28]

Visual representations of the balsam trees are less helpful in the process of identifying the species of plant that once grew in Matarea. Two main reasons can be given for this. First, with one exception, the depictions of the balsam trees were done as illustrations to texts. In other words, they were not conceived independently, but serve to give visual form to a written description. Second, most of the illustrations – whether in the form of manuscript paintings, engravings, woodcuts or mosaic – were not done by artists who had actually seen the trees at first-hand. While this is also the case for some of the textual accounts surveyed above, there is a fundamental difference: authors could simply repeat the information in an earlier source (making such embellishments as might be thought necessary), but the illustrators of manuscripts often had no visual model upon which to rely.

The fundamental source on the appearance of the balsam tree throughout the medieval period, the pharmacological encyclopedia of Dioscorides, was not initially designed to carry illustrations. From the sixth century there exist lavish copies of the *De materia medica* with extensive illustrations of plants and mineral products. The most famous, the manuscript made for the Byzantine princess Anicia Juliana in c. 512, is notable for the highly naturalistic quality of the plant illustrations. This manuscript contains no depiction of the balsam tree, however, and the plant does not feature commonly in later Byzantine manuscripts of Dioscorides' text. The only possible sixth-century representation is to be found on the mosaic map within the church of St George in Madaba (Fig. 2.11). The bushes tentatively identified as balsam plants are clearly distinguished from the date palms that dot the surrounding areas of landscape, though little can be inferred from the simple designs. The most important features are the shape and dimensions and the dark green trifoliate leaves.

The earliest Islamic example is in an Arabic translation of *De materia medica*, dated 475/1083, and probably written in Bukhara or Samarqand. It is the most complete Arabic Dioscorides manuscript.[29] Following the common convention for the illustration of plants in pharmacological texts, the balsam tree is shown complete with its roots exposed as if it has been pressed between the pages of the book (Fig. 4.1). The marginal annotation, written in a different hand to the main text, confirms the identification of the plant: *balasān*. The illustrator has included two cutting tools piercing the bark with a pair of vessels placed underneath to catch the liquid flowing from the incisions. Branches spring from the slender trunk of the tree, and each branch carries

Figure 4.1 Balsam tree from the Arabic Dioscorides, dated 1083. Possibly Samarqand. University of Leiden Library: Or. 289, fol. 12r. HIP / Art Resource, NY.

long ovoid leaves. Interspersed among the leaves are small round fruit. The lowest branch on the right hand side also carries a drooping branch, perhaps with more fruit. Differences in the drawing style in this section (note, for example, the lack of a clear black outline around the individual fruit) suggest that this feature may be a later addition.

If one were to compare this painting with the masterpieces of naturalistic botanical illustration found in Greek manuscripts, such as those made for Juliana Anicia or the tenth-century copy now in the Morgan Library & Museum, it would be easy to dismiss Leiden illustration as the work of an unskilled artist unable to emulate the illusionistic techniques of modelling achieved by the finest artists of Constantinople. Minta Collins has established, however, that from an early date there existed two distinct approaches to plant illustration. One was naturalistic in character, trying to reproduce the actual appearance of living plants. The other was designed to provide a precise visual complement to the text. Like a diagram of an electrical circuit or the map of the London underground, these plant illustrations did not need to mimic the physical appearance of things they represented. Rather, the intention was to illustrate the relationships between such features as trunk and stems, stems and leaves, and groupings of the fruit or flowers.[30]

Returning to the Leiden manuscript, it can be seen how well this approach works. The Central Asian artist is unlikely to have seen a living specimen of a balsam tree, but his painting accurately conveys much of the pertinent information in Dioscorides' text. This more schematic approach predominates in later illustrated Dioscorides manuscripts produced in the Islamic world. Another painting of the balsam tree appears in a Dioscorides manuscript now in the collection of the shrine of Imam Reza in the Iranian city of Mashhad (Fig. 4.2). While the manuscript is undated (the style of the paintings suggest a date in the early thirteenth century), it is based on the translation of Mihran ibn Mansur after a Syriac translation of the Greek by Hunayn ibn Ishaq (d. 873). Mihran's translation was made for the Artuqid ruler Najm al-Din Alpi (r. 1152–76), who ruled over regions of south-eastern Turkey and northern Iraq. Importantly, this is a different Arabic translation from that of the Leiden Dioscorides (which is a direct Arabic rendition of the Greek text undertaken initially by Istifan ibn Basil and corrected by Hunayn ibn Ishaq and others), and indicates that the two manuscripts and their

THE BALSAM TREE AND BALSAM 'OIL' | 129

Figure 4.2 Balsam tree being harvested. From an Arabic Dioscorides manuscript, late twelfth or early thirteenth century, Mesopotamia. Museum of the Shrine of Imam Reza, Mashhad, Iran. Drawing: Marcus Milwright.

illustrations belong to different traditions.[31] Another broadly contemporary depiction of a balsam tree can be found in the *Kitāb al-diryāq* ('Book of Antidotes') dated to 595/1199 (Fig. 4.3). Believed in the medieval period to be the work of Galen, the *Kitāb al-diryāq* is thought to have been written by an unknown tenth-century author.[32]

Comparing the three illustrations it is the commonalities that are most striking. All three artists represent balsam as a relatively small tree. The human figures in the Mashhad manuscript suggest a height for the tree of about 3 m (taller than is indicated in the text of Dioscorides). The root system of the plants appears similar in the two Dioscorides manuscripts (Leiden and Mashhad), and all three images show a tree with a slender trunk and branches. In all cases the long ovoid leaves spring directly from the branches without intermediary stems, and the fruit is small and round. The Mashhad Dioscorides shows slight projections on both the trunk and the branches,

Figure 4.3 Balsam tree being harvested. From *Kitāb al-diryāq* (Book of Antidotes), dated 1199, Mesopotamia or Iran. Bibliothèque Nationale de France, Paris: Ms Arabe 2967.

perhaps indicating the places where the plant has been pruned. The greatest difference to be seen in the later versions is the addition of human figures making incisions into the bark of the trees and collecting the *opobalsamum*. This practice of 'inhabiting' scientific illustrations can be seen in some Greek

THE BALSAM TREE AND BALSAM 'OIL' | 131

Figure 4.4 Balsam tree within a walled garden with guards. From a herbal produced in c. 1440, Northern Lombardy. British Library, London. British Library Board / Robana / Art Resource, NY.

Dioscorides manuscripts, and becomes common in later medical manuscripts both in the Islamic world and in medieval Europe.[33]

The illustrations in medieval European manuscripts are considerably less helpful. They were made by artists who had not seen the balsam plantation of Matarea for themselves, and the images are also subject to flights of fancy. Examples of this genre dating to the thirteenth and fourteenth centuries can be found in manuscripts of the *Sacra Salernitana*, and in herbals such as the *Tractatus de herbis* (Figs 1.7, 1.8 and 4.4). The painters all chose to locate the trees within a walled enclosure, and in each case care has been taken to show the vessels that hung from the trees to collect the 'oil'. Unfortunately, these illustrations give no meaningful clues concerning the plants themselves. More detailed is the painting of a balsam tree in a fifteenth-century copy of the *Book of Simple Medicines* attributed to Matthaeus Platearius (d. c.1161). Although the surrounding landscape bears no obvious relation to Matarea,

Figure 4.5 Balsam tree in the *Book of Simples* of Matthaeus Platearius. France, fifteenth century. Bibliothèque Nationale de France ms. Fr. 12322. Snark / Art Resource, NY.

the tree itself accords more closely to the Islamic illustrations (Fig. 4.5).[34] The height of the tree is, like the example of the Mashhad Dioscorides manuscript, nearly twice that of a man. Unlike the Islamic versions, however, the leaves do not spring from the main branches but from thinner, slightly curved stalks.

Woodcut and engraved images of the balsam tree were made for inclusion in printed books between the sixteenth and the eighteenth centuries. Prosper Alpin includes a woodcut illustrating the branch of a balsam tree in his *De balsamo dialogus* (1591). The branch has smaller stalks springing from it, each bearing three, five or seven leaves (Fig. 4.6).[35] At the end of the branch are what appear to be small flowers and seed pods. This illustration can be compared to the woodcuts that appear in the third book of John Gerard's (d. 1612) *Herball, or Generall Historie of Plantes* (1597). These depict the fruit (*balsami fructus*) of the tree, the dry branches stripped of their leaves (*xylobalsamum*) and lastly *carpobalsamum* (Figs 4.7 and 4.8). The last of these has a caption reading 'The fruite of one of the Balsame trees', perhaps

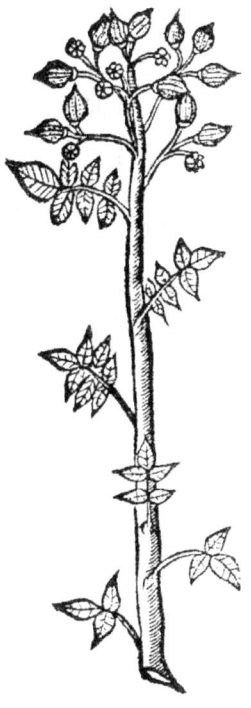

BALSAMI RAMVM.

Figure 4.6 Woodcut illustration of a branch from a balsam tree. From the 1591 edition of Prosper Alpin, *De balsamo dialogus*. Private collection.

indicating some confusion about the precise identification of this product.[36] On this 'fruit' he writes:

> This tree saith *Garcias* that beareth the fruit *Carpobalsamum*, is also one of the Balsame trees: it groweth to the height and bignes of the Pomegranate tree, garnished with very many branches: whereon doe growe leaues like those of Rewe, but of colour whiter, alwaies growing greene: among which come foorth flowers, whereof we haue no certaintie: after which commeth fruite like that of the Turpentine tree, which in shops is called *Carpobalsamum*, of pleasant smell; but the liquor which floweth from the wounded tree, is much sweeter: which liquor of some is called *Opobalsamum*.[37]

Gerard was reliant upon others to bring him botanical samples like this from the 'Indies', and he appears to have procured fruit and branches from more than one species identified at the time as a 'balsam' (Chapter 5). The fruit and the liquid derived from them are described in some later sources, though it is not clear how many authors of the seventeenth century and later had actually seen them first-hand.[38]

More reliable is the woodcut illustration of an entire balsam plant in the 1640 edition of Alpin's *De plantis Aegypti* (Fig. 4.9). Presumably following the illustration in *De balsamo dialogus*, the engraver represents the

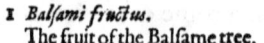

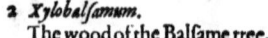

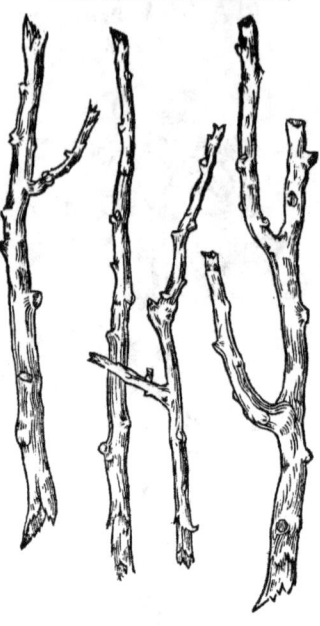

Figure 4.7 Illustrations of the fruit and wood of the balsam tree. From John Gerard, *Herball, or Generall Historie of Plantes* (1597), book III, p. 1344. Courtesy of the McPherson Library, University of Victoria.

Figure 4.8 Illustration of the fruit of the balsam tree. From John Gerard, *Herball, or Generall Historie of Plantes* (1597), book III, p. 1345. Courtesy of the McPherson Library, University of Victoria.

leaves attached on stems in groups of three, five or seven. The small, star-like flowers and associated seed pods also look much like the woodcut in his *De balsamo dialogus*. The complete tree is also illustrated in the *Histoire générale des drogues* by Pierre Pomet, published in Paris in

Figure 4.9 Woodcut illustration of a balsam tree. From Prosper Alpin, *De plantis Aegypti* (1640). After Prosper Alpin, *Plantes d'Égypte*, trans. Raymond de Fenoyl (1980).

1694 (Fig. 4.10).[39] In each case balsam is depicted as a bushy plant about the height of a man, with relatively slender ovoid leaves and small flowers appearing at the ends of the branches. These features recur in Benoit de Maillet's *Description de l'Égypte* (1735), which makes use of the illustration in Alpin's *De plantis Aegypti*, but places the tree next to a diminutive version of the pharaonic obelisk of Heliopolis (Fig. 4.11).[40]

Modern Botanical Studies

It will be apparent from the descriptions given in the previous section that the 'oil' (*opobalsamum*) derived from the trees of Matarea was, in fact, a type of resin or, more precisely, an oleo-resin. These oleo-resins are contained within the schizogenous or schizolysigenous ducts of the plant and are part of its defence mechanisms. In other words, the ejection of the oleo-resin from these ducts occurs when the bark of the plant is injured. The oleo-resin of the balsam trees of Matarea was strongly aromatic and remained in a

Figure 4.10 Illustration of a balsam tree. From Pierre Pomet, *Histoire générale des drogues* (1694). Courtesy of the Syndics of Cambridge University Library.

liquid state for some time after its initial extraction because of the relatively high concentrations of volatile oils mixed with the resin. Within the larger group of oleo-resins is a category known to biologists as 'balsams'. These balsams are distinguished from other oleo-resins by the high proportions of balsamic acids such as benzoic or cinnamic acid.[41] Plants that liberate these balsams include balsam of Peru (also known as balsam of Tolu, *Myroxylon pereirae* [Royle] Klozsch) and the Middle Eastern species of myrrh (either *Commiphora molmol* Engl. or *Commiphora myrrha*), 'Levant' galbana (*Ferula galbaniflua* Bossier and Buhse), labdanum (or ladanum; *Cistus ladanifer* L.), and bdellium (*Balsamodendron mukul* Hooker). Frankincense actually comprises a number of oleo-resins drawn from the genus *Boswellia* (see also Chapter 2).[42]

While each of the Middle Eastern resin-producing trees mentioned above can be correlated with references in antique and medieval pharmacological sources, it remains uncertain whether the tree from which *opobalsamum* was

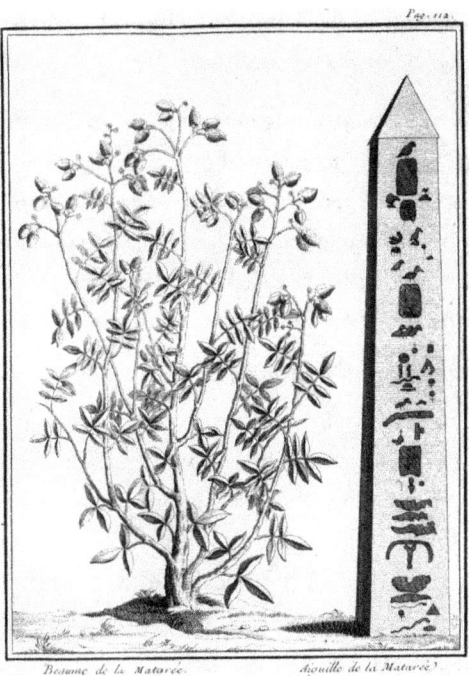

Figure 4.11 Illustration of a balsam tree. From Benoît de Maillet, *Description de l'Égypte* (1735). Courtesy of the Syndics of Cambridge University Library.

gathered can be linked with a living species. As already noted, medieval Arabic writers distinguish between *balasān* and the inferior *bashām* that was found in Arabia. Nevertheless, it was to the western coast of Arabian (the Hijaz) that sultans and governors of Egypt looked when they needed to restore the gardens of Matarea. The resin-producing plants of Arabia began to receive the attention of European scientists in the second half of the eighteenth century. Pehr (or Peter) Forsskål, a botanist with the Danish expedition to Arabia in 1762–3, was the first European to record the tree from which 'balm of Mecca' (probably corresponding to the medieval *bashām*) was extracted in mountainous areas north-west of Taʿizz. He died on the journey, but his results were brought back to Europe and published by the surviving member of the expedition, Niebuhr. Forsskål notes that the inhabitants in the region of Taʿizz were unaware of how to draw out the resin from it, but some knowledge of this product probably existed elsewhere in Hijaz.[43] The spy Domingo Badía y Leblich (d. 1818), who wrote under the pseudonym of

'Ali Bey Abbasi, made the following observations based on his time in Mecca in the early years of the nineteenth century:

> The celebrated balm of Mecca is not made there; it is, on the contrary, very scarce, and it is only to be found in the country when the Bedouins, or other parties of Arabs, bring it down by chance. A man, who appeared tolerably well informed, told me that it was obtained principally from the territory of Medina; that it was called *belsan*; and that his countrymen did not know the tree which produced it by the name of Gilead.[44]

According to Max Meyerhof (d. 1945) this same aromatic resin was also available in the markets of Cairo in the early twentieth century. In Yemen it is sometimes known as 'Hadramawt myrrh' while in Somalia it is called *habbak daseino* (i.e. gum of the *daseino* tree).[45] More recent research has provided further evidence for the physical characteristics and geographical range of the species seen by Forsskål. In botanical studies this tree (often designated as a shrub because of its relatively small size) is most commonly called either *Commiphora gileadensis* (L.) C. Chr. or *Commiphora opobalsamum* (L.) Engl. (Fig. 4.12).[46] The plant is a relative of the myrrh tree within the family of Burseraceae (composed of about 540 species and seventeen or eighteen genera). *Commiphora gileadensis* grows in semi-arid regions on sandy plains and hillsides. It flourishes from sea level to altitudes of 750 m. An aromatic and virtually colourless oleo-resin is collected from the tree. Its geographical range encompasses southern Arabia (Saudi Arabia, Yemen, Oman), south-east Egypt, north-east Sudan, Djibouti, Eritrea, Ethiopia and Somalia. The northernmost range of *Commiphora gileadensis* is the foothills between the Arabian towns of Jidda and Yanbu'.[47]

Was this Arabian tree the same species as those growing in Matarea, and further back in the plantations in Palestine? Considerable uncertainty surrounds the identification of the 'balm of Gilead' (*zori*) referred to in the Old Testament (Chapter 2), and recent suggestions have included the resins of the terebinth tree and the Aleppo pine. The Old Testament also mentions an imported 'spice' known as *bosem* which might have some relationship to balsam. Detailed descriptions of balsam plants given by classical sources such as Theophrastus, Pliny the Elder and Dioscorides (see above) provide a firmer basis for further study of the plant cultivated in Palestine, at least from the

Figure 4.12 Mecca balsam (*Commiphora opobalsamum*): entire plant. Line engraving by James Heath (d. 1834), 1 October 1804. Wellcome Collection. Attribution 4.0 International (CC BY 4.0).

third century BCE. Starting with the question of scale, there is a clear disparity between the small shrub (standing no more than 1.5 m in height) mentioned by Dioscorides and the Arabian *Commiphora gileadensis*. The latter is much larger, growing to a height of about 4 m, although modern botanical studies note its lower range as about 1.5 m. Another major difference relates to the oleo-resin gathered from the trees. While Pliny extols *opobalsamum* as the finest of scents, and its aromatic qualities are greatly praised elsewhere, modern observers have been rather less impressed by the smell and taste of 'balm of Mecca'.

There are also considerable similarities between the wild and cultivated trees. In common with the written descriptions and the more accurate illustrations of the balsam trees, *Commiphora gileadensis* has long slender branches without spines, and a reddish (or greyish) bark. Other features are noted in modern botanical descriptions of *Commiphora gileadensis*. The leaves are arranged in groups of three or five on short shoots. The leaves themselves are either smooth or have a fine downy surface. The flowers are small (2–3 mm across) and arranged in clusters, with ellipsoid petals. Comparing these features with, for example, the illustration of the balsam trees in Alpin's *De balsamo dialogus* (1591), Pomet's *Histoire générale des drogues* (1694) and de Maillet's *Déscription de l'Égypte* (1735) (Figs 4.6 and 4.9–4.11) it is apparent that there are significant, though inconclusive correlations.

Reconciling the Evidence

Several hypotheses can be advanced on the basis of the evidence reviewed in the previous sections. First, the balsam trees cultivated in Matarea, and before that in Palestine, constitute an extinct species that is distinct from any living resin-producing plant. Second, the plants of Matarea can be identified with a living species – such as *Commiphora gileadensis* – and the disparities between the living plants and their compatriots in the Egyptian garden and the plantations of Palestine can be attributed to inaccuracies in the descriptions given by authors and illustrators. A third possibility is that practices of selective cultivation over an extended period of time resulted in the creation of a plant which diverged significantly from its wild ancestors.

Of these three options, the second seems to be least likely. There are simply too many detailed written descriptions to dismiss their veracity out of hand. While one can certainly point to anomalies in this evidence, the commonalities encountered in the most accurate textual sources are surely of greater significance. To this one might add that writers like Dioscorides give precise accounts of other, living species of plant that accord well with modern botanical observations. It is difficult to imagine why Dioscorides would have dealt with the balsam tree in a less systematic manner than other plant species contained within *De materia medica*. The first option – that the species grown in Matarea is now extinct – remains a plausible, but ultimately unproveable hypothesis. An intriguing piece of evidence in this respect is the small ceramic jug excavated at the caves of Qumran (Fig. 2.7). It remains unknown whether this stoppered vessel actually held balsam from the plantations at En-Gedi, but it is worth noting researchers were unable to find a modern correlate for the resinous compound contained within it. One future avenue might be to compare the chemical analysis of the Qumran resin with samples from other potential surviving samples of balsam (see below, and Chapters 5 and 8).

The last hypothesis finds greatest support in the available evidence. It is quite feasible for a wild plant species to be radically altered – in characteristics of height, the shape and colour of its flowers, or the quality of its scent – through long-term selective breeding. By the time Pliny and Dioscorides recorded their own observations about balsam, the plant could have been grown as a distinct cultivar for more than 400 years. Dioscorides claims that the plants were only found in the Palestinian plantations; had he been referring to a wild plant such as *Commiphora gileadensis*, he presumably would have noted its wider geographical range (at least, that it also grew in Arabia). That there might be some relationship between balsam and a larger wild counterpart is perhaps suggested in Theophrastus' account: he claims that left without pruning the balsam trees would naturally grow taller. Centuries of selective breeding might have resulted in more than one cultivar, and Pliny describes three types of balsam, each with rather different characteristics.

If one turns to later writers, there is further evidence of the effects of selective breeding. Al-Biruni claims that the balsam trees did not produce seeds and had to be propagated by means of cuttings (Pliny makes much the same observation). Although it represents no more than a legend, it is intriguing that Coptic accounts of the visit of the Holy Family to Matarea (Chapter 1) contain similar assertions; in some versions, a section of Joseph's staff – itself cut from a tree in the region of Jericho – was planted in the soil by Christ and miraculously sprang into leaf as a balsam tree. Al-Biruni's claim is brought somewhat into question, however, by the statement in the *Kitāb al-mufrādāt* (*Book of Simples*) written by al-Ghafiqi (d. 1165) and revised by Bar Hebraeus (d. 1286) that, in order to prevent its cultivation elsewhere, no parts of the seeds (sing. *ḥabb*) of the balsam tree in the sultan's gardens at ʿAyn Shams were exported.[48] The most pertinent description is given by an author who had the opportunity to study the trees first-hand. ʿAbd al-Latif al-Baghdadi writes:

> The oily balsam tree (*al-balasān al-duhnī*) does not bear fruit (*lā yuthmiru*): they take cuttings of the tree which, planted in the month of Shubat

(i.e. February), take root and grow. The wild male (*dhakar*) tree has one fruiting, but gives no oil. It is found in the Najd, in the Tihama, the Arabian deserts, and the maritime regions of Yemen and Persia. It is known under the name of *bashām*.[49]

Importantly, al-Baghdadi establishes a clear relationship between two types of plant: one the 'oily' tree in Matarea that is sterile (bears no fruit) and has to be grown from cuttings, and the other wild 'male' tree that produces an annual crop of fruit but yields no 'oil' (*duhn*). In other words he believes that the two are both from the same species. Furthermore, the male tree, *bashām*, grows wild in the Arabian regions of Najd, Tihama and Yemen, as well as the coastal zones of Iran.[50] Further confirmation that the two groups of plants were from the same species is given in sixteenth-century accounts that the Mamluk sultan Qansawh al-Ghawri, and subsequent Ottoman governors of Egypt, brought seeds or saplings from the Hijaz in order to replenish the trees of Matarea. Notably, some travellers claim that the plants in Matarea had to be covered with cloths in winter to protect them from the cold. Such a precaution would hardly have been necessary had they been native to Lower Egypt. Al-Baghdadi's account also agrees with al-Biruni in that the propagation was carried out by means of cuttings. Presumably these cuttings could either be placed directly into the ground or grafted onto stocks (which might sometimes have been the wild Arabian *bashām*).

The wholesale replacement of dead trees in Matarea for new trees from the Hijaz – as seems to have occurred during the rule of al-Ghawri and several more times during the sixteenth century – adds a further complication, however. If the long-term cultivation of the trees in the plantations of Palestine and Egypt had resulted in the creation of one, or – as Pliny suggests – three cultivars that possessed characteristics not shared by the wild *Commiphora gileadensis* of Arabia, southern Egypt and the Horn of Africa, then the destruction of the trees in Matarea at the end of the fifteenth century represents a crucial watershed. Following the restorations by al-Ghawri, the garden of Matarea must have contained trees producing an oleo-resin unlike that described by authors of the medieval and antique periods. It is perhaps significant that Prosper Alpin, who must have seen only trees of Arabian provenance at Matarea, writes that the smell exuded by *opobalsamum* when it is first extracted is 'very strong and special' and 'acute and violent', and that it could provoke headaches or nosebleeds.[51] After a time the smell fades and, in his words, 'becomes more pleasant'. This seems a far cry from Pliny's claim that balsam was the most valued fragrance of the ancient world. Conversely, Alpin's comments resonate with descriptions of the rather harsher odour of *Commiphora gileadensis* given by travellers and botanists in the nineteenth and twentieth centuries.

A final perspective on this topic comes from the survival of traces of balsam (probably in the form of myron; see Chapter 8) on the surfaces of medieval relics and reliquaries. Hartmann Grisar (d. 1932) records the presence of hard deposits of reddish resinous material on reliquary crosses and icons in the Sancta Sanctorum, the personal chapel of the popes. He notes that this could be dissolved with alcohol, and that this liberated a strong aroma that he suggests might be balsam. The potent smell of old balm was also detected while trying to open the doors of the shrine, and this provided some discomfort to those who experienced it. This last observation brings to mind Alpin's comment about the headaches and nosebleeds that could occur when balsam was in its freshest state.[52] An avenue for future research would be to submit some of these resinous accretions to scientific analysis.

Harvesting Balsam in Ancient and Medieval Times

Opobalsamum, the 'oil' of balsam, was gathered from scoring into the bark of the trunk and larger branches. This same process can still be seen in the harvesting of myrrh and other tree resins in the Middle East. It is clear, however, that the harvesting of balsam was a more complex process circumscribed by beliefs and rituals. For example, while some simply state that a 'bent piece of iron' or other iron implement could be employed for the scoring into the bark, the use of iron is prohibited by other writers. Quite when and where this aversion to the use of iron tools originates is unclear. Josephus recommends a sharpened stone for the purpose,[53] and other sources describe the employment of knives of bone or glass. A claw-like implement used for scraping into the bark of a balsam tree is illustrated alongside a balsam container in a ninth- or tenth-century Latin translation of Dioscorides.[54] It is unlikely that the illustrator would have seen actual instruments used for this purpose in En-Gedi or Matarea, however. Knives (with blades of unknown material) also appear in the earliest illustration of the balsam tree in an Arabic Dioscorides manuscript (Fig. 4.1).

The Greek and Latin writers of the antique period are vague about the stages involved in moving from the 'raw' sap collected from the trees to the finished balsam 'oil'. In this respect, the archaeological analysis undertaken in the processing plant at En-Gedi is more informative (Chapter 2). By contrast, the manufacturing processes are dealt with at some length by several medieval scholars.[55] In addition, they also furnish us with information concerning the beliefs that surrounded the collection and subsequent treatment of this precious crop. One of the most detailed descriptions of the harvesting process at Matarea is given by Abu al-Makarim. He writes that this was started in the month of Barmuda (Parmoute), which equates to April. He continues:

> Three men are charged [with this task], the first making three incisions into each branch, with the aid of a sharp stone, and not an iron [tool]; another who captures the oil on a wad of cotton, which he then expresses into a receptacle meant to hold all that is recovered; and a third who dresses the cuts using leaves brought from Ashmun Tanah and al-Daqahliyya – and nowhere else – and these are leaves of papyrus and other than that.[56]

The fifth-century Aramaic inscription from the synagogue of En-Gedi refers to *zvwtyh*, possibly meaning palm fibres (Chapter 2) that were employed instead of papyrus leaves or cotton wads. The collection of the oil into bottles is also mentioned by the eleventh-century Persian traveller, Nasir-i Khusraw.[57]

A rather different version of the harvesting technique is provided by ʿAbd al-Latif al-Baghdadi. He locates the time of the harvest as near the rise of al-Shaʿari (Sirius, the Dog Star), and writes that it starts with stripping the leaves from the branches. Incisions were then made in the trunk with a sharp stone, but he cautions that this must be done carefully in order to split only the bark and the inner layer. The tree would give forth no liquid if the incision was made too deeply, piercing the wood. He claims that the oleo-resin was then gathered with the finger as it flowed from the tree. The harvester would then wipe his finger on the edge of a horn. When full, the contents of the horn were poured into a glass bottle. Climatic conditions could affect the extent of the harvest, with humid days being the most productive. Unlike

Abu al-Makarim he follows the process beyond the initial collection to the extraction of the pure 'oil'. Of the second phase he writes:

> Then they take the bottles and bury them in the earth until the full heat of the summer, when they retrieve them from the ground and put them in the sun. Each day they visit them and find the oil which floats on a watery substance, mixed with particles of earth. They take the oil, and put the bottles back in the sun. This they repeat until there is no more oil. When this point is reached, they take all the oil and cook it secretly without anyone to assist in this operation: this they transport to the owner's store. The quantity of pure oil gained from the sap amounts when all is done to one tenth of the total [volume]. An experienced man assured me that they receive about 20 *ratl*s of oil.[58]

The application of mild heat (from the sun) clarified the liquid from the balsam trees and allowed for the extraction of the pure 'oil'. Abu al-Makarim indicates that the 'oil' represented a relatively small fraction of the total volume of sap: for example, he writes that 150 Egyptian *ratl*s of balsam juice were extracted from the trees of Matarea in 509/1115–16, but that each *ratl* only produced a *waqiyya* of balsam 'oil'. An Egyptian *ratl* is the equivalent of 449 g, and there are 12 *waqiyya* in a *ratl*. Thus, it can be calculated that in the harvest of 1115–16 about 5.5 litres of 'oil' was derived from a little over 67 litres of sap.[59] Al-Baghdadi suggests that the ratio between sap and finished oil is ten to one, and he gives rather different figures for the annual crop. In the passage quoted above the total amount of 'oil' could be 20 *ratl*s (therefore requiring somewhere between 200 and 240 *ratl*s of sap). Elsewhere he reports on a poor year (596/1199–1200) resulting from the lack of humidity that yielded a harvest of only 20 *ratl*s.[60] Presumably, he is referring to the amount of sap and not the finished product. It is not clear how these figures can be compared to the earlier testimony of Theophrastus, Pliny and Dioscorides. Both Theophrastus and Pliny claim that the daily quota from a single tree was only a 'shell-full' of liquid, while the former also adds that the larger of the two Judaean plantations yielded about 17 litres from 1.6 hectares of trees. Dioscorides writes of a crop of 6–7 *congii* (16–19 litres), but does not specify how many trees were required for this quantity.[61] The antique authors do not state whether the quantities are for the raw sap or the fraction of balsam 'oil'.

Several accounts of the cultivation and harvesting of the balsam trees exist from the period of Mamluk rule. Ludolph von Sudheim's description tallies in many important respects with those of Abu al-Makarim, al-Baghdadi and other Arabic sources. Of the harvesting of the oleo-resin, Ludolph von Sudheim writes:

> At the beginning of March, when the time of ripening is at hand, it is watched yet more carefully, and when it is ripe the shoots and shrubs are cut and wounded, as the vines are pruned, and their wounds are bound up with muslin. From these wounded shoots the balsam drips out, as water does from a cut vine, and oozes into the muslin bound around the wound. Beneath each wounded branch and bandage there hangs a silver cup, into which the best balsam drops.[62]

His reference to the use of vessels hung from the trunk and larger branches correlates with illustrations in Arabic and European manuscripts, as well as later printed books such as Pomet's *Histoire générale des drogues* (Fig. 4.10). One of the manuscript copies of von Sudheim's text also contains a similar drawing. After a brief discussion of the operation of the sultanic monopoly over the site, von Sudheim turns his attention to the collection of liquid from the branches (i.e. *xylobalsamum*):

> Afterwards, when all of the (true and good) balsam has thus oozed out, the guardians of the shrubs cut off the ends of the shoots which belong to them, boil them in water, and then whatever balsam was left in the tops of the shoots boils out like fat, and swims upon the top of the water like oil, whence it is taken up with a spoon, put into a vessel, and left for some time. Even this balsam is of great value, albeit has been boiled, and it is of a reddish colour, with some mixture of black; but the crude balsam which drips forth naturally is of the colour of wine.[63]

Thus, there seems to be considerable agreement in the medieval sources concerning the methods used in the extraction of both *opobalsamum* and *xylobalsamum*, and the clarification of the former in the heat of the sun. Abu al-Makarim indicates that the finest balsam underwent additional processing beyond simple clarification. In the late Fatimid period this was done in a house owned by the Coptic patriarchate. Under the Ayyubids, direct control of the garden and its products was transferred to the sultan. At this time the last stages of processing were moved to the royal treasury in Cairo.[64]

Notes
1. Josephus, *Jewish Antiquities*, 6:6.
2. For example, ʿAbd al-Latif al-Baghdadi, *The Eastern Key*, pp. 44 (Arabic), 45 (English). For an Arabic edition, see ʿAbd al-Latif al-Baghdadi, *Kitāb al-ifāda wa'l-i'tibār*, ed. Ahmad Sabunu (Damascus: Dar Qutaiba, 1983), p. 24. See also Abu Muhammad ʿAbdallah b. Ahmad ibn al-Baytar, *Kitāb al-jāmiʿ li-mufradāt al-adwīya wa'l-aghdīya* (Bulaq: El-Amiriya Press, 1291/1874), I, p. 109. For a French translation of this chapter of the text, see Ibn al-Baytar, *Traité des simples*, trans. Lucien Leclerc, in *Notices et Extraits des Manuscrits de la Bibliothèque Nationale* 23.1 (1876): 255–8.
3. On the Arabic names for the plant, see Schweinfurth, *Arabische Pflanzennamen*, pp. 14, 87, 136, 163.
4. Löw, *Die Flora der Juden*, I, p. 300; Groom, *Frankincense and Myrrh*, pp. 126–7. Also Crone, *Meccan Trade*, p. 65.
5. Theophrastus, *Enquiry into Plants*, 9:1.2.
6. Ibid. 9:1.6.
7. Ibid. 9:6. The quoted section comes from 9:6.1.
8. Ibid. 9:6.4.
9. Ibid. 9:6.3.
10. Diodorus Siculus, *Bibliotheca historica* 3:46.2.
11. These sources are reviewed in Chapter 2.
12. Pliny, *Natural History*, 12:112–13.
13. Ibid. 12:114–15.
14. Ibid. 12:119.
15. Theophrastus, *Enquiry into Plants*, 9:6.2; Pliny, *Natural History*, 12:115; Tacitus, *Histories* 5:6.
16. Dioscorides, *De materia medica*, I:19. For the original Greek, see *De materia medica libra quinque*, ed. Wellmann, I.1, pp. 24–6. The English translation given here comes from *Pedanios Dioscorides of Anazarbus. De materia medica*, trans. Lily Beck, Altertumswissenschaftliche Texte und Studien 38 (Hildesheim, Zürich and New York: Olms – Weidmann, 2005), I:19 (pp. 19–20).
17. John Riddle, *Dioscorides on Pharmacy and Medicine* (Austin, TX: University of Texas Press, 1985), pp. 75–7. See also discussion in Chapter 5.

18. Muhammad ibn Ahmad al-Biruni, *Al-Biruni's Book of Pharmacy and Medicine*, ed. and trans. Hakim Said (Karachi: Hamdard Academy, 1973), I, p. 73.
19. 'Abd al-Latif al-Baghdadi, *The Eastern Key*, pp. 40 (Arabic), 41 (English).
20. Yaqut, *Jacut's geographische Wörterbuch*, IV, pp. 564–5.
21. Leo Africanus, *The History and Description of Africa*, III, p. 879.
22. On Alpin's use of Dioscorides in his assessment of balsam and related New World species, see Jerry Stannard, 'Dioscorides and Renaissance materia medica', *Analecta Medico-historica* 1 (1966): 13. On the influence of Dioscorides in European pharmacological writing, see Jerry Stannard, 'Medieval herbals and their development', *Clio Medica* 9 (1974): 23–33.
23. From the French translation: Alpin, *Plantes d'Égypte*, pp. 79–80 [53–4]. The complete section on balsam appears on pp. 71–87 [48–59]. Much the same information appears in his *Histoire du baulme*, pp. 41–51. See also Prosper Alpin, *De balsamo dialogus. In quo verissima balsami plantae, opobalsami, carpobalsami, et xilobalsami cognitio plerisque* (Venice: Signum Leonis, 1591). For additional information on botanical scholarship on balsam at this time, see Karen Reeds, *Botany in Medieval and Renaissance Universities* (New York and London: Garland Publishing, 1991), p. 18.
24. William Lithgow provides another late description of the tree, though it is less detailed and accurate (he records that Christians and Jews were not in his time permitted to enter the walled plantation). He writes: 'The tree itself is but of three foot height, which keepeth evermore the colour green, having a broad three-pointed leaf; which being thrice a year incised in the body and branches, it yieldeth a red water that droppeth down in earthen vessels, which is the natural balsam'. See his *The Rare Adventures and Painful Peregrinations*, p. 173.
25. Alpin, *Plantes d'Égypte*, p. 80 [54]. These observations are repeated in Thomas Greenhill, Νεκροκηδεια, *or the Art of Embalming, wherein is shewn the Right of Burial, the Funeral Ceremonies, and the several Ways of preserving dead Bodies in most Nations of the World*... (hereafter *Nekrokideia*) (London: Printed by the author, 1705), p. 210.
26. Pierre Pomet, *Histoire générale des drogues* (Paris: Jean-Baptiste Loyson and Augustin Pillon, 1694), p. 276. The sixteenth-century traveller Pierre Belon du Mans claims the smell is like that of cardamom. See his *Observations du plusieurs singularitez et choses mémorables trouuées en Grece, Asie, Iudée, Égypte, Arabie et autres pays estranges* (Paris: G. Corrozet, 1553), p. 111. Also de Maillet, *Description de l'Égypte*, pp. 111–12.
27. Alpin, *Plantes d'Égypte*, pp. 80–1 [54–5]; Alpin, *Histoire du baulme*, pp. 45–7.

28. Alpin, *Plantes d'Égypte*, p. 73 [49–50]. See also González, *Voyage en Égypte*, I, p. 62. He discusses the activities of 'Messinor', and concludes that balsam originates in Arabia and not in Egypt.
29. On the Arabic translations of Dioscorides, see Mahmoud Sadek, *The Arabic Materia Medica of Dioscorides* (St Jean-Chrysostome, Quebec: Éditions du Sphinx, 1985); Collins, *Medieval Herbals*, pp. 115–47.
30. Collins, *Medieval Herbals*, pp. 49–50, 85–92.
31. Sadek, *The Arabic* Materia Medica, pp. 9–13.
32. The 595/1199 copy is available in facsimile as Anon. (Pseudo-Galen), *Kitāb al-Diryāq (Thériaque de Paris)*, with commentary by Marie Guesdon et al. (Sansepolchro: Aboco Museum, 2008). On the illustrations, see also Oya Pancaroğlu, 'Socializing medicine: Illustrations of the *Kitāb al-diryāq*', *Muqarnas* 18 (2001): 155–72 (on the authorship, see pp. 165–6).
33. Collins, *Medieval Herbals*, pp. 66, 85–8. The earliest Dioscorides manuscripts to include human figures are the eighth-century copy in the Bibliothèque Nationale in Paris (gr. 2179) and M 652 in the Morgan Library & Museum, probably produced between 925 and 975 in the Byzantine court.
34. Matthaeus Platearius (attributed), *Le Livre des simples médicines d'après le manuscrit français 12322 de la Bibliothèque Nationale de Paris*, ed. Ghislaine Malandin (Paris: Éditions Ozalid et Textes Cardinaux, 1986), pp. 222–3.
35. Alpin, *Plantes d'Égypte*, figure on p. 88 [60]. See also illustrations in Alpin, *De balsamo dialogus*, page facing 1r and p. 23r.
36. John Gerard, *The Herball, or Generall Historie of Plants* (London: Edmund Bollifant, 1597. Reprinted in The English Experience 660B, Amsterdam and Norwood, NJ: Walter J. Johnson Inc. and Theatrum Orbis Terrarum, 1974), pp. 1343–6 (book III, chapter 139). Much of his information was derived from the work of the Dutch scholar Rembert Dodoens (d. 1585).
37. Gerard, *The Herball*, p. 1344. 'Garcias' can probably be identified as the Portuguese physician Garcia de Orta (d. 1568). Of the other 'fruit' (Fig. 4.6), Gerard writes (p. 1343): 'It is a fruite very crooked, and hollowed out like the palme of an hand; two inches long; halfe an inch thicke; couered with a thicke smooth rinde, of the colour of a dry Oken leafe; wherein is contained a kernell (of the same length and thicknes, apt to fill the said shell or rinde) of the substance of an Almond; of the colour of ashes; fat, and oilie; of good smell, and very vnpleasant in taste'.
38. For example, Moyse Charas, *The Royal Pharmacopoea Galenical and Chymical* (London: John Starkey and Moses Pitt, 1678), part 2, book 1, pp. 144–5. He

writes, 'fix'd to the plant with a cup; to be large, weighty, picquant and sharp in taste, cover'd with a small membrane of a deep yellow-colour, inclining to red; lin'd within, with other membranes thicker then that without, and which contains within a yellow honey-like substance, with a pleasing scent like to that of *opobalsamum*'.

39. A slightly adapted version of this illustration appears in Richard Cartwright's *An Essay upon the Virtues of the Balm of Gilead* (1760). Illustrated in Hepper and Taylor, 'Date palms and opobalsam', p. 40, fig. 4.
40. De Maillet, *Description de l'Égypte*, p. 112.
41. George Trease and William Evans, *Pharmacognosy*, tenth edition (London: Ballière Tindall, 1972), pp. 156–7; Thomas Wallis, *Textbook of Pharmacognosy*, fourth edition (London: J. and A. Churchill, 1960), p. 500.
42. Majno, *The Healing Hand*, pp. 217–18; R. Rao et al., 'Toxicity studies in mice of *Commiphora molmol* oleo-gum-resin', *Journal of Ethnopharmacology* 76 (2001): 151. On the chemistry of myrrh, see Dieter Martinez, Karlheinz Lohs and Jörg Janzen, *Weihrauch und Myrrh. Kulturgeschichte und wirtschaftliche Bedeutung. Botanik. Chemie. Medizin* (Stuttgart: Wissenschaftliche Verlaggesellschaft, 1989), pp. 169–80.
43. Groom, *Frankincense and Myrrh*, p. 127 (the original citation is not given in the endnotes). The entry on *amyris opobalsamum* appears in Forsskål, *Flora Aegyptiaco-Arabica*, pp. 79–80 (no. 48). Also pp. xc, xcv. For *amyris kataf*, see p. 80 (no. 49). Also Nigel Hepper, 'Current research on the plant specimens from the Niebuhr and Forsskal Yemen expeditions, 1761–63', *Proceedings of the Seminar for Arabian Studies* 17 (1987): 81–90; Hepper and Friis, *The Plants of Pehr Forsskal's 'Flora Aegyptiaco-Arabica'*, pp. 15–16, 90.
44. 'Ali Bey 'Abbasi, *Travels of Ali Bey: In Morocco, Tripoli, Cyprus, Egypt, Arabia, Syria, and Turkey between the Years 1803 and 1807* (London: Longman, Hurst, Rees, Orme and Brown, 1816. Reprinted Farnborough: Gregg, 1970), I, p. 112.
45. Max Meyerhof, 'Der Bazar der Drogen und Wohlgeruche in Kairo', *Sonderabdruck aus Archiv für Wirtschaftforschung im Orient* 3.4 (1918): 198, no. 297.
46. Other names are employed in earlier studies including *Balsamodendron gileadensis, Balsamodendron ehrenbergianum, Amyris gileadensis, Amyris opobalsamum* and *Balsamea meccanensis*.
47. There are reports that the trees have been identified as far south as the coastal regions of Kenya, and also in India. See Kaj Vollesen, 'Burseracaeae', in *Flora of Ethiopia 3: Pittosporaceae to Araliceae*, eds Inga Hedberg and Sue Edwards

(Addis Ababa and Uppsala, 1989), pp. 475–77; Jan Gillett, *Burseracaeae*, Flora of East Africa (Rotterdam: Bulkema, 1991), pp. 84–6. See also comments in Harold and Alma Moldenke, *Plants of the Bible*, New Series in Plant Sciences 28 (Waltham, MA: Chronica Botanica, 1952), pp. 84–6; Desmond Vesey-Fitzgerald, 'Vegetation of the Red Sea Coast south of Jedda, Saudi Arabia', *Journal of Ecology* 43 (1955): 485–6; Michael Zohary, *Geobotanical Foundations of the Middle East*, Geobotanica Selecta 3 (Stuttgart and Amsterdam: Gustav Fischer and Swets & Zeitlinger, 1973), I, pp. 242, 244. Additional synonyms are given in Groom, *Frankincense and Myrrh*, pp. 126–30; George Post, *Flora of Syria, Palestine and Sinai*, second edition revised by John Dinsmore (Beirut: American University in Beirut Press, 1932–3), I, p. 284; Lutfi Boulos, *Flora of Egypt. Volume Two: Geraniaceae – Boraginaceae* (Cairo: Al Hadra Publishing, 2000), pp. 68–9. The present northern range of *Commiphora opobalsamum* in Arabia is in the foothills between Jedda and Yanbuʻ. See Desmond Vesey-Fitzgerald, 'Vegetation of the Red Sea Coast north of Jedda, Saudi Arabia', *Journal of Ecology* 45 (1957), p. 552.

48. Abu al-Faraj (Bar Hebraeus), *The Abridged Version of* 'The Book of Simple Drugs', pp. 58 (Arabic), 247 (English).
49. ʻAbd al-Latif al-Baghdadi, *The Eastern Key*, pp. 44 (Arabic), 45 (English).
50. Ibid. pp. 44 (Arabic), 45 (English). With the exception of Iran, the geographical range of al-Baghdadi's *bashām* accords fairly well with the distribution of *Commiphora gileadensis* (allowing for the fact that the thirteenth-century author may not have had access to reliable information about the flora of the Horn of Africa and the coastal areas further south).
51. Alpin, *Plantes d'Égypte*, p. 80 [54].
52. Hartmann Grisar and Moriz Dreger, *Die römische Kapelle Sancta Sanctorum und ihr Schatz. Meine Entdeckungen und Studien in der Palastkapelle der Mittelalterichen Päpste* (Freiburg im Breisgau: Herder, 1908), pp. 88, 92.
53. Josephus, *Jewish War*, 1:138. Kottek, *Medicine and Hygiene*, p. 127.
54. Illustrated and discussed in John Murdoch, *Album of Science: Antiquity and the Middle Ages*, Albums of Science (New York: Charles Scribner's Sons, 1984), p. 274.
55. Adomnán (d. 704) records Arculf on the harvesting of balsam in the gardens of Jericho. This must be anachronistic, though the comments correlate with accounts of the practices in Matarea. See Adomnán, *The Pilgrimage of Arculfus*, p. 78: 'There the opobalsamum is produced, which we name thus with an affix because the husbandmen, with sharp stones, cut slender channels through the

bark, in which the balsam is generated, so that the sap, after distilling slowly through those caverns, collects in beautifully bedewed tears . . .' This section does not appear in a more recent translation. See Wilkinson, trans., *Jerusalem Pilgrims before the Crusades*, pp. 106–7. The description of Jericho appears in part 13:1 of the text.

56. Abu al-Makarim translated in Ugo Zanetti, 'Matarieh', pp. 37–8. Also Abu al-Makarim, *History of the Churches*, p. 46.
57. Nasir-i Khusraw, *Book of Travels*, p. 51.
58. 'Abd al-Latif al-Baghdadi, *The Eastern Key*, pp. 42 (Arabic), 43 (English). Cf. Oliver of Paderborn in Gavignan, trans., *Christian Society and the Crusades*, pp. 117–18 (chapter 60); Marino Sanudo, *Secrets for True Crusaders*, p. 59. The latter author claims that the bottles of sap were buried in pigeon droppings.
59. Abu al-Makarim translated in Zanetti, 'Matarieh', p. 38. Also Abu al-Makarim, *History of the Churches*, p. 46.
60. 'Abd al-Latif, *The Eastern Key*, pp. 42 (Arabic), 43 (English).
61. Theophrastus, *Enquiry into Plants*, 9:6.2, 4; Pliny, *Natural History*, 12:117; Dioscorides, *De materia medica* 1:19.1. For a translation, see Beck, trans., *De materia medica*, p. 19.
62. Von Sudheim, *Description of the Holy Land*, p. 68.
63. Ibid. p. 69.
64. Abu al-Makarim translated in Zanetti, 'Matarieh', pp. 34, 35, 37. Also Abu al-Makarim, *History of the Churches*, pp. 42, 43, 45.

5

Diplomacy and International Trade

Felix Fabri makes the striking claim that balsam was sent by the sultan of Egypt as gifts to Prester John, Frederick Barbarossa and the emperor of China. The oil was placed within gold or silver containers, often ornamented with precious stones.[1] Clearly this statement cannot be accepted uncritically, any more than the remark found in dramatic retellings of the life of Rodrigo Diaz de Vivar, prince of Valencia (known as El Cid, r. 1094–9) that he had been sent balsam and myrrh by the 'sultan of Persia'.[2] The first of Fabri's notional recipients, Prester John (or Presbyter John), is a mythical figure who came into being in the twelfth century as the Christian king who ruled over a fabulously wealthy land somewhere to the east, or occasionally the south, of the Islamic world.[3] It is conceivable that Frederick Barbarossa (r. 1150–92) may have received some balsam from Saladin. What, however, is the reader to make of Fabri's assertion that this precious commodity was sent as far afield as China?

Fabri can surely have had no way of knowing whether sultans of Egypt did, in fact, send balsam to the emperor of China (he describes him as the 'Mongol Khan of Cathay'), but his idea is not as outlandish as it may first appear. As noted in Chapter 2, at least one writer of Tang dynasty China was aware of a product from Syria (Fu-Lin) known as *a-pʻo-tsʻan*, which could be equated with the balsam grown around En-Gedi until about the sixth century.[4] Other Chinese writings exhibit knowledge concerning theriacs that might have contained balsam (Chapter 7). The exchange of diplomatic gifts between the Islamic world and China can be demonstrated from as early as the eighth century, though there is little to indicate that Muslim rulers of Egypt made extensive efforts to engage with their counterparts in China. While most of the diplomatic traffic with China was conducted with Islamic polities of Iran and Central Asia, the entire Middle East was a significant consumer of porcelain and other manufactured goods from Southeast Asia.[5]

In a broader sense, however, Fabri is correct in his belief that balsam was frequently employed by the sultans of Egypt in their exchanges with other rulers, particularly those of Europe, and with the representatives of the different Christian Churches. The monopoly over the supply of balsam was well established under the Ayyubid sultans of the early thirteenth century. In common with the practices of the Jewish Hasmonean and Herodian dynasties and the Roman empire after 70 CE (Chapter 2), the sultans of Egypt tried to ensure that the supply of balsam never fully met the demand. In this way balsam retained its status as a much sought-after luxury commodity, the allocation of which remained under the tight control of the sultan and his officials. Products from the trees of Matarea were available on the open market, however, and travellers' accounts, mercantile handbooks, trading archives and inventories illuminate the trade in balsam in the Mediterranean and Europe. This chapter assesses the textual evidence for the exchange of balsam by means of diplomacy, state-sponsored redistribution and trade.[6]

Gifts of Caliphs and Sultans

Where the Romans appear to have desired the control of the plantations of Jericho and En-Gedi largely for their economic value, Muslim rulers of Egypt seem to have been more concerned with the symbolic potential of the monopoly on the supply of balsam. Unlike the Jewish kings, the Fatimid caliphs and sultans of the Ayyubid and Mamluk dynasties had no use for balsam in their own religious or royal rituals. The only reference to balsam in a Muslim religious context is Ludovico di Varthema's (d. 1517) odd claim that jars of balsam were placed on either side of the door of the Kaʿba in Mecca. He continues that the balsam 'is shown on the day of Pentecost. And they say that the balsam is part of the treasures of the sultan'.[7] Di Varthema is perhaps referring to ʿArafa, the ninth day of the month of Dhu al-Hijja. His report about the jars is not confirmed in other sources.

Even though the Mamluk sultans had little use for balsam in their own rituals, they were clearly aware of the central role of balsam 'oil' in Christian liturgy and the anointing practices of kings and emperors in medieval Europe. This knowledge of the power exerted by the sultans of Egypt is captured eloquently by the chronicler and bureaucrat al-'Umari (d. 1347), who observes:

> Some of it [balsam] is sent as ceremonial gifts, and the Christian kings (*malik*, pl. *mulūk*) of Habash, al-Rum, and the Franks vie with each other to receive presents from the master (*ṣāḥib*) of Egypt. They believe that one has not become fully Christian except if one is immersed in water of baptism, and they believe that a little oil of balsam (*duhn al-balasān*) must be added to the water. They call it *mīrūn*.[8]

Al-'Umari's account is broadly confirmed by a contemporary, Ludolph von Sudheim. He claims that the annual extraction of the oleo-resin from the trees would usually be attended by the sultan (Chapters 3 and 4). The audience for this ceremony would also include 'legates and ambassadors of certain kings and princes from foreign parts'. Each would be given a small glass container of balsam. This was perceived by the sultan to be 'the richest gift jewel that he could give'.[9] Al-'Umari continues his description, noting that the sultan also sent supplies of balsam from the treasury for use in 'the castles (sing. *qal'a*) of Syria' and in hospitals.[10] It is not specified, however, whether this is the finest 'oil' or lower grades, such as *xylobalsamum* or *carpobalsamum*.

The 'kings' mentioned in al-'Umari's account are those of the Solomonic dynasty of Abyssinia (Habash), the emperor of Byzantium (al-Rum) and the Christian rulers of Europe (comprising both kings and the Holy Roman emperor). The author makes no mention of European royal and imperial anointing ceremonies that were performed with the oil of consecration (chrism) or oil of catechumens, both of which contained balsam. Al-'Umari's main concern is with the role of *mīrūn* (from the Greek myron, which equates to the Latin word chrism) in the fundamental Christian ritual of baptism, though he mistakenly asserts that myron is simply made from 'oil of balsam' (Chapter 8).

An early record for the use of balsam in an Islamic diplomatic exchange comes from the rule of the Abbasid caliph Harun al-Rashid (r. 786–809). The Frankish emperor Charlemagne (r. 768–814) had sent three emissaries to Baghdad in about 800. Only one of the three, a Frankish Jew named Isaac, survived the trip and was given the responsibility of making the return journey with the most famous of the caliph's gifts, an elephant, known as

Abu'l-'Abbas. Isaac and the elephant arrived on the Italian coast late in 801 and were presented at the court in Aachen on 20 July 802. An account of these events is given in the latter part of the ninth century by a monk, Notker the Stammerer (d. 912). He claims that the 'Persian' envoys were overwhelmed by the magnificence of Charlemagne's court, proclaiming, 'Until now we have only seen men of clay: now we see golden men'. It is commonplace to find such sentiments placed into the mouths of foreign ambassadors by dutiful court historians, but of greater interest is the list of gifts. In addition to the elephant, these apparently comprised 'some monkeys, balsam, nard, unguents of various sorts, spices, scents and a wide variety of medicaments'. The chronicler continues: 'They seem to have despoiled the East so that they might offer all these gifts to the West'.[11]

The veracity of Notker's list is difficult to assess given that no corresponding information on these events survives in the Arabic written sources of the period. Comparison with other known diplomatic exchanges of the Umayyad and Abbasid periods yields some significant points. Expensive animals are indeed a staple of elite gift-giving at this time, as they were in later periods. The eleventh-century text known as *The Book of Gifts and Rarities* (*Kitāb al-hadāyā wa'l-tuḥaf*) includes mentions of horses, camels, elephants and saluki dogs. Slaves, eunuchs and Turkish soldiers (sing. *mamlūk*) also feature in the lists, along with fine textiles, furs and sought-after manufactured goods, such as carved rock crystal and Chinese glazed ceramics. Ambergris, musk, aloe wood and other perfumed goods appear regularly along with products held to have medicinal qualities. Balsam is not a feature of the exchanges listed in *The Book of Gifts and Rarities*.[12] One explanation for this omission is that the oleo-resin had limited meaning in the context of diplomacy between Muslim rulers, or in contacts with China and India. The text also records, however, gifts exchanged with Christian rulers, most notably the emperor in Constantinople; in such cases one might have expected balsam to have been mentioned given its role in liturgy.

Key components of a successful gift were overwhelming scale and the knowledge that the items were desirable to the recipient.[13] These features are exemplified in the report of a gift sent by Caliph al-Ma'mun to the Byzantine emperor. The caliph commanded that the items he sent should reflect the glory of Islam by being one hundred times greater than those received from

Constantinople. Al-Ma'mun continues with a telling question: 'What do they value most?' Having ascertained these products, the caliph ordered that his gift also be augmented by 200 sable pelts and 200 *raṭls* (about 87 kg) of musk.[14] We can imagine the same processes at work in the inclusion of balsam into the package sent from Baghdad to Aachen. Balsam was evidently a difficult product for Europeans to procure; the account of the pilgrimage of Willibald indicates that it was sometimes necessary to resort to subterfuge in order to carry the substance beyond the borders of the Islamic world (Chapter 2).

Evidence is lacking for the use of balsam as a diplomatic gift by Egyptian rulers during the Tulunid (868–905), Ikhshidid (935–69) and Fatimid dynasties. Balsam is counted among the possessions of Christian nobles in Europe and the Crusader states, but the written sources do not reveal the mechanisms of exchange in these cases.[15] During his visit to Cairo the fifteenth-century ambassador Gilbert de Lannoy apparently received the gift of a vial of fine balsam from a patriarch.[16] Under the Ayyubids the balsam plantation came fully under Muslim authority. Christian rulers were furnished with their supplies of this precious substance during embassies, while the representatives of the Churches had to come to Cairo in order to buy their supplies direct from the treasury. Balsam was also sent in a lavish gift by Salah al-Din to his Zengid overlord, Nur al-Din (r. 1154–74).[17]

Mamluk sultans made extensive use of balsam in diplomatic exchanges. The commodity appears in a well-documented sequence of exchanges between the court of Aragon and the sultan al-Nasir Muhammad ibn Qalawun. Contact was instigated by Jaime II (as king of Aragon, r. 1291–1327) in 1300, and continued through to the reign of his successor, Alfonso IV (r. 1327–36). Eight embassies are recorded in all, the last occurring in 1330. Letters from Aragon reveal a consistent set of concerns relating to the granting of privileges to trade for Aragonese merchants operating in Egypt, the right to perform pilgrimage to Jerusalem, allowing mendicant orders patronised by Aragon to be involved in the liturgy of the Church of the Holy Sepulchre, improvement in the treatment of the Copts and other eastern Christians, and the liberation of Christian prisoners held by the sultan. The sixth embassy requested three relics: fragments of the True Cross, the chalice used by Christ at the Last Supper and the body of St Barbara. The first was among the items taken from the Crusader army by Salah al-Din following the battle of Hattin in 1187. While it was not unreasonable to assume these revered items still resided in the treasury in Cairo, it is less clear why the court of Aragon believed the chalice of Christ was located there. It is doubtful too whether the body of St Barbara was within al-Nasir Muhammad's gift given that the church in Old Cairo holding her remains had been razed during anti-Christian riots in 1318.[18]

Following common diplomatic practice, the court of Aragon identified gifts that would please their intended recipient. The Mamluk sultan was known for his fondness for hunting, and the gift of falcons (sing. *sunqūr*) in the eighth embassy in 1330 was evidently well received. The response sent from Cairo even notes, 'we have ordained their delivery from the bearers with redoubled gratitude and our praise for the excellent birds which he [Alfonso IV] has chosen'. The information about gifts sent by the sultan appears as part of the third embassy. Jaime II had dispatched Neymerich Dusay to Cairo on 1 September 1305 with a letter for the sultan. The reply is dated 1 Sha'ban 705/16 February 1306, and contains an extensive list, including bows, crossbows and a range of fine textiles. The consignment also included incense sticks meant for oral hygiene and a glass container (*fuqqā'a zajāj*) filled with 120 *mithqāl* of balsam 'oil' (*duhn al-balasān*). This equates to nearly half a kilogram of the finest balsam, a princely gift in its own right.[19]

Dusay and the Mamluk emissary, Fakhr al-Din 'Uthman, were due to set sail from Alexandria in the company of a group of freed captives. The journey was delayed because of a report that the captives included the son of a Christian monarch. Thinking of the ransom that could be levied on this individual, al-Nasir Muhammad decided to remove him from the group agreed in the embassy. Dusay's reaction to this breach of protocol was to have far-reaching consequences. He seized all of Fakhr al-Din's possessions and cast him adrift on a barge. Dusay sought refuge in Sicily with Frederick II, and diplomatic contact between Aragon and Cairo ceased for the next eight years. Balsam appears in the same period in a gift to another ruler on the Iberian peninsula, Ferdinand IV of Castile (r. 1295–1312).[20] This commodity also formed part of diplomatic exchanges between the Mamluk sultanate and Mahmud Shah (r. 1436–69), the sultan of Malwa in northern India, the Abdalwadid dynasty of Tlemcen and perhaps also the kingdom of Ethiopia.[21]

The first of these is worthy of comment in that Sultan Qaytbay's gift was in direct response to a request from Mahmud Shah for substances used in theriacs and aphrodisiacs, including the dried flesh of the skink (Chapter 7).[22]

Some of the best documented collections of Mamluk diplomatic gifts come from the last decades of the Mamluk sultanate. Those sent to Italy contained lavish gifts. For example, the items sent in 1487 by Sultan Qaytbay to Lorenzo de' Medici in Florence are enumerated in a letter sent to his sister, Clarice Orsini de' Medici (d. 1488). This missive claims the sultan's ambassador (identified in Arabic sources as Ibn Mahfuz) brought with him animals, including a horse, goats and fat-tailed sheep, though other sources mention a giraffe and a lion. These last two creatures can also be seen in Giorgio Vasari's painting of the event in the Palazzo Vecchio, begun in 1559 (Fig. 5.1). In common with many of the later Mamluk diplomatic gifts, Chinese glazed ceramics (*porcellana*; probably referring both to porcelain

Figure 5.1 Giorgio Vasari, Lorenzo de' Medici receiving gifts from the ambassador of the Mamluk sultan, Sala di Lorenzo Magnifico, Palazzo Vecchio, Florence, 1559. HIP / Art Resource, NY.

and celadon wares) feature prominently along with expensive textiles. Most interesting in the present context are the aromatic and medicinal goods, comprising musk, benzoin, aloe wood, myrobalan, ginger and balsam. The last of these is described in the letter as '*una grande ampolla di balsamo*', indicating that it corresponded to the container sent more than a century earlier to the king of Aragon.[23]

The most intense diplomatic activity was with Venice, reflecting the commercial significance of the trade between the Italian city and the ports of Egypt and Syria. One such negotiation was represented in an anonymous painting, now dated to c. 1511, known as the *Reception of the Venetian Ambassadors*. In this case, the location can clearly be identified as Damascus, with the seated dignitary being the governor (*nā'ib al-salṭana*) of Syria rather than the sultan himself (Fig. 5.2).[24] Missions were sent in 1442, 1461, 1465, 1473, 1490, 1499 and 1503 from Cairo to Venice with the intention of maintaining lucrative trading arrangements.[25] Other notable exchanges in this period occurred with Charles V of France in 1447 and Catherine Cornaro of Cyprus in 1476.[26] In all these cases Chinese porcelain featured in the gifts sent from Cairo. The prominence of these imported goods is somewhat ironic

Figure 5.2 Reception of the Venetian ambassadors in Damascus, after 1511. School of Gentile Bellini. Musée du Louvre, Paris. Erich Lessing / Art Resource, NY.

given that the increasing intensity of these exchanges can be attributed in part to the erosion of the Mamluk monopoly over the maritime trade routes with South and Southeast Asia. In 1498 Vasco da Gama (d. 1524) arrived in India, having sailed around the Cape of Good Hope, an event that signalled the end of Egypt's lucrative role in the transmission of luxury goods from the Indian Ocean to the Mediterranean.[27]

During the fifteenth and early sixteenth centuries, the Mamluks had to contend with the rising power of the Ottoman sultanate. Embassies between the two powers commenced in 1388, during the rule of Sultan Barquq (r. 1382–9, 1390–9) and continued through to the last year of the reign of Qansawh al-Ghawri. As might be expected, the gifts from the Mamluk sultan differ in significant respects from those sent to members of the European political elite. Animals, especially fine horses, are prominent in the lists of gifts, and they are sometimes accompanied by gilded saddles or even bales of special fodder. *Mamlūk*s and slave girls appear along with references to the porters who must have helped tend the animals and carry the other objects. Silks and other textiles are important components, as well as furs, silverware, gold coins, jewels and weaponry.[28]

Balsam appears only twice, first in an exchange between sultans Jaqmaq (r. 1438–53) and Murad II (r. 1421–44, 1446–51) in 843/1440 and the second between sultans Sayf al-Din Inal (r. 1453–61) and Mehmed II Fatih (r. 1444–6, 1451–81) in 857/1453. The listing of Jaqmaq's consignment starts with an ancient Qur'an believed to have been 'written in the hand of Imam 'Uthman b. 'Affan' (r. 644–56) and continues with elaborate weapons and armour, turban clothes, carpets with golden thread, velvets and saddles. Inal's gift follows a remarkably similar pattern, and was accompanied by a letter congratulating Mehmed on his conquest of Constantinople.[29] The lack of prominence given to the containers of balsam oil can be attributed to the fact that its utility in a Muslim context was largely restricted to the realm of medicine (Chapters 6 and 7). By contrast, Christian rulers will have valued the oleo-resin more highly for its central role in church liturgy and royal rituals.

Even in the last decades of the life of the trees in the plantation of Matarea, balsam continued to appear in records of diplomatic exchanges. Following the common practice for such gifts, balsam was included among many other items, such as spices, exotic animals and fine textiles. One significant innovation from the second half of the fifteenth century onward was a substance known in European sources as *terra lemnia* or *terra sigillata* ('stamped earth'). This earth was gathered in an annual ceremony from a site on the Greek island of Lemnos. The ceremony itself is recorded in numerous antique sources, but had fallen into abeyance some time after the second century CE. Mehmed II revived the annual collection of the clay following his conquest of the island. Formed into tablets, each authenticated by an official stamp, *terra lemnia* was widely valued for its medicinal applications (most importantly in the treatment of poisons and venoms). Pottery vessels were also made from the clay, and it was believed that these would sweat if brought into contact with poison. Balsam, another medicament with a perceived efficacy as an antidote, was included with *terra lemnia* and the theriac Mithridatium (Chapter 7). *Terra lemnia* and balsam appear together in a gift sent in 1574 to the Doge of Venice. The French ambassador to the Sublime Porte, Jean de Montluc (d. 1579), was given some of the theriac along with balsam and *terra sigillata* by the immensely wealthy Grand Vizier Rüstem Pasha (d. 1561).[30]

Balsam of Matarea in International Trade

Dioscorides claims that balsam sold for twice its weight in silver. In fact, his information may relate to earlier centuries, for his near contemporary Pliny offers higher estimates in his *Natural History*. He asserts that six *sextarii* (about 3.3 litres) of the finest balsam could be obtained from the emperor's personal treasury (*fiscus*) for the sum of 1,000 *denarii* (silver coins). The merchants buying this commodity would then sell it on – probably adulterated with other plant oils, gums and resins – at 300 *denarii* per *sextarius*, yielding a considerable profit of 800 *denarii* on the initial purchase.[31] From this one can infer that the price per litre in the marketplaces of Rome was at least 548 *denarii*, or (assuming the liquid had approximately the specific gravity of water) 0.548 *denarii* per gram. Given the weight of the *denarius* in Pliny's time (one seventy-second of a Roman pound, or about 4.5 g) this means that the best balsam retailed for two and a half times its weight in silver.[32] These calculations do not account, of course, for the additional costs accrued as the result of shipping, land transport and customs.

That adulteration (or the deceptive practice of substituting cheaper oleo-resins or oils for balsam) was commonplace is suggested by the careful notes that Dioscorides provides for identifying pure balsam (Chapter 4). According to Pliny, the liquid made from boiling the branches of the balsam tree (*xylobalsamum*) also generated annual profits of 800,000 *sesterces* for the *fiscus*.[33] He does not specify the quantities in this case, but it presumably refers to the 'oil' generated from the total harvest of pruned branches from the trees in the imperial plantations around En-Gedi. The practice of boiling branches for oil is also described in Arabic sources: for example, al-Biruni writes:

> People purchase its boughs from druggists, who peel off the bark of the boughs before handing them over to customers, especially since the bark is used as a calorifacient. The buyers then extract oil from the boughs, as we have just said. The self-same oil is then exported to foreign lands.[34]

It is difficult to assess quite how the prices paid for balsam changed between Pliny's time and the great expansion of Mediterranean mercantile activity in the mid-eleventh century. Both luxury commodities and bulk goods continued to be traded across the Mediterranean in the later Roman period, and even the collapse of the Western Roman empire in 476 did not curtail the traffic of ships plying the routes from the eastern Mediterranean and North Africa to ports in southern Europe. While the volume of traffic diminished from the fifth century CE, the rulers and wealthy inhabitants of Western Europe were still willing to pay for imported spices, silks, papyrus and olive oil.[35]

The presence of balsam in some of the cargoes coming from Egypt to Italy in the sixth century is confirmed by the references (along with nard, storax and stacte, the fragrant oil produced from myrrh) in the *Liber Pontificalis*.[36] Balsam was also sent from Rome to Ravenna.[37] The *Book of the Prefect* (*eparch*), a commercial manual probably dating to the late tenth century, lists balsam (*barzi*) among the substances sold in Constantinople.[38] Although it is not stated specifically, balsam and many of the other listed aromatics would have been supplied to the city by merchants operating in the Middle East. The *Book of the Prefect* devotes a chapter to those who brought goods from Syria and Baghdad.[39] Balsam may have been available further north; a letter from Elias III, patriarch of Jerusalem (r. 897–907), to Alfred the Great, ruler of the English kingdom of Wessex (r. 871–99), recommends the product in the treatment of chest ailments.[40]

A new chapter in Mediterranean trade opened in the eleventh century, with Italian ports, such as Amalfi, Genoa, Pisa, Noli and Venice, aggressively developing trading opportunities. Marseilles was another port city to prosper. These maritime powers looked in all directions, including the Islamic regions of the Iberian peninsula, North Africa and the Middle East. The archaeological record provides ample evidence of this contact, with high-quality manufactured goods – most notably glazed pottery and enamelled glass – cropping up regularly across Europe, even as far north as England.[41] Access to Egypt provided Italian merchants with the chance to buy goods from more distant places. While many of the organic materials – nutmeg, ginger, pepper and other spices – have long since been consumed (or have rotted in the soil), remnants of these international trade routes endure, including the fine glazed ceramics, particularly porcelains and stonewares, produced in China and in other kilns in Southeast Asia. The earliest documented complete vessel is the Fonthill vase, an elegant piece of Qingbai porcelain that was given to Louis the Great of Hungary (r. 1342–82) by a Chinese embassy travelling to meet Pope Benedict XII (r. 1334–42) in 1338.[42]

Excavated pottery provides additional evidence about the trade in plant resins at this time. Organic residues detected in the bases of amphorae and other storage vessels recovered from the Red Sea port of Quseir were subjected to infrared spectroscopic analysis. Although these samples did not allow for conclusive identification, the researchers were able to draw conclusions concerning the presence of resins and tree-based pitches, also known as 'wood tar'. Among the former group were residues that could be either pine resins or resins from the family Burseraceae, such as olibanum and bdellium. The fact that this sample is described as being 'devoid of aromatic character' seems to exclude balsam.[43] The archive of fragmentary documents associated with the structure known as the 'Sheikh's house' provided supporting evidence for the trade in resins. Although the bulk of the trade passing through Quseir comprised grain and other staples, one document mentions *sandarūs*. This can be identified as the resin of the Sandarac tree (*Tetraclinis articulata* [Vahl] Mast.), a native of north-west Africa and the Iberian peninsula. The aromatic resin enjoyed applications in medicine.[44]

Many goods were passed along the land and maritime trade routes of the medieval period, with some travelling long distances and others being circulated in more restricted areas. Long-distance land transport obviously concentrated largely on products that enjoyed a high unit cost (at least in their intended market). The situation with maritime transport is more complex due to the requirement to fill the ship both with high-value goods and with heavier items that could function as ballast. This could take the form of sacks of grain, amphorae filled with olive oil, consignments of glazed pottery or, in the case of the eleventh-century wreck discovered at Serçe Limanı, broken glass (cullet) and glass waste.[45] Balsam existed at the other end of this spectrum as a valuable commodity, yielding high profits for the merchant.[46]

The oleo-resin was also ideally suited to international trade as it could be bottled up into small, durable containers. These containers might be made of glass, though there is also evidence for balsam 'oil' being transported in bottles made of lead or pewter. Vessels of this type had been used for centuries for the transport of other precious liquids, including spent olive oil from lamps at holy sites in Palestine. Ancient examples are found in the churches of Monza and Bobbio in Italy (Fig. 5.3).[47] Pilgrim flasks bear some similarities to the metal containers fixed to the trunk of the balsam tree in Pomet's *Histoire générale des drogues* (Fig. 4.10). Similar vessels were employed in the nineteenth century for the storage of water from the well of Zamzam in Mecca (Fig. 5.4). Pomet claims to have received from Madame de Villefavin two lead bottles of balsam 'as it came from Grand Cairo' that contained a hardened material with a golden yellow colour. The author likens this to the turpentine harvested on the Greek island of Chios.[48]

Although it was published some decades after the death of the last balsam tree, Pomet's text provides a clear description of the different types of balsam that were traded to Europe. The author laments the fact that the oleo-resin is extremely difficult to obtain. The substance was only available from ambassadors of the Porte, as gift from the sultan, or via the janissaries who guarded the plantation. He continues that 'several Cheats pretend to sell true Balsam is nothing but white Balsam of Peru, which they prepare with Spirit of Wine rectified, or with some Oils distill'd'.[49]

Pomet devotes his next section to the liquid made from the berries and seeds, known as *carpobalsamum*. The berries were evidently available for sale

Figure 5.3 Pilgrim ampulla, Palestine, sixth century. Museo del Duomo, Monza, Italy. Bildarchiv Foto Marburg / Art Resource, NY.

Figure 5.4 Metal flask containing Zamzam water. Brought back from Mecca by Sir Richard Burton in 1853. British Museum: OA+3740.

in France, though they were not highly regarded: 'they are of some medicinal Use, but principally for the great Treacle wherein they require no other Preparation but to be chose true, and freed from their little Stalks, empty Shells, and such as are Worm-eaten amongst them'.[50] John Gerard was able to purchase in England branches and fruit of balsam, though he may have obtained samples from different species of plant (Chapter 4).[51] Already in the thirteenth century Roger Bacon (d. 1292) notes the difficulty of obtaining in England organic commodities such as aloe, musk and pure balsam.[52] Christoph Harant, a contemporary of Gerard, claims that a liquid was derived from the leaves and that this was sold to Christians in great quantities. This product was available in the pharmacies of Prague.[53]

The 'great Treacle' referred to by Pomet is the antidote prepared in Venice and sold extensively across Europe (Chapter 7). The scarcity of *carpobalsamum* is noted by Moyse Charas (d. 1698) in his *Royal Pharmacopoea Galenical and Chymical* (1678).[54] Pomet concludes with a brief discussion of the wood of the tree (*xylobalsamum*). This was brought from Cairo to Marseilles in the form of faggots of branches. The best wood had a reddish bark and many knots. The principal application for these was in troches (pastilles), combining a binder such as honey with the active medicinal ingredients.[55] These medicines are referred to in ancient Greek medical texts, and continued to be manufactured through the medieval and early modern periods. Balsam twigs and leaves could be burned in order to make aromatic smoke (on the medicinal applications of smoke, see Chapter 7). Fabri mentions one further product, the ash made from burning branches. He names this powder as *lachobalsamum*, without giving further indication as to its commercial or practical value.[56]

With these basic distinctions in mind, the remainder of this section deals with the textual evidence for the trade and distribution of products of the balsam trees between the twelfth and the seventeenth centuries. The evidence concerning the cost and transport of *opobalsamum* can be briefly summarised. Writing in the early thirteenth century, 'Abd al-Latif al-Baghdadi quotes the Spanish pharmacologist Ibn Samajun (d. 1002) to the effect that balsam traded for twice its weight in silver.[57] This estimate is perhaps drawn from Dioscorides (see above) and may not reflect the commercial realities of Ayyubid Egypt. In the sixteenth century Ibn Iyas claims that the finest balsam was traded for as much as its weight in gold, and this general observation is confirmed in other sources, including the well-known fourteenth-century trade manual (*La pratica della mercatura*) of Francesco Balducci Pegolotti. Venetian merchants appear to have been accustomed to paying for balsam 'oil' according to its weight in gold.[58] The association between the two precious commodities even appears in aphorisms, such as Ambroise's (fl. 1190s) observation in his account of the Third Crusade that 'prowess outvalues gold and balm'.[59]

Different grades of liquid balsam circulated around the Mediterranean.[60] Other products, such as sugar, were also offered at variable prices according to quality.[61] A document dated 1347 records the purchase by a Venetian merchant, Pignol Zucchelo, of a consignment of 27 kg of wood (*xylobalsamum*) for six *dinār*s.[62] As noted above, this commodity was still traded in the seventeenth century. Pomet's testimony is repeated later in the first volume of Savary de Brûlons' *Dictionnaire universel de commerce*, published in 1723, though it is doubtful that any genuine balsam wood was still available by that date.[63] Alternatives such as balm of Mecca seem more likely, or the branches from the South American balsams.

The annual crop of the finest balsam oleo-resin was a sultanic monopoly, and the majority must have been distributed via non-commercial avenues. Unfortunately, it is impossible to be certain about the mechanisms by which balsam found its way from Egypt to Europe or the Crusader polities. Johannes Schiltberger's (d. c. 1440) account of Matarea suggests an active trade in balsam that benefited the Mamluk ruler. He writes: 'The king-sultan enjoys a large income from this balsam. The infidels often adulterate it, and merchants and druggists often mix it, and this they do to make more profit'.[64] Representatives of different churches purchased their supplies of balsam from the treasury in Cairo.[65] These, and other types of commercial transactions, might, therefore, account for the presence of balsam in church treasuries, including Augsburg, Bamberg, Merseburg, Staffelsee, Wilten, Haberstadt, Canterbury, Barling (Essex), Salisbury and St Paul's cathedral in London.[66] Traces of balsam exist in the Sancta Sanctorum in the Vatican. Balsam was also employed as a perfumed product in fifteenth-century Italy.[67]

Mercantile archives present more tangible evidence of trade. For example, balsam appears in a document dated 1369 listing the contents of a ship sailing from Alexandria to Genoa. Cases such as this allow one to gauge the relative economic significance of balsam against other high-value commodities. The shipment of 1369 contained goods such as pepper, cinnamon, ginger, saffron and brazil wood. Those with the largest value (as a percentage of the total) are pepper (45.5 per cent), ginger (11.5 per cent) and saffron (3 per cent). By contrast, the precious balsam makes up only c. 0.05 per cent of the total monetary value.[68] This disparity might simply reflect the difficulty of obtaining large quantities of balsam, though it is also a useful reminder that international trade in luxury commodities in this period was much more focused on spices, dyes, sugar and manufactured goods, including silks, glass and metalwork.

Substitutes and Fakes

The high prices fetched for balsam, particularly the oleo-resin, must have stimulated the manufacture and sale of imitations. One aspect of this activity was the legitimate search for other plant oils and resins that were believed to possess similar medicinal properties. This would have been necessary given that the total harvest from the balsam gardens of Matarea can never have fully satisfied the demand. Furthermore, the restrictions placed on the finest balsam by the governments of Egypt exacerbated an already challenging situation in the marketplaces of the Mediterranean. The other aspect is that there were extensive profits to be made by selling to unsuspecting buyers either diluted balsam or out-and-out fakes.[69] Potential purchasers could arm themselves with knowledge in order to tell the real products from the fakes.

The eleventh-century Byzantine physician Simeon Seth records information about the identification of balsam oleo-resin that derives largely from Dioscorides.[70] The ancient scholar's influence is also readily apparent in Arabic pharmacological literature. For example, both al-Ghafiqi and Ibn al-Baytar offer translations of substantial sections of Dioscorides' chapter on balsam, before providing commentaries and additions drawn from the work of later Greek and Arabic scholars.[71] Dioscorides places the relevant remarks directly after his comments on the harvesting process, the volume produced annually, the price, and the smell and taste of the best oleo-resin. He writes that adulteration was achieved with a range of plant oils: terebinth, henna, mastic, lily and *metópion* (an ointment produced in Egypt).[72] Oil of myrtle was also used for this purpose when mixed with honey or wax. There is a warning concerning substitutes for the fruit of balsam; in this case, the culprit is the seed of the ground-pine (Yellow bugle, or *Ajuga chamaepitys*) that grows in the region of Petra in Jordan. This counterfeit could be spotted because 'it is larger, emptier, less strong, and tastes like pepper' while the genuine article, by contrast, would burn the tongue and give off the fine aroma of the balsam oleo-resin. Warnings also appear in books of market law (*ḥisba*), including that of the thirteenth-century Syrian jurist al-Shayzari. Oil of lily might be sold as balsam.[73] Other jurists note the practice of diluting balsam oil (*duhn al-balasān*).[74]

Al-Ghafiqi was not content with simply recording the words of earlier authors. In his book of simples, abridged by the Syrian Christian chronicler Bar Hebraeus (d. 1286), there are comments by the Spanish physician Ibn Juljul (d. c. 994) and others that deal with the issue of differentiating balsam (Arabic: *balasān*) from *bashām*, or 'balm of Mecca' (Chapter 4). Ibn Juljul notes that the chief cause of confusion was the seed/grain of balsam sold by druggists, which he claims came exclusively from the wild *bashām*. The trees of the Egyptian plantation in ʿAyn Shams (Matarea) did not, according to him, bear fruit. Hence, only the wood and oleo-resin were derived from the balsam tree. In his own commentary, al-Ghafiqi disagrees with this interpretation, noting that merchants would often present consignments of balsam wood with the fruit and seeds attached. In his view this indicates that they come from the one type of tree, which he identifies as the balsam cultivated in ʿAyn Shams. He then provides his own description of the tree, likening it to one called *shubrum* (tithymalus; *Euphorbia pithyusa* L.) with small and thin leaves resembling willow or spurge. The fruit form in clusters at the end of the branches and are the same size as peppercorns (but with a different colour). Al-Ghafiqi notes the existence of a plant in Spain that was often mistaken for *bashām*. The seeds of this plant were sold as if they came from the balsam tree.[75]

Ibn al-Baytar also concerns himself with medicinal substitutes, employing a range of Greek and Arabic sources. He argues that balsam could be replaced by ben oil (deriving from the seeds of *Moringa oleifera*, also known as the drumstick tree or horseradish tree), mature olive oil or camphor water. Seed of balsam could be substituted for half its weight in cinnamon or ten times the amount of mace.⁷⁶ The efficacy of ben oil is disputed, however, by ʿAbd al-Latif al-Baghdadi.⁷⁷ On the authority of the Tunisian physician Ibn al-Jazzar (d. 979), Ibn al-Baytar claims that the wood of balsam (*xylobalsamum*) could stand in for its fruit, though more of the former was required to achieve the same medicinal effect.⁷⁸ The seventh-century physician Paul of Aegina also indicates differences between the two, giving oil of myrtle as a substitute for *opobalsamum* and liquid myrrh (stacte) for *carpobalsamum*.⁷⁹

One branch of pre-modern medical literature deals exclusively with the isolation of alternatives to products specified in simple and compound medicines. A work attributed to a medic named Pythagoras (Arabic: Badighuras; fl. sixth or seventh century CE?), which was subsequently translated into Arabic by Hunayn ibn Ishaq (also Chapter 6), concerns itself solely with simple remedies, and offers several substitutes for balsam. Other examples of this genre were produced by the Jewish physician and translator Masarjawayh (fl. late seventh century) and al-Razi (d. 925 or 932). The latter's work is interesting in that balsam also appears as a substitute for other plant-based medicaments.⁸⁰ This suggests that the financial dimension of substitution was not the only criterion driving the creation of such texts.⁸¹

European scholars and travellers also concerned themselves with adulterated balsam and substitutes. For example, Schiltberger notes the dilution of balsam in order to maximise the profits of 'merchants and druggists', and he provides his readers with methods for identifying the true liquid.⁸² These issues took on an additional urgency from the sixteenth century as the supplies of true balsam began to dwindle. The practice of restocking the garden with trees imported from Arabia raised further suspicions about the uniqueness of the species located in the plantation of Matarea. Prosper Alpin's treatise of balsam includes an entire chapter dealing with the markets where balsam could be purchased and the methods used in spotting forgeries. An earlier traveller, Pierre Belon, found seeds and branches of balsam for sale in Cairo, but reports that they had been brought from Arabia.⁸³ Pierre Pomet addressed the important problem of distinguishing the true balsam from others, particularly balsam of Mecca (*bashām*). Balsam of Mecca shared the astringent qualities of its more illustrious relative, and found applications in the treatment of venereal disease. Pomet was also aware of other substitutes that had come onto the market since the European colonisation of South

America.[84] Charas mentions balsam of Peru, relating that there was no way to tell it apart from Egyptian balsam (though elsewhere in his work he describes the American oleo-resin as 'inferiour in goodness and beauty'). For medical purposes, such as the making of treacles, he allows that *opobalsamum* could be substituted one-to-one with oil of nutmeg. For the seeds of balsam Charas recommends the use of cubeb (or tailed pepper; *Piper cubeba*) from Java.[85]

Both Alpin and Charas provide tests for balsam, including placing a drop into milk and passing the oleo-resin through a cloth.[86] Dioscorides is the principal source concerning the detection of fraudulent copies of balsam (translated in Chapter 4).[87]

This is not the only point in the book where Dioscorides discusses the question of adulteration; a total of forty examples have been identified with seven types of test employed in order to root out the fraudulent products. As Ernst Stieb has demonstrated, these range from those using the senses – tactile qualities, visual properties, smell and taste – to botanical examinations of specific components of given plants. Testing could involve comparative observations with other species, a pharmacological measurement of strength and efficacy, and a chemicophysical demonstration.[88] The last of these is relevant in the case of balsam, both *opobalsamum* and *carpobalsamum*, for some of the most valuable properties could not be discerned simply through an assessment of the colour, texture, smell or taste. As John Riddle observes, the tests outlined by Dioscorides aim to establish a central characteristic of balsam: that it had a latex base (Chapter 4).[89]

The tests outlined by Dioscorides appear in numerous sources of the medieval period, either in part or quoted in their entirety. Other claims were also made for balsam when it was placed in liquids.[90] The details could well have been perplexing for consumers, and the confusions are suggested in the elaborate account found in the fictitious travels of Sir John Mandeville. Adulteration is dealt with in some detail with the anonymous author listing aromatic plant products – turpentine, cloves and spikenard – that were commonly mixed with balsam. The 'Saracens' are the chief offenders, passing off adulterated liquids to fool Christians.[91] The pure product could be ascertained by its colour and fine aroma, and the potential consumer was to avoid those that were 'cloudy or red or blackish'. Further tests could also be administered. The author continues:

if you place a little balm in your palm [and hold it] toward the sun, if it is good and pure, you will not be able to bear holding your hand in the sun's heat. Also, take a little balm with the point of a knife and touch it to flame and if it burns that is a good sign. Then take a drop of balm as well and put it into a bowl or goblet where there is goat's milk, and if it is real balm the milk will immediately curdle and congeal. Or place a drop in clear water in a silver goblet or in a clean basin and move it vigorously with the clear water, and if the balm is genuine the water will not be cloudy, and if it is adulterated the water will become cloudy. And if the balm is pure it will sink to the bottom of the vessel as if it were quicksilver [mercury], for pure balm is twice as heavy as adulterated balm.[92]

Presumably readers in the fourteenth century and later would seldom have had the chance to evaluate the usefulness of the tests outlined by the author of Mandeville's travels. Physicians and others who had a professional interest in establishing the purity of balsam must have placed greater weight on scientific writing deriving from Dioscorides. Merchants may well have gained information by oral transmission. What comes through clearly from the account in Mandeville is that the high commercial and cultural value of the balsam of Matarea stimulated the creation of a web of data, some of which possessed a demonstrable validity.

Notes
1. Felix Fabri, *Evagatorium*, III, p. 16. Translated in French as Fabri, *Voyage en Égypte*, I, pp. 393–4.
2. Robert Southey, trans., *The Chronicle of the Cid, Translated from the Spanish by Robert Southey with an Introduction by U. S. Pritchett and Illustrations by René Ben Sussan* (Haarlem: Joh. Enschedé en Zonen for the Members of the Limited Editions Club, 1958), p. 172; *The Chronicle of the Cid* (London: Longman, Hurst, Rees and Orme, 1808), pp. 330–1. This translation is based on sixteenth-century versions of this popular epic.
3. His identity was later conflated with the Mongol conquerors of Asia, and faint echoes can be detected in the first European reports of the victory of the Central Asian warlord Temür (Tamerlane) over the Ottoman sultan Bayezid I Yıldırım at the battle of Sivas in 1400. On the legend of Prester (or Presbyter) John, see Igor de Rachewiltz, *Prester John and Europe's Discovery of East Asia*

(Canberra: Australia National University Press, 1972); Robert Silverberg, *The Realm of Prester John* (Garden City, NY: Doubleday, 1972). On the oral reports about the battle of Sivas, see Donald Nicol, *The Last Centuries of Byzantium, 1261–1453*, second edition (Cambridge: Cambridge University Press, 1993), pp. 313–15.

4. Berthold Laufer, *Sino-Iranica*, pp. 429–34.
5. On trade between China, the Middle East and Europe during the medieval period, see Donald Richards, ed., *Islam and the Trade of Asia: A Colloquium*, Papers on Islamic History 2 (Oxford: Bruno Cassirer and University of Pennsylvania Press, 1970); David Whitehouse, 'Chinese porcelain in medieval Europe,' *Medieval Archaeology* 16 (1972): 63–78; David Whitehouse, 'Chinese stoneware from Siraf: the earliest finds', in Norman Hammond, ed., *South Asian Archaeology: Papers from the First International Conference of South Asian Archaeologists Held in the University of Cambridge* (Park Ridge, NJ: Noyes, 1973), pp. 241–55; Marco Spallanzani, *Ceramiche orientali a Firenze nel Rinascimento* (Florence: Cassa di Risparmio di Firenze, 1978); Janet Abu Lughod, *Before European Hegemony*; Ellen Laing, 'A report on the Western Asian glassware in the Far East', *Bulletin of the Asia Institute* New Series 5 (1991): 109–21; John Carswell, *Blue and White*.
6. For discussions on the circulation of balsam in the pre-modern world, see Wilhelm Heyd, *Histoire du commerce du Levant au Moyen Âge*, trans. Furcy Reynaud (1885–6. Reprinted, Leipzig: Harrassowitz, 1923), II, pp. 575–80; Milwright, 'Balsam in the mediaeval Mediterranean'.
7. Ludovico di Varthema, *The Travels of Ludovico di Varthema in Egypt, Syria, Arabia Deserta and Arabia Felix, Persia, India, and Ethiopia*, A.D. *1503 to 1508*, trans. John Jones and ed. George Badger, Works issued by the Hakluyt Society (London: Hakluyt Society, 1863), p. 40.
8. Al-'Umari, *L'Égypte, la Syrie, le Ḥiğāz et le Yémen*, p. 68.
9. Von Sudheim, *Description of the Holy Land*, pp. 68–9. Similar observations are made earlier by Oliver of Paderborn. See Gavignan, trans., *Christian Society and the Crusades*, pp. 117–18 (chapter 60).
10. Al-'Umari, *L'Égypte, la Syrie, le Ḥiğāz et le Yémen*, p. 68. The same basic information is repeated verbatim by the fifteenth-century Egyptian author al-Maqrizi. See his *al-Khiṭaṭ*, IV, p. 100.
11. Notker, in Einhard and Notker the Stammerer, *Two Lives of Charlemagne*, trans. Lewis Thorpe (London: Penguin Classics, 1986), pp. 145–6.
12. Ghada al-Hijjawi al-Qaddumi, trans., *Book of Gifts and Rarities: Kitāb al-Hadāya*

wa al-Tuḥaf, Harvard Middle Eastern Monographs 29 (Cambridge, MA: Harvard University Press, 1996).

13. On gift-giving, see Anthony Cutler, 'Gifts and gift exchange as aspects of Byzantine, Arab, and related economies', *Dumbarton Oaks Papers* 55 (2001): 247–78; Linda Komaroff, ed., *Gifts of the Sultan: The Arts of Giving at the Islamic Courts* (Los Angeles: Los Angeles Museum of Art, 2011).
14. Al-Qaddumi, trans., *Book of Gifts and Rarities*, p. 77, no. 31.
15. For example, A.-M. Chazaud, 'Inventaire et comptes de la succession d'Eudes, comte de Nevers (Acre, 1266)', *Mémoires de la Société Nationale des Antiquaires de France* 32, ser. 4, vol. 2 (1871): 192, 201.
16. See the translator's notes in Schiltberger, *Bondage and Travels*, pp. 207–9, n. 23, 23a. See also Louis Villecourt, 'Un manuscrit arabe', p. 6.
17. Taqi al-Din Ahmad b. ʿAli al-Maqrizi, *Kitāb al-mawāʿiẓ waʾl-iʿtibār fī dhikr al-khiṭaṭ waʾl-āthār* (Bulaq: El-Amariya Press, 1270–2/1853–5), II, p. 68.
18. ʿAziz Atiya, *Egypt and Aragon: Embassies and Diplomatic Correspondence between 1300 and 1330 A.D.*, Abhandlungen für die Kunde des Morgenlandes 23.7 (Leipzig: F. A. Brockhaus, 1938). The references to the Christian relics occur during the sixth and seventh embassies. See pp. 44–6, 56–7. For specific references to balsam, see pp. 28, 32 (third embassy).
19. Atiya, *Egypt and Aragon*, pp. 20–5. Also Behrens-Abouseif, *Practicing Diplomacy*, pp, 99, 100.
20. Behrens-Abouseif, *Practicing Diplomacy*, p. 96.
21. Ibid. pp. 47–8, 51, 54–5. The Ethiopian gift (p. 51) mentions two bottles of *al-zayt al-ṭayyib* (literally, 'good oil'), that Behrens-Abouseif tentatively identifies as balsam. It would, of course, have been a suitable gift to send to a Christian ruler because of the role of balsam in the creation of the oil of consecration (see Chapter 8).
22. The dried flesh of the skink was used in the preparation of Mithridatium. See Adrienne Mayor, *The Poison King: The Life and Legends of Mithradates, Rome's Deadliest Enemy* (Princeton, NJ and Oxford: Princeton University Press, 2009), p. 242.
23. John Wansbrough, 'A Mamluk commercial treaty concluded with the Republic of Florence in 894/1489', in Samuel Stern, ed., *Documents from Islamic Chanceries*, Oriental Studies: First Series 3 (Oxford: Bruno Cassirer, 1965), pp. 39–41.
24. On this painting, see Julian Raby, *Venice, Dürer and the Oriental Mode*, Hans Huth Memorial Studies 1 (London: Islamic Art Publications, 1982), pp. 55–65;

Caroline Campbell and Alan Chong, eds, *Bellini and the East* (London and Boston: Yale University Press for the National Gallery Company, London, and the Isabella Stewart Gardner Museum, 2005), pp. 22–3.

25. Heyd, *Histoire du commerce*, II, p. 679; Arthur Lane, *Italian Porcelain* (London: Faber & Faber, 1954), p. 1; Nurhan Atasoy and Julian Raby, *Iznik. The Pottery of Ottoman Turkey* (London: Thames & Hudson, 1989), p. 28; John Wansbrough, 'A Mamluk letter of 877/1473', *Bulletin of the School of Oriental and African Studies* 24 (1961): 209; Sanudo, *I diarii Marino Sanuto*, II, p. 605; V, p. 92. Also Marcus Milwright, 'Pottery in written sources of the Ayyubid-Mamluk period (*c*.567–923/1171–1517)', *Bulletin of the School of Oriental and African Studies* 62.3 (1999): 516.

26. Jean-Charles Davillier, *Les origines de la porcelaine en Europe* (Paris: Librairie de l'Art, 1882), pp. 9–10 (quoting Matthieu de Couchy, ms. 434, Sorbonne); Behrens-Abouseif, *Practicing Diplomacy*, pp. 106, 117.

27. On the economic decline of the late Mamluk period, see Eliyahu Ashtor, *Levant Trade in the Later Middle Ages* (Princeton, NJ: Princeton University Press, 1983), pp. 433–512; Petry, *Protectors or Praetorians?*; Jean-Claude Garcin, 'The regime of the Circassian Mamlūks', in Carl Petry, ed., *The Cambridge History of Egypt, Volume I: Islamic Egypt, 640–1517* (Cambridge: Cambridge University Press, 2008), pp. 296–9; Rosamond Mack, *Bazaar to Piazza: Islamic Trade and Italian Art, 1300–1600* (Berkeley, CA and London: University of California Press, 2002), pp. 20–2.

28. Elias Muhanna, 'The Sultan's new clothes: Ottoman-Mamluk gift exchange in the fifteenth century', *Muqarnas* 27 (2010): 189–207; Behrens-Abouseif, *Practicing Diplomacy*, pp. 84–94.

29. Muhanna, 'The Sultan's new clothes', pp. 192–3 (*duhn balasān ṣamr baṭar* [?]), 194 (*raṭl zujāj ḍammahā duhn al-balasān*); Behrens-Abouseif, *Practicing Diplomacy*, pp. 87–8.

30. Julian Raby, '*Terra Lemnia*', pp. 316–17; Ernest Charrière, *Négociations de la France dans le Levant* (Paris: Imprimerie Nationale, 1848–60), III, p. 558. He served as Grand Vizier to Sultan Süleyman between 1544–53 and 1555 until his death in 1561.

31. Pliny, *Natural History*, 12:117–18.

32. Dioscorides, *De materia medica*, 1:19; Pliny, *Natural History*, 12:111, 123; Cotton and Eck, 'Ein Staatsmonopol'.

33. Pliny, *Natural History*, 12:111. In Pliny's time the *sestertius*, or *sesterce*, was the largest copper denomination and was worth one quarter of a *denarius*.

34. Al-Biruni, *Book of Pharmacy*, I, p. 74 (citing al-Khutaybi).
35. Lopez, 'Mohammed and Charlemagne', 26–8. On the decline of papyrus and the rise of paper, see Joseph von Karabacek, *Arab Paper*, trans. Don Baker and Suzy Dittmar (London: Archetype and the Don Baker Memorial Fund, 2001), pp. 5, 8–13; Bloom, *Paper before Print*, pp. 27–9, 42–5.
36. Duchesne, ed., *Le Liber Pontificalis*, I, pp. 174, 177–8, 183; Raymond Davis, trans., *The Book of the Pontiffs (Liber Pontificalis): The Ancient Biographies of the First Ninety Roman Bishops to AD 715* (Liverpool: Liverpool University Press, 1983), pp. 17, 19, 20. Also Atchley, *Use of Incense*, p. 141.
37. Atchley, *Use of Incense*, pp. 144–5.
38. Edwin Freshfield, trans., *Roman Law in the Later Roman Empire: Byzantine Guilds, Professional and Commercial. Ordinances of Leo VI, c. 895 from the Book of the Eparch* (Cambridge: Cambridge University Press, 1938), p. 30 (chapter X).
39. Ibid. pp. 19–20 (chapter V). Also Marlia Mango, 'Byzantine maritime trade with the East (4th–7th centuries)', *Aram* 8, 1–2 (1996): 148. On Byzantine trade, see also Cécile Morrisson, ed., *Trade and Markets in Byzantium, Dumbarton Oaks Byzantine Symposia and Colloquia* (Washington, DC: Dumbarton Oaks Research Library and Collection, 2012).
40. Voigts, 'Anglo-Saxon plant remedies', p. 260 (citing the *Leechbook* of Bald). The other eastern Mediterranean/Middle Eastern ingredients mentioned by Elias are scammony, ammoniacum, gum tragacanth, galbanum and petroleum. On the exchange of such commodities in early medieval Europe, see Voigts' comments on pp. 259–61.
41. John Clark, 'Medieval enamelled glass from London', *Medieval Archaeology* 28 (1983): 152–6; David Whitehouse, 'Islamic pottery and Christian Europe from the tenth to the fifteenth century. The thirteenth Gerald Dunning Memorial lecture', *Medieval Ceramics* 21 (1997): 3–12; Andrew Petersen, 'The archaeology of Islam in Britain: Recognition and potential', *Antiquity* 82.318 (2008): 1080–92; Milwright, 'Pottery in written sources', pp. 506–7; Marcus Milwright, *An Introduction to Islamic Archaeology*, New Edinburgh Islamic Surveys (Edinburgh: Edinburgh University Press, 2010), p. 167.
42. Arthur Lane, 'The Gagnières-Fonthill vase: A Chinese porcelain of about 1300', *The Burlington Magazine* 103.697 (1961): 124–33; Whitehouse, 'Chinese porcelain'.
43. Curt Beck and Larry Moray, 'Organic residues', in Donald Whitcomb and Janet Johnson, eds, *Quseir al-Qadim, 1978: Preliminary Report* (Princeton, NJ:

American Research Center in Egypt, 1979), pp. 253–6 (see particularly p. 254). My thanks to Katherine Strange Burke for alerting me to this report.

44. Li Guo, *Commerce, Culture, and Community: The Arabic Documents of Quseir*, Islamic History and Civilization: Studies and Texts 52 (Leiden and Boston: Brill, 2004), pp. 43–4. Other items on the same list – *fāghira* (a type of prickly ash of the *Zanthoxylum* genus) and *maḫlab* (*Prunus mahaleb* L.) – have been demonstrated to possess medicinal properties, and appear in ancient and Islamic pharmacological texts.

45. George F. Bass et al., *Serçe Limanı. Volume 2: The Glass of an Eleventh-Century Shipwreck* (College Station, TX: Texas A&M University Press, 2009).

46. Curiously, balsam is absent from the published records of Mediterranean trade in the Geniza archive. This suggests that balsam was not an important commodity for Jewish merchants between the eleventh and the thirteenth centuries. See Shlomo Goitein and Paula Sanders, *A Mediterranean Society: The Jewish Communities of the Arab World as portrayed in the Documents of the Cairo Geniza. Volume VI: Cumulative Indices* (Berkeley, CA and Los Angeles: University of California Press, 1993, reprinted 1999).

47. On these vessels, see André Grabar, *Ampoules de Terre Sainte (Monza-Bobbio)* (Paris: C. Klinksieck, 1958). Also: David Buckton, ed., *Byzantium: Treasures of Byzantine Art* (London: British Museum Press, 1994), pp. 188–9, cat. no. 203; Helen Evans and Brandie Ratliff, eds, *Byzantium and Islam: Age of Transition, 7th–9th Century* (New Haven, CT and London: Yale University Press and Metropolitan Museum of Art, 2012), pp. 91–2, cat. no. 59.

48. Pierre Pomet, *Histoire générale des drogues*, p. 276. Translated as *A Compleat History of Druggs: Written in French by Monsieur Pomet, Chief Druggist to the Present French King; to which is added what is further observable on the same subject, from Messrs. Lemery, and Tournefort, divided into three classes, vegetable, animal and mineral . . .*, trans. J. Browne (London: R. Bonwicke et al., 1712), pp. 204–5.

49. Pomet, *A Compleat History of Druggs*, p. 204.

50. Ibid. p. 205.

51. Gerard, *The Herball*, pp. 1343–6 (book III, chapter 139).

52. Quoted in Jerry Stannard, '". . . findet man in den apotecken": Notices concerning the available of medicamenta in medieval *Fachliteratur*', in Peter Dilg, ed., *Perspektiven der Pharmaziegeschichte: Festschrift für Rudolf Schmitz zum 65. Geburstag* (Graz: Akademische Verlag, 1983), p. 371, n. 4. Also mentioned in this list is *petrolium*.

53. Christophe Harant de Polzic in Brejnik, trans., *Voyage en Égypte*, p. 88. On the availability of commodities in fifteenth-century German pharmacies, see Stannard, 'Medicamenta in medieval *Fachliteratur*'.
54. Moyse Charas, *The Royal Pharmacopoea*, part 2, book 1, pp. 144–5. This work is a translation of the French original, published in 1676.
55. Pomet, *A Compleat History of Druggs*, p. 205.
56. Fabri, *Evagatorium in Terrae Sanctae*, III, p. 15; Fabri, *Voyage en Égypte*, I, p. 391.
57. 'Abd al-Latif al-Baghdadi, *The Eastern Key*, pp. 44 (Arabic), 45 (English).
58. Ibn Iyas, *Die Chronik des Ibn Ijas*, IV, p. 149; Francesco Balducci Pegolotti, *Pratica della mercatura*, ed. Allan Evans (Cambridge, MA: Harvard University Press, 1936), pp. 70, 286, 414.
59. Ambroise, *The Crusade of Richard Lion-Heart*, trans. Merton Jerome Hubert with notes by John La Monte (New York: Columbia University Press, 1941), p. 370.
60. For example, see comments in Alpin, *Histoire du Baulme*, pp. 58–69.
61. Pegolotti, *Pratica della mercatura*, pp. 295, 363, 365; Ashtor, 'Levantine sugar industry', p. 97.
62. Document cited in Eliyahu Ashtor, *Histoire des prix et des salaires dans l'Orient médiéval*, École Pratique des Hautes Études – Vie Section. Monnaie. Prix. Conjoncture 8 (Paris: SEVPEN, 1969), p. 338.
63. Jacques Savary de Brûlons, *Dictionnaire universel de commerce* (Paris: Jacques Estienne, 1723–30), III, p. 399. See also comments in I, pp. 310–11; III, pp. 54–5.
64. Schiltberger, *Bondage and Travels*, p. 60. For another source mentioning the sale of balsam from Matarea, see Michael Heberer, *Voyages en Égypte de Michael Heberer von Bretten, 1585–1586*, trans. Oleg Volkoff, Collection des Voyageurs Occidentaux en Égypte 18 (Cairo: Institut Français d'Archéologie Orientale, 1976), p. 135.
65. For example, Schiltberger, *Bondage and Travels*, p. 92. He writes of the Armenian church that 'the patriarch gives the sultan a large price for the balm, which he sends to his bishopric'.
66. Avinoam Shalem, *Islam Christianized: Islamic Portable Objects in Medieval Church Treasuries of the Latin West* (Frankfurt-am-Main: Peter Lang, 1996), pp. 21–2.
67. Grisar and Dreger, *Die Römische Kapelle Sancta Sanctorum*, pp. 89–97; Evelyn Welch, *Art and Society in Italy, 1350–1500*, Oxford History of Art (Oxford: Oxford University Press, 1997), p. 44, fig. 18.

68. Document quoted in Danielle Jacquart and Françoise Micheau, *La Médecine arabe et l'Occident médiévale*, Collection Islam-Occident 7 (Paris: Maisonneuve and Larose, 1990), p. 226.
69. An ancient trade in medicaments, see Vivian Nutton, 'The drug trade in Antiquity', *Journal of the Royal Society of Medicine* 78.2 (1985): 138–45 (on the adulteration and imitation of expensive plant and mineral imports, see pp. 142–4).
70. Simeon Seth, *Syntagma per elementorum ordinem, de alimentorum facultate* (Petrum Pernam: Basle 1561), pp. 19–20. These include the methods used for detecting fakes.
71. Dioscorides 1:19 (for Lily Beck's translation, see Chapter 4); Abu al-Faraj (Bar Hebraeus), *Book of Simple Drugs*, pp. 245–8; Ibn al-Baytar, *al-Mufrāda*, I, pp. 107–9.
72. On this ointment, see Dioscorides, *De materia medica*, 1:59. For a translation, see Dioscorides, *De materia medica*, trans. Beck, p. 43.
73. 'Abd al-Rahman b. Nasr al-Shayzari, *The Book of the Market Inspector:* Nihāyat al-rutba fī ṭalab al-ḥisba (Utmost Authority in the Pursuit of Ḥisba), trans. Ronald Buckley, Journal of Semitic Studies Supplement 9 (Oxford and New York: Oxford University Press, 1999), p. 68. For further comments on the identification of balsam and its substitutes from a fourteenth-century Egyptian source, see Louis Villecourt, trans., 'Le livre du chrême. Ms. Paris arabe 100', *Le Muséon: Revue des Études Orientales* 41 (1928): 70.
74. For example, see the Moroccan scholar Muhammad b. Abi Muhammad al-Saqati, *Un manuel hispanique de hisba. Traité d'Abu 'Abd Allah Muhammad b. Abi Muhammad as-Sakati de Malaga sur la surveillance des corporations et la répression des fraudes en Espagne musulmane*, ed. and trans., Georges Colin and Evariste Lévi-Provencal, Institut des Hautes-Études Marocaines Publications 21 (Rabat: Institut des Hautes-Études Marocaines, 1931), p. 42.
75. Abu al-Faraj (Bar Hebraeus), 'The Book of Simple Drugs', pp. 247–8. On the sale of *bashām* in early-nineteenth-century Mecca, see 'Ali Bey 'Abbasi, *Travels of Ali Bey*, I, p. 112 (discussed more fully in Chapter 4).
76. Ibn al-Baytar, *al-Mufrāda*, I, p. 109.
77. 'Abd al-Latif al-Baghdadi, *The Eastern Key*, pp. 44 (Arabic), 45 (English). Oil of nutmeg is another product that is suggested as a substitute for balsam. See Charas, *The Royal Pharmacopoea*, pp. 134, 138–9.
78. Ibn al-Baytar, *al-Mufrāda*, I, p. 109.
79. Paul of Aegina, *The Seven Books of Paulus Aegineta*, trans. with commentary by Francis Adams (London: Sydenham Society, 1844–7), 7:25 (III, p. 604).

80. These texts are collected in Martin Levey, *Substitute Drugs in Early Arabic Medicine with Special Reference to the Texts of Masarjawaih, al-Razi, and Pythagoras*, Veröffentlichungen der Internationalen Gesellschaft für Geschichte der Pharmazie. Neue Folge 37 (Stuttgart: Wissenschaftliche Verlagsgesellschaft, 1971), pp. 16, 42, 51. The substitutes comprise cassia bark cinnamon and fennel for balsam berries (p. 16); cassia bark cinnamon for balsam wood (p. 16); oil of screw pine, coconut and old olive oil for 'balm of Gilead' (p. 16); oil of radish for balsam oil (p. 42); and larch oil, coconut oil and old olive oil for balsam oil (p. 51). Also 'balm of Gilead' appears as a substitute for black and white naphtha (p. 30), while oil of balsam is a substitute for Oriental anacardium (p. 49).
81. On al-Razi, see Manfred Ullmann, *Islamic Medicine*, Edinburgh Islamic Surveys 11 (Edinburgh: Edinburgh University Press, 1978, reprinted 1997), pp. 36–8, 43–4, 82–5, 108–9; Peter Pormann and Emilie Savage-Smith, *Medieval Islamic Medicine* (Washington, DC: Georgetown University Press, 2007), pp. 115–19.
82. Schiltberger, *Bondage and Travels*, pp. 60–1. He writes that a drop of genuine balsam placed on one's hand would grow very hot if exposed to the sun, a drop placed on a knife would burn if placed over a fire, and that a silver cup filled with goat's milk would curdle if a drop was placed into it.
83. Pierre Belon du Mans, *Voyage en Égypte*, p. 111a.
84. Pomet, *A Compleat History of Druggs*, pp. 204, 205–6.
85. Charas, *The Royal Pharmacopoea*, pp. 144–5. On the different types of balsam that were available, see also Savary, *Dictionnaire universel*, I, pp. 310–11; Denis Diderot and Jean d'Alembert, eds, *Encylopédie, ou dictionnaire raisonné des sciences, des arts, et des métiers* (Paris: Briasson et al., 1751–80), II, pp. 163–6, 509, 510–11.
86. Alpin, *Plantes d'Égypte*, I, pp. 80–1 [55]; Charas, *The Royal Pharmacopoea*, p. 143.
87. Dioscorides, *De materia medica* 1:19.
88. Ernst Stieb, 'Drug adulteration and its detection in the writings of Theophrastus, Dioscorides and Pliny', *Journal Mondial de Pharmacie* 2 (1958): 628–34.
89. John Riddle, *Dioscorides on Pharmacy and Medicine*, pp. 75–7.
90. For example, Fabri, *Evagatorium*, III, p. 17.
91. Higgins, trans., *The Book of John Mandeville*, pp. 31–2. By comparison, Fabri lists the oils of terebinth, nard, privet, lentisk, balans, myrtle and galbanum as common adulterants for balsam. See Fabri, *Evagatorium*, III, p. 18; Fabri, *Voyage en Égypte*, I, p. 397.
92. Higgins, trans., *The Book of John Mandeville*, p. 32.

6

Balsam in Medicine: From Greek to Arabic

Even after the disappearance of the last specimen in Matarea in 1615, the reputation of balsam as a medicament remained strong in Egypt. This is captured well by the surgeon and embalmer Thomas Greenhill (d. 1740):

> There is no medicine more generally us'd by the *Egyptians* than the *True Balsam*, which they esteem as a kind of Panacea for all Diseases, both external and internal, curing therewith diverse sorts of Wounds, as also the bitings of venomous Creatures. They use it moreover as a Preservative against the Plague, and to drive away Agues or Fevers that proceed from Putrefaction.[1]

Similarly enthusiastic appreciations can be found in travel accounts (Chapter 1). Travellers mix together plausible medical information along with more fanciful claims; for example, that a drop of balsam dropped into the eye would conserve its state permanently.[2] Greenhill overplays his hand in his assertion that the 'true balsam' was a type of panacea, however. It is clear that balsam was not used in the treatment of all illnesses, as the word implies; a survey of the pre-modern medical literature reveals that the products derived from this rare plant were employed in the treatment of a broad, but demarcated range of medical conditions.

The present chapter surveys the earlier medical history of balsam, starting with its appearance in ancient Greek and Latin texts through to the sixth century CE. The second half of the chapter looks at the translation of Greek medical knowledge into Syriac, and then, during the so-called 'Translation Movement', into Arabic. This process of translation was not, of course, a passive activity, and new observations relating to the employment of balsam were made during this time. In order to provide context for this historical survey, the first section of this chapter evaluates briefly research on the intrinsic medicinal qualities of tree resins.

Medicinal Characteristics of Tree Resins

One of the recurrent problems encountered by scholars studying the medical traditions of the ancient and medieval worlds is that of the efficacy, or otherwise, of the simple and compound medicines described by physicians. There can be little doubt that, for the most part, the authors discussed in this chapter believed sincerely that their medicines would alleviate the symptoms of the illnesses and physical complaints they sought to treat. To modern readers, however, much of what they claim looks outlandish, likely to do as much harm as good. To what extent, therefore, did the medicines described in the Greek, Latin, Syriac and Arabic texts actually help in the treatment of disease? Robert Irwin questions whether a patient prior to the advent of modern medical practices in the late seventeenth century would have been better off consulting a physician schooled in Galenic scholarship or the herbal knowledge of a local 'wise woman'.[3] Should we then dismiss this entire corpus of ancient and medieval scholarship as no more than elaborate hocus-pocus, studying it solely as a formative phase in the evolution of scientific thought? This is not a question that admits to a simple answer, though it is possible to make some general observations relating to the medicinal applications of plant resins based on modern scientific research.

As noted in Chapter 3, there is an early reference to 'balm' (*zori*) from the lands of Gilead.[4] Whether or not this 'balm of Gilead' is actually balsam is less important for present purposes than the fact that the reference in Jeremiah implies the usefulness of the substance in the treatment of wounds. Resins are specified in the creation of salves for wounds in the Ebers papyrus, an Egyptian medical text written in c. 1550 BCE.[5] Requests for supplies of myrrh in other documents of the second millennium BCE suggest that it was much used in military medicine. A specific reference to this use of myrrh appears in the description by Herodotus of a naval battle between the Greeks and the Persians in 480 BCE.[6] By contrast, the references in the Old Testament laud myrrh as a fragrance.[7]

Guido Majno suggests some of the reasons why myrrh and other tree resins have enjoyed such a long history in the treatment of wounds and other skin complaints.⁸ Two of his ideas relate to observable characteristics of the resins themselves. First, they are generated when the bark of a tree is cut, and the resin fills up and 'heals' the fissure. Thus, it would not represent a major leap of faith to assume that it might have the same effect upon the cuts made into human skin. Second, resins do not readily decay. Again, by analogy, one might conclude that the placing of a tree resin on a wound might render it in a state of stasis. A third characteristic of resins, and particularly the oleo-resins, is that they exude a powerful odour. Prior to the invention of modern antisepsis by Joseph Lister (d. 1912), one of the most unpleasant aspects of wounds was the smell; the powerful aromas emanating from resins would, at least, counteract this problem.⁹

The last idea advanced by Majno is at first sight the most straightforward of all: resins were employed by the ancients in the treatment of wounds because they actually aided in the process of healing. In order to test the claims made for myrrh as an antiseptic agent, a bacteriologist placed a suspension of myrrh on a petri dish with cultures of three bacteria, *Staphylococcus aureus* (a common bacterium in wounds), *Bacillus subtilis* and *E. coli*. Myrrh was an effective bacteriostatic against the first two strains. Only *E. coli* remained unaffected. This property relates to the presence of volatile oils that produce the aromatic qualities of many resins. The greater the percentage of volatile oils the more intense the antiseptic effect. Myrrh is, in fact, not highly perfumed, but others, such as balsam of Peru (or Tolu) are sufficiently potent in antisepsis to warrant their inclusion in modern medicine.¹⁰

Modern analytical processes confirm the antiseptic properties observed by physicians and scholars in earlier historical periods. This is certainly not the only occasion when such causal links can be claimed. For example, Vitruvius (d. after 15 CE) remarks that terracotta pipes were healthier than lead pipes for the transport of water. He reasons that the water passing through the former tasted better, and also notes the unwholesome pallor of the skins of lead sheet workers.¹¹ Vitruvius did not know about the physiological damage caused by the ingestion of lead, but he was able to correlate the physical symptoms of lead workers (their skin colour) with the likely cause (long-term exposure to the metal). That said, it did not stop the Romans making extensive use of lead in numerous aspects of daily life. Returning to medical practice, John Riddle discusses the efficacy of garlic in the thinning of blood. When fresh, this plant has been found in modern experiments to contain active agents that inhibit the aggregation of platelets in the blood. Some active agents in fresh garlic are able to withstand the enzymes in the digestive system and pass into the bloodstream. Given this characteristic it is intriguing that Dioscorides should claim that garlic 'cleans the arteries'.[12]

The interpretation of the comments of Dioscorides on the benefits of garlic are problematic. While Dioscorides connects the arteries and garlic, he was ignorant of the primary function of the arteries in the circulation of blood; it was commonly believed in Dioscorides' time that the veins contained blood but that the arteries contained largely air, and only a little blood.[13] Hence, the ancient scholar was hardly in a position either to identify the role of garlic as an inhibitor of platelet aggregation or to understand the dangers of cholesterol. Riddle acknowledges these difficulties, but points to the role of external symptoms in the pre-modern diagnosis and treatment. Ancient medics were in a position to observe shortness of breath, one of the symptoms of arteriosclerosis. This was perhaps significant given the belief that the arteries carried the life-giving *pneuma* (air).[14] An association might have been made between the extensive consumption of garlic and the alleviation of shortness of breath. Originating in the realm of folk medicine, such symptomatic relief could then have been picked up by Dioscorides and given a more theoretical foundation.

A chain of events like this is plausible, and it seems likely that ancient scholars did benefit from tried-and-tested remedies. The selection of one positive correlation between ancient and modern medical practice does not explain, however, the longer lists of pharmacological applications that are often attributed to a single plant. The chapter in *De materia medica* on garlic recommends its use as a diuretic, as an antidote to poison, in the treatment of an intestinal parasite (broad worms) and what may be either diarrhoea or amoebic dysentery.[15] Some plants do indeed have a value in the treatment of a wide variety of illnesses, but the ambitious lists found in ancient and medieval medicine are to be viewed with caution. The classification of the intrinsic characteristics of 'simple medicines' (i.e. single plant, animal, or mineral products) according to their respective degrees of heat, coldness, dryness and wetness may have offered some logic to the minds of ancient and medieval scholars, but these distinctions have no basis in modern medical practice. If the claimed values of simples are not always to be trusted, additional difficulties are presented by compound medicines. Here one encounters sometimes dizzyingly long lists of ingredients in which the active qualities of a single substance might well be dissipated or counteracted by one or more of the other ingredients. This problem is particularly evident in the preparation of antidotes (Chapter 7).

Medical authorities of the stature of Dioscorides, Galen and al-Razi were neither unintelligent nor credulous. Their scholarship did not merely consist of collating the observations of others, and it would be perverse to assume that they were not passionately concerned with the treatment of illness. Just as Dioscorides could demonstrate a variety of ways to test the authenticity of balsam, so one finds the best physicians and pharmacologists of the pre-modern world seeking ways to test accepted wisdom and finding new applications for simple and compound medicines. One even finds the forerunner of modern case notes in the writings of al-Razi.[16] Whether this effort actually resulted in more effective treatment of disease than might be gained from folk medicine is a more difficult point to resolve.

With these reservations in mind, some comments can be made about the results of clinical experiments using extracts of *Commiphora molmol* (myrrh), *Commiphora gileadensis* ('Mecca balsam') and other species of *Commiphora*. The first of these, myrrh, is employed in traditional medicine for the treatment of inflammation and tumours, and as an antiseptic, an antipyretic, a stimulant and a mouthwash. Some of these claims have been subjected to scientific scrutiny, and myrrh has indeed been found to have anti-inflammatory, antipyretic, antihistaminic and antiarthritic qualities. It was also found to have potential in the treatment of gastric ulcers and tumours. In one experiment mice given regular dosages of myrrh experienced greater weight gain and increased production of red blood cells when compared to a control group. Myrrh was found to have no significant degree of toxicity.[17] Myrrh has been employed in traditional medicine in the Middle East and elsewhere in Asia for the treatment of stomach complaints, and conditions such as tonsillitis, pharyngitis and gingivitis.[18] *Commiphora mukul*, an Indian plant, has also been found to have notable anti-inflammatory qualities when tested on arthritic lesions induced in rats.[19] Experimental data from other species of *Commiphora* indicate the efficacy of oleo-resins as muscle relaxants, anti-inflammatories and analgesics. They may also have hypolipidemic qualities (i.e. reducing levels of blood cholesterol) and inhibit fertility. *Commiphora gileadensis* is still employed in traditional medicine in the Middle East for the alleviation of pain and as a laxative and diuretic. Given in an aqueous extract to rats, *Commiphora gileadensis* had the effect of reducing blood pressure (hypotension) and slowing the heart rate (bradycardia). The researchers concluded that these qualities might well explain the common use of the substance in the treatment of headache, urinary retention and constipation.[20]

Balsam in Ancient Medicine

The extensive corpus of ancient Greek medicine establishes the main areas of treatment in which balsam was commonly employed, either as a simple or as part of a compound drug. Late antique scholars of medicine have left numerous encyclopedic works that gather together and summarise the earlier writing. One somewhat eccentric example of this genre is an anonymous Hermetic collection known as the *Cyranides*. Probably compiled in the fourth century CE, this work remained popular through the medieval period, being translated, either as a whole or in part, into Latin and Old French. Book 5 of the *Cyranides* also provides a short chapter devoted to balsam (*balsámon*). Oddly categorising balsam as a 'herb' (*botáni*) rather than a tree or shrub, the author claims that balsam has heating and drying properties, and that it is efficacious in the treatment of cloudiness of the eye (i.e. glaucoma or cataract), earache, coughing and the spitting up of blood (consumption), pleurisy, pneumonia and the breaking up of kidney stones. It helps in aborting foetuses, facilitating periods and reducing coldness of the womb. In another section of the text, balsam is said to aid in the expulsion of afterbirth. When mixed with wine it is a diuretic, and with honey it could be rubbed onto the skin in order to treat ulcers. Trembling could be treated if the sufferer ingested olive oil and balsam before an attack. Lastly, balsam was also used as an antidote against poisons, particularly the stings of scorpions.[21] Elsewhere balsam is recommended in helping conception and in enhancing sexual pleasure.[22]

If one compares this list of treatments with the chapter on balsam penned by Dioscorides (Chapter 4), considerable points of similarity emerge.[23] The earlier author recognises that balsam can be used for the treatment of ailments of similar organs, or regions of the body, including the eyes, lungs, skin and the female reproductive system. The role of balsam in the counteracting of poison is emphasised in both works. Dioscorides and the *Cyranides* both note that balsam has a heating quality, though the latter also mentions its drying capacity. References to heating and drying locate these books within the tradition of humoral medicine, whereby diseases were understood in relation to imbalances within the body of the four humours: blood, black bile, yellow bile and phlegm. Each humour was associated with an element, its related sensual characteristics, and with a specific organ of the body: air/warm and moist/liver (blood), fire/warm and dry/gall bladder (yellow bile), earth/cold and dry/spleen (black bile) and water/cold and moist/brain and lungs (phlegm). The humoral system was first codified in the writings of Hippocrates (d. c. 370 BCE) and his followers. Aristotle (d. 322 BCE) further elaborated the system, adding behavioural concepts: sensuous pleasure (blood), acquisitive (black bile), moral virtue (yellow bile) and logical investigation (phlegm). In the second century CE the great classical physician Galen established human temperaments as part of this system: sanguine (blood), melancholic (black bile), choleric (yellow bile) and phlegmatic (phlegm). In contrast to the Hippocratic approach, Galen believed that disease was an imbalance of the humours not throughout the body, but rather within an individual organ.[24]

This framework allowed simple medicines to be categorised in the same way (heating, drying, cooling and moistening) with their inherent qualities serving to counteract the excess of a specific humour in part of the body. Simples could possess more than one characteristic (such as cooling and moistening). Dioscorides classifies balsam as a powerful heating agent, but he does not offer a means to quantify this dominant characteristic. A more rigorous system of classification appears in the writings of Galen.[25] According to Galenic pharmacology, balsam is defined as heating to the second degree. Galen and his followers in the antique and medieval periods also believed the products derived from the balsam tree to be drying to the second degree.[26] This greater precision facilitated the employment of agents as simples, but also their more accurate integration into compound medicines. The heating and drying qualities of balsam meant that it addressed illnesses deriving from an excess of cold or moisture in the body. Balsam warms specific organs; for example, compound medicines containing balsam, myrrh, saffron, terebinth and styrax were employed for this purpose and for fighting the inflammations caused by an excess of cold.[27] The drying qualities of *opobalsamum* are indicated by its inclusion in desiccating concoctions, such as the one known as the 'antidote of Esdra'.[28]

The magical and popular qualities of the *Cyranides* exist in equal measure with its employment of the humoral system. Balsam appears in several preparations, but often with outlandish ingredients, including the gall bladders of quail, eagle, vulture and types of fish.[29] These qualities place the text at the fringes of the classical medical tradition, though it clearly draws upon the major authorities. The works of the great compilers of late antiquity – Oribasius (d. 400), Aetius of Amida (fl. sixth century), Alexander of Tralles (d. c. 605) and Paul of Aegina (d. 641) – offer a more conventional picture of the employment of balsam in medical practice. These authors drew heavily on Galen, and other influential physicians and pharmacologists of earlier centuries, and adhered more closely to humoral principles.

Many of the preparations involving balsam in these compilations were applied to the skin in the form of restorative ointments (*acopon*), poultices and plasters. Paul of Aegina lists several of the first category in which balsam plays an active part, though with other plant-based oils, including privet, marjoram, iris and nard, as the major component.[30] These appear in a chapter including warming plasters, and it is likely that the ingredients of the ointments were also meant to warm the skin. Plasters were commonly designed to fight inflammation and pain associated with cold humour. Among these plasters was one called Gallus, attributed to Oribasius. Some of these were for general use, while others were applied to specific parts of the body. For example, one soothing poultice (*malagma*) was intended for chronic inflammations of the abdomen.[31] Paul of Aegina also describes plasters for the healing of wounds, that worked to both dry and bind together the damaged area. Balsam is listed in these contexts for its heating and drying powers.[32]

Dioscorides lists several examples of the employment of balsam in gynaecology. It was suitable for the treatment of 'uterine chills' when combined with a thick ointment (cerate) of roses. It could also be made into a fumigant or be utilised when bathing. The latter activity helped to dilate the cervix and reduce excess moisture. These treatments are consistent with the heating and drying characteristics of balsam. Dioscorides also notes the ability of balsam to 'draw down both the afterbirth and foetuses'.[33] Book 16 of the *Tetrabiblon* of Aetius of Amida is devoted to gynaecology and obstetrics, and provides numerous treatments featuring balsam. The product appears in the composition of fumigants used for aborting the foetus and the removal of the placenta.[34] Balsam appears in two unguents, one using spikenard as its major ingredient and the other wild grapes, and in a suppository that was designed to induce menstruation.[35] Hysteria was attributed in ancient medicine to the strangulation of the uterus. A suppository containing a variety of aromatic resins, spices and other components is recommended by Aetius for the treatment of this condition.[36]

A carved stone seal used for stamping collyria (pastilles that could be dissolved in order to create a medicated eyewash), once in the collection of nineteenth-century gem dealer Bram Hertz, carries the image of the goddess Roma and the words 'Herophili opo[balsamum]'.[37] The first part of this inscription probably refers to the name of the Roman oculist for whom it was carved, though it also evokes the illustrious figure of Herophilus (d. 280 BCE), an Alexandrine scholar who influenced later pharmacological writing.[38] Galen attributes a compound for cataracts and dim sight to one 'Hermophilus', perhaps a corruption of Herophilus.[39] This eye treatment is one of many to contain *opobalsamum* in the Galenic corpus.[40] Dioscorides too was aware of the capacity of balsam to treat cataracts, writing that it could remove 'the elements that cast a shadow over the pupils of the eyes'.[41] Later Greek physicians also include balsam in collyria. For example, Alexander of Tralles recommends it in a treatment for ulceration of the eye, while Paul of Aegina in his medical compendium describes a compound medicine to be used against cataracts.[42] The latter physician also includes a collyrium with balsam for sharpening sight. Aetius of Amida treats lacrimal fistula (an abnormal duct connected to the lacrimal sac of the eye) when it becomes pustulent with a compound remedy comprising equal parts of balsam resin, myrrh, spruce resin, natron scum and colophonium (pine resin), mixed with paste of lily.[43] Most treatments took the form of liquids that were applied in drops to the eye itself, but other techniques are mentioned, including a *xerocollyrium* containing balsam that was applied to the eyelids.[44]

Pliny the Elder makes clear Roman consumers greatly valued balsam for its fine scent (Chapters 2 and 8). Its fame is also registered in the poetry of Virgil (d. 19 BCE) even before the Roman conquest of Palestine. In the *Georgics* he writes:

> Each nation has specific trees. None but the Indies grow black ebony, none but Arabia its sticks of incense. What need is there for me – because you already know it – to mention the fragrant resin exuded by the balsam or the pods of the evergreen acacia?[45]

Medical sources record a variety of perfumes and other scented products.[46] These preparations were not just meant for olfactory pleasure, however, and ancient authorities offer considerable detail about the medical dimensions of scent. Paul of Aegina notes the value of perfume in warding off pestilential disease and describes the perfumes that can act as deobstruents, removing catarrh when inhaled.[47] Balsam appears also in preparations meant for internal consumption. These could take the form of powders, such as one recommended by Alexander of Tralles for the treatment of gallstones and dysuria (painful urination). The same author describes the preparation of pills containing styrax, opium, myrrh, balsam and saffron that were to be taken before sleeping. A variety of medicines aided appetite and digestion.[48] A *picra* (bitter remedy), attributed to Galen, contains *xylobalsamum*, and is meant for gastric issues, including colic.[49] This recipe appears in his chapter on theriacs, though it is worth noting that these functioned as more than antidotes to poisons and animal venoms. For example, Paul of Aegina claims that one theriac is valuable against dysentery, kidney complaints and dimness of sight (presumably cataracts).[50]

Balsam (in the forms of *opobalsamum*, *carpobalsamum* and *xylobalsamum*, and sometimes in combination) appears in numerous Greek recipes for antidotes. In *De antidotis* Galen distinguishes between the three types of antidote destined for internal consumption. These comprise compounds to counteract the effects of poisons, those for counteracting venoms and those which are used to fight ailments. Some antidotes, like Mithridatium and Galene (see below), were held to be effective in all three areas of treatment.[51] The belief in balsam as a potent antidote to venom was widespread in the ancient world. For example, the traveller Pausanias (fl. second century CE) makes a striking claim concerning the balsam trees of Arabia:

> Those vipers in Arabia that nest around the balsam trees (*pálsama*) have, I know, the following peculiarities. The balsams are about as big as a myrtle bush, and their leaves are like those of the herb marjoram (*Origanum marjorana* L.). The vipers of Arabia lodge in certain numbers, larger and smaller, under each tree. For the balsam juice is the food they like most, and moreover they are fond of the shade of the bushes.
>
> So when the time has come for the Arabians to collect the juice of the balsam, each man takes two sticks to the vipers, and by striking them together they drive the vipers away. Kill them they will not, considering them sacred to the balsam. And even if a man should have the misfortune to be bitten by the vipers, though the wound is like the cut of a knife, nevertheless there is no fear from the poison. For as the vipers feed on the most fragrant perfumes, their poison is mitigated and less deadly.[52]

Clearly this account should not be taken literally, but it may well have been folk tales of this nature that encouraged the employment of balsam in antidotes.

Nicander of Colophon (fl. c. 200 BCE) gives perhaps the earliest recipe for a theriac, which is described by him as a general panacea. This preparation contains numerous plant elements, including balsam, along with freshwater crab and curds.[53] One of the most celebrated ancient theriacs was Mithridatium, so named because it had reputedly been taken daily by Mithradates VI Eupator, king of Pontus (r. c. 119–63 BCE) owing to his fear of being poisoned (Fig. 6.1).[54] The many ingredients for the theriac were crushed, then mixed with honey and formed into tablets (troches). In the first century CE Aulus Cornelius Celsus (d. c. 50 CE) records the list of substances required to make Mithridatium along with the required weight of each component.[55]

A piece about the size of an almond was to be taken with wine as an antidote to poisoning. This cannot have been an easy recipe to follow: not only were the weights of each substance strictly specified (a point that Pliny remarks upon with some incredulity),[56] but many were expensive and drawn from diverse regions of the Mediterranean basin and Middle East.[57] The active trade in perfumes and incense from Arabia (Chapter 2) certainly facilitated those wealthy enough to follow Celsus' recipe, however. The Mithridatium

Figure 6.1 Fragmentary head of Mithradates VI Eupator. From Delos, Greece. Musée du Louvre, Paris. Erich Lessing / Art Resource, NY.

recorded by Celsus, Galen and others may have shared many of the ingredients of its illustrious forebear, but it cannot have been identical to that consumed by Mithradates himself. Not only is the original recipe lost,[58] but also it is known that one of the main reasons for its supposed efficacy was the inclusion of minute quantities of toxic plant, animal and mineral compounds. Mithradates discovered that regular and long-term ingestion of tiny doses of specific toxins gradually raises the body's immunity. For example, Pliny records that the blood of Pontic ducks was included in Mithridatium. These ducks, he claimed, fed on hemlock (*Conium maculatum* L.) causing their flesh and blood to become toxic. Other possible inclusions in the original recipe may have been the honey from Pontus (believed to be mildly toxic) and parts of poisonous reptiles such as skinks, salamanders and vipers.[59]

Tree resins, including *opobalsamum*, myrrh, frankincense, turpentine, nard and storax, play a prominent role. Such resins might have aided against poisoning, offering some protection against infection, inflammation, allergic reaction and a rise in body temperature. Oleo-resins of the *Commiphora* genus have been found to act as analgesics, and this quality was also noted by ancient authors in connection to balsam. The same reason would also account for the presence of 'tears of poppy' (opium). Another notable ingredient is the herb hypericum (St John's wort). Experiments have found that it causes the liver to produce an enzyme effective against several toxic compounds.[60] Thus, even without the addition of traces of specific poisons, pastilles of Mithridatium could well have provided limited protection against a range of organic and mineral toxins.

Figure 6.2 Portrait of Emperor Nero from the obverse face of an *aureus*. Drawing: Marcus Milwright.

A later ruler, the Roman emperor Nero (r. 54–68 CE; Fig. 6.2), is associated with the other great ancient theriac: Galene (Greek: *galíni*), meaning 'tranquillity'. Said to have been invented by his personal physician, Andromachus the Elder, Galene may be thought of as a refinement of Mithridatium. According to the accounts of it in *De theriaka ad pisonem*, and other writings by Greek physicians, Andromachus omitted some of the ingredients of the earlier theriac, and added more of his own. This resulted in a compound made up of sixty-four separate elements. Significantly, he added the dried flesh of vipers that was crushed to a powder and combined with the plant-based ingredients before being formed into tablets with honey.[61] A simpler recipe for the so-called 'troches of hedychroum' involved balsam (both *opobalsamum* and *xylobalsamum*) and a range of perfumed plant products, and is frequently mentioned in the medical literature.[62] The manufacture of theriacs evolved into a major industry in late medieval Europe (Chapter 7).

Balsam in Syriac Medicine

Scholars in the Middle East had been translating Greek scientific treatises into Syriac since the fourth century. The greatest late antique Syriac translator was Sergius of Resh 'Ayna (d. 536). Sergius worked on both philosophical and medical literature, the latter subject dominated by the works of Galen.[63] Other prominent scholars of medicine responsible for translations into Syriac include Jacob of Edessa and Yahya ibn Sarafyun (fl. ninth century). The first of these is credited with an original work on uroscopy, while the latter's reference work on medicine enjoyed wide circulation when translated into Arabic and Latin.[64]

A wide-ranging multi-volume Syriac text known as the *Book of Medicines* contains numerous compound medicines and treatments involving products of the balsam tree. The undated text contains material that can be placed in the sixth or seventh century.[65] The sources of information are diverse, ranging from folk medicine to the works of Galen. Balsam appears in some uncomplicated remedies: warm oil of balsam poured into the ears to cure diseases and a mixture of pounded balsam wood and honey for persistent coughs. For colds and 'protracted ailments of the head' a mixture of wax, oil of nard and oil of balsam is recommended either as an ointment or impregnated into a bandage applied to the head.[66] Another ointment, containing storax, stacte, wax, oil of balsam and oil of nard, is applied to the body with a cloth in cases of rigidity, paralysis of the nerves, pain in the excretory organs and kidneys, and hemiplegia (the paralysis of one side of the body after a stroke).[67] Hardness of the liver is treated by a draught of balsam infused with rue and dill.[68] Large numbers of ingredients also appear in the preparation of a kohl for increasing the production of moisture in the eyes, and in a collyrium for dimness of sight and dryness of the eye. Composed of wolf's gall, opopanax, peppercorns, olive oil, 'oil' of balsam, tincture of aniseed, cadmin and liquid honey, this collyrium is smeared on the eyelids.[69]

Other compound medicines are to be ingested by the patient. Examples include the *hiera* of Theodoretus and another compound containing oil of balsam that is known as *arkadya* or *beldor*.[70] Oil and wood of balsam appear in *polykaryou*, a remedy for muscle spasms. A recipe contained dried roses, frankincense, laurus malabathrum, resin, myrrh, oil of balsam, bdellium, amomum, spikenard and a last ingredient called *estumka*, and was designed to combat breathing difficulties.[71] The most complex preparations in the Syriac *Book of Medicines* are the antidotes. One example, made principally with lichen, contains a total of forty-four ingredients, including 'oil' of balsam.[72]

Galen is referenced in another antidote, recommended for long-term liver pain. This is made principally with crocus, and also numbers balsam among its many components.[73] Containing both *opobalsamum* and *carpobalsamum*, the *hiera* of Theodoretus is useful against dementia, delirium, vertigo, elephantiasis, leprosy, gout, constipation, and diseases of the liver, spleen, kidneys, colon and womb.[74]

Translating Medicine into Arabic

The fragmentary surviving evidence about traditional medical practices in Arabia before the advent of Islam through to the end of the first Islamic dynasty, the Umayyad caliphate (661–750) suggests that knowledge concerning the applications of balsam was largely reliant upon the acquisition of Greek scientific writing. Balsam (*balasān*) is absent from the Qur'an. To the best of my knowledge, later compilations such as the *ḥadīth* and the corpus of medical writings known as *al-Ṭibb al-nabawī* ('Medicine of the Prophet') also make no mention of balsam.[75]

The impetus to translate Greek knowledge predates Islam. Under the patronage of Khusraw I Anushiravan (r. 531–79), scholars, many of them Nestorian Christians, translated works into Pahlavi. This activity has traditionally been associated with an academic centre and hospital in Gondeshapur (Arabic: Jundaysabur), located in south-west Iran in the province of Khuzistan, though the evidence is circumstantial. This translation project extended beyond Greek to encompass works in Syriac, Sanskrit and Chinese languages. The focus was scientific writing, though literary works such as the *Pancatantra*, a collection of Indian animal fables, were also rendered into Pahlavi.[76] Nestorian physicians were employed by the Umayyad caliphs, and they were also set the task of producing translations of medical texts.[77] It was under the early Abbasid caliphs that this activity was given more formal state support. Sources mention the foundation of the 'House of Wisdom' (*bayt al-ḥikma*) by Caliph al-Ma'mun in Baghdad, though this too may be more legend than solid fact. The caliph did, however, seek out ancient Greek scientific and philosophical treatises, both within his own lands and from the Byzantine empire. Translations were also made from Pahlavi in the ninth century. The translators working in Iraq during this period included a strong Christian presence, mainly Nestorians and

Jacobites. Translations were made directly from Greek into Arabic, while others were done first into Syriac.[78]

The process of translating from Greek into Arabic was not straightforward, and required the creation of neologisms for words and concepts that had not previously been expressed in the latter language. Arabic underwent important changes during this phase, facilitating the subsequent evolution of Islamic scientific scholarship. The potential difficulties are illustrated by the attempts to produce a workable Arabic version of the pharmacological reference work of Dioscorides. According to Ibn Juljul and the Iraqi bookseller Ibn al-Nadim (d. 995 or 998), the first attempt to render *De materia medica* into Arabic was undertaken during the reign of Caliph al-Mutawakkil (r. 847–61) by Istifan ibn Basil. This translation of the five-book recension of the Dioscorides text was hampered by the fact that not all the Greek plant names possessed a corresponding word in Arabic. Istifan took the pragmatic step of simply transliterating the Greek terms with Arabic characters. This approach resulted in a text of questionable value for Arabic-speaking scholars, and was soon revised by Hunayn ibn Ishaq. The son of a pharmacist, Hunayn was in a better position to provide informative Arabic botanical terminology.[79] According to a later translator, Mihran ibn Mansur, Hunayn had also produced a Syriac translation of the Dioscorides text. His revision comprised seven *maqālāt* (treatises), the first five by Dioscorides, with the sixth and seventh (on animals and poisons) possibly additions by Hunayn or his nephew, Hubaysh. This translation circulated across the Islamic world.[80]

Ibn Juljul reports on a second translation attempted at the Umayyad court in Cordoba, stimulated by the gift of an illustrated Greek manuscript of Dioscorides from Romanos II (r. 945–59 as co-emperor, and 959–63 as sole emperor) to Caliph ʿAbd al-Rahman III (r. 912–61). Three years later the emperor sent a monk, Nicholas, to assist in the identification of the plants for which Cordoban scholars were unable to find Arabic names. It is unclear whether a complete translation resulted, and there is little to indicate that this Cordoban initiative had a wider influence.[81] An Arabic Dioscorides manuscript in Leiden, dated 475/1083, provides evidence for an adaptation of the translation produced by Istifan ibn Basil and Hunayn ibn Ishaq. This is one of the earliest surviving illustrated Islamic manuscripts (Fig. 4.1), and according to its colophon, is based on a revision undertaken by one Abu 'Abdallah al-Natili in 380/990–1, at the court of Simjur, perhaps in Samarqand. Al-Natili describes his text as a 'rectification' (*iṣlāḥ*), signalling to the reader that he had exercised the freedom to adjust the original. Most notably, this involved the addition of 108 plant species not found in Greek versions of Dioscorides.[82]

Two more Arabic translations or redactions (sing. *taḥrīr*) were made in northern Mesopotamia in the twelfth century. The first of these was undertaken, according to Mihran ibn Mansur, by Abu Salim al-Malti for the Artuqid ruler of Kayfa, Fakhr al-Din Kara Arslan (r. 1148–74). Two copies of this translation are known in the hand of a later scribe, Bihnam al-Mawsili. One of these, now located in the Bibliothèque Nationale in Paris, is significant for the fact that it is the only Arabic Dioscorides to be written on parchment, suggesting a closer relationship with Greek prototypes. Al-Malti's version was soon recognised to have been written in poor Arabic, and a new translation was commissioned by another Artuqid, Najm al-Din Alpi, ruler of Mardin. The translator in this case was Mihran ibn Mansur, a scholar also known for his work on Aristotle. He employed the Syriac translation produced by Hunayn ibn Ishaq. Two copies of the Ibn Mansur translation are known.[83]

The commissioning of new translations by Fakhr al-Din Kara Arslan and Najm al-Din Alpi should be seen in the wider context of Artuqid scholarly and artistic patronage. The dynasty exhibited a fascination with the art and architecture of classical antiquity, even to the extent of incorporating figural elements on some of their coinage.[84] They were also enthusiastic patrons of scholarship, much of which had its roots in classical antiquity. The engineer al-Jazari (d. 1206) worked under the Artuqids, adapting and expanding on the achievements of earlier scholars, such as Philo of Byzantium (fl. third century BCE) and Hero of Alexandria (d. c. 70 CE).[85] This inclination towards classical art and learning is also seen in other contemporary dynasties in Syria, northern Iraq and Anatolia, and helps to explain the cross-cultural quality of Arabic manuscript illustration. The double frontispiece of the 626/1229 Dioscorides manuscript depicts the eminent scholar seated in a wicker throne in the manner of a classical scholar or Christian evangelist, but with a turban on his head. The Islamic context is further emphasised by the students presenting their copies of the master's text to be authenticated

Figure 6.3 Dioscorides and student holding a mandrake plant. Arabic Dioscorides, dated 1229. Topkapı Museum Library: Ahmed III 2127, fol. 2v. HIP / Art Resource, NY.

(a process known as *ijāza*). A second frontispiece with Dioscorides holding a mandrake derives from a late antique prototype, but replaces the classical personification of invention or discovery (Heuresis) with that of a seated male student (Fig. 6.3).[86]

George Saliba and Linda Komaroff question the usefulness of the term 'translation' to describe some of the surviving Arabic manuscript copies, unillustrated and illustrated, of the pharmacopoeia of Dioscorides. They note that much of this activity can be understood as the creation of commentaries and redactions (*iṣlāḥ* and *taḥrīr* respectively) of the original text, reflecting the needs of physicians and patrons. New plants could be added when necessary, or sections of text omitted. The popularity of Dioscorides is not in doubt, but there was no need to reproduce the Greek text with an antiquarian regard for completeness and accuracy. Hence, later Arabic pharmacological compilers quote large sections of the *De materia medica*, but provide the annotations and observations attributed to later authors. This process can be seen in the works of al-Ghafiqi and Ibn al-Baytar. In the case of Ibn al-Baytar, it is possible that the author glossed the Istifan ibn Basil/Hunayn ibn Ishaq translation of Dioscorides with information from Galen's *Simple Medicines*.[87] The two chapters devoted to balsam cite numerous Greek and Arab authorities post-dating Dioscorides, including Galen, Pythagoras (Arabic: Badighuras), Theodoros Priscianos (fl. fourth century), Ibn Juljul, ʿAli b. Rabban al-Tabari (d. after 864), Ibn Abi al-Ashʿath (d. 975), al-Razi, Ibn ʿImran (fl. tenth century) and Ibn Jazzar (d. 979).[88] Significantly, al-Ghafiqi expresses scepticism about some of the information he records from earlier sources. Al-Razi is another scholar who questioned the validity of classical scholarship when it failed to tally with his own clinical observations, even penning a book entitled *al-Shukūk ʿalā Jānīnūs* ('Doubts about Galen').[89]

Balsam appears in other translations undertaken by Hunayn ibn Ishaq, including the book on substitute drugs penned by Pythagoras.[90] His work as a translator also fed into his own medical writing, including his influential *al-Masā'il fi'l-ṭibb* ('Introduction to medicine', or *Isagoge*). His important contributions to the field of ophthalmology were contained within *al-ʿAshar maqālāt fi'l-ʿayn* ('Ten treatises on the eye'). Here again, the influence of Greek medicine is apparent. An example is a collyrium for cataracts and dimness of vision, containing galls, juice of fennel, honey, the gum of ferula persica, asafoetida, scapwort, balsam oil (*duhn al-balasān*), pepper and rock salt. This preparation derived from the work of the late antique compiler Paul of Aegina, rather than directly from Galen.[91] Hunayn, like many of those who came after him, was able to sift through the corpus of translated Greek texts, choosing and rejecting information as he felt necessary.

In conclusion, some general points can be made about the most significant medical applications of balsam prior to the Arab conquests of the seventh century, and the ways in which writing on this substance was received. Dioscorides and Galen are dominant figures, with the latter frequently quoted by Islamic authorities. Such was Galen's status in the medieval world that his name was attached to broadly 'Galenic' texts penned by others. Antique scholarship had already been brought together in encyclopedic form in late antiquity, meaning that the subsequent Islamic acquisition was mediated partly through the likes of Alexander of Tralles and Paul of Aegina. The process of translation from Greek into Syriac and Arabic, discussed above, is another factor that complicates the relationship between Islamic medicine and its classical predecessor.

Aside from specific medical applications and compound recipes, the scholars of the Islamic world inherited a comprehensive framework – humoral medicine – through which they understood the functioning of the body, disease pathology, and the active qualities of plant, animal and mineral medicaments. Again, much of this knowledge came through the writings of Galen; particularly significant in the present context was his emphasis on the classification of simples according to both their principal actions in the humoral system and their relative potency. Hence, a substance like balsam (whether as oleo-resin, fruit or wood) could be employed on its own, but also combined with a variety of other products following a schema that was rational, at least in its own terms. While both the framework and the more fine-grained information in the Greek medical corpus were enthusiastically received, it is clear that Islamic scholars did so in a relatively critical manner, testing claims, comparing testimony of different authorities and adding new observations. This process was, of course, not restricted to the domain of medicine and pharmacology, but extended to all other areas of scientific and philosophical discourse across the Islamic world.

Notes
1. Greenhill, *Nekrokideia*, p. 210.
2. For example, Felix Fabri, *Evagatorium*, III, p. 17; Von Sudheim, *Description of the Holy Land*, pp. 69–70.
3. Irwin, *For Lust of Knowing*, p. 33.
4. Genesis 37:25; Jeremiah 8:21–2, 46:11.
5. For examples, see Ebbell, *The Papyrus Ebers*; Kamal, *A Dictionary of Pharaonic Medicine*.
6. Discussed in Majno, *The Healing Hand*, p. 215.
7. For example: Proverbs 7:17; Song 4:14.
8. Majno, *The Healing Hand*, pp. 215–17. On the ancient trade and use of resins from Arabia, see Potts, *The Arabian Gulf*, I, p. 349; II, pp. 9–10, 149. See also Roland Harrison, *Healing Herbs of the Bible* (Leiden: Brill, 1966), pp. 43, 45–6; Juris Zarins, 'Mesopotamia and frankincense'.
9. Majno (*Healing Hand*, p. 216) cites the example of a concoction of burnt resin, cassia, cinnamon and myrrh – all of them perfumed substances – that Theophrastus

recommends to reduce the inflammation of a wound. Theophrastus, *Concerning Odours* 8:35.

10. Majno, *Healing Hand*, pp. 217–19. Balsam of Peru was still being employed in US military hospitals into the 1960s. Other perfumed substances, such as thyme, could offer similar bacteriostatic qualities when used in sufficient concentrations.

11. Vitruvius, *On Architecture* 8:6.1–11. This passage is translated in John Humphreys et al., *Greek and Roman Technology: Annotated Translations of Greek and Latin Texts and Documents* (London and New York: Routledge, 1998), pp. 295–7.

12. John Riddle, 'The medicines of Greco-Roman Antiquity as a source for medicines today', in Bart Holland, ed., *Prospecting for Drugs in Ancient and Medieval European Texts: a Scientific Approach* (Amsterdam: Harwood Academic Publishers, 1996), pp. 7–17. A contrary view is given in Plinio Prioreschi et al., 'A quantitative assessment of ancient therapeutics: Poppy and pain in the Hippocratic corpus', *Medical Hypotheses* 51 (1998): 325–51.

13. Sir William Harvey (d. 1657) is commonly associated with the discovery of the circulation of blood, though Ibn al-Nafis (d. 1288–9) earlier made similar observations. See Sami Haddad and Amin Khairallah, 'A forgotten chapter in the history of the circulation of the blood', *Annals of Surgery* 104.1 (1936): 1–8.

14. On these issues, see David Furley and J. S. Wilkie, trans. and eds, *Galen on Respiration and the Arteries: An Edition with English Translation and Commentary of* De usu respirationis, An in arteriis natura sanguis contineatur, De usu pulsum, *and* De causis respirationis (Princeton, NJ and Guildford: Princeton University Press, 1984).

15. On garlic in ancient medicine, see Biljana Petrovska and Svetlana Cekovska, 'Extracts from the history and medical properties on garlic', *Pharmacognosy Review* 4.7 (2010): 106–10.

16. On al-Razi's diagnostic practice and clinical notes, see Pormann and Savage-Smith, *Medieval Islamic Medicine*, pp. 115–17.

17. M. Tariq et al, 'Anti-inflammatory activity of *Commiphora molmol*', *Agents and Actions* 17 (1986): 381–2; Rao et al., 'Toxicity studies in mice'. Also Martinez et al., *Weihrauch und Myrrh*, pp. 169–80.

18. Richard Wren, *Potter's New Cyclopaedia of Botanical Drugs and Preparations*, revised and rewritten by Elizabeth Williamson and Fred Evans (Saffron Walden: The C. W. Daniel Company Limited, 1988), p. 198.

19. R. Arora, V. Taneja, R. Sharma and S. Gupta, 'Anti-inflammatory studies on a crystalline steroid isolated from *Commiphora mukul*', *Indian Journal of Medical Research* 60 (1972): 929–31.

20. A.-S. Abdul-Ghani and R. Amin, 'Effect of aqueous extract of *Commiphora opobalsamum* on blood pressure and heart rate in rats', *Journal of Ethnopharmacology* 57 (1997): 219–22.
21. There are several variants of this text. The following citatons come from Dimitri Kaimakis, ed., *Die Kyraniden*, Beiträge zur klassischen Philologie 76 (Meisenheim am Glan: Anton Hain, 1976), 5:2 (pp. 300–1). For the Latin and Old French versions of the *Cyranides*, see Louis Delatte, ed., *Textes latins et vieux français relatif aux Cyranides*, Bibliothèque de la Faculté de Philosophie et Lettres de l'Université de Liège, fasc. 93 (Paris: Société d'Édition des Belles Lettres, 1942).
22. Kaimakis, ed., *Die Kyraniden*, 1:18 (p. 86).
23. Dioscorides, *De materia medica* 1:19. Translated in Dioscorides, *De materia medica*, trans. Beck, pp. 19–20. Quoted in full in Chapter 4.
24. Ullmann, *Islamic Medicine*, pp. 57–60.
25. For a discussion of the theoretical basis of Galenic pharmacology, see Owsei Temkin, *Galenism. Rise and Decline of a Medical Philosophy*, Cornell Publications in the History of Science (Ithaca, NY and London: Cornell University Press, 1973), pp. 112–14.
26. Paul of Aegina, *Seven Books* 7:3 (III, p. 67).
27. Alexander of Tralles, *Oeuvres médicales d'Alexandre de Tralles. Le dernier auteur classique des grands médicins grecs de l'antiquité*, trans. Félix Brunet, Médicine et Thérapeutique byzantines (Paris: Librairie orientaliste Paul Geuthner, 1933–7), 7:8 (IV, pp. 18–19).
28. Paul of Aegina, *Seven Books* 7:11 (III, pp. 517–18).
29. Kaimakis, ed., *Die Kyraniden*, 3:1a (p. 191); 3:38 (p. 227); 4:39 (p. 273). All are medicines for eye complaints.
30. Paul of Aegina, *Seven Books* 7:20 (III, pp. 594–7).
31. Ibid. 7:19 (III, p. 585); Alexander of Tralles, *Oeuvres médicales* 3:1 (III, pp. 54–5); 7:8 (IV, pp. 18–19).
32. Paul of Aegina, *Seven Books* 7:17 (III, pp. 556–7); 7:18 (III, p. 558).
33. Dioscorides, *De materia medica* 1:19. See translation given in Chapter 4.
34. Aetius (Aetios) of Amida, *The Gynaecology and Obstetrics of the VIth Century, A.D. Translated from the Latin Edition of Cornarius, 1542 and Fully Annotated*, trans. and ed. James Ricci (Philadelphia and Toronto: The Blakiston Company, 1950), chapters 18–24 (pp. 26–35). For the fumigant, see chapter 122 (pp. 117–19).
35. Ibid. chapters 55, 105, 106 (pp. 58–9, 114–15). Spikenard is an essential oil

made from *Nardostachys jatamansi* (D. Don) DC (a member of the valerian family).
36. Ibid. chapter 69 (pp. 74–5). On the ancient, Islamic and Medieval European conceptualisations of hysteria, see Helen King, 'Once upon a text: Hysteria from Hippocrates', in Sander Gilman et al., *Hysteria beyond Freud* (Berkeley, CA: University of California Press, 1993), pp. 3–64.
37. Bram Hertz, *Catalogue of the Collection of Assyrian, Babylonian, Egyptian, Greek, Etruscan, Roman, Indian, Peruvian, and Mexican Antiquities formed by B. Hertz* (London: 11 Great Marlsborough Street, 1851), p. 44, no. 852; Heinrich von Staden, ed. and trans., *Herophilus: The Art of Medicine in Early Alexandria* (Cambridge and New York: Cambridge University Press, 1989), p. 583.
38. Von Staden, ed. and trans., *Herophilus*, pp. 583–4. Traces of his writings are to be found in later medical sources, including Apollonius Mys (probably first century BCE) and Demosthenes Philalathes (first century CE).
39. Galen, *De compositione medicamentorum secundum locos* 4:8. See Kühn, ed., *Opera omnia*, XII, p. 781.
40. Galen, *De Compositione medicamentorum* 2:4.7. See Kühn, *Opera omnia*, XII, pp. 781–5, 787–8). See also Harald Nielsen, *Ancient Ophthalmological Agents: A Pharmacologico-historical Study of Collyria and the Seals for the Collyria during Roman Antiquity, as well as the Most Frequent Components of the Collyria*, Acta Historica Scientiarium Naturalium et Medicinalium 31 (Odense: Odense University Press, 1974), p. 17.
41. Dioscorides, *De materia medica* 1:19.
42. Alexander of Tralles, *Oeuvres médicales* 2:1 (III, pp. 23–4); Paul of Aegina, *Seven Books* 7:16 (III, p. 554).
43. Aetius of Amida, *Tetrabiblia* 7:87. Translated in Julius Hirschberg, *The Ophthalmology of Aëtius of Amida*, translated with commentary by Richey Waugh, Hirschberg History of Ophthalmology. The Monographs 8 (Leipzig: Viet & Co., 2000), p. 125. Also Paul of Aegina, *Seven Books* 7:16 (III, p. 554). Aetius also provides a long description of the different ways of preparing 'dressing of nard', each of which contains balsam. See Aetius (Aetios) of Amida, *Libri medicinales [I–VIII]*, ed. Alexander Olivieri, 2 vols (Leipzig: B. G. Teubneri, 1935–50), I, pp. 67–9; text and translation in Hirschberg, *Ophthalmology*, pp. 155–8.
44. Paul of Aegina, *Seven Books* 7:16 (III, p. 555). This preparation is attributed by the author to Galen.
45. Virgil (Publius Vergilius Maro), *Georgics* 2:115–18. According to the translation

in Peter Fallon with notes by Elaine Fantham, Oxford World's Classics (Oxford and New York: Oxford University Press, 2006). An alternative translation is: 'Alone India bears black ebony, alone the Sabaeans their rod of spice. Why should I rehearse to thee the scented wood that drips with balm, and the clusters of the evergreen thorn?' See *The Eclogues and Georgics of Virgil*, new edition, trans. John McKail (London and New York: Longmans, Green and Co., 1915), p. 62.

46. One example of the latter is goose fat scented with *xylobalsamum*. See Dioscorides, *De materia medica* 2:91. Alexander of Tralles gives the recipe for a finely scented unguent containing balsam. See his *Oeuvres médicales* 7:3 (III, pp. 210–11).
47. Paul of Aegina, *Seven Books* 7:21–2 (III, pp. 598–600). Cf. comments by Ibn Ridwan, quoted in Chapter 7. See also Alexander of Tralles on the treatment of viscous humour in the lungs. See his *Oeuvres médicales* 5:4 (III, p. 146).
48. Alexander of Tralles, *Oeuvres médicales* 5:4 (III, p. 148).
49. Paul of Aegina, *Seven Books* 7:11 (III, p. 520).
50. Paul of Aegina, *Seven Books* 7:11 (III, pp. 511–12).
51. Galen, *De antidotis* 1:1. See Kühn, ed., *Opera omnia*, XIV, pp. 3–5. See also Gilbert Watson, *Theriac and Mithridatium: A Study in Therapeutics*, Publications of the Wellcome Historical Medical Library. New Series 9 (London: The Wellcome Historical Medical Library, 1966), p. 4.
52. Pausanius, *Description of Greece* 9:28.3–4. See Pausanias, *Description of Greece. Vol. IV: VIII:22–X*, trans. and ed. William Jones, Loeb Classical Library 297 (Cambridge, MA: Harvard University Press, 1935, reprinted 2014), pp. 292–3.
53. Nicander of Colophon, *Theriaka*, ll. 935–56. Translated in Martin Levey, 'Medieval Arabic toxicology: The *Book on Poisons* of Ibn Waḥshīya and its relation to early Indian and Greek texts', *Transactions of the American Philosophical Society* 56.7 (1966): 18.
54. On this theriac and its connection to Mithradates, see Adrienne Mayor, *Poison King*, pp. 58, 239–47. On the development of ancient and Medieval theriacs, see Watson, *Theriac and Mithridatium*, pp. 1–100.
55. With the weights converted to grams, this comprises: costmary 1.66 g, sweet flag 20 g, hypericum, gum, sagepenum, acacia juice, Illyrian iris, cardamom 8 g each, anise 12 g, Gallic nard, gentian root, dried rosemary leaves 16 g each, poppy tears and parsley 17 g each, cassia, saxifrage, darnel, long pepper 20.66 g each, storax 21 g, castoreum, frankincense, hypocistis juice, myrrh and opoponax 24 g each, malabathrum leaves 24 g, flower of round rush, turpentine resin, galbanum, Cretan carrot seeds 24.66 g each, nard and opobalsamum 25 g each,

shepherd's purse 25 g, rhubarb root 28 g, saffron, ginger, cinnamon 29 g each. See Celsus, *De medicina* 5:23. A slightly different version with a larger dose of opium and the addition of wine appears in Galen, *De antidotis* 2:1–4. See Kühn, ed., *Opera omnia*, XIV, pp. 108–29. Also Watson, *Theriac and Mithridatium*, pp. 5–6.

56. Pliny, *Natural History* 8:24. He concludes of Mithridatium, 'Which of the Gods, in the name of Truth, fixed these absurd proportions? No human brain could have been sharp enough. It is plainly a showy parade of the art, and a colossal boast of science'. Quoted and discussed in Carla Nappi, 'Bolatu's pharmacy theriac in early Modern China', *Early Science and Medicine* 14.6 (1997): 748–9.

57. On the use of rare or regionally specific commodities in these recipes, see Laurence Totelin, 'The world in a pill: Local specialties and global remedies in the Graeco-Roman world', in Rebecca Kennedy and Molly Jones-Lewis, eds, *The Routledge Handbook of Identity and the Environment in the Classical and Medieval Worlds*, Routledge Handbooks (London and New York: Routledge, 2016), pp. 151–70.

58. Laurence Totelin, 'Mithradates' antidote – a pharmacological ghost', *Early Science and Medicine* 9.1 (2004): 1–19. Also Mayor, *Poison King*, pp. 240–1, 289. It may never have been committed to written form. Alternatively it might either have been destroyed by Pompey (Gnaeus Pompeius Magnus, d. 48 BCE) or kept as a secret by the physicians of the Roman emperors.

59. Mayor, *Poison King*, pp. 241–2.

60. Linda Moore et al. 'St John's Wort induces hepatic drug metabolism through activation of the Pregnane X receptor', *Proceedings of the National Academy of Sciences of the United States of America* 97.13 (2000): 7500–2; Mayor, *Poison King*, p. 242.

61. Galen, *De theriaka ad pisonem* 6–7. See Kühn, ed., *Opera omnia*, XIV, p. 233. Also *Claudius Galen, De theriaca ad pisonem: Testo Latino*, ed. and trans. Enrico Coturri and Michele Nardi, Biblioteca della 'Rivista di Storia della Scienze Mediche et Naturali' 8 (Florence: Olschki, 1959), pp. 120–6; Watson, *Theriac*, pp. 45–9.

62. *De theriaca ad pamphilinum*. This work is no longer attributed to Galen. See Kühn, ed., *Opera omnia*, XIV, p. 306. Also Paul of Aegina, *Seven Books* 7:11 (III, p. 510).

63. Ullmann, *Islamic Medicine*, pp. 15–16; Pormann and Savage-Smith, *Medieval Islamic Medicine*, pp. 18–19. On the presence of Galen's work in Syriac writing, see Rainer Degen, 'Galen im Syrischen: Eine Übersicht über die syrische

Überlieferung der Werke Galens', in Vivian Nutton, ed., *Galen: Problems and Prospects* (London: The Wellcome Institute for the History of Medicine, 1981), pp. 133–66.
64. Ullmann, *Islamic Medicine*, p. 16.
65. Ernest Wallis Budge, trans., *Syrian Anatomy, Pathology and Therapeutics, or 'Book of Medicines'* (Oxford and New York: Oxford University Press, 1913). On the date of this work, see Pormann and Savage-Smith, *Medieval Islamic Medicine*, pp. 19–20.
66. Budge, trans., *'Book of Medicines'*, 3:37 (II, p. 64).
67. Ibid. 8:8 (II, pp. 149–50).
68. Ibid. 16:5 (II, p. 417).
69. Ibid. 5:6 (II, p. 95).
70. Ibid. 15:8 (II, pp. 349–50). *Hiera* is a warming substance designed for the expulsion of bile and phlegm from the body.
71. Ibid. 13:7 (II, p. 262).
72. Ibid. 16:5 (II, pp. 404–6).
73. Ibid. 16:5 (II, pp. 428–9).
74. Ibid. 3:30 (II, pp. 51–2). Paul of Aegina also recommends *hiera* for elephantiasis. See his *Seven Books* 4:1 (II, p. 2).
75. For example, see Muhammad b. Abi Bakr ibn Qayyim al-Jawziyya, *Medicine of the Prophet*, trans. Penelope Johnstone (Cambridge: Islamic Texts Society, 1998).
76. Dimitri Gutas, *Greek Thought, Arabic Culture: The Graeco-Arabic Translation Movement in Baghdad and Early 'Abbāsid Society (2nd–4th/8th–10th Centuries)* (London and New York: Routledge, 1998), pp. 25–7.
77. Collins, *Medieval Herbals*, p. 115.
78. Franz Rosenthal, *The Classical Heritage in Islam*, trans. Emile and Jenny Marmorstein (Berkeley, CA and Los Angeles: University of California Press, 1975), pp. 4–9; Gutas, *Greek Thought, Arabic Culture*, pp. 53–60, 77–104. On the role of Hebrew in the transmission of Galen, see Elinor Lieber, 'Galen in Hebrew: The transmission of Galen's works in the mediaeval Islamic world', in Vivian Nutton, ed., *Galen: Problems and Prospects* (London: The Wellcome Institute for the History of Medicine, 1981), pp. 167–86.
79. On the issue of terminology and the identification of plants, see Penelope Johnstone, 'Galen in Arabic: The transformation of Galenic pharmacology', in Vivian Nutton, ed., *Galen: Problems and Prospects* (London: The Wellcome Institute for the History of Medicine, 1981), pp. 200–2.

80. Sadek, *Arabic* Materia Medica, pp. 7–9, 12–13; Collins, *Medieval Herbals*, pp. 115–16; George Saliba and Linda Komaroff, 'Illustrated books may be hazardous for your health: A new reading of the Arabic reception and rendition of the *Materia Medica* of Dioscorides', *Ars Orientalis* 35 (2008): 8–9. For a translation of Ibn Juljul's account, see also Rosenthal, *Classical Heritage*, pp. 194–7.
81. Sadek, *Arabic* Materia Medica, pp. 9, 12–13; Collins, *Medieval Herbals*, pp. 116–18; Saliba and Komaroff, 'Illustrated books', pp. 9–10.
82. Sadek, *Arabic* Materia Medica, pp. 11–12, 13; Collins, *Medieval Herbals*, pp. 118–24; Saliba and Komaroff, 'Illustrated books', pp. 17–18.
83. Sadek, *Arabic* Materia Medica, pp. 9–13; Collins, *Medieval Herbals*, pp. 124–7; Saliba and Komaroff, 'Illustrated books', p. 9. The example in the Museum of the Shrine of Imam Riza in Mashhad is the most complete and has been identified as an original produced in Diyar Bakr for Najm al-Din Alpi.
84. On these coins, see Nicholas Lowick, 'The religious, the royal and the popular in the figural coinage of the Jazīra', in Julian Raby, ed., *The Art of Syria and the Jazīra, 1100–1250*, Oxford Studies in Islamic Art 1 (Oxford: Oxford University Press, 1985), pp. 159–74.
85. Donald Hill, *Islamic Science and Engineering*, Edinburgh Islamic Surveys (Edinburgh: Edinburgh University Press, 1993), pp. 122–48. For al-Jazari's treatise, see *The Book of Knowledge of Ingenious Mechanical Devices (Kitāb fī maʿrifat al-ḥiyal al-handasiyya)*, trans. Donald Hill (Dordrecht and Boston: D. Reidel, 1974). Al-Jazari was also reliant upon earlier Islamic engineers, such as the Banu Musa working in Abbasid Baghdad.
86. Also omitted from the thirteenth-century painting is the dog, despite the prevalent belief that this animal was needed in order to extract the medicinal root from the ground. The exclusion can probably be explained by the ritually unclean status of the dog in Islamic law. On the relationship between these frontispieces and late antique parallels, see Eva Hoffman, 'The author portrait in thirteenth-century manuscripts', *Muqarnas* 10 (1993): 6–20; Collins, *Medieval Herbals*, pp. 127–9, pl. X.a, b. For more on the classical heritage in Arabic book illustration, see Kurt Weitzmann, 'Greek sources of Islamic scientific illustration', in George Miles, ed., *Archaeologica Orientalia. In Memoriam Ernst Herzfeld* (Locust Valley, NY: J. J. Augustin, 1952), pp. 244–66; Eva Hoffman, 'The beginnings of the illustrated Arabic book: An intersection between art and scholarship', *Muqarnas* 17 (2000): 37–52.
87. Saliba and Komaroff, 'Illustrated books', pp. 18–20, 39–40.

88. Ibn al-Baytar, *al-Mufrāda*, I, p. 109; Abu al-Faraj (Bar Hebraeus), The Book of Simple Drugs, pp. 57–9 (Arabic), 243–5 (English). On the influence of Dioscorides in Islamic scholarship, see Sadek, *Arabic* Materia Medica, pp. 48–50. Pythagoras may have been a Greek physician employed by the Sasanian dynasty. See Ullmann, *Islamic Medicine* (1997), p. 18.
89. On the translation of Galen, see Gotthard Strohmaier, 'Galen in Arabic: Prospects and projects', in Vivian Nutton, ed., *Galen: Problems and Prospects* (London: The Wellcome Institute for the History of Medicine, 1981), pp. 187–96; Johnstone, 'Galen in Arabic'.
90. Levey, *Substitute Drugs*.
91. Hunayn ibn Ishaq, *The Book of the Ten Treatises on the Eye Ascribed to Hunain ibn Is-Hâq (809–877 A.D.). The earliest existing systematic text-book on ophthalmology*, ed. and trans. Max Meyerhof (Cairo: The Government Press, 1928), pp. 121–2 and notes (Arabic text: p. 189). The chapter also mentions bleeding of the veins of the eye and the application of leeches to the temples. On the medicinal qualities of ferula persica, see Zohreh Sattar and Mehrdad Iranshahi, 'Phytochemistry and pharmacology of *Ferula persica* Boiss.: A review', *Iran Journal of Basic Medical Sciences* 20.1 (2017): 1–8.

7

Balsam in Medieval and Early Modern Medicine

The increased recognition of the site from the beginning of the twelfth century is partly a product of the upsurge of Mediterranean trade (Chapter 5) and the promotion of Crusading, but also correlates well with the beginnings of the translation of Arabic scholarship in Europe. This scholarly activity has its origins in Salerno and Montpellier, but spread to other centres of learning across the continent. Medical and pharmacological knowledge was avidly sought after, and this naturally increased the understanding of balsam both as a simple and as part of compound preparations.

This chapter offers a selective approach to this vast array of texts, identifying authors and works that illustrate significant points in the transmission and elaboration of knowledge about balsam. The first part evaluates the ways in which balsam features in Arabic pharmacological and medical literature until the sixteenth century. The second part deals with the understanding of balsam and its medical applications in European sources. This part includes the discussion of the product in early medieval European medicine, though the focus is on the acquisition and processing of the Arabic medical and pharmacological tradition from the late eleventh century onwards.[1] The third part deals with the recipes for theriacs, also known in English as treacles.

Arabic Medical Writing

As noted in the previous chapter, scholars such as Ibn al-Baytar reproduced the principal content of Dioscorides' reference work, updating it with relevant late antique and Islamic sources. Ibn al-Baytar's approach to the subject is that of a compiler, offering little explicit critique of the information provided by his chosen authorities. Other Arabic scholars were more analytical in their treatment of earlier sources. The extent to which Greek knowledge had been incorporated into Arabic scholarship is demonstrated by al-Biruni's chapter devoted to balsam in his *Kitāb al-ṣaydala* ('Book of Pharmacy'). In this case, the author cites data drawn from Dioscorides, Galen, Oribasius, Paul of Aegina, 'Nicholos' (perhaps Nicolaus Damascenos, d. 4 BCE) and a range of Arab authors, that are necessary to build his argument about the precise identification and characteristics of the plant. Al-Biruni exhibits no partisanship in his treatment of Greek, Syriac and Arabic sources, sifting through all of them for the best information; for example, he notes that Paul of Aegina and al-Razi both recommend myrrh as a substitute for balsam (Chapter 5), though he adds that the latter also suggests a mixture of the oils of *kāzī* (a fragrant species of screw pine), coconut and olive.[2]

Ibn al-Baytar and al-Biruni favoured an alphabetic arrangement of data, but the presentation of pharmacological information could take other forms. For example, the book of simples by al-Ishbili (d. 1134), a physician attached to the Zirid dynasty (972–1148) in Tunisia, organises the organic and mineral commodities according to the part of the body being treated. The simples themselves are carefully classified along humoral lines, with balsam noted as heating and drying to the third degree. The author claims its efficacy in the treatment of convulsions that derive from an abundance of humidity and phlegm, as well as epilepsy and vertigo. Balsam was also good for the stomach, and prepared as a decoction it would arrest dyspepsia. The wood of the tree (*'ūd al-balasān*) and the seed (*ḥabb*) are both characterised as heating to the second degree and drying to the first (i.e. less powerful than the oil). The seed of balsam is recommended for the treatment of asthma and other respiratory disorders.[3] Ibn al-Baytar also views balsam as being valuable for breathing difficulties, citing the work of Ibn 'Amran.[4] Another genre that contained information about simples was glossaries of larger works. For example, in the thirteenth century, Ibn al-Hashsha' produced a glossary based on the *Kitāb al-manṣūrī fī'l-ṭibb* of al-Razi. Entitled *Mufīd al-'ulūm wa-mubīd al-humūm*, the work contains a substantial chapter devoted to balsam, giving information about where it was found ('Ayn Shams), the products derived from it and their applications in medical practice.[5]

Ibn Sina's *Qānūn fi'l-ṭibb* ('Canon of Medicine') comprises five books and covers all topics from the theoretical foundations to pathology and the preparation of compound medicines. The *Qānūn* was extensively copied and remained a standard reference work in the Islamic world and Europe through to the early modern period. Ibn Sina's scholarship is notable both for its encyclopedic range and for the consistent application of humoral principles. Information about balsam is located principally in books 2 (*materia medica*) and 5 (formulary, dealing with the preparation of compound medicines), though references appear in other contexts (see below).[6] In the *Urjūza fi'l-ṭibb*, Ibn Sina provides a summary of the information in the five-volume *Qānūn*. The versed form of the *Urjūza fi'l-ṭibb* had a mnemonic function, while the brevity of the composition ensured its popularity as a medical handbook. In the pharmacological section balsam appears among the astringent drugs, and as one that could heat without purging the body. This work was translated into Latin under the title *Cantica Avicennae* and widely circulated in Europe.[7]

The Egyptian physician and astronomer Ibn Ridwan (d. c. 1061) suggests the burning of the following mixture of aromatic plants during winter months:

> If the air is cold, put stoves in the living rooms and furnish them with branches, leaves, and warm flowers, such as narcissus, gilly-flower, sweet basil, wild thyme, citron, camomile leaves, sweet marjoram, sticks of balsam and its leaves, lily of the valley, jasmine, musk rose and its branches and leaves, leaves of Abraham's balm, soft-haired basil, wormwood, southernwood, dog's fennel, camomile, and aquatic mint.[8]

This mixture was not to be used simply for its pleasurable aroma. Contained within his treatise on the prevention of illnesses, Ibn Ridwan was drawing on an ancient idea that fumigants could combat disease; Paul of Aegina (Chapter 6) discusses the role of these treatments in the preservation of the body against 'pestilential disorders', noting also how inhalation could remove catarrh and other obstructions, clear the brain, and combat respiratory and liver complaints originating from coldness.[9] Maimonides (Moses ben Maimon, d. 1204) suggests another use for fumigants; one recipe including balsam is recommended for alleviating haemorrhoids.[10]

Most important in this context, however, is the notion that disease, and particularly plague, was carried in the air. Arabic sources refer to *wabā'*, with the definition given as corruption or an unwholesomeness of the air. The word *ṭā'ūn* is often used synonymously, though it seems more precise to refer to the human afflictions caused by *wabā'*. Galen and his followers saw this from a humoral perspective, noting that patients might fail to respond to treatments if the air around them affected the balance of the humours in the body.[11] For Ibn Ridwan, therefore, the quality of air was an issue of public health; while the plants in the fumigant had different humoral qualities, balsam, at least, neutralised coldness with its capacity to heat and dry the body. These characteristics were valued in later centuries (see below).[12]

According to al-'Umari, the Mamluk sultan distributed the substance to the hospitals of the empire for the treatment of 'those suffering from illnesses of cold [humour] (*li-mu'ālajat al-mabrūdīn*)'.[13] Numerous references to balsam in the treatment of diseases associated with cold appear in Islamic medical literature. The Tunisian physician Ibn al-Jazzar recommends the product for the warming of cold parts of the body and notes its ability to drive out vapours collected in the organs.[14] Al-Kindi's (d. c. 873) formulary includes balsam in the preparation of an enema (*ḥuqna*) used for a variety of purposes, including warming the kidneys and increasing sexual potency.[15] Al-Biruni claims that coldness of the uterus and strangury is treated through the use of a cerecloth impregnated with balsam and rose oil.[16] Ibn al-Baytar records a treatment for stroke (*al-sakta*) caused by coldness of the brain given by Ibn Abi al-Ash'ath, the physician to the Hamdanid (890–1004) court in Mosul. The head was to be covered with a cloth soaked in a mixture of balsam and oil of lily (*duhn al-zanbaq*). Citing one al-Taymi, Ibn al-Baytar claims burnt balsam wood mixed with honey warms the stomach and removes excess humidity.[17]

A range of other treatments can be found in Arabic medical writings. Balsam helped the evacuation of excess moisture and removed blockages. Ibn Ridwan writes that balsam promotes urination, and also claims that it aids in breaking up bladder stones (sing. *al-ḥaṣā*).[18] Following Dioscorides, al-Biruni and Ibn Sina note the role of balsam as a deobstruent, also encouraging the expulsion of a foetus and the placenta.[19] Balsam oil is also an ingredient in a number of ophthalmological remedies by 'Ali ibn 'Isa (d. 1010).[20] Ibn Sina provides a compound remedy for the eye containing old olive oil, balsam and fennel juice that relates closely to those given by Paul of Aegina and Hunayn ibn Ishaq.[21] Al-Biruni writes that balsam removes cloudiness from the eye.[22] Ibn Abi al-Ashʿath too recommends balsam as an eyewash to counteract the development of cataracts. The same author suggests a mixture of balsam, almond oil and honey in the treatment of convulsions, trembling, facial tics, paralysis, weak pulse and slowness of movement.[23] Balsam appears both as a simple and in compound medicines used in the relief of paralysis, lethargy, spasms, convulsions and vertigo.[24] Balsam calms the stomach, easing digestion,[25] and is an analgesic for back pain, headache, toothache and earache.[26] The Jewish physician Yaʿqub b. Ishaq al-Israʾili (d. 1208) writes that ash of burnt balsam wood could be mixed with vinegar and applied to the skin to remove warts (sing. *thūlūl*).[27] Maimonides even recommends the seeds of balsam as an aphrodisiac.[28]

The Antiochene scholar Daʾud al-Antaki (d. 1599) is regarded as the last significant authority of the tradition of classical Islamic medicine. Blind from birth, he is said to have mastered Greek and to have travelled widely, living in Damascus, Cairo and Mecca. His medical scholarship relied on the pharmacological writing of Ibn al-Baytar, though he also cites a number of Greek and Arab authors, including Galen, Dioscorides, al-Kindi and Ibn ʿAmran. His major work is the *Tadhkirat ulī al-albāb wa jāmiʿ lil-ʿajab al-ʿujāb*, though he also wrote shorter summaries and commentaries on medicinal issues, philosophy, astrology and magic.[29] He devotes a section of the *Tadhkirat* to balsam 'oil' (*duhn al-balasān*), repeating many of the treatments described by Ibn al-Baytar and other sources discussed above.[30]

Medieval and Early Modern European Medicine

Balsam and other imported aromatics were known in Europe in the pre-Salernitan period, at least among the political/religious elites and scholars of medicine. Evidence for this comes from texts such as the Carolingian compendium, the *Lorscher Arzneibuch*. Composed in the late eighth or early ninth centuries, this work contains numerous references to balsam, illustrating the ways in which this valuable commodity could be employed in medical practice. In the foreword to the text there is a reference to 'balm of Gilead' in the healing of wounds in Jeremiah 8:22 (see also Chapters 2 and 6). The author associates this with the balsam of his own day, noting the product's role in the treatment of wounds and scars.[31] A later section deals with information drawn from the medical saints Cosmas and Damian, and the antique authorities Hippocrates and Galen. The text alludes to the role of 'Arabia, the Indus of fragrances' in providing significant medicaments such as myrrh, frankincense, balsam, cinnamon, spikenard and saffron. Balsam appears in a complex antidote, containing both locally available plants, including parsley, henbane, lovage and dill, as well as more exotic imports. Sometimes the text states how a given antidote could be used; for example, the theriac of Theodoret (Theodoretus; Chapter 6) contains balsam, and is recommended in the treatment of dyspnea, dizziness, trembling, oral and stomach ailments, and illnesses of the kidney and liver.[32]

According to the *Lorscher Arzneibuch*, a salve of balsam or of liquid pitch treats excessive catarrh and the build-up of liquid in the head. Lastly, the book enumerates a variety of ointments and oils, in which balsam is included. Some of these medicaments are simply described as 'soothing', perhaps indicating that they are primarily designed for skin complaints or localised pain. The celebrated 'winter remedy' is claimed as a panacea.[33] The text describes this 'Great Hygieia', and notes its potency as an analgesic and pyretic, as well as its use against 'paralysis on one side' (i.e. stroke). One ointment is particularly effective against stomach ache, hypothermia and fever brought on by chills. The recipe for 'must oil' contains balsam wood and treats neck cramp and other forms of muscle contraction. Others to make use of balsam wood are the recipes for 'nard oil' and 'spikenard oil'. 'Myrtle oil' treats outgrowths on the head, dandruff and hair loss, as well as suppressing sweating.[34]

The *Leechbook of Bald* (also *Medicinale anglicum*) was probably composed in the second half of the ninth century. This Old English text combines local plant lore with information drawn from an international scholarly context.[35] The *Leechbook* also brings in magico-medical elements, including treatments offering protection against enchantments and the malicious attentions of elves. Notably, myrrh is counted in one protection against these dangers, indicating that the understanding of imported aromatics was not circumscribed by the medical and pharmacological knowledge of antiquity.[36] The exotic ingredients mentioned in the *Leechbook* include commodities such as myrrh, frankincense, spikenard and balsam. The last of these appears in an eye salve with pure honey. Another salve contains mugwort and rue, though the text also recommends the addition of honey and, when available, balsam.[37] The remaining references to balsam appear in a section of the text that ends with the following note: 'Lord Helias [i.e. Elias], patriarch of Jerusalem ordered all this to be said to King Alfred'. This part of the text mentions several Middle Eastern commodities, including the minerals petroleum and sal ammoniac, that presumably were sent to the English king. Ointment of balsam is 'for all infirmities which may be on a man's body, for fever, and against phantasms and against all deceptions'. The patriarch also recommends madness can be treated through marking the sign of the cross on the limbs with petroleum and on the forehead and top of the head with balsam. This suggests a link to practices of chrismation in the eastern Churches (Chapter 8).[38] The Anglo-Saxon authors of the *Leechbook* probably drew information on balsam from the *Physica Plinii*, a fourth-century pharmacological compilation mostly derived from the *Natural History* of Pliny.[39]

The 'Translation Movement' preserved and dispersed antique texts in Arabic translations, but it also generated important critical syntheses and novel works by Islamic physicians and pharmacologists. The acquisition of this knowledge beyond the borders of the Islamic world required the translation of Arabic works, a process that occurred from the eleventh century. Simeon Seth was doctor to the Byzantine emperor Michael VII Doukas (r. 1071–8), but is perhaps best known for his revision of the study on the properties of foods, composed by his contemporary, the historian Michael Psellos (d. after 1078). Seth's revised text shows his critical stance towards Galen and his knowledge of Aetius of Amida, and Arabic, Persian and Indian medical sources. In one section he describes the balsam tree and the nature of the oleo-resin drawn from it (suggesting a reliance upon Dioscorides). He continues with observations about the medicinal properties of balsam, including its effectiveness against snakebite and the stings of scorpions. Other applications noted by Seth are the breaking of bladder stones, stemming of excessive bleeding, alleviation of ear pain, and the treatment of illnesses associated with cold and 'childhood diseases'.[40] These ideas correlate closely with the classical formulation of balsam as a heating and drying agent.

Salerno had established a medical school, the Schola Medica Salernitana, in the ninth century, but it was in the eleventh century that the institution rose to prominence. In particular, this was driven by the translation of Graeco-Arabic medical texts. This project was led by the North African physician known as Constantine the African (d. c. 1098), who arrived in Salerno in 1077 and spent the latter part of his life in the Benedictine monastery of Monte Cassino. One of his most important translations was of the *Kitāb al-Malikī* of ʿAli ibn al-ʿAbbas al-Majusi (in Europe, Haly Abbas; d. 994), which was given the Latin title *Pantegni* or *Liber regius*. He also created Latin versions of works by such luminaries as Hunayn ibn Ishaq, al-Razi, Ibn al-Jazzar, Galen and Hippocrates.[41] Constantine's work facilitated the development of medical scholarship in Salerno through the late eleventh and twelfth centuries. Among the notable achievements of this phase are the herbal *Circa instans*, probably composed by Matthaeus Platearius,[42] the *Antidotarium Nicolai* and the gynaecological writings of Trotula (or Trota). The *Practica brevis* is also associated with the Platearius family, and may have been written by Giovanni (Johannes), the father of Matthaeus.

Constantine the African's translations and independent works contain numerous references to balsam. His ophthalmological tome, the *Liber de oculis*, contains a chapter dealing with cataracts and dimness of sight that draws upon the *Ten Treatises on the Eye* by Hunayn ibn Ishaq (Chapter 6). Constantine writes that the head and body should be purged, and the sufferer placed on a light diet. The collyrium he recommends corresponds largely with that of Hunayn ibn Ishaq, including such ingredients as honey, juice of fennel, asafoetida (known as 'devil's dung') and balsam.[43] The text of Constantine's *Liber de Coitu* ('Book on Intercourse') is known in several variants. One of these mentions balsam in relation to an unguent for the genitalia.[44] Constantine's book of simples contains a chapter dealing with balsam, with information on the characteristics of the plant and the products derived from it. The chapter singles out Dioscorides, though the range of suggested treatments illustrates his familiarity with Arabic sources. He notes the heating and drying qualities of balsam, and how the product can be applied in medical procedures, including the expulsion of a foetus from the womb, the driving out of phlegm, urinary complaints such as strangury, and dizziness. Balsam's role in the treatment of wounds is mentioned, as is its value in alleviating dysentery.⁴⁵ While none of these are original observations, Constantine's summary helped disseminate knowledge about balsam to European physicians.

The capture of Toledo in 1085 brought a wealth of Arabic scholarship into Christian Europe. Under the patronage of Peter the Venerable, abbot of Cluny (d. 1156), the first Latin translation of the Qur'an was completed along with translations of other works of Islamic history and law (known as the 'Toledan collection').⁴⁶ Scientific and philosophical works, both Arabic translations of Greek originals and new works by Islamic scholars, were also placed into Latin during this phase. Gerard of Cremona was one of the most prolific translators of the twelfth century, coming to Toledo in 1167 initially in search of the *Almagest* of Ptolemy. Through his collaboration with Mozarabic and Jewish translators, Gerard produced editions of key texts covering the topics of algebra, optics, geometry, astronomy and ethics. Among his translations are several important works devoted to medicine, including Ibn Serapion (fl. ninth century), Ibn Ridwan and al-Razi. One of his greatest contributions to medieval European medicine was the translation of the *Qānūn* of Ibn Sina (known in Europe as Avicenna). Its enduring relevance to medical discourse is shown by the production of several printed editions from the late fifteenth to the seventeenth centuries. As noted above, balsam appears numerous times in the preparation of salves and ingestible drugs.⁴⁷

The achievements of the translators of Salerno and Toledo had a major impact upon the theory and practice of medicine elsewhere in Europe. Some Salernitan texts, such as the influential *Practica brevis* of Platearius, were translated from Latin so as to broaden their readership in northern Europe. The author of *Practica brevis* notes the usefulness of balsam in the treatment of kidney stones and rheumatic pain, a condition held to result from an excess of choleric blood and phlegmatic humour. The treatment for rheumatic pain required pills that included *carpobalsamum* and *xylobalsamum* along with other imports like nard and mastic.⁴⁸ A balm (*baume*) is recommended in the treatment of stomach pain, though it is not clear whether the text specifies balsam or some other soothing product.⁴⁹ Compound medicines that normally contained balsam are also mentioned in this work; for example, Mithridatium, the popular theriac, treats both diarrhoea (*lienterie*) and toothache.⁵⁰ 'Balm' (*basme*) is also found in the Anglo-Norman verse translation of work on women's health by Trotula. In a section devoted to 'Oribaces' (Oribasius), the warming quality and fine odour of this commodity is noted, along with others such as storax and rose.[51]

A few other examples can illustrate the ways in which this new knowledge was appreciated and used from the twelfth to the fourteenth centuries. Balsam was discussed in reference works such as the herbal produced by the Italian monk Rufinus soon after 1287 and in the encyclopedic *De proprietatibus rerum* ('On the Properties of Things') by the English scholar Bartholaeus Anglicus (d. 1272).[52] The Benedictine abbess and mystic Hildegard of Bingen (d. 1179) devotes short chapters to frankincense (*thus*), myrrh (*myrrha*) and balsam (*balsamon*) in her *Physica*. Such imported aromatics were evidently familiar to her, and must have been in use in monastic infirmaries. In each case, she starts by locating the resin in humoral terms: balsam being classified as 'very hot and moist'. The latter characteristic stands in contrast to the more common understanding that balsam had a drying action. This disparity suggests Hildegard of Bingen did not have direct access to translations of the standard works of Arabic medicine. She notes the powerful qualities of balsam, stressing the need to employ it with caution. It is 'strongly feared by all natural things'. At a practical level, she recommends the application of an unguent formed of balsam, olive oil and deer marrow for fevers of the stomach. This combination is also found earlier in the *Lorscher Arzneibuch* in an ointment for alleviating fatigue, pain and the build-up of phlegm. Echoing the treatment ascribed to the Patriarch Elias in the *Leechbook of Bald*, Hildegard writes that madness could be healed by anointing the sufferer with this same unguent on the temples and neck (though not the top of the head).[53]

Benvenutus Grassus (or Grapheus) was one of the most influential medieval European scholars of ophthalmology. Little is known of his biography, though he may have studied in Salerno in the thirteenth century. His *De probatassima arte oculorum* refers to Galen, Hippocrates and scholarship from Salerno, quotes Hunayn ibn Ishaq's work directly and may have made use of the work of 'Ali ibn 'Isa.[54] Balsam appears in the text in relation to a purge that was used prior to the application of a plaster over an infected eye.[55] In his commentary to the *Antidotarium Nicolai*, Jean de Saint Amand (d. 1303), a teacher at the University of Paris and an early champion of the experimental method in science, outlines ways of testing the efficacy of medicines that build on recommendations in the *Qānūn* of Ibn Sina.[56] The commentary deals with the treatment of the stomach and medicines that contribute to the healthy state of the liver and spleen. Balsam is recommended for its beneficial effect on the liver.[57] Henri de Mondeville (d. c. 1320) is an interesting figure in the history of surgery, though his treatise *Cyrurgia* was seldom copied.[58] Rejecting the ancient practice of encouraging suppuration, de Mondeville championed a 'dry' treatment, involving the cleaning, suturing and dressing of the wound. The linen dressing is soaked in wine, and periodically changed by the surgeon. De Mondeville also sought substances to combat sepsis, listing these in the *antidotarium* (book 5). Significantly, both balsam oil and *carpobalsamum* are listed, having both heating and drying qualities.[59]

Prosper Alpin's comprehensive analysis of the balsam plant gives a useful insight into the early modern understanding of its medical applications. Many of these are familiar from the texts reviewed above and in Chapter 6. For example, he notes the usefulness of balsam against illnesses associated with cold and for the treatment of internal blockages. This latter point can also be associated with his recommendation, following Galen, of balsam in an enema to treat female hysteria. Balsam was good for digestion and reducing flatulence. Despite its common characterisation as a calorifacient, Alpin claims that balsam would reduce fevers, as well as acting as a preventative against plague. The presence of the fruit or wood of balsam in Egyptian theriacs was, according to the author, the reason why they were superior to their Italian counterparts (see below).[60] Alpin's publications came at the time of the final demise of the balsam trees of Matarea; the dwindling of supplies of balsam hardly encouraged the creation of innovative medical writing on its use. There are references to different grades of balsam in pharmacological and mercantile encyclopedias (Chapter 5) throughout the seventeenth and eighteenth centuries, but their concern is largely with the creation of theriacs.

From *diryāq* to Treacle: Medieval and Early Modern Antidotes and their Uses

Hunayn ibn Ishaq provides probably the earliest references to the use of theriacs in Arabic medical writing in his *Masā'il fī'l-ṭibb* ('Questions on Medicine').[61] The subject was developed in greater detail by the Iberian physician and pharmacologist Ibn Juljul. His main preoccupation was with Galen's presentation of the theriac of Andromachus (Galene). Ibn Juljul analyses the mathematical relationships between the different measurements and, on this basis, offers criticisms of Galen's methods.[62] Theriacs also appear in later Islamic sources, including Ibn Sina and Ibn Rushd (Averroes, d. 1198). While the latter was familiar with the recipes recommended by Galen, his approach was more theoretical in nature, considering the qualities of theriacs and their diverse employment both against venom and in the treatment of diseases. He advised caution against repeated use of theriacs, particularly for the purposes of prophylaxis, because of their transformative characteristics. Hence, Ibn Rushd concludes that in such circumstances the human body would gradually take on the nature of poison.[63]

Balsam appears in treatments for animal venom and plant poisons. For example, according to al-Tabari, the author of the early Arabic compendium *Firdaws al-ḥikma* ('Paradise of Wisdom'), and his student, al-Razi, the stings of scorpions (sing. *ladgh al-ʿaqrab*) could be treated with balsam.[64] This point is also made by the Byzantine physician Simeon Seth.[65] Al-Biruni mentions balsam in the treatment of hemlock poisoning.[66] Maimonides is another author who concerned himself with theriacs, with balsam included in one recipe.[67] Surprisingly, balsam appears both in the preparation of poisons and as an antidote (for example, following the ingestion of poisonous plants like spurge) in the work of the ninth- or tenth-century scholar Ibn Wahshiyya. Many of his recipes have a magical quality, however, and it is not clear to what extent their actions should be understood according to humoral classification. Some comparison could be made with the mixing of magic and medical lore in the *Cyranides* (Chapter 6).[68]

Elements of magic can also be detected in other Islamic texts. The illustration of the balsam tree in the 595/1199 copy of the *Kitāb al-diryāq* ('Book of Antidotes') has already been discussed in Chapter 4. Products of the balsam plant feature in the theriacs listed in this manuscript. While the authorship of the text is unknown, many of the recipes can be traced to classical sources.[69] The 1199 copy is unusual in that the bulk of the information – at least, as it survives in its present condition – is not in standard pages of text, but in diagrammatic form. Balsam appears in different forms in these diagrams, including wood (*ʿūd*), oil, berry and stem/branch (*ʿirq*) of balsam.

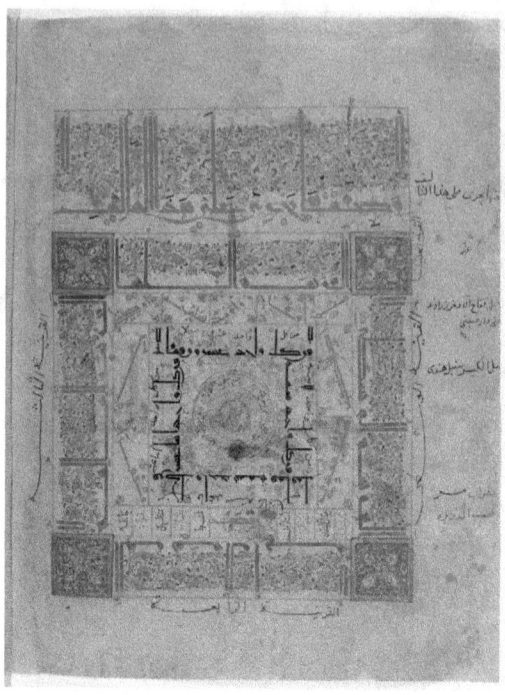

Figure 7.1 Diagram showing the recipe for pastilles of Hedychroum. From *Kitāb al-diryāq* (Book of Antidotes), dated 1199, Mesopotamia or Iran. Bibliothèque Nationale de France, Paris: Ms Arabe 2967.

This distinction between the wood and the stems or smaller branches is one that is not found elsewhere. Balsam products appear in four of the diagrams. The first outlines the components for making pastilles of Hedychroum (*iqrāṣ al-āthār al-kharūn*), which could then be added into other theriacs (Fig. 7.1). Two more deal with the famous Galene, the first providing the ingredients and the second, the beneficial uses of the compound drug. The last illustration is the Galenic improvement of Andromachus (Fig. 7.2), including balsam wood, berries and oil at several points around this ornate stellate design.[70]

Knowledge about theriacs found its way to China during the T'ang dynasty (618–907), apparently by way of a Byzantine embassy. The first reference to them in a Chinese medical text is in the pharmacological treatise, *Xinxiu bencao*, of Su Jing (fl. 656–60). Theriac (*diyejia*) is said to treat many serious illnesses, including intestinal blockages, and diseases associated

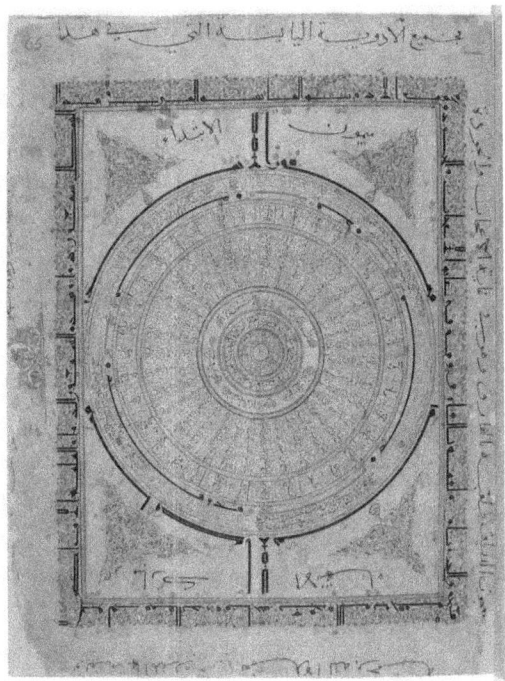

Figure 7.2 Diagram showing the theriac of Andromachus. *Kitāb al-diryāq* (Book of Antidotes), dated 1199, Mesopotamia or Iran. Bibliothèque Nationale de France, Paris: Ms Arabe 2967.

with childhood. The author continues that the pills were very costly and brought to the country by foreigners (*huren*). The expense was, however, justified because 'experiments have shown it to be effective'.[71] These 'foreigners' must have been both merchants and medical professionals; references to Soghdian, Persian and Arab physicians appear in Chinese sources, their skills in ophthalmology and the treatment of dysentery being particularly noted.[72] Textual sources of the sixteenth century allude to the introduction of Greek medicine into Tibet in the seventh and eighth centuries. The extent of the absorption of Greek ideas at this early date has been questioned, however, with more tangible relationships existing between Tibetan medical writings on urology and Ibn Sina's *Qānūn*. One dimension of this contact was the production of theriacs in the country.[73]

There are references to theriacs in Europe in the eighth century.[74] The exotic ingredients were finding their way to England in the late ninth century (see above), and must have been more common in southern Europe because of the greater proximity to Mediterranean trade routes. Arabic scholarship on theriacs spread to Europe through translations by Constantine the African, Gerard of Cremona and others.[75] The production of theriacs came to be associated with several urban centres across Europe. Commonly known as 'treacles' (from the French, *triacle*), the most famous type was produced in Venice and derived from Galene.[76] The production was overseen by the municipal authorities in order to combat adulteration and other cost-saving measures. Those pharmacists allowed to make the theriac raised their own vipers and cultivated many of the herbs. The days set aside for the annual manufacture of the theriac were attended by solemn ritual and public festivals. As was common in many other European cities, the diverse ingredients were displayed for examination, with the cooking process overseen by physicians. The finished product was placed into decorated vessels. Only those belonging to the office of the theriac makers (*Triacanti*) were permitted to produce Venice Treacle (Figs 7.3 and 7.4).[77]

Figure 7.3 Pewter container for theriac, Venice, 1603. Wellcome Collection.

Figure 7.4 Theriac stamp, Venice, 1601–80. Science Museum, London. Attribution 4.0 International (CC BY 4.0).

Fraudulent copies of Venice Treacle were commonplace.[78] Glazed ceramic and pewter containers bearing titles such as 'Theriaca', Mithridatum' and 'Mitridatium' were made for the producers of these compounds across early modern Europe (Figs 7.5 and 7.6). While they may have enjoyed less prestige in international trade, the treacles of other European cities were often made in tightly regulated fashion. For example, there was an inspector of theriacs in The Hague and the certification of approved apothecaries in Amsterdam. Noted treacles were produced in Genoa, Montpellier, Nuremburg, Istanbul, London and Edinburgh.[79] Demand for theriac in seventeenth-century England outstripped that of local producers, and additional supplies were imported from Europe, Egypt and Turkey. The extent of the importation may also have been affected by economic considerations, with the English theriacs costing more than their foreign rivals. This led to accusations that producers in Europe took less care than their English counterparts in ensuring the quality of their ingredients (Genoa being singled out for harsh criticism in this respect).[80]

Figure 7.5 Drug jars for holding Mithridatium. The largest vessel is Lambeth Delft ware, seventeenth century. Wellcome Collection. Attribution 4.0 International (CC BY 4.0).

Alpin describes the manufacture of theriacs in late-sixteenth-century Cairo.[81] He writes that the theriac was made annually in May in the most celebrated 'temple' in the city, called '*Morestan*' (i.e. *maristān*, or hospital), by order of the prefect (presumably, the *wazīr*) and the royal physician (*archiâtre*) that he calls '*Achim-Bassi*'.[82] The preparation was presided over by a pharmacist, with the mixture finally being made into pastilles. The Egyptian recipe was a closely guarded secret. Alpin does, however, claim to have a local source of information, one 'Mohamed ebne Haly' (Muhammad ibn 'Ali). On the basis of this source, Alpin provides a list of the components of the theriac called '*Tharachfaruc*', that was sent annually from Egypt to the Ottoman sultan.[83] This comprised sixty separate items, including both balsam 'oil' (*debenbalassan*, i.e. *duhn al-balasān*) and the fruit of the plant (*ab balassan*), and expensive aromatics such as saffron, Indian nard, terebinth and cinnamon. Another notable addition is stamped earth/clay (*tinmactum*, i.e. *ṭīn makhtūm*). This product was gathered from several sites, most notably the

Figure 7.6 Glazed albarello for storing theriac, Italy 1641. Wellcome Collection. Attribution 4.0 International (CC BY 4.0).

Greek island of Lemnos, and was believed to counteract poisons. Balsam and *terra lemnia* ('earth of Lemnos') were employed in diplomatic gifts during the early Ottoman period (Chapter 5).[84]

Treacles were best known for their use as antidotes to toxins, and for this reason they were popular among members of political elites. Henry VIII (r. 1509–47) and Elizabeth I (r. 1558–1603) were among the English monarchs to have taken tablets of theriac every day, and the kings of France were also avid consumers.[85] The *Antidotarium Nicolai*, a twelfth-century Salernitan medical compendium, suggests other uses for Mithridatium and Galene. A late-thirteenth-century version describes the creation of the so-called 'first lady (*primadonna*) of medicine', the 'Great Theriac of Galen'. This contained viper flesh, balsam, myrrh, cinnamon, storax and opium, and was recommended for a wide range of problems, including epilepsy, catalepsy, headache, migraine, arthritis, constrictions of the chest, asthma, kidney stones, colic, difficult menstruation, and the treatment of animal bites and venoms. In more general terms the theriac promoted the health of the heart, brains, lungs, liver and stomach. The discussion of Mithridatium in the same work gives more emphasis to analgesia.[86]

The Black Death (c. 1347–51) was the greatest pandemic of the medieval period, though the inhabitants of Europe endured periodic waves of plague both before and after. The role of theriacs in the treatment of pestilential disease has been the subject of some debate. Practitioners of Galenic medicine did not entirely commend their use in this context, because plague induced heat as did many of the simples found in theriacs. In the view of Gentile da Foligno (d. 1348), author of an influential commentary on Ibn Sina's *Qānūn*, this disadvantage was offset by the drying capacity of theriacs, allowing them to combat 'putridity'.[87] Recent scholarship has demonstrated that theriacs were employed in the alleviation of fever, pain, coughing, vomiting and diarrhoea, all of which were associated with plague. Recovery would also have been facilitated by treatments that eased skin inflammations (boils and ulcers) and inhibited bacterial and fungal infections. While one can only speculate on the efficacy of theriac tablets in these respects, the individual components of famous theriacs, such as balsam, myrrh, opium, wormwood, rue and camphor, possess active properties that are pertinent to the treatment of the symptoms listed above.[88] One last application of theriacs is revealed in an eighteenth-century record of Venice Treacle being taken to reduce the symptoms of seasickness during a voyage across the Aegean.[89]

Although there are references to balsam oil in some of these compound medicines, it was the fruit of balsam (*carpobalsamum*) that probably found the most extensive employment in the late medieval and early modern European treacle industry.[90] An eighteenth-century dictionary of trade even goes as far as claiming that, beyond its use in Venice Treacle, 'it has no other use in physic'.[91] Writers of the seventeenth and eighteenth centuries were, however, well aware that commodities marketed as *carpobalsamum* and *xylobalsamum* could well come from other species, such as 'balm of Mecca' (Chapter 5).

The efficacy of treacles was questioned by William Heberden (d. 1801) in a pamphlet entitled *Antitheriaka*. The author argues that the panoply of different components was unlikely to have any useful effect in treating poisons. Indeed, it was also possible that some ingredients might counteract one another, rendering the whole either useless or actually harmful to the patient.[92] His intended target was the Royal College of Physicians, the group responsible from 1618 for the publication of the *Pharmacopoeia*, listing all of the authorised simples and compound medicines for use by apothecaries. Heberden's objections did not have any immediate effect; Mithridatium, Galene and other theriacs remained in the *Pharmacopoeia* until 1746.[93]

Theriacs gradually lost their appeal in the latter part of the eighteenth century. Perhaps the quasi-magical character of many recipes sat uneasily with the scientific rationalism of the Enlightenment?[94] Other than their possession of ancient pedigrees, there was little to recommend the efficacy of Mithridatium and Galene as antidotes. These complex compound medicines did not entirely disappear from European medical literature, however. Mithridatium was still being employed in some regions through to the mid-nineteenth century, while Galene is listed in German and French pharmacopoeias in 1872 and 1884 respectively. Treacles were also recommended in manuals for farmers and farriers in the late eighteenth and early nineteenth centuries.[95] Theriacs spread to early modern India, perhaps as the result of the export of the product from Venice, Cairo or Istanbul, and Charles Doughty (d. 1926) also hears of theriac ('*tiryâk*') in Arabia.[96]

The medical applications of balsam surveyed in this chapter stayed largely true to the principles established in Greek scholarly writings, though innovations do appear in areas such as the treatment of wounds and the prevention of plague. The humoral classification of balsam as heating and drying defined many of its roles in combating ailments associated with an overabundance of cold or wet in the bodily organs. The use of balsam in theriacs was also well understood, with recipes attributed to the likes of Andromachus and Galen reproduced by Islamic and European authors. This transmission of information was ensured through the process of translating Arabic texts into Latin in Salerno and other centres of learning across Europe. This phase of translation brought original works by the likes of Hunayn ibn Ishaq, 'Ali ibn 'Isa, Ibn Sina and Ibn Butlan (d. c. 1038)[97] to the attention of European physicians, but it also made available Arabic translations of Greek originals. Works such as the *Lorscher Arzneibuch* and the *Leechbook of Bald* demonstrate, however, that elements of antique learning were available prior to the twelfth century. These texts also include information from northern European medical popular traditions, as do the writings of Hildegard of Bingen. There are also religious overtones in some accounts that can be related to the important role of balsam in Christian liturgical oils (Chapter 8).

Notes

1. For surveys of Islamic and Byzantine medicine, see Ullmann, *Islamic Medicine*; Pormann and Savage-Smith, *Medieval Islamic Medicine*. For biographical summaries of many figures discussed below, see Plinio Prioreschi, *Byzantine and Islamic Medicine*, History of Medicine 4 (Omaha, NE: Horatius Press, 2001, reprinted 2004), pp. 47–103, 213–344.
2. Al-Biruni, *Book of Pharmacy and Medicine*, I, pp. 73–5.
3. Umayya b. 'Abd al-'Aziz b. Abi al-Salt al-Dani al-Ishbili, *Livre des simples*, ed. and trans. Barbara Graille, Bulletin d'Études Orientales: Supplément 50 (Damascus: Institut Français du Proche-Orient, 2003), pp. 92–3, 116–17, 164–5, 186–7, 220–1, 238–9.
4. Ibn al-Baytar, *Mufrada*, I, p. 109.
5. Ahmad b. Muhammad ibn al-Hashsha', *Glossaire sur la Mans'uri de Razès*, ed. Georges Colin and Henri-Paul Renaud, Collection de textes Arabes publiée par l'Institut des Haute-Études Marocaines 11 (Rabat: Institut des Haute-Études, 1941), pp. 16–17.
6. Although it is not an ideal point of reference, I have cited below examples from the Latin translation of the *Qānūn*. See Gerard of Cremona, trans., *Avicennae*

arabum medicorum principis, Canon medicinae, annotations by Giovanni Costeo et al. (Venice: Apud Iuntas, 1608). For an edition and translation of the first book, see *The Canon of Medicine (al-Qānūn fī'l-ṭibb), vol. 1*, ed. Laleh Bakhtiar and trans. Oskar Gruner and Mazhar Shah, Great Books of the Islamic World (Chicago: Kazi Publications, 1999).

7. Abu 'Ali al-Husayn b. 'Abd Allah ibn Sina, *Avicenne: Poème de la médicine*, ed. and trans. Henri Jahier and Abdelkader Nourredine (Paris: Société d'édition des belles lettres, 1956), pp. 79, 80 (ll. 1038, 1055). On the book, see also Henri Jahier and Abdelkader Nourredine, '*Urguza fī't tibb – Cantica (Poème de la médicine)* d'Avicenne', *Bulletin de l'Association Guillaume Budé* 3 (1954): 95–7.

8. Abu al-Hasan 'Ali ibn Ridwan, *Medieval Islamic Medicine: Ibn Ridwan's Treatise 'On the Prevention of Bodily Ills in Egypt'*, trans. with introduction by Michael Dols, Arabic text edited by Adil Gamal (Berkeley, CA and London: University of California Press, 1984), p. 113 [40a–40b] (from the chapter, 'On the means of improving the badness of air, water, and food in Egypt', pp. 131–7).

9. Paul of Aegina, *Seven Books* III, p. 599.

10. Moses b. Maymun (Maimonides), *Treatise on Poisons, Hemorrhoids and Cohabitation. Maimonides' Medical Writing*, trans. Fred Rosner (Haifa: Maimonides Research Institute, c. 1984), p. 51.

11. On this issue, see Lawrence Conrad, '*Ṭā'ūn* and *wabā*': Conceptions of plague and pestilence in early Islam', *Journal of the Economic and Social History of the Orient* 25.3 (1982), pp. 286–307. For more on these issues, see Michael Dols, *The Black Death in the Middle East* (Princeton, NJ: Princeton University Press, 1977).

12. Thomas Greenhill (*Nikrokideia*, p. 210) notes the value of balsam against plague, and 'Agues or Fevers that proceed from Putrefaction'.

13. Al-'Umari, *L'Égypte, la Syrie, le Ḥiğāz et le Yémen*, p. 68. See also comments in Chapter 5.

14. Abu Ja'far b. Abi Khalid ibn al-Jazzar, *Ibn al-Jazzār on Sexual Diseases and Their Treatment. A Critical Edition of Zād al-musāfir wa-qūt al-ḥāḍir. Provisions for the Traveller and Nourishment for the Sedentary, Book 6*, trans. and ed. Gerrit Bos (The Sir Henry Wellcome Asian Series, London: Wellcome Institute, 1997), pp. 218, 303.

15. Abu Yusuf Ya'qub b. Ishaq al-Kindi, *The Medical Formulary or Aqrabadhin of al-Kindi*, trans. and ed. Martin Levey (Madison, WI: University of Wisconsin Press, 1966), p. 146.

16. Al-Biruni, *Book of Pharmacy*, I, p. 75.
17. These two sources are quoted in Ibn al-Baytar, *Mufrada*, I, p. 109. Al-Taymi is perhaps Fakhr al-Din al-Razi, who died in Herat in 1209.
18. Abu Hasan ʿAli ibn Ridwan, *Kitāb al-kifāya fiʾl-ṭibb*, ed. Salman Qataya (Baghdad: Maktabat al-Wataniyya, 1981), p. 81. On the humoral interpretation of urinary complaints and its application in medieval medicine, see Diana Luft, 'Uroscopy and urinary ailments in medieval Welsh medical texts', *Transactions of the Physicians of the Myddfai Society* 2018: https://www.ncbi.nlm.nih.gov/books/NBK540246/ (last consulted: 2 October 2019).
19. Al-Biruni, *Book of Pharmacy*, I, p. 75; Ibn Sina, *Canon medicinae*, I, p. 279 (Book 2, tract 2, cap. 84).
20. ʿAli ibn ʿIsa al-Kahhal, *Memorandum Book of a Tenth-century Oculist for the Use of Modern Ophthalomologists*, trans. and ed. Casey Wood (Chicago: University of Chicago Press, 1936), pp. 181–3. See also Martin Levey, *Early Arabic Pharmacology* (Leiden: Brill, 1973), p. 128.
21. Ibn Sina, *Canon medicinae*, II, p. 323 (Book 5, summa 2, tract 2). On the recipes of Paul of Aegina and Hunayn ibn Ishaq, see Chapter 6.
22. Al-Biruni, *Book of Pharmacy*, I, p. 75. On the understanding of trachoma, see Emilie Savage-Smith, 'Ibn al-Nafis's *Perfected Book on Ophthalmology* and his treatment of trachoma and its sequelae', *Journal of the History of Arabic Science* 4.1 (1980): 147–206. Ibn al-Nafis mentions the use of frankincense, myrrh, gum ammoniac and oil of rose, but not balsam.
23. Quoted in Ibn al-Baytar, *Mufrada*, I, p. 109.
24. For example, Ibn Ridwan, *Kifāya*, p. 81; al-Biruni, *Book of Pharmacy*, I, p. 75; Ibn al-Baytar, *Mufrada*, I, p. 109.
25. For example, Ibn Sina, *Canon medicinae*, I, p. 279 (Book 2, tract 2, cap. 84).
26. For example, al-Biruni, *Book of Pharmacy*, I, p. 75; Ibn al-Baytar, *Mufrada*, I, p. 109. See also Budge, trans., *Syrian Anatomy, Pathology and Therapeutics*, 7:2 (II, pp. 111–14); Alexander of Tralles, *Oeuvres médicales* 3:1 (III, pp. 54–5).
27. Quoted in Ibn al-Baytar, *Mufrada*, I, p. 109.
28. Maimonides, *Treatise on Poisons*, p. 176. No reference to balsam appears in his work on symptomatic medicine, though he recommends 'balm gentle' (*Melissa officinalis*) in the treatment of palpitations and hot temperament. See Maimonides (Moses b. Maymun), *Moses Maimonides on the Causes of Symptoms*, ed. J. Liebowitz and Shlomo Marcus (Berkeley, CA and Los Angeles: University of California Press, 1974), p. 111.
29. For his biography and writings, see Raphaela Veit, 'Dāʾūd al-Anṭākī',

Encyclopaedia of Islam 3 (2010). See also Nicola Ziadeh, 'al-Antāqi and his *Tadhkira*', *Aram* 11–12 (1999–2000): 503–8.

30. Da'ud al-Antaki, *Tadhkirat ulī al-albāb wa jāmi' lil-'ajab al-'ujāb*, ed. Muhammad al-Falaki, 3 vols in 1 (Cairo: Shakirat Maktaba wa Matba'a Mustafa al-Babi al-Halabi, 1952, reprinted 1982), I, p. 369. On his pharmacological method, see Ephraim Lev, 'The contribution of the sixteenth-century Turkish physician Daud al-Antaki to the research of medical substances in use in the Levant (Bilad al-Sham)', *Turkiye Klinikleri Journal of Medical Ethics* 13 (2005): 74–80. Lev identifies *zaqqūm* (cf. Qur'an 17:60; 37:62–8; 44:43 and 56:52) as 'Egyptian balsam' (*Balanites aegyptiaca*). See pp. 75–6, table 1.
31. *Lorscher Arzneibuch* (Staatsbibliothek Bamberg Ms. Med.1), fol. 1v. The manuscript is available online, with a modern German transcription, at: http://digital.bib-bvb.de/view/bvbmets/viewer.0.6.4.jsp?folder_id=0&dvs=1560631547288-410&pid=4685473&locale=en&usePid1=true&usePid2=true# (last consulted: 15 June 2019). On this manuscript and the context of Carolingian medicine, see Meg Leja, 'The sacred art: Medicine in the Carolingian Renaissance', *Viator* 47.2 (2016): 1–34.
32. *Lorscher Arzneibuch*, fols 5r, 44r.
33. Ibid. fols 23r, 46v, 68r.
34. Ibid. fols 68v, 69v–70v.
35. On this text, and other medical works of the period, see Voigts, 'Anglo-Saxon plant remedies'; Cameron, *Anglo-Saxon Medicine*, pp. 30–64. The *Leechbook of Bald* was published in Oswald Cockagne, ed. and trans., *Leechdoms, Wortcunning, and Starcraft of Early England. Being a Collection, for the most Part never before printed, illustrating the History of Science in this Country before the Norman Conquest* (London: Longman, Green, Longman, Roberts and Green, 1864).
36. *Leechbook of Bald* II, 65:4 (fols. 107v–108r). See Cockagne, ed. and trans., *Leechdoms*, II, 295–7. Myrrh is also mentioned in more conventional medical contexts: I, 1:1; II, 65:10, 11, 18, 19. For frankincense, see I, 64:5 (fol. 52v); II, 37:2 (fol. 92r).
37. *Leechbook of Bald*, I, 2:2, 3. See Cockagne, ed. and trans., *Leechdoms*, p. 29. On the acquisition of imported medicaments, see John Riddle, 'The introduction of eastern drugs in the early Middle Ages', *Archiv für Geschichte der Medizin und der Naturwissenschaft* 49 (1965): 185–98.
38. *Leechbook of Bald*, II, 64:1. See Cockagne, ed. and trans., *Leechdoms*, II, p. 289.

39. Cameron, *Anglo-Saxon Medicine*, pp. 85–6. He cites two salves for the eye that follow closely *Physica Plinii* 17:3, 8.
40. For the Latin translation, see Seth, *Syntagma*, pp. 19–20. On Seth and his methods, see Owsei Temkin, 'Byzantine medicine: Tradition and empiricism', *Dumbarton Oaks Papers* 16 (1962): 95–115 (particularly pp. 108–9).
41. On Constantine's practices of translation, see Charles Burnett and Danielle Jacquart, *Constantine the African and 'Alī ibn al-'Abbās al-Maǧūsī. The Pantegni and Related Texts*, Studies in Ancient Medicine 10 (Leiden and New York: Brill, 1994).
42. This work was often copied in the Middle Ages. For example, see Platearius, *Le Livre des simples médecines*. For discussion of balsam, and an illustration of the balsam tree (also discussed in Chapter 4), see pp. 222–3. Another example of this genre is Arnold Pfister, ed. with introduction to the facsimile edition, *De simplici medicina. Kräuterbuch-Handschrift aus dem Letzen Viertel des 14. Jahrhunderts im Besitz der Basler Universitäts-Bibliothek Hugo Berchten* (Basel: Sanz AG, 1960). See text and illustrations on fol. 5v.
43. Dominique Haefeli-Till, trans., *Der 'Liber de oculis' des Constantinus Africanus: Ubersetzung und Kommentar*, Zürcher Medizingeschichtliche Abhandlungen, Neue Reihe 121 (Zurich: Juris Druck und Verlag 1977), p. 92 (12:13). Following Hunayn, Constantine also recommends bleeding the patient and the application of leeches to the temples.
44. Enrique Cartelle, ed., *Constantini Liber de Coitu. El tratado de andrologiá de Constantino el Africano*, Estudio y edicion critica. Monografias de la Universidad de Santiago de Compostela 77 (Santiago de Compostela: Europa Artes Gráficas 1983), chapter 17, 1:10. The version in Constantine's collected works (*Opera*, pp. 299–307) contains no reference to balsam. For an English translation, see Paul Delaney, 'Constantinus Africanus' *De Coitu*: A translation', *The Chaucer Review* 4.1 (1969): 55–65.
45. Constantine the African, *Liber de gradibus simplicium*. In *Opera* (Basle: H. Petrus, 1536–9), I, pp. 342–87. The section on balsam appears on pp. 356–7.
46. On this, see James Kritzeck, *Peter the Venerable and Islam*, Princeton Studies on the Near East (Princeton, NJ: Princeton University Press, 1964, reprinted 2016).
47. For example, his translations of ophthalmic treatments containing balsam appear in Ibn Sina, *Canon medicinae*, II, pp. 319–24. Antidotes are dealt with in II, 265–83. On the texts chosen by Gerard and his contemporary, Domenicus Gundissalinus, see Charles Burnett, 'The coherence of the Arabic-Latin

translation program in Toledo in the twelfth century', *Science in Context* 14.1/2 (2000): 249–88.
48. Platearius, *Practica brevis* 12:3; 15. In Tony Hunt, ed., *Anglo-Norman Medicine, Volume I: Roger Frugard's* Chirurgia, *The* Practica brevis *of Platearius* (Woodbridge and Rochester, NY: D. S. Brewer, 1994), pp. 236–8, 246–8. On the uncertainties concerning the identity of the author of the *Practica brevis* and the date of composition, see pp. 149–50.
49. Platearius, *Practica brevis* 8:5. In Hunt, ed., *Anglo-Norman Medicine, Volume I*, pp. 213–15.
50. Platearius, *Practica brevis* 6:3, 9:4. In Hunt, ed., *Anglo-Norman Medicine, Volume I*, pp. 194–6, 223–4 (9:4 also mentions another antidote, Adrianum).
51. Women's Health of 'Trotula'. In Tony Hunt, ed., *Anglo-Norman Medicine, Volume II: Shorter Treatises* (Cambridge and Rochester, NY: D. S. Brewer, 1997), p. 94, l. 467.
52. Bartholomaeus Anglicus, *On the Properties of Things. John Trevisa's Translation of Bartholomaeus Anglicus* De proprietatibus rerum. *A Critical Text*, ed. Michael Seymour et al. (Oxford: Clarendon Press, 1975–88), 17:18 (II, pp. 916–17); Rufinus, *The Herbal of Rufinus*, ed. Lynn Thorndike (Chicago: University of Chicago Press, 1946), pp. 50–2.
53. Hildegard of Bingen, *Hildegard von Bingen's* Physica: *The Complete English Translation of her Classic Work on Health and Healing*, trans. Priscilla Throop (Rochester, VT: Healing Arts Press, 1998), chapter 177 (pp. 82–3). She describes balsam as having a 'royal nature', though she does not elaborate on this point. Myrrh and frankincense are dealt with in chapters 175 and 176 respectively (p. 82). On the combination of deer marrow and balsam, see *Lorscher Arzneibuch*, fol. 68r.
54. Benjamin Kedar, 'Benvenutus Grapheus of Jerusalem, an oculist in the era of the Crusades', *Korot: The Israel Journal of the History of Medicine and Science* 11 (1995): 14*–41* (the quoted observation appears on p. 19). Kedar describes him as having a 'slim' grasp of theoretical knowledge. On his methods and conclusions, see Laurence M. Eldredge, 'A thirteenth-century ophthalmologist, Benvenutus Grassus: His treatise and its survival', *Journal of the Royal Society of Medicine* 91 (1998): 47–52.
55. Laurence M. Eldredge, ed., Benvenutus Grassus. *The Wonderful Art of the Eye. A Critical Edition of the Middle English Translation of his 'De Probatissima Arte Oculorum'*, Medieval Texts and Studies 19 (East Lansing, MI: Michigan State University Press, 1996), l. 815. 'Ali ibn 'Isa's work had been translated

in Salerno as the *Tractatus de oculis*. Balsam is mentioned in this text. For example, see *Chirurgia parua. Guidonis. Cyrurgia Albucasis c≠ cauterijs [et] alijs instrumentis. Tractatus de oculis Iesu Hali. Tractatus de oculis Canamusali* (Venice: Schott, 1500), *Tractatus de oculis*, book 4, p. 17 (no. 42). Available online: https://wellcomelibrary.org/item/b12954044#?c=0&m=0&s=0&cv=4&z=0.5646%2C0.2771%2C0.418%2C0.2626 (last consulted: 30 September 2019).

56. For a brief assessment of his place in the development of clinical methodology, see D. Craig Brater and Walter J. Daly, 'Clinical pharmacology in the Middle Ages: Principles that presage the 21st century', *Clinical Pharmacology and Therapeutics* 67.5 (2000): 447–50 (particularly p. 449). For his work on magnets, see Lynn Thorndike, 'John of St Amand on the magnet', *Isis* 36.3/4 (1946): 156–7.

57. Jean de Saint Amand, *Die Areolae des Johannes de Sancto Amando*, ed. Julius Pagel (Berlin: Georg Reimer, 1896), p. 54.

58. On his biography and methods, see Jacques Vrebos, 'Thoughts on a neglected French medieval surgeon: Henri de Mondeville (ca. 1260–1320)', *European Journal of Plastic Surgery* 34 (2011): 1–11 (particularly pp. 7–9 on the treatment of wounds).

59. Henri de Mondeville, *Die Chirurgie des Heinrich von Mondeville (Hermondaville) nach Berliner, Erfurter und Pariser Codices* (Book 1 of *Leben, Lehre und Leistungen des Heinrich von Mondeville [Hermondaville]. Ein Beitrag zur Geschichte der Anatomie und Chirurgie*), ed. Julius Pagel (Berlin: August Hirschwald, 1892), p. 567 (*Antidotarius* 9:121, 122). By contrast, the classical scholar Celsus lists balsam as one of the products that could promote suppuration. See the commentary by Francis Adams in Paul of Aegina, *Seven Books* III, p. 67 (7:3).

60. Prosper Alpin (Alpinus), *La médecine des Égyptiens*, trans. Raymond de Fenoyl, Collection des voyageurs occidentaux en Égypte 21 (Cairo: Institut Français d'Archéologie du Caire, 1980), pp. 291 [383], 302 [402], 308 [411–12], 314 [423–4], 319 [431–2], 322–3 [438–9]; Prosper Alpin (Alpinus), *Histoire naturelle de l'Égypte par Prosper Alpin, 1581–1584*, trans. Raymond de Fenoyl and ed. Raymond de Fenoyl and Serge Sauneron, Collection des voyageurs occidentaux en Égypte 20 (Cairo: Institut Français d'Archéologie du Caire, 1979), pp. 191–2 [369–70].

61. Joëlle Ricordel, 'Le traité sur la thériaque d'Ibn Rushd', *Revue d'Histoire de la Pharmacie* 48.325 (2000): 81.

62. Joëlle Ricordel, 'Ibn Djuldjul: "propos sur la thériaque"', *Revue d'Histoire de*

la Pharmacie 48.325 (2000): 73–80. On Arabic writings on theriacs and their relationship to Galen, see Penelope Johnstone, 'Galen in Arabic', pp. 207–10.

63. Georges Anawati, 'Le traité d'Averroes sur la thériaque et ses antécédents grecs et arabes', *Quaderni di Studi Arabi* 5–6 (1987–8): 26–48. Anawati identifies references to Galen's *De antidotis* and *De theriaka ad Pison*, and the pseudo-Galenic *De theriaka ad Pamphilianum*. Also Abu al-Walid Muhammad b. Ahmad ibn Rushd (Averroes), *Rasā'il Ibn Rushd al-ṭibbiyya* (Les traités médicaux d'Averroes), ed. Georges Anawati and Sa'id Zayed (Cairo: Centre de l'Édition de l'Héritage Culturel, 1987), pp. 289–322. For his comments on poisons and the body, see Ricordel, 'Ibn Rushd', p. 87.

64. 'Ali b. Sahl Rabban al-Tabari, *Firdausu'l-hikmat or paradise of wisdom*, ed. Muhammad Siddiqi (Berlin: Buch und Kunstdruckerei, 1928), p. 403; al-Razi cited in Ibn al-Baytar, *Mufrada*, I, p. 109. On the former, see Max Meyerhof, 'Alî at-Tabarî's "Paradise of Wisdom", one of the oldest Arabic compendiums of medicine', *Isis* 16.1 (1931): 6–54.

65. Seth (Sethis), *Syntagma*, p. 20.

66. Al-Biruni, *Book of Pharmacy and Medicine*, I, p. 75.

67. Maimonides, *Treatise on Poisons*, p. 51.

68. Muhammad b. 'Ali ibn Wahshiyya, *Medieval Arabic Toxicology: The Book of Poisons of Ibn Wahshiya and its Relation to Early Indian and Greek Texts*, trans. and ed. Martin Levey, American Philosophical Society Transactions, New Series 56 viii (Philadelphia: American Philosophical Society, 1966), pp. 55, 58, 69, 71, 79, 88, 102, 108.

69. Françoise Micheau, 'The medicinal value of the Book of Theriac', in *Kitab al-diryaq (Thériaque de Paris), édition en facsimilé du manuscrit arabe 2964 de la BnF* (Sansepolcro: Aboca Museum Edizioni, 2009), pp. 49–75. See also: Pancaroğlu, 'Socializing medicine'.

70. My thanks to Zahra Kazani for sharing her research on this important text.

71. Nappi, 'Bolatu's pharmacy theriac', p. 746. The author also cites studies on the reception of theriacs in Tibet. On the Byzantine embassy in 667, see Edward Schafer, *The Golden Peaches of Samarkand: A Study of T'ang Exotics* (Berkeley, CA: University of California Press, 1963), p. 184. For balsam, see pp. 187–8. The ninth-century writer Tuan Ch'eng-shi reports that the substance would cure acariasis, and claims that its cost in China was 'double that of gold'. He gives the Syriac name of the plant as *apursāmā*.

72. Christopher Beckwith, 'The introduction of Greek medicine into Tibet in the seventh and eighth centuries', *Journal of the American Oriental Society* 99.2

(1979): 297, 311, n. 6. Balsam may be mentioned in a ninth-century text, the *Yu yan tsa tsu* (Chapter 2), suggesting further evidence of Chinese scholarly engagement with the rare medicaments of western Asia and north-eastern Africa.

73. Beckwith, 'The introduction of Greek medicine into Tibet'; Ronit Yoeli-Tlalim, 'Revisiting "Galen in Tibet"', *Medical History* 56.3 (2012): 355–65. On theriacs, see Christopher Beckwith, 'Tibetan treacle: A note on theriac in Tibet', *The Tibetan Society Bulletin* 15 (June 1980): 49–51.

74. Christiane Fabbri, 'Treating medieval plague: The wonderful virtues of theriac', *Early Science and Medicine* 12 (2007): 253. The work cited is the Carolingian pharmacological compendium *Lorscher Arzneibuch*. For the theriacs in this text with balsam, see *Lorscher Arzneibuch*, fols 58r–v, 61r–v.

75. For example, see Ibn Sina's recounting of Greek theriac recipes in Ibn Sina, *Canon medicinae*, IV.1.1 (II, pp. 265–83). Those containing balsam can be found on pp. 265–7 (theriacis magnis), 267–8 (Ars trochiscorum de viperis), 268–9 (Mithridatium).

76. Watson, *Theriac and Mithridatium*, pp. 98, 101. The word even finds its way into English translations of the Bible in the sixteenth century, replacing 'balm'. For example, see Jeremiah 8:22 from the 1538 version produced by Matthew Coverdale: 'Is there no treakle in Gilead? No physician there?' See J. P. Griffin, 'Venetian treacle and the foundation of medicines regulation', *British Journal of Clinical Pharmacology* 58.3 (2004): 318.

77. Watson, *Theriac and Mithridatium*, pp. 103–5. Also Mayor, *Poison King*, pp. 244–5.

78. The English translation of Pomet (*A Compleat History of Druggs*, p. 278) remarks, 'and to promote or recommend the Sale of this, they cover the Pots with a printed Paper, wherein are two *Vipers* that compose a Circle, crown'd with a *Fleur-de-lis*, which contains this Title, *Fine Venice Treacle*, tho' it is made at *Orleans* or *Paris*'.

79. Watson, *Theriac and Mithridatium*, pp. 104–8, 146–8. On the industry in Montpellier, see François Granet, 'La thériaque de Montpellier', *Revue d'Histoire de la Pharmacie* 229 (1976): 75–83. On the ingredients, including 'balm of Mecca', see pp. 76–7. On the evolving scholarship on theriacs in Montpellier, see Michael McVaugh, 'Theriac at Montpellier, 1285–1325 (with an edition of the "*Questiones de tyriaca*" of William of Brescia)', *Sudhoffs Archiv. Zeitschrift für Wissenschaftsgeschichte* 56.2 (1972): 113–44.

80. Watson, *Theriac and Mithridatium*, pp. 120–1.

81. Alpin, *La médecine*, pp. 285–93 [375–86]. For his comparison of modern theriacs and the recipe attributed to Andromachus, see pp. 294–302 [387–402].
82. Ibid. p. 288 [376]. The name of the *maristān* is not given, though he may be referring to the complex founded by Sultan Qalawun (r. 1279–90).
83. Ibid. p. 288 [376]. I have been unable to identify Muhammad ibn ʿAli. On medicine in Ottoman Egypt, see Sherry Gadalrab, 'Medical healers in Ottoman Egypt, 1517–1805', *Medical History* 54.3 (2010): 365–86.
84. Alpin, *La médecine*, pp. 290–3 [381–6]. On *terra lemnia* in gifts, see Raby, '*Terra Lemnia*', pp. 316–17.
85. Watson, *Theriac and Mithridatium*, pp. 106–8, 115–16; Mayor, *Poison King*, p. 244.
86. These details about the text are recorded in Fabbri, 'Treating medieval plague', pp. 257–8, n. 34. For the ingredients of Galene and Mithridatium in a Latin version of the *Antidotarium Nicolai* see Hunt, ed., *Anglo-Norman Medicine, Volume I*, pp. 319–21, nos 54 (Yerapigra Galyeni) and 56 (Metridatum).
87. Watson, *Theriac and Mithridatium*, p. 100. Da Foligno also acknowledges the 'occult virtue' of these compound medicines.
88. Fabbri, 'Treating medieval plague', pp. 247–83. See particularly pp. 269–74, table 1. Watson downplays the role of theriacs in the treatment of plague. See his *Theriac and Mithridatium*, pp. 99–100, et passim.
89. Watson, *Theriac and Mithridatium*, p. 150.
90. Pomet (*A Compleat History of Druggs*, p. 205 [chapter 45]) observes that this product was 'principally for the great Treacle wherein they require no other Preparation but to be chose true, and freed from their little Stalks, empty Shells, and such as are Worm-eaten amongst them'.
91. Savary de Brûlons, *Dictionnaire universel*, entry on balsam (unpaginated text). The same source notes the employment of balsam wood in the making of 'troches of Hedychroum'.
92. Of Mithridatium he writes, 'Among the many eminent services which the authority of this learned and judicious Body has done to the practice of Physic, it might not be the least that it had driven out this medley of discordant Simples; which has no better title to the name of *Mithridates*, than as it so well resembles the numerous, undisciplined forces of a barbarous King, made up of a dissonant crowd collected from different countries, mighty in appearance, but in reality, an ineffective multitude, that only hinder one another'. William Heberden, *Antitheriaka: An Essay on Mithridatium and Theriaca* (London?: no publisher

given, 1745), p. 19. This work is discussed in detail in Watson, *Theriac and Mithridatium*, pp. 136–43. Also Griffin, 'Venetian treacle', pp. 323–4.

93. Theriacs were omitted from the next edition of 1788. See Watson, *Theriac and Mithridatium*, p. 150.
94. See comments in Griffin, 'Venetian treacle', pp. 321–4.
95. Watson, *Theriac and Mithridatium*, p. 150. He also mentions that Mithridatium and Galene were still being utilised regularly in the hospital of Montpellier through to the end of the eighteenth century.
96. Watson, *Theriac and Mithridatium*, p. 108; Charles Doughty, *Travels in Arabia Deserta*, new edition in one volume (New York: Random House, 1937), II, p. 27. On the use of theriacs in early modern China, see Nappi, 'Bolatu's pharmacy theriac', pp. 746–63.
97. His most famous work, the *Taqwīm al-ṣiḥḥa* ('Maintenance of Health') was translated into Latin as the *Tacuinum sanitatis*. This work is known in numerous manuscript copies, often provided with extensive cycles of illustrations.

8

Religious and Royal Dimensions to Balsam

Levinus Lemnius' (d. 1568) *An Herbal for the Bible* takes as its subject matter the plant species mentioned in the Old and New Testaments. A physician by training, Lemnius was well aware of the curative properties of aromatic resins and gums such as myrrh, stacte, frankincense and ammoniac.[1] The book also comments on the religious symbolism attached to specific plants. He writes about the passages containing references to 'Balme', noting that the product appears in scripture 'to signifie high honor and excellencie of vertue, and most sweete and comfortable perfumes of heavenly love and doctrine, wherewith the mind of man is most graciously inspired and divinely indued'.[2] In a discussion of the times when Christ likens Himself to different species of tree, Lemnius cites the first part of Ecclesiasticus 24:15, translating it as: 'I have given a smell in the streets as cinnamon and Balme'.[3]

The conjunction of beautiful aroma with holiness is, of course, commonplace in medieval Christian literature, particularly hagiographies. For example, those written about the seventh-century saint Lambert of Maastricht make clear that the holy body emanated a 'sweet' (*dulcis*) smell from the time of the celebration of the funeral rites onward. This pleasing quality, according to a twelfth-century account, 'refreshed all who came near'.[4] A contrast is drawn between the normal processes of decomposition undergone by a human corpse and the miraculous preservation of the bodies of deceased holy men and women. This preserved state also allowed the cadaver to give off not the stench of putrefaction, but rather the 'odour of sanctity'. The release of the soul of a saint at the moment of death was also believed to be accompanied by a sweet perfume.[5]

The olfactory dimension of Middle Eastern shrines is noted by the twelfth-century pilgrim Saewulf; he claims that visitors to the tombs of the patriarchs in Hebron (al-Khalil) 'are greeted by the smell of balsam and the very precious spices with which the holy bodies were anointed'.[6] Numerous medieval accounts record the fragrant oil that dripped miraculously from the tomb of St Catherine, located in the monastery bearing her name in the Sinai.[7] The source of this exudate is not specified, though it seems to have derived from a practice of regularly anointing the saint's relics with oil, mixed with aromatic agents such as balsam or myrrh. The reverence paid to the resting places of saints, and to places associated with the life of Christ, also led pilgrims to collect spent olive oil from lamps. This liquid would be placed into ceramic or pewter ampullae, sometimes decorated with religious motifs and inscriptions. Examples of these vessels survive, dating from the sixth century onwards (Fig. 8.1; for other types of pilgrim container, see Figs 5.3 and 5.4).

As can be seen in the chapters devoted to medicine (6 and 7), the premodern understanding of balsam combines aspects of its physical attributes,

Figure 8.1 Ceramic ampulla with relief images of St Menas and camels. Egypt, 395–643. Musée du Louvre: E24445, AF 7035. RMN-Grand Palais / Art Resource, NY.

such as the powerful smell, with more symbolic dimensions. Theriacs are an example of this phenomenon, containing as they do more than a hint of magic (Chapter 7). This chapter reviews the ways in which balsam was employed in a range of ritualistic functions, from the treatment of dead bodies to anointing ceremonies conducted in ancient and medieval times.

Embalming and Incense

The pleasing smell of balsam is bound up with the experience of the dead bodies of saints and patriarchs. This opens the question concerning the possible role of balsam in the practice of embalming. The close relationship in English between the words 'balm' (often used as a synonym for balsam) and 'embalm' appears, at first sight, to indicate a straightforward connection between the products of the balsam tree and the procedures associated with preserving a cadaver. The word 'embalm' is, in fact, first employed in English only in the sixteenth century, with the earlier form of the word in Middle English being *embaumen*, deriving from the Old French *embaumer* (also *embausmer*).[8] Despite the relatively recent lineage of these words, some writers of the early modern period advanced the claim that balsam had long played a role in embalming. For example, the French surgeon and scholar Ambroise Paré (d. 1590) provides a detailed description of the process, noting the use of both minerals and organic products (including balsam) in filling the body cavity following the removal of the internal organs.[9]

In *Nekrokideia* (1705), Greenhill specifies the role of balsam in 'preserving the dead Bodies of Kings and Princes; from which Quality, and on account of its Analogy with *Embalming*, the Art itself deriv'd its Name from it'.[10] Balsam could act as a 'preservative' against diseases and fevers 'that proceed from Putrefaction'.[11] Although there is some truth in this statement, given the antibacterial qualities of aromatic tree resins, Greenhill might well have been aware of the claims in European travel writing that balsam could conserve indefinitely the state of bodily organs.[12] Popular literature also alludes to this quality of balsam; a striking example is the story of the eleventh-century ruler of Valencia known as El Cid (Chapter 5), whose dead body was sent into battle propped up in the saddle of his horse. Balsam was one of the resins employed to obstruct the natural processes of decay, allowing for his miraculous appearance on the battlefield.[13]

One of the dedicatory poems in the preface to *Nekrokideia* alludes to this almost magical ability to halt the processes of decay.[14] Greenhill makes more tangible comments about balsam in the practice of embalming, citing Pliny on the anointing of the washed corpse with 'Odiferous and Aromatick Ointments'. He reviews ancient practices of anointing and embalming the dead, with some using 'Compositions either of *Salt, Nitre, Asphalt, Bitumen, Cedar, Balsam, Gypsum, Lime, Petrole, Naptha, Turpentine, Rosin*, or the like . . .'[15]

Elsewhere he contrasts the differences in the materials used to pack the cavities of cadavers. Poorer clients would make use of pissasphalt (or mummia, a tarry intermediate between petroleum and asphalt), where the embalming of the wealthy elite had access to rarer commodities, such as myrrh, aloes, cinnamon, balsam and saffron, for the same purpose.[16] He also references Diodorus Siculus on the employment of 'Balsam of Cedar' (probably meaning oil of cedar; see below) as an initial embalming agent, prior to the application of myrrh, cinnamon and other aromatics.[17] Dipping the winding cloths in balsam would, according to Greenhill, serve 'like Glue to stop the Pores, and hinder the Dissipation of the volatil parts of the Aromatics, as well as the Penetration of the Air'.[18]

Despite the confidence expressed by authors of early modern Europe, there is little textual or physical evidence to support the widespread employment of balsam in ancient embalming practices. Herodotus (d. c. 425 BCE) provides a detailed account of the methods used in Egypt. He starts with the extraction of the brain and of the contents of the abdomen. The account continues:

> the cavity is then thoroughly cleansed and washed out, first with palm wine and again with an infusion of pounded spices. After that it is filled with pure bruised myrrh pounded up with cassia and every other aromatic substance with the exception of frankincense, and sewn up again, after which the body is placed in natron, covered entirely over, for seventy days . . .[19]

The body was subsequently washed before being wound with strips of fine linen smeared with gum. Diodorus is critical of Herodotus, though his account agrees largely in its listing of the products employed to wash and fill the body cavity.[20] Herodotus relates the cheaper methods of embalming involving the filling of the abdomen with oil of cedar (*kedros*). This was applied with syringes and did not require the removal of the intestines and other organs. The same technique is described by Pliny.[21]

Archaeology and archaeological science provide additional insights into the practices of embalming in ancient Egypt. Excavations conducted by Theodore Davis (d. 1915) led to the discovery of embalming materials thought to have been employed in the funeral of Tutankhamun (r. c. 1332–1323 BC). These included winding clothes and sacks containing natron and chaff, but little that bears on the resins and perfumed substances used to preserve cadavers.[22] Embalming material, dating to c. 1500 BC, was unearthed at Deir al-Bahri. This contained chemical components that are consistent with wood tar oil, known as cedar oil (as described by Herodotus and Pliny).[23] Scientific examination of mummies has revealed further evidence on the mummification process. CT scanning demonstrated the extensive use of resinous materials, though this technique does not permit more accurate differentiation. Resin was also soaked into the linen rags around the bodies. The scans also showed the use of mud, sand, small rocks and organic packing that might have been either chaff or sawdust, and plant seeds. Resin blackens through age, and has mistakenly been identified in earlier studies as pitch. One study did, however, suggest the presence of myrrh.[24]

In summary, both textual and physical evidence confirm the use of tree resins and other organic materials in the embalming processes of Pharaonic Egypt. Myrrh is mentioned, with aloes, in connection with the embalming of the body of Christ (Chapter 2).[25] Myrrh has proven antiseptic qualities, aiding in the preservation of human tissue. Balsam would have performed a similar role, but there is no evidence that it was commonly employed for the purposes of embalming in the ancient world. The practice of using balsam as a preservative against decay may originate in the late antique period. Agnellus's ninth-century account of the opening of the tomb of Peter Chrysologus (bishop of Ravenna from 433 until c. 450) records that the smell of myrrh and balsam was so potent that it lingered in the church for more than a week. More specific references to balsam in embalming appear in descriptions of the preparation of the bodies of emperors Justinian (r. 527–65) and Charlemagne in 565 and 813 respectively.[26] Hildegard of Bingen writes that balsam could be employed for a short period to counteract the putrefaction of a corpse, and a similar claim appears in the *Tractatus de herbis*.[27]

The attractive smell attributed to true balsam naturally contributed to its use in perfumes.[28] This practice appears to have been most prevalent in the Roman empire. Pliny notes the employment of balsam in several types of unguent sold in the city, and elsewhere in the empire. 'Bryon' (probably made from the buds of white poplar) and oil of balanus formed the basis of a number of unguents, though many other aromatics could be added. For example, Mendesian unguent contained a variety of ingredients, including myrrh, metopion (an Egyptian oil extracted from bitter almonds), cardamom, sweet rush, honey, wine, seed of balsam, galbanum and resin of terebinth.[29] Pliny writes in exasperated tones about the overuse of perfumes in his own time, seeing these practices as a sign of the corruption of society.[30] In his ribald novel, *The Golden Ass*, Apuleius of Madaura (d. c. 170) cites balsam as a perfume, both to be worn on the body and to fragrance interior and exterior spaces.[31] The tenth-century *Book of Eparch* includes information about the guild of perfumers in Constantinople, indicating the continued interest in scents, including balsam, for personal use.[32] Perfumes remained popular in domestic settings across the early Islamic world. Al-Tanukhi (d. 854/55), the tenth-century Iraqi judge, records the practice of making pods of fabric from cotton rags. These were soaked in oil of balsam (*duhn al-balasān*) and other expensive aromatic oils before being burnt in stone or clay censers during the celebration of Nawruz (new year).[33] Aromatic substances are regularly mentioned in pre-Islamic and early Islamic poetry.[34]

It might be that the Roman fixation with perfumes led to their rejection among the leaders of early Christian communities. Only in the fifth and sixth centuries did aromatics become more commonplace in a Christian context, principally in the form of incense. The *Liber Pontificalis* provides evidence for importation from Egypt of perfumed products, including balsam, nard, storax and stacte (liquid myrrh).[35] There was annual benefaction of nard, balsam and spices to the church of saints Marcellinus and Peter in Rome, these products being burnt in the presence of the bodies of the saints. The ingredients for incense were also sent from Rome to other churches; Gregory the Great (Pope Gregory I; r. 590–604) sent gifts, including balsam, to Secundus of Non, deacon of Ravenna, as an offering to the holy martyrs of the city.[36] Such uses drew upon Old Testament precedents; myrrh and frankincense are mentioned in connection to incense, while the former is also described as a fumigant.[37] A passage in Babylonian Talmud, probably dating to the seventh century, also claims that balm (ẓori) was burnt within the Temple. The author may have assumed that ẓori actually referred to Judaean balsam (see also Chapters 2 and 4).[38] Myrrh and frankincense continued to be employed as incense into the early modern period; for example, George III (r. 1769–1820) had these fragrant resins burned in the royal chapels during ceremonies.[39]

Religious Oils

Felix Fabri was well aware of the symbolic dimensions of the finest oleo-resin, writing:

> balsam, which when mixed with oil and consecrated by a bishop, becomes chrism that is used for anointing during baptism and at the confirmation and reception into Holy Orders. It is the same for the anointing of popes, bishops, emperors and their kings.[40]

Similar comments can be found in the work of the fourteenth-century author al-'Umari.[41] Fabri uses the word 'chrism', deriving from the Greek *chríu*, meaning 'to anoint'. 'Chrism' is the word employed by several fathers of the early Church and by Christians in the Latin West in later centuries. Among the eastern Churches, the word myron (*míron*) was generally preferred. This oil was distinguished from others, such as that used for the unction for the sick (extreme unction), by the inclusion of balsam.[42] While balsam had a special status as the result of its rarity, rich historical associations stretching back to Solomon and the Queen of Sheba, and many applications in medicine, its vital place in Christian liturgical practice was dependent upon the process of consecration. This consecration of the mixture of balsam and oil took place in a ceremony presided over by a bishop and held on Maundy Thursday.

Bar Hebraeus gives an account of the ceremony of the consecration of myron in the Syrian church.[43] The church would contain singers, arranged in groups occupying the sanctuary, the *bema* and the *questroma*.[44] In the first part of the service the bishop, wearing white robes, reads the main prayer (Sedro) before making a procession through the nave with a censer. Following the reading of selected passages from the Old Testament and the litany by the archdeacon, the bishop enters the sanctuary alone in order to mix 'balsam oil with perfumed olive oil'. The bishop then carries the bottle of myron through the church in solemn procession, accompanied by twelve priests, twelve deacons and twelve sub-deacons. The archdeacon cries out, 'Depart those who are to leave' and the procession returns towards the sanctuary. The bottle is placed on the altar and covered with a veil. This starts the second part of the ceremony in which the bishop, surrounded by the priests, deacons and sub-deacons, performs the service in the manner of the Holy Eucharist. The veil is removed from the bottle as prayers and the Epiklesis (part of the Eucharistic prayer, or Anaphora) is recited. During this time the bishop waves his hands over the myron. The bishop ascends the *bema* in order to exalt the bottle and then blesses the people with it. A litany by the deacon concludes the ceremony.

The recipe for myron seems relatively simple; it comprises only balsam and 'perfumed olive oil'. Bar Hebraeus does not in this passage indicate what aromatics were employed to create the 'perfumed olive oil', though it is clear from other sources that the list of ingredients employed by the eastern Churches could be complex. Paulos Menevisoglou collected together accounts relating to the Orthodox Church.[45] The earliest, dating to the eighth century, lists twelve ingredients, including balsam.[46] Forty-seven components, in addition to wine and oil, are enumerated in a seventeenth-century manuscript. This text contains an acknowledgement that necessary supplies of balsam might not be available, and allows for substitution with nutmeg oil combined with fragrant herbs and flowers.[47] The mixture would be stored for forty days before being macerated on Palm Sunday, and cooked with oil and wine over the following week.[48] The mid-nineteenth-century *Order of the Holy Myron*, issued by the patriarchate in Constantinople, enumerates fifty-seven ingredients. This includes 'oil of *carpobalsamum*', though another entry uses a substitute: 'Meccan balsam, that is balsam oil'.[49] In the seventeenth century balsam was very difficult to obtain commercially, and there was considerable confusion about the commodity sold under the name of *carpobalsamum* (Chapter 5).

Another set of instructions on the preparation of myron is provided in a letter sent to Pope Leo X (r. 1513–21) in 1514 by the patriarch of the Maronite church. This process was undertaken in the presence of seventy-two priests, seven prelates and other members of the clergy. In addition to the six pounds (*libras*) of olive oil and twenty-one measures (*mensuras*) of balsam, the mixture was perfumed with saffron from Genoa, styrax, gum, white incense, rose, linseed, cinnamon and a grated root (possibly saponaria or liquorice). The mixture was heated and passed three times through silk before being poured into pots. A curious additional feature of this involved process was that the fire to heat the oil was provided by the boards and leaves of illuminated books.[50]

The Coptic Church also employed elaborate recipes, only preparing the myron on an occasional basis when stocks needed to be replenished. This ritual is undertaken in the cathedral of St Mark in Alexandria. One of these rare events was captured by the celebrated director, Youssef Chahine (d. 2008), in a short documentary film entitled *'Īd al-mīrūn* ('The Feast of Myron'), first broadcast in 1967.[51] A fourteenth-century Arabic manuscript, known as the *Livre du chrême* ('Book of Chrism'), contains extensive information about the ingredients, preparation and consecration of both myron and the oil of catechumens. The work was written by a Coptic prelate for the Jacobite suffragan bishop to the region of Mosul, Anba Ya'qub, and completed in 1346 or soon after.[52] The author cites Biblical sources for oils, including the anointing oil of Moses (see below), before moving to descriptions of different ways to make myron.[53] These all have in common the olive oil base, but not all include balsam. The lists of aromatic products also vary, though cinnamon, nard, cloves, calamus, cloves, rose, crocus and styrax are mentioned in most versions. Myrrh, a conspicuous feature of the Old Testament oil, is not included in the Coptic preparations.[54] The author mentions the maceration and cooking of the ingredients, emphasising the recitation of prayers during the processes. The fathers of the church kept back one-third of their existing supply each year, and added this to balsam and newly prepared perfumed oil. In this manner, the fine odour of the oil apparently never diminished.

The preparation of chrism in the Catholic Church was a simpler matter, comprising only the oil and balsam. This formulation was also adopted in the Protestant Churches.[55] For all of the complication of the recipes recorded in the eastern Churches, however, the primary distinction is always between the oil (perfumed by a variety of aromatics) and balsam. The symbolic dimension of this combination preoccupied theologians, allowing them to make connections with the Holy Spirit, Christian virtue and the unity of the Church.[56] Jacob of Edessa and George of the Arabs view the principal elements of myron as standing symbolically for the incarnate Christ, who combined both humanity (oil) and divinity (balsam).[57] Moses Bar Kepha's commentary on myron further develops these arguments. He cites a letter of St Severus in which myron is said to signify the Holy Spirit, but Moses argues that it should be considered as symbolising the 'divine Christ'.[58] He makes specific connections between myron and the Word of God. Among these is the fragrance attached to both, and the fact that this property is at first concealed and then revealed to the faithful:

> When the bottle [of myron] is opened and poured into another bottle, it is known from the fragrance it gives out. Similarly was God the Word also. When He was in the bosom of the Father, He was hidden and veiled. But when he was poured out into the Virgin, it was known that He is God incarnate, as it is written: *Your name is the myron poured out* (Songs 1:3) and as the Apostles had said: *He emptied Himself and received the death of his servant* (Philippians 2:7).[59]

He distinguishes the symbolic qualities of olive oil and balsam, with the former representing the humanity of Christ and the latter his divinity, or the union of flesh and God the Word. Of balsam Moses remarks that it

> does not need to receive fragrance from other oils, as it naturally possesses fragrance and imparts fragrance to other oils. So God the Word does not receive holiness from others, and he gives [holiness] to others, [so that they might] become holy.[60]

Comparable ideas are expressed later by Dionysius Bar Salibi, bishop of Mardin (d. 1171). Of balsam, he writes:

> [From] the balsam we understand the eternity of the Word. As this oil that oozes and flows from a stem, is simple and naturally possesses a fragrance, the Word, who is from the Father, is simple in His eternal glory. He has no need to enrich His naturally possessed magnificence, from another [source].[61]

Similar sentiments are expressed by Catholic scholars in Europe at the same time; for example, in her mystical work, the *Scivias*, Hildegard of Bingen equates the oozing of the balsam from a tree to the Virgin birth and the integrity of the church.[62]

The principal use for myron/chrism was in baptism and confirmation (Chrismation). These fundamental Christian ceremonies required the two physical components: water for the baptism and oil or myron/chrism for the act of anointing. The Synoptic Gospels all record the descent of the Holy Spirit after the baptism of Christ, while Luke adds the words of John the Baptist, contrasting his practice of baptising simply with water with the one who would 'baptise you with the Holy Spirit and Fire'.[63] The lecture on baptism attributed to Cyril of Jerusalem (d. 386) exhorts the reader to 'regard the spiritual grace that is given by the water', and makes clear the dual role of the water in purifying the corporeal body and allowing the Spirit to seal the soul.[64] Philoxenus of Mabbug (d. 523) asserts that the Holy Spirit is received through both the water and the oil. This understanding is common in later writing, though in the East Syrian rite the priest could give the newly baptised the sign of the cross on the forehead without the use of oil/myron.[65] Sebastian Brock notes that the earliest Syriac sources only talk about anointing with oil (*meshho*). John Chrysostom (d. 407), whose works were translated into Syriac, refers to myron and oil (*elaion*), while the preference for myron is confirmed in sources of the fifth century and later.[66] Anointing can occur both before and after the immersion in water, though prior to the fifth century it appears only as a pre-baptismal practice.[67] In later times, the act of applying myron/chrism was largely transferred to the post-baptism phase.[68]

Additional uses were found in the eastern Churches for the oil of consecration. Myron was used for the consecration of altars, processional crosses, reliquaries and other liturgical items.[69] Relics could be marked with oil; for example, the fragment of the True Cross in Santa Croce in Gerusalemme in Rome was periodically anointed with balsam or myron.[70] A document in the monastery of St Macarius at Wadi al-Natrun in Egypt records the marking of new icons with myron.[71] This was not a canonical practice, though it became widespread after the time of the Seventh Ecumenical Council convened in Nicaea in 787 by the Patriarch Tarasios (d. 806). This council restored the veneration of icons to the Orthodox Church. On the basis of these events Pope Hadrian I (r. 772–95) writes an opinion in favour of the consecration of holy paintings with chrism.[72] An example of a contrary opinion on anointing is provided by a later scholar of the Orthodox tradition, Nicodemos the Hagiorite (d. 1809). He notes that the adoration of an icon allows the worshipper to be 'analogically lifted up and carried back to the honour of the original through the name of the icon'. Thus, the icon represents the means to adore the prototype (the saint depicted), and this process does not require the sanctification through anointing of the icon itself. In his justification he also takes the opportunity to criticise the papal practices of saying prayers over icons and anointing them.[73]

Some ceremonies probably had their roots in pre-Christian practices; for example, the *History of the Patriarchs of Alexandria* records the ceremony in which a mixture of water and myron in a pottery vessel was blessed and then floated in the Nile river. This ritual was meant to facilitate the annual flooding of the river, an event of crucial importance to the agricultural economy of Egypt. The miraculous effect of myron on water is alluded to in other episodes, and draws comparison with claims made by Gregory of Tours (see Introduction).[74] At the level of metaphor, at least, myron is imbued with magico-medical qualities in that the consecrated oil is claimed to drive out sickness from the body.[75] The Acts of Thomas, the third-century Syriac text, provides an example of oil eradicating the wounds and sores from a woman, while Jacob of Serugh (d. 521) claims that the leprous marks on the face of Emperor Constantine I were removed with anointing oil prior to his baptism.[76] Moses Bar Kepha records that if myron is rubbed on an unclean animal, such as a vulture, it will die.[77] This fluid boundary between religious practice and magic is also reflected in popular beliefs among Coptic Christians concerning liturgical oils, as well as the spent olive oil collected from lamps employed in the shrine of St Menas. The oils (oil of catechumens and myron) employed during the Coptic baptismal service are specifically identified as being protective against demons and their sorcery.[78]

Royal Practices

In May 1941 a bomb landed on the deanery at Westminster Abbey. Among the valuable items lost during the explosion was a small vial containing the anointing oil that had been used since the coronation of Edward VII (r. 1901–10). A new batch of oil had to be created in 1952 for the coronation of Elizabeth II the following year, based on the one made by Peter Squires (d. 1884), druggist to Queen Victoria (r. 1834–1901). Although the precise formulation of the ingredients remains secret, the principal ingredients are known. In addition to the olive oil (or sesame oil) base, the anointing mixture contains ambergris, civet, orange flowers, rose, jasmine, cinnamon, musk and benzoin. This mixture of aromatics can be traced to the reign of Charles I (r. 1625–49), who commissioned it for his coronation in 1626. Previously, monarchs had been anointed with chrism, though this had to be periodically replaced when the oil coagulated. Notably, Mary I (r. 1553–8) ordered for new oil to be prepared due to her concerns that the existing supply might have been corrupted through handling by Protestant clergy. Her successor, Elizabeth I, is reported to have complained of the greasiness and unappealing odour of the chrism.[79] The golden ampulla in the Royal Collection was designed for holding the chrism, and has been used from the time of the coronation of Charles I. Its companion, the silver gilt anointing spoon, is considerably older, having been manufactured in the twelfth century (Fig. 8.2). The ridge along the bowl of the spoon allowed the priest to run two fingers through the oil that would then be marked on the forehead of the monarch.[80]

The fragrant anointing oil used since the seventeenth century is differentiated from the oil of consecration employed in the Church of England, both in composition and in preparation. The former has been created for the last two centuries at least not by religious officials, but by the royal-appointed Surgeon-Apothecary. It is only afterwards that the oil is consecrated by a bishop in the chapel of St Edward the Confessor (r. 1042–66). Thus, the role of the anointing oil is defined as much in the context of royal ritual, even though it is consecrated prior to use and applied during the coronation by the archbishop of Canterbury. The anointing of the monarch on the palms of the hands, head and breast is, however, considered the holiest part of the ceremony, and in the case of the coronation of Elizabeth II was not captured publicly on film or in photographs.

The quasi-religious nature of such coronations is significant, illustrating the interconnections between secular authority and the Church. This

Figure 8.2 Bird-shaped gold ampulla, made in 1661 by Sir Robert Viner (d. 1688) and the coronation spoon. Silver gilt with pearls, twelfth century. RCIN31732, RCIN 31733. Royal Collection Trust / © Her Majesty Queen Elizabeth II 2020.

overlapping of the royal and religious domains is an ancient one, and is closely tied to the practice of anointing. There is disagreement concerning the extent to which anointing was widely practised in Middle Kingdom Egypt; a study by Stephen Thompson found only one clear example of a pharaoh anointing one of his officials.[81] The pharaohs themselves appear to have been anointed with a liquid made from the fat from sacred crocodiles, and this practice is illustrated on carved reliefs (Fig. 8.3). Thompson's argument casts some doubt on the assumption that it was from Egypt that the practice of anointing moved to other royal lines, including that of the Jewish kings. It has been speculated that these practices of anointing came from the Canaanites.[82] What is most relevant in the present context is that the references to anointing in the Old Testament provide a template for the practices of Christian rulers through the medieval and early modern periods.

The earliest Biblical example of a royal anointing is the one performed by the Prophet Samuel upon Saul: 1 Samuel describes the pouring of olive oil

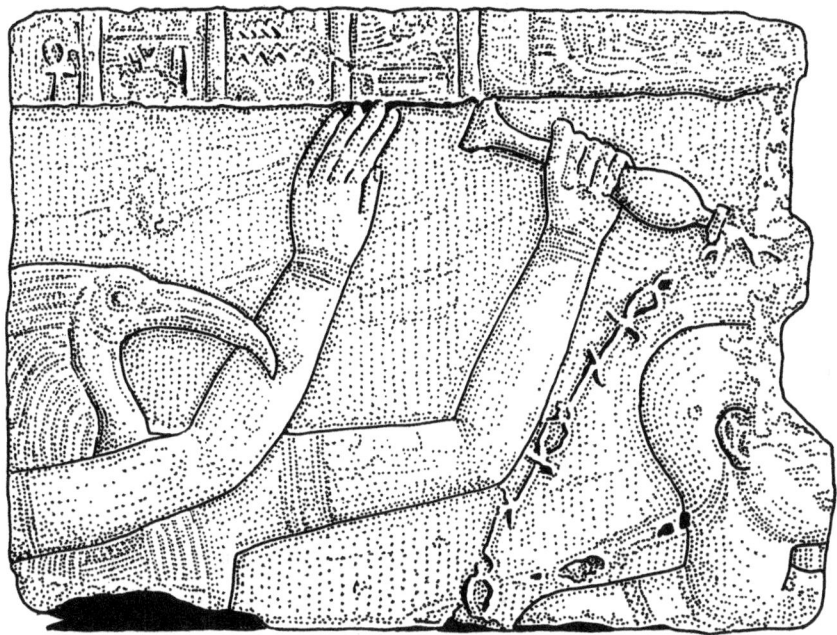

Figure 8.3 Cornice block showing the anointing of a pharaoh, temple of Harendotes ('Horus the Avenger'), Philae Island, Egypt, 41–68 CE. Metropolitan Museum. Rogers Fund 1911: 11.154.3. Drawing: Marcus Milwright.

over the head of Saul. Samuel kisses him and pronounces, 'Has not the Lord anointed you ruler over His inheritance?'[83] This mandate to rule is, however, temporary, and Samuel tells Saul that God has rejected him as the legitimate ruler. A later passage recounts the exchange between God and Samuel in which the latter is instructed to fill his horn with oil and go with a sacrificial heifer to Jesse of Bethlehem. It is here that the youngest son, David, is identified by God as the chosen king of Israel. This episode concludes, 'So Samuel took the horn of oil and anointed him in the presence of his brothers, and from that day on the spirit of the Lord came powerfully on David'.[84] David receives a second anointing by 'the men of Judah', and again by the 'elders of Israel'. Each event marks an acceptance of his legitimacy to rule over an expanded domain: first Judah and then the entire land of Israel.[85]

These examples are described as having a political rather than divine quality, and the same can be said of the anointing by supporters of the rebel Absalom.[86] The priestly class is also mentioned in these rituals of kingship, such as the anointing of Solomon by the High Priest Zadok (with the Prophet Nathan) and Joash by Jehoiada.[87] The status of anointed ruler is also extended in the Old Testament to the sixth-century BC Persian emperor Cyrus the Great,[88] as it is through his conquest of Babylon that the Jews were able to return from exile and rebuild the Temple. The idea of anointing appears again in the title Christ (from the Greek *christós*, and equating to the Hebrew *mashiah*), meaning 'the anointed one'. This epithet for Jesus appears in the letters of Paul and the Gospels. For followers of Christ, he represented the fulfilment of the Jewish prophecies of an anointed saviour of the Davidic line.[89]

The anointing of Saul was undertaken using simple olive oil, but the Old Testament indicates that more complex formulations were usually employed. Moses is instructed by God about the recipe for anointing oil:

> Then the Lord said to Moses, 'Take the following fine spices: 500 shekels of liquid myrrh, half as much of fragrant cinnamon, 250 shekels of cassia [i.e. cinnamon] – all according to the sanctuary shekel – and a *hin* of olive oil. Make these into a sacred anointing oil, a fragrant blend, the work of the perfumer.[90]

The following verses indicate the physical items to be consecrated with this oil, including the tent of meeting, the ark of the covenant and the altar of incense, but it is also apparent that it is meant especially for use on the body. God's words continue:

> Anoint Aaron and his sons and consecrate them so they may serve me as priests. Say to the Israelites, 'This is to be my sacred anointing oil for the generations to come. Do not pour it on anyone else's body and do not make any other oil using the same formula. It is sacred, and you are to consider it sacred. Whoever makes perfume like it and puts it on anyone other than a priest must be cut off from their people'.[91]

The exclusion of balsam from the Mosaic recipe is notable, particularly given the archaeological evidence for the cultivation of the plant in royal plantations in Jericho (Chapter 2). Josephus claims that the connection between the Jewish kings and balsam can be traced back to the time of Solomon, though archaeological and textual sources suggest that the trees were first introduced about four or five centuries later (Chapter 2). The Hasmonean and Herodian dynasties were active in the patronage of the agricultural land around Jericho, and Pliny explicitly describes the balsam plantations as being under royal control.[92] While balsam might well have been used for a variety of purposes by these dynasties, as well as forming a potential cash crop for export, there remains the possibility that balsam was incorporated into anointing oils. Contemporary textual evidence is lacking on this issue, though post-Biblical Jewish sources claim the use of balsam in the anointings of several ancient kings, as well as the priests Aaron, his sons, and Zadok.[93] The anointing of an ancient king is also mentioned in a Hebrew Alexander Romance.[94] This elevation of the status of balsam is seen in other contexts in the first centuries of the Common Era. For example, the elaboration of the four rivers of paradise (Exodus 2:10–14) in the Apocalypse of Moses states that these run beneath the thrones of the pious, and contain honey, milk, wine and balsam respectively. The stream of balsam is also mentioned in Rabbinic literature.[95]

The Pagan Roman emperors made no use of anointing oils in their ceremonies of investiture, and the practice was only adopted latterly by the Christian emperors of Constantinople, perhaps after 1204. The pouring of oil by Samuel onto the head of David is depicted in Byzantine art, illustrating the divine right to rule (Figs 8.4 and 8.5), and this event was invoked by the patriarch at the coronation of Emperor Manuel II and Helena Dragas in 1392. Manuel was anointed on this occasion with an unguent of nard, before the crown was placed on his head.[96] Evidence for royal anointing in Europe dates back at least to the seventh century among the Visigothic kings of Spain. Pepin I (r. 751–86) was the first of the Frankish kings to be anointed at his coronation. The introduction to England of royal anointing occurs in the aftermath of the visit of the churchman Alcuin of York (d. 804) to the court of Charlemagne in 781; Offa, king of Mercia (r. 757–96), ordered that his son, Ecgfrith (r. 787–96), be anointed when he was designated as successor to the throne. The example of Alfred the Great shows that anointing could occur prior to coronation. He was inoiled in 853 by Leo IV (r. 847–55) at the time he was given the status of a Roman consul. When he ascended the throne in 871 there was evidently no need to repeat an anointing already given at the hands of the pope. The practice of the pope anointing rulers

Figure 8.4 Samuel anointing David. Silver plate, 629–30. Found in Cyprus. Metropolitan Museum: 17.190.398. Metropolitan Museum of Art. Image Source: Art Resource, NY.

begins with the coronation of the Holy Roman emperor Louis II (r. 844–55, with Lothair I, and 855–75 as sole ruler).[97]

Practices of anointing varied across Europe. The Anglo-Saxon kings of England were marked on the head with chrism, though other ceremonies across Europe involved the application of the oil also on the breast, shoulders and joints of the arms. Charlemagne's corpse was embalmed with a variety of aromatics, and his coronation also featured an elaborate anointing in which he was covered over his entire body with oil. There are variations in the type of oil employed, with the German kings being anointed with the lesser oil of catechumens. This issue was taken up by the papacy in a decretal issued in 1204 by Innocent III (r. 1198–1216). He notes that episcopal and royal authority were differentiated in the act of anointing: chrism on the head for the clergy and oil of catechumens on the arms and shoulders for kings.[98]

The distinction between chrism and oil of catechumens was not the only one that existed among the royalty of medieval Europe. The kings of

RELIGIOUS AND ROYAL DIMENSIONS TO BALSAM | 259

Figure 8.5 Samuel anointing David, Theodore Psalter, Constantinople, 1066. British Library Add. Ms. 19353, fol. 190r.

France possessed an anointing oil that surpassed all others, and was believed to date back to the baptism of the Merovingian king Clovis I (r. 488–511) on Christmas Day 508. For Gregory of Tours the importance of this baptism was that it marked the rejection by Clovis and his troops of the Arian faith and their embrace of Catholicism.[99] The anointing was done by St Remi (or Remigius) with 'holy ointment', but for Gregory this item has no special character. Later representations give this part of the narrative greater attention. A late-ninth-century ivory plaque, possibly a book cover, now in the Musée de Picardie in Amiens, contains a panel depicting Clovis in the baptismal font. Above his head is an ampulla held in the beak of a dove, symbolising the Holy Spirit (Fig. 8.6). This scene can be connected with the removal by Hincmar, archbishop of Rheims (d. 882), of two vials containing aromatic oils from the tomb of St Remi. Hincmar connected these vessels to the baptism of the Merovingian ruler, thus creating the legend of the Sainte Ampoule.

Figure 8.6 Drawing of a detail from an ivory plaque with baptism of Clovis, c. 850. Musée de Picardie, Amiens. Drawing: Marcus Milwright.

A legendary twelfth-century account claims that the container of oil was brought from heaven by an angel.[100] The propaganda value of this 'celestial oil' was not lost on supporters of the French crown: a thirteenth-century work entitled *La Vie de saint Remi* asserts that this unique oil gave the rulers of France a spiritual superiority because other kings were left to purchase the ingredients for their coronations 'in a pharmacy'.[101] The English chronicler Matthew Paris (d. 1259) agrees, claiming that the French monarchs were counted as the finest of the earthly kings because they were anointed with an oil brought from heaven. An early-fourteenth-century illustration shows the act of anointing, with the French king about to be marked on the forehead with the sign of the cross. The bishop is shown holding the bottle in one hand and the brush laden with the oil in the other.[102] The kings of England sought to redress this imbalance through the acquisition of similar heavenly liquid. Edward II (r. 1307–27) was the recipient of such an oil; correspondence with

Pope John XXII (r. 1316–34) reveals that the container sent to the king had reputedly been given to St Thomas Becket (d. 1170) during his years of exile from 1164 to 1170. Becket had received this miraculously from the hand of the Blessed Virgin, and the pope's letter continued with more about the adventures of the ampulla.[103]

Whether shop bought or heaven sent, the role of anointing in the conferral of kingship was well understood across Europe, and had an authority built on Old Testament precedents and the Christian understanding of Jesus as 'the anointed one'. The spiritual and political dimensions of anointing are a theme in Shakespeare's *Richard II*. In one speech the king reflects on the inalienable quality of kingship, and that no worldly factor can remove the anointing oil employed during the coronation: 'Not all the water in the rough rude sea can wash the balm from an anointed king'. What becomes apparent, however, is that the king himself can strip away these signs of authority, and later Richard laments: 'With mine own tears I wash away my balm. With mine own hands I give away my crown'.[104] English Reformation scholars also point out that the oil is only a physical manifestation of the spiritual act of anointing. For example, Thomas Cranmer, archbishop of Canterbury (d. 1556), writes that a king is 'God's Anointed, not in respect of the oil which a bishop useth, but in consideration of their power which is ordained'. He concludes, 'The oil, if added, is but a ceremony: if it be wanting, that King is yet a perfect monarch notwithstanding, and God's Anointed as well as if he were inoiled'.[105]

Given the historical and archaeological evidence for balsam cultivation in Jericho and En-Gedi, it is surprising that balsam is not more strongly associated in primary sources with Jewish ritual practice. Balsam appears as an unguent in the Talmud, though there is no indication that the oleo-resin had any designated religious role in Rabbinic Judaism.[106] The aroma could also have a negative ethical connotation; for example, the Midrash contains a passage dealing with the sinful daughters of Zion that features balsam.[107] Textual evidence suggests that Christians adopted balsam – in incense and, more importantly, in myron/chrism – in the late fourth or fifth centuries. Its symbolic importance was magnified in eastern Christianity, at least, through the production of treatises on myron and baptism. The translation of anointing to the royal domain establishes itself among the rulers of Europe, and, again, balsam played a significant role. This reliance upon a luxury aromatic from Egypt had political implications, evidence of which is seen in the long record of diplomatic gifts between sultans of Egypt and the Christian rulers of Europe (Chapter 5). The decline in balsam cultivation at Matarea affected both Church authorities and European royal houses, and substitutes were sought. For example, a papal bull issued by Pius V (r. 1566–72) in 1571 allowed clergy in the Americas to use balsam of Peru in the preparation of liturgical oils.[108]

The reluctance to adopt balsam into Muslim religious practice must be partially due to the fact that its Christian context was well established by the seventh century. Scented products play an important role in Islamic culture, however, with the Prophet sanctioning the use of perfumes (*ṭīb*) for men. Prophetic medicine (*al-ṭibb al-nabawī*) mentions the medicinal value of perfumes in general, singling out well-known aromatics, such as aloe wood (*'ūd*), ambergris (*'anbar*), frankincense (*lubān*) and musk (*misk*).[109] While it was occasionally burned either as a form of incense for domestic purposes, or as a means to combat the spread of disease (Chapter 7), balsam does not feature in any religious context. Muslim dynasties in Egypt made use of other aromatic oils for ritual purposes, most notably *khalūq*, a mixture made up principally of olive oil and saffron. *Khalūq* was employed in the annual perfuming of the Nilometer, a practice that long predates the Islamic era but was actively patronised by the Fatimid caliphs and the sultans of the Ayyubid and Mamluk periods.[110] There is earlier evidence for the Islamic use of *khalūq*, a mixture including saffron and olive oil, in the anointing of the exposed rock within the Dome of the Rock during the Umayyad caliphate. This again seems to have picked up on earlier practices; the unnamed fourth-century CE 'Bordeaux Pilgrim' records the anointing by the Jews of Jerusalem of a 'perforated rock' on the Temple Mount, though the nature of oil used in this ritual is not specified.[111]

Notes

1. Or ammoniacum, a gum derived from the herb *Dorema ammoniacum*.
2. Levinus Lemnius, *Herbarum atque arborum quae in Bibliis passim obviae sunt et ex quibus sacri vates similitudines desumunt.* Published in English as *An Herbal for the Bible; Containing a Plaine and Familiar Exposition of such Similitudes,*

Parables and Metaphors, both in the Olde Testament and the Newe, trans. Thomas Newton (London: Edmund Bollifant, 1587), pp. 121–3 (the quoted passage appears on p. 123).

3. Lemnius, *Herbal for the Bible*, p. 127. In the King James Bible the verse from this apocryphal book (also known as the Book of Sirach) is translated as: 'I gave a sweet smell like cinnamon and aspalathus, and I yielded a pleasant odour like the best myrrh, as galbanum, and onyx, and sweet storax, and as the fume of frankincense in the tabernacle'. The same passage is quoted by the German pilgrim Felix Fabri. See his *Evagatorium*, III, p. 18.

4. Catherine Saucier, 'The sweet sound of sanctity', *The Senses and Society* 5.1 (2010), pp. 10–27; The tenth- and twelfth-century hagiographies mentioned above are dealt with on p. 15.

5. Constance Classen, *The Color of Angels: Cosmography, Gender and the aesthetic Imagination* (London and New York: Routledge, 1998), pp. 45–6; Saucier, 'Sweet sound', pp. 15–16. Classen notes the Graeco-Roman roots of the 'odour of sanctity' in the stories about ambrosia, the sweet-smelling food of the classical gods (see p. 44).

6. Saewulf, *A Reliable Account of the Situation of Jerusalem*, 26, in Wilkinson, trans., *Jerusalem Pilgrimage, 1099–1185*, p. 110.

7. The first writer to discuss the tomb in the monastery is Thietmar in 1217. The date of the 'discovery' (*inventio*) of St Catherine's body is unknown, though it may have occurred in the tenth century. The first resting place for the bones was a chapel on Jabal Katrin. On this issue, see Christine Walsh, *The Cult of St Katherine of Alexandria in Early Medieval Europe* (Aldershot and Burlington, VT: Ashgate, 2007), pp. 39–46.

8. 'Embalm, *v.*', in *Oxford English Dictionary Online*. https://www.oed.com (last consulted: 6 October 2019). Geoffrey Chaucer makes use of the older form, enbaume, while Shakespeare employs embalme.

9. He writes, 'and then that there may be space to put in the aromaticke powders; and then the whole body shall be washed over with a spunge dipped in aqua vita and strong vinegar, wherein shall be boyled wormewood, aloes, coloquintida, common salt and alume. Then these incisions, and all the passages and open spaces of the body and the three bellyes shall be stuffed with the following spices grossely powdered. Rx pul rosar, chamomile, balsami, menthe, anethi, salvia, lavend, rorismar, marjoran, thymi, absinthi, cyperi, calami aromat, gentiana, ireosflorent, assacederata, caryophyll, nucis moschat, cinnamoni, styracis, calamita, benjoini, myrrha, aloes, santel, omnium quod

sut ficit. Let the incisions be sowed up and the open spaces that nothing fall out; then forthwith let the whole body be anointed with turpentine, dissolved oyle of roses and chamomile, adding if you thinke it fit, some chymicall oyles of spices, and then let it be againe strewed over with the aforementioned powder; then wrap it in a linnen cloath, and then in ceare-cloathes. Lastly, let it be put in a coffin of lead, sure soudred and filled up with dry sweete hearbes.' This quote comes from the English translation of the works of Ambroise Paré. See *The Works of that Famous Chirurgion Ambrose Parey, translated out of Latine and compared with the French by Th. Johnson* (London: Th. Coates and R. Young, 1634), pp. 748–50 (book 28: 'On the manner howe to embalme the dead'). The quoted passage appears on p. 749. Quoted in Edward Johnson et al., 'The origin and history of embalming', in Robert Mayer, ed., *Embalming: History, Theory and Practice*, fifth edition with a foreword by John Reed (New York: McGraw Hill Medical, 2012), p. 479.
10. Greenhill, *Nekrokideia*, p. 211.
11. Ibid. p. 210.
12. For references, see the introduction to Chapter 5.
13. Southey, trans., *The Chronicle of the Cid* (1958), pp. 180–3. A drink made of balsam and myrrh was given to him every day during his fatal illness. The text remarks that 'every day after he did this, his body and his countenance appeared fairer and fresher than before, and his voice clearer, though he waxed weaker and weaker daily, so that he could not move in his bed'. After death his body was anointed with balsam and myrrh.
14. 'The *Balm* and *Eastern Odours* you employ, / The Noxious *Vapours* of the *Vault* destroy; / You reconcile us to the Things we loath, / We feel the *Flesh* is firm, the *Features* smooth; / We see, we smell, by e'ry *Sense* we try / Your *Skill*, and are no more afraid to *Die*'. Poem by J. Oldmixon in Greenhill, *Nekrokideia* (unpaginated preface). The next poem, by one B. B., begins by lauding 'Fragant *Arabian Gums*'.
15. '*Babylonians* either anointed their Dead with, or laid them in Hony. The *Persians* and *Scythians* did the same with Wax. The *Aethiopians* with a sort of Parget'. Greenhill, *Nekrokideia*, p. 63. Greenhill cites Pliny, *Natural History* 12:1.
16. Greenhill, *Nekrokideia*, p. 278.
17. Ibid. p. 282. On oil of cedar, see p. 287.
18. Ibid. p. 289.
19. Herodotus, *Histories* 2:86. Quoted in Robert Loynes, *Prepared for Eternity: A Study of Human Embalming Techniques in Ancient Egypt Using Computerised*

Tomography Scans of Mummies, Archaeopress Egyptology 9 (Oxford: Archaeopress, 2015), pp. 1–2; Zahi Hawass and Sahar Saleem, *Scanning the Pharaohs: CT Imaging of the New Kingdom Royal Mummies*, ed. Sue D'Auria (Cairo and New York: The American University in Cairo Press, 2016), pp. 193–4.

20. Diodorus Siculus, *Bibliotheca historica* 1:91.2. Quoted in Loynes, *Prepared for Eternity*, p. 2.
21. Herodotus, *Histories* 2:87. Quoted in Loynes, *Prepared for Eternity*, p. 2. For Pliny, see his *Natural History* 16:52. He uses the term *cedrium*.
22. On this evidence, see H. E. Winlock, *Materials Used at the Embalming of King Tūt-ʿAnkh-Amūn*, The Metropolitan Museum of Art Papers 10 (New York: Metropolitan Museum of Art, 1941. Reprinted New York: Arno Press, 1973). See particularly pp. 8–11, pls III, IV. Embalming materials from the Valley of the Kings are also illustrated in Hawass and Saleem, *Scanning the Pharaohs*, pp. 193–4, fig. 89.
23. J. Koller et al., 'Herodotus' and Pliny's embalming materials identified on ancient Egyptian mummies', *Archaeometry* 47.3 (2005): 609–28.
24. Hawass and Saleem, *Scanning the Pharaohs*, pp. 196–9; Loynes, *Prepared for Eternity*, pp. 180–1, 184. Similar findings on mummification materials are also reported in John Taylor and Daniel Antoine, *Ancient Lives, New Discoveries: Eight Mummies, Eight Stories* (London: The British Museum Press, 2014). For a survey of Egyptian techniques of embalming, see Johnson et al., 'Origin and history', pp. 469–75.
25. John 9:39.
26. Atchley, *Use of Incense*, pp. 101–2, 107. For Charlemagne, see Martin Bouquet, *Recueil des historiens de Gaules et de la France*, vol. 5 (Paris: Les Libraires Associés, 1744), p. 186.
27. Hildegard of Bingen, *Hildegard von Bingen's* Physica, chapter 177 (pp. 82–3); Anon., *A Medieval Herbal*, fol. 12r (British Museum Egerton 747). The content is summarised by Minta Collins in her introduction. See p. 18. The same passage recommends balsam for the treatment of illnesses of the womb, bladder stones, earache and toothache.
28. *Bosem*, which could equate to balsam, is mentioned several times in the Old Testament as an imported fragrance or spice. See Exodus 25:6, 1 Chronicles 9:29, Song 4:10, 16, 5:13, Esther 2:12 and Isaiah 3:24. *Ẓori*, however, is not mentioned in relation to perfumes. On *bosem* and *ẓori*, see also Chapter 2, with references.

29. Pliny, *Natural History*, 13:2. See also comments in Virgil's *Georgics*. Quoted in Chapter 6.
30. Pliny, *Natural History*, 13:4–5. He claims that personal uses included perfuming the soles of the feet and the addition of bitter-tasting aromatics into food and drink. Another practice he condemns is the perfuming of military standards. On the use of perfumes in the antiquity, see Paul Faure, *Parfums et aromates de l'antiquité*, Nouvelles études historiques (Paris: Fayard, 1987). For balsam, see pp. 87–8, 240, 246–7. On the addition of balsam to wine, see also Kottek, *Medicine and Hygiene*, p. 127.
31. Apuleius of Madaura, *The Golden Ass* 6:11–13, 24. See Apuleius, *The Metamorphoses, or Golden Ass*, trans. H. E. Butler, vol. 1 (Oxford: Clarendon Press, 1910), pp. 170, 181.
32. Balsam is included in the list of aromatics. See Freshfield, trans., *Roman Law in the Later Roman Empire*, p. 30 (chapter X).
33. Abu 'Ali al-Muhassin al-Tanukhi, *The Table Talk of a Mesopotamian Judge, Being the First Part of the Nishwār al-muḥādarah*, vol. 1, ed. Abood Shalchy (Beirut: Dar Sadir, 1971), p. 293 (chapter 157). Translated in al-Tanukhi, *The Table Talk of a Mesopotamian Judge*, trans. David Margoliouth, Oriental Translation Fund. New Series 28 (London: Royal Asiatic Society, 1922), pp. 156–7. Also Muhammad Ahsan, *Social Life under the Abbasids 170–269A.H./786–902A.D.* (New York and London: Longmans, 1979), p. 288.
34. Anya King, 'The importance of imported aromatics in Arabic culture: Illustrations from pre-Islamic and early Islamic poetry', *Journal of Near Eastern Studies* 67.3 (2008): 175–89.
35. Duchesne, ed., *Le Liber Pontificalis*, I, pp. 174, 177–8, 183; Davis, trans., *The Book of the Pontiffs*, pp. 17, 19, 20.
36. Duchesne, ed., *Le Liber Pontificalis*, I, p. 183; Atchley, *Use of Incense*, pp. 141–2, 144–5.
37. Exodus 30:23, 34, Leviticus 2:2, Song 3:6. Also Jones, 'Balm', pp. 573–4.
38. Babylonian Talmud: Kerithoth 6a. Judeo-Christian Research: https://juchre.org/talmud/kerithoth/kerithoth1.htm#6a (last consulted: 21 May 2018).
39. Moldenke, *Plants of the Bible*, p. 84.
40. Fabri, *Evagatorium*, III, p. 14. Translated in French as Fabri, *Voyage en Égypte*, I, p. 390.
41. Al-'Umari, *L'Égypte, la Syrie, le Ḥiǧāz et le Yémen*, p. 68. Also al-Maqrizi, *al-Khiṭaṭ*, IV, p. 100.
42. 'Chrism', in Frank Cross and Elizabeth Livingstone, eds, *The Oxford Dictionary*

of the Christian Church, third edition (Oxford: Oxford University Press, 1997), p. 332. The early sources who discuss chrism include Tertullian, Ambrose and Theodoret.

43. Paul Bedjan, ed., *Nomocanon Gregori Barhebraei* (Paris and Leipzig: Harrassowitz, 1898), 3.4, pp. 31–4. Translated in the introduction to Dionysius Bar Salibi, *Commentaries on Myron and Baptism*, ed. and trans. Baby Varghese, Moran 'Eth'o 29 (Kottayam: St Ephrem Ecumenical Research Institute, 2006), pp. 7–8.

44. The *questroma* is located between the sanctuary and the nave and is employed for the celebration of daily offices. The *bema* is the raised area in the middle of the nave.

45. Paulos Menevisoglou, Το Αγιον Μύρον εν τη ορθοδόξω ανατολικη εκκλησία (The Holy Chrism in the Eastern Orthodox Church)', ed. Panayotis Christou, Analecta Vlatadon 14 (Thessaloniki: Patriarchal Institute for Patristic Studies, 1972), pp. 33–40. My thanks to Evanthia Baboula for translating this section of the text.

46. Ibid. pp. 33–4 (citing Codex Barberini Greek ms 336).

47. Oil of nutmeg appears as a substitute for balsam in Arabic pharmacological texts. See Chapter 5.

48. Menevisoglou, *Το Αγιον Μύρον*, pp. 35–6 (citing ms 328 in the Synodic library, Moscow).

49. Ibid. pp. 37–40 (and see n. 1 on p. 39 with a French translation of the ingredients).

50. The original letter is transcribed in Giovanni Mansi et al., eds, *Sacrorum conciliorum nova, et amplissima collectio* (Venice: Antionium Zatta, 1759–98. Reprinted Paris: H. Welter, 1901–27), 32, cols 1005–6. Summary based on a translation made by Francesco Celi in Donceel-Voûte, 'Traces of fragrance', p. 100.

51. I was shown a video copy of this documentary by Ibrahim Fawal in Oxford in about 1996. My thanks to him for making me aware of it.

52. On the manuscript (Bibliothèque Nationale ms arabe 100), see William MacGuckin de Slane, *Catalogue des manuscrits arabes de la Bibliothèque Nationale* (Paris: Imprimerie Nationale, 1883–95), I, p. 23, no. 100 (he does not provide an Arabic title for the work); Louis Villecourt, 'Un manuscrit arabe sur la Saint Chrême dans l'Église Copte', *Revue d'Histoire Ecclésiastique* 16–17 (1921): 501–14 (see particularly 501–2 for the attribution and date). Additional analysis is offered in the second part of this article by the same author

in *Revue d'Histoire Ecclésiastique* 18 (1922), pp. 1–19. For Louis Villecourt's French translation, see 'Le livre du chrême'.

53. Villecourt, 'Le livre du chrême', pp. 63–5 (citing Exodus 30:22–5).
54. By contrast, it does appear in the nineteenth-century list issued by the Patriarchate in Constantinople. See Menevisoglou, *Το Άγιον Μύρον*, pp. 38–9, n. 1.
55. The present practice in the Church of England is to create chrism only from olive oil consecrated during the service on Maundy Thursday.
56. See examples cited in 'Chrism', *Oxford Dictionary of the Christian Church*, p. 332. Augustine and Duns Scotus claim that the use of chrism goes back to the time of the life of Christ, even though no mention of it appears in the New Testament. The same assertion also appears in Moses Bar Kepha, *Commentary on Myron*, trans. with introduction by Baby Varghese, Texts from Christian Late Antiquity 34 (Piscataway, NJ: Gorgias Press, 2014), pp. 8–9 (chapter 2).
57. Sebastian Brock, *The Holy Spirit in the Syrian Baptismal Tradition*, The Syrian Churches Series 9 (Poona: Anita Printers, 1979), p. 106.
58. Moses Bar Kepha, *Commentary on Myron*, pp. 14–15 (chapter 5). Also comments in Brock, *The Holy Spirit*, pp. 16–17. He notes that it is the olive oil (*meshha*) rather than balsam that is associated with the Holy Spirit. The play on words between the Syriac *meshha* and *mshiha* ('the anointed', i.e. Christ) leads the fourth-century theologian Ephrem the Syrian to write, 'From whatever angle I look at the oil, Christ looks at me from it'.
59. Moses Bar Kepha, *Commentary on Myron*, pp. 16–17 (chapter 6). Also Dionysius Bar Salibi, *Commentaries*, pp. 32–3 (chapter 17).
60. Moses Bar Kepha, *Commentary on Myron*, pp. 20–21 (chapter 7). Also Dionysius Bar Salibi, *Commentaries*, pp. 26–7 (chapter 12).
61. Dionysius Bar Salibi, *Commentaries*, pp. 30–1 (chapter 14).
62. Hildegard of Bingen, *Scivitas*, trans. Columba Hart and Jane Bishop, The Classics of Western Spirituality (New York: Paulist Press, 1985), book 2, vision 3, part 13 (p. 174): 'As the balsam oozes from a tree, and powerful medicines pour from an onyx vessel in which they are stored, and bright light streams without impediment from a diamond, so the Son of God, unopposed by corruption, was born of the Virgin; and so too the Church, His Bridge, brings forth her children without being opposed by error, yet remains a virgin in the integrity of her faith'.
63. Matthew 3:14–17; Mark 1:9–11; Luke 3:15–22.
64. Cyril of Jerusalem, Catechetical Lectures 3: On Baptism, 3–4. Translated by

Leo MacCauley and Anthony Stephenson, *The Works of Saint Cyril of Jerusalem*, Fathers of the Church. A new Translation 8 (Washington, DC: The Catholic University of America Press, 1969–70), I, pp. 109–11 (the entire lecture is on pp. 108–18).
65. Quoted in Brock, *The Holy Spirit*, p. 25.
66. Ibid. p. 25.
67. Ibid. pp. 23–5.
68. While the eastern Churches hold the Sacrament of Chrismation directly after baptism, the Catholic and Protestant Churches allow for the child to make the rational decision to become Christian.
69. The anointing of the altar draws upon Old Testament practices, as described in Exodus 30:26–9 (see below). For evidence of solidified balsam accreted onto reliquary crosses in the Sancta Sanctorum (the personal chapel of the popes), see Grisar and Dreger, *Die römische Kapelle Sancta Sanctorum*, p. 88.
70. Grisar and Dreger, *Die römische Kapelle Sancta Sanctorum*, p. 91. This section also refers to the giving of gifts of balsam to the bodies of loved ones in the Roman catacombs.
71. Evelyn White, *The Monasteries of Wadi'n Natrûn, Part III: The Architecture and Archaeology*, Publications of the Metropolitan Museum of Art Expeditions 8 (New York: Metropolitan Museum of Art, 1933), p. 69 and n. 5. This evidence comprised a note attached to a door in the monastery that included a passage from a text entitled *The Book of Reasonable Paradise*.
72. Grisar and Dreger, *Die römische Kapelle Sancta Sanctorum*, p. 92.
73. Nicodemus the Hagiorite, *Prologue to the Seventh Ecumenical Council*, in Nicodemus the Hagiorite and Agapius the Monk, *The Rudder (Pedalion) of the Metaphorical Ship of the One Holy Catholic and Apostolic Church of the Orthodox Christians, or All the Sacred and Divine Canons*, trans. Denver Cummings (Chicago: Orthodox Christian Educational Society, 1957), pp. 930–3.
74. Sawirus ibn Muqaffaʿ and continuators, *History of the Patriarchs*, III, p. 282 (Arabic text: p. 162, ll. 22–3). It deals with the year 1702–3. For the water rising when coming into contact with consecrated water and potsherds, see II, pp. 282–4.
75. Brock, *Holy Spirit*, pp. 103–5. He quotes, for example, the Maronite litany for the oil: 'May God cause his glorious, splendid and hidden light to dwell in the oil and may it drive out from them sicknesses and diseases, both hidden and invisible . . .'
76. Ibid. pp. 103–4. The story about Constantine appears in Jacob's homily on the

baptism of the emperor. The treatment is undertaken by the priest so that the leprosy is not introduced into the font.

77. Moses Bar Kepha, *Commentary on Myron*, pp. 18–19 (chapter 6). The editor suggests that this may be drawn from Gregory of Nyssa's commentary on the Song of Songs. Also Dionysius Bar Salibi, *Commentaries*, pp. 22–5 (chapter 10).
78. Gérard Viaud, *Magie et coutumes populaires chez les Coptes d'Égypte*, Le soleil dans le cœur (Saint-Vincent-sur-Jabron: Éditions Présence, 1978), pp. 62–5 (sections from the baptismal service are quoted on p. 64).
79. Vivian Rich, *Cursing the Basil and Other Folklore of the Garden* (Victoria, BC: Horsdal and Schubart, 1998), pp. 167–9.
80. On these items, see G. Younghusband and Cyril Davenport, *The Crown Jewels of England* (London: Cassell and Co., 1919); Hervey Sitwell, *The Crown Jewels and Other Regalia in the Tower of London*, ed. Clarence Winchester (London: Published by the Viscount Kemley at the Dropmore Press, 1953).
81. Stephen Thompson, 'The anointing of officials in ancient Egypt', *Journal of Near Eastern Studies* 53.1 (1994): 11–25.
82. Ibid. p. 16. The scholar who advances this idea is Roland de Vaux.
83. 1 Samuel 10:1.
84. 1 Samuel 16:13.
85. 2 Samuel 2:4, 5:3; 1 Chronicles 11:3.
86. 2 Samuel 19:10.
87. 1 Kings 1:39; 2 Kings 19:16. The account in 2 Chronicles 23:11 mentions that Joash was anointed by 'Jehoiada and his sons'. George Frideric Handel's composition 'Zadok the Priest' is used as the coronation anthem for the British monarch.
88. Isaiah 45:1–3.
89. For example, 1 Corinthians 4:15; Romans 12:5; Matthew 1:16; Mark 16:16. The Greek version of 2 Maccabees (1:10) uses the term *christós* to refer to the High Priest.
90. Exodus 30:22–5. A *hin* is a unit of volume, equating to about 3.8 litres. The information concerning the anointing of sacred objects appears in Exodus 30:26–9.
91. Exodus 30:30–2.
92. Pliny, *Natural History* 12:111.
93. Louis Ginzberg, *The Legends of the Jews*, trans. Henrietta Szold (Philadelphia: Jewish Publication Society of America, 1909–38), VI, p. 72. The kings listed are Saul, David, Joash and Jehoash.

94. Saskia Dönitz, 'Alexander the Great in medieval Hebrew traditions', in David Zuwiyya, ed., *Companion to Alexander Literature in the Middle Ages* (Leiden and Boston: Brill, 2011), p. 36. The episode involves the visit of Alexander to the grave of King Altimos, who had been anointed with balsam from Jericho.
95. Ginzberg, *Legends*, I, p. 20; II, p. 315; V, p. 29. The Apocalypse of Moses (also known as the Life of Adam and Eve) is known in versions dating from the third to the fifth century CE, though its origins may date back to the first century. In its present form 2 Enoch 8:6 has references to oil, though no specific mention of balsam: 'And two springs come forth which send forth honey and milk, and their springs send forth oil and wine, and they separate into four parts, and go round with quiet course, and go down into the Paradise of Eden, between corruptibility and incorruptibility'. The Qur'anic account replaces the oil with pure water (47:16–17).
96. The account of the coronation is given in Charles Brand, ed., *Icon and Minaret: Sources of Byzantine and Islamic Civilization* (Englewood Cliffs, NJ: Prentice-Hall, 1969), pp. 10–13. My thanks to Evanthia Baboula for this reference. For Byzantine images of the anointing of David by Samuel, see Evans and Ratliff, eds, *Byzantium and Early Islam*, pp. 16–17, cat. 6.A (one of the early-seventh-century 'David plates'); Buckton, ed., *Byzantium*, pp. 154–5, cat. 168 (Theodore Psalter, dated 1066, British Library Additional ms 19352, fol. 190r); Paris Psalter, tenth century, Bibliothèque Nationale de France ms grec 139, fol. 3v
97. Percy Schramm, *A History of the English Coronation*, trans. Leopold Wickham Legg (Oxford: Clarendon Press, 1937), pp. 8–9, 14–16.
98. Ibid. pp. 37, 120–1; Ernst Kantorowicz, *The King's Two Bodies: A Study in Mediaeval Political Theology* (Princeton, NJ: Princeton University Press, 1957), p. 74. On the differences between the anointing practices of priests and royalty, see pp. 319–20.
99. Gregory of Tours, *History of the Franks* 2:31. Reproduced in the Medieval Sourcebook: https://sourcebooks.fordham.edu/source/gregory-clovisconv.asp #n31 (last consulted: 24 May 2019).
100. Théodor Godefroy, *Le cérémonial françois* (Paris: S. and G. Cramoisy, 1649), I, pp. 18, 26, 36, 137; Schramm, *English Coronation*, p. 131.
101. Kantorowicz, *King's Two Bodies*, pp. 335–9. The author of the poem is simply known as Richier.
102. *Ordo* of the Coronation Ceremony of the Kings of France. Bibliothèque Nationale de France ms. Lat. 1246, fol. 17. Illustrated in Marc Bloch, *Feudal*

Society, II: Social Classes and Political Organization, trans. L. A. Manyon (London: Taylor & Francis, 2005), p. 90, pl. XI. On the ceremony, see Godefroy, *Le ceremonial*, I, pp. 36, 58, 75, 196.
103. Schramm, *English Coronation*, pp. 130–1.
104. These two passages come from William Shakespeare, *The Life and Death of Richard the Second*, act 3, scene 2 and act 4, scene 1.
105. Kantorowicz, *King's Two Bodies*, p. 318.
106. Louis Rabinowitz, 'Oils', *Encyclopaedia Judaica*, second edition (Detroit: Macmillan Reference USA, 2007), XV, pp. 395–6.
107. 'She would place the balsam between her heel and her shoe and, when she saw a band of young men, she pressed upon it so that the perfume seeped through them like snake poison'. Lamentations Rabbah 4:18 quoted in Jehuda Feliks, 'Balsam', *Encyclopaedia Judaica*, second edition (Detroit: Macmillan Reference USA, 2007), III, pp. 95–6.
108. Heyd, *Commerce du Levant*, II, p. 580 n. 2.
109. Geert Jan Van Gelder, 'Four perfumes of Arabia: A translation of al-Suyūtī's al-*Maqāma al-miskiyya*', *Res Orientales* 11: *Parfums d'Orient* (1998): 203–4; Ibn Qayyim al-Jawziyya, *Medicine of the Prophet*, pp. 199–200, 238, 243–5, 271–2, 276.
110. William Popper, *The Cairo Nilometer: Studies in Ibn Taghrî Birdî's Chronicles of Egypt I*, University of California Publications in Semitic Philology 12 (Berkeley, CA and Los Angeles: University of California Press, 1951), pp. 71–3; Shalem, *Islam Christianized*, pp. 19–21.
111. Julian Raby, 'In vitro veritas: Glass pilgrim vessels from 7th-century Jerusalem', in Jeremy Johns, ed., *'Abd al-Malik's Jerusalem*. II: Jerusalem and early Islam, Oxford Studies in Islamic Art 9.2 (Oxford: Oxford University Press, 2000), pp. 168–71. On the account of the Bordeaux Pilgrim, see John Wilkinson, ed. and trans., *Egeria's Travels in the Holy Land*, revised edition (Warminster: Aris & Phillips, 1981), p. 157 (for the complete translated section of the Bordeaux pilgrim's account, see pp. 153–63).

9

Conclusion

This book charts a path through four main themes: medieval and early modern perceptions of the site of Matarea; the historical narrative of balsam cultivation from ancient Judaea to the ultimate demise of the last Egyptian tree in 1615; the botanical identification of the balsam plant; and the place of the products derived from the tree in the economic, cultural and intellectual life of Europe, North Africa and the Middle East. The available information on the plant could be organised in different ways, and there are sources and questions that have received less coverage than they deserve. For example, medieval Jewish scholarship is likely to contain more information than is suggested by the previous chapters, and merits further examination both in its own right and in the context of the transmission of knowledge from Greek to Arabic and from Arabic to Latin. The writings of the Armenian Church have only been dealt with tangentially, and other eastern Churches have been entirely omitted. Alchemy has not been analysed in depth, though its overlaps with medieval medicine have been noted. One reason for this is that references to 'balsams' in alchemical texts of the medieval and early modern periods are not necessarily to the products of the trees from Matarea. Rather, the term is understood in a more metaphorical sense (see Introduction) and, as such, has limited relevance to the principal questions addressed in this book. For the same reason I have not undertaken a survey of the treatment of the words 'balsam' and 'balm' in poetry, church sermons and other literary genres.

The question of value was raised in the Introduction, and is worth revisiting. The book has provided many examples of the ways in which balsam was valued. This can be expressed in relation to gold or silver coinage, but is more usefully understood as a product of its applications in medicine, liturgy and royal ceremonies, and the diverse socio-cultural environments in which it appears. This expanded sense of 'use value' relies on anthropological scholarship, and considers the processes by which a product is perceived in specific cultural settings, and how these perceptions might change over time.[1] In the Introduction it was argued that the relative worth cannot be computed solely on the basis of intrinsic properties, but must also take into account the circulation of information. This body of information naturally fluctuates across regions and periods, with specific components being added or subtracted for a variety of reasons. This can often have an ideological dimension, with the restriction of access to 'esoteric knowledge' being used to create or accentuate divisions between elites and other societal groups.[2] The analysis of travel writing and Coptic traditions (Chapter 1) showed that descriptive material recovered in texts is sometimes problematic for the modern researcher, mixing objective observation with hearsay and folk tales. This challenge is to be found elsewhere too, and the presentation of medical and pharmacological writing (Chapters 6 and 7) illustrates the coexistence of empirical data collection, dogmatic adherence to prior authority and willingness to embrace quasi-magical dimensions of healing.

What remains, however, is the role of information in defining value. It is scarcely likely that purchasers would have been willing to expend their wealth on balsam had there not been a broadly shared sense that the substance possessed qualities that were not available in other aromatic resins. As noted in Chapter 6, myrrh occurs in more treatments than balsam, but was not traded for the same high prices. Clearly the associations built up around balsam were important in establishing its value. The other significant factor is the enduring sense of rarity, given that 'true' balsam was cultivated in very few locations (Jericho and En-Gedi in ancient times, and later in the walled plantation at Matarea). Scarcity will certainly increase value, but only when the commodity is already held to be desirable.

Chapter 4 discussed the relationship between the balsam of Matarea (*balasān*) and the cheaper *bashām*, probably referring to 'balm of Mecca'. This information was used in order to argue for an identification of balsam as a highly cultivated strain of the wild plant (*Commiphora gileadensis*, also *Commiphora opobalsamum*), but the distinction also has implications for understanding the generation of relative value. Medieval authors make clear that *balasān* from Egypt was much more expensive than the similar *bashām* from western and southern Arabia, and it is productive to reflect on the processes involved in establishing the 'authenticity' of one product against another. Dioscorides is a key source both for his accurate description of the balsam plant, and for outlining the tests that might establish whether a sample of the oleo-resin was genuine. Ensuring authenticity was, of course, an issue of pressing concern given the prevalence of fakes and adulterated balsam in the markets of the Mediterranean and Middle East (Chapter 5). The tests would not, however, have been sufficient to tell balsam from the resin produced by its wild forebear, *Commiphora gileadensis*, though a buyer could perhaps rely on the reputed differences in the fragrances of the two commodities.

Pre-modern conceptions of authenticity are, at least in part, a cultural construct, which rely upon the acceptance of authority and the use of systems of classification.[3] The former component is relatively straightforward, in that the stature of a scholar like Dioscorides ensured that his claims were readily accepted by later physicians and pharmacologists. As noted in Chapters 6 and 7, antique scholarship was not always taken at face value, but the general picture prior to the seventeenth century is one of transmission and elaboration of the existing corpus. This point can also be made about the reception of other aspects of classical learning, such as philosophy, astronomy, engineering and geography, both in the Islamic world and in medieval Europe. For European scholars there was also a secondary process of reception in the acquisition, through the translations produced in Salerno, and other centres of learning, of works by great scholars of the Islamic world.

The second component offers us intriguing insights into the methods used by pre-modern scholars in forming qualitative distinctions between physical things, whether natural or man-made. Provenance was clearly an important issue in establishing the high value of balsam, first in Jericho and En-Gedi, and later in Matarea. In the case of the Egyptian garden, the importance of the site was magnified, for Christians at least, through the Coptic narratives concerning the visit of the Holy Family (Chapter 1). These narratives are notably absent from the first descriptions of Matarea by Arab geographers, though they are acknowledged by Muslim authors in later centuries (Chapter 3). The role of provenance in the evaluation of the quality, or intrinsic properties of a commodity can be seen in other aspects of medieval society. For example, pre-modern Arabic and Persian writers might identify the place of manufacture of textiles from a combination of the qualities of pattern, colouration and the fibres employed. Crucially, descriptions of textiles usually omit what precise qualities actually contributed to the identification of the provenance; simply naming a textile as being from a given town or region was presumably sufficient for the educated reader to know what type of fabric was being referenced.[4] Provenance also plays a role in trade, with mercantile manuals providing the places where a given commodity – sugar is a good example of this process – was made, and noting the variant prices for each one. Location acts as a powerful marker, denoting to the potential purchaser the perceived relative quality of the item being sold.[5]

The medieval market place was, however, an environment where claims of quality had to be amenable to independent tests. Examples appear in technical treatises devoted to the working of precious metals. Items of particular concern in this respect are the ways of establishing the purity of gold and silver and of measuring accurately the weight of consignments of metal.[6] Such issues were matters of practical significance, as is demonstrated by descriptions of legal interrogations of potential fraud; in one recorded case from seventeenth-century Jerusalem, the claims of a silversmith about the *dirham* weight and purity of metal used in a sword sheath were tested by a *qāḍī* (judge) who ordered the metal to be melted down by another from the same guild.[7] The authenticity of materials employed by artisans is a recurrent theme in texts devoted to market law (*ḥisba*). In some cases this was the simple question of ensuring that consumers received what they paid for, and were not tricked with cheaper substitutes. Authors of *ḥisba* manuals also note that there should be no difference between the promises in a contract and the goods delivered to the consumer. Beyond these issues, however, the *muḥtasib* (market inspector) had to root out unethical behaviour in the public sphere; the relevance of this in the present context is the need to detect the use of materials that contravened Islamic law (such as blood and products derived from carrion and 'unclean' animals).[8]

Some forms of testing found in medieval sources, such as those the establishing the purity of metal, could be reproduced today in a laboratory while others evidently relied on intellectual frameworks that have little in common with modern scientific discourse. For example, the circulation of relics in medieval Europe required a set of criteria for establishing authenticity. Provenance played a clear role in this respect, but the spiritual potency of a given body part or attribute of a saint could also be measured by its ability to intervene in worldly affairs. Hence, truly powerful relics promoted miraculous events, including resisting attempts to move them from their chosen resting place. In cases where relics were spirited to a new church by means of subterfuge, the recipients needed to establish a narrative in which devout prayer in the presence of relics persuaded the saint to allow for the transfer to take place.[9] Similar points can be made about the veracity of the image of a saint in an icon; numerous legends exist in which the 'true' form of a saint appears to a painter in a vision. In other examples, the outline of the subject is miraculously inscribed onto the gesso, leaving the painter to provide the necessary colour and tone. These acts occur through the action of the long-deceased saint. The notion of 'inscribing' the human form takes on a further dimension in that unambiguous identification, at least after the Iconoclastic phase (c. 726–843), required the addition of an inscription naming the depicted holy person.[10]

The validity of forms of religious knowledge could also be subjected to tests. A well-known example of this process is the evaluation of the sayings and actions attributed to the Prophet Muhammad and the early Muslim community (ḥadīth). The centrality of this corpus to Islamic culture, and particularly to the articulation of Islamic law, necessitated the creation of a methodology for establishing the authenticity of specific ḥadīth, including the assessment of the chains of transmission (isnād).[11] This preoccupation with the probable veracity of the source material is illustrated by the fact that two of the four canonical early compilations of Sunni ḥadīth, by al-Bukhari (d. 870) and Muslim ibn al-Hajjaj (d. 874–5) are both commonly known simply by the name ṣaḥīḥ, meaning 'correct', 'sound' or 'authentic'. In this context it can be seen that the invoking of earlier authorities in the discussion of balsam goes further than slavish medieval academic practice, and reflects a desire to augment the appearance of authenticity around the products from Matarea. Where this process differs from the evaluation of isnād is in the shifting ground of the source material available to medieval scholars. The authentication of information about balsam also involved reaching out to works by members of other confessional groups, including the pagans of antiquity.

Beyond the narrow question of authenticity, the medieval discourse around balsam also relates to the larger problem of how to classify natural and man-made things. The humoral system was clearly crucial in demarcating the perceived actions of balsam 'oil', *carpobalsamum*, and *xylobalsamum*, with the observations of Greek physicians and pharmacologists forming a template for medical practice between the seventh and the sixteenth centuries. Classification according to their heating, drying, cooling and hydrating qualities allowed all simples to be graded according to the same scale, also facilitating the development of compound remedies. This humoral viewpoint could, of course, be extended to consider human temperament and the natural world. This concern with systems of classification is found in many aspects of medieval literature. The epistles (*rasā'il*) of the Ikhwan al-Safa', for example, attempt to provide consistent methods to distinguish between natural and man-made objects. Within this second group, the authors offer the means to distinguish different types of materials – such as 'raw' (*hayūlā*) and 'ready for use' (*mawḍū'*) – and consider the process of manufacture that leads to finished items, organising categories such as its contribution to society and inherent nobility.[12] This sensitivity to materials is shown in the discussion of metals in the nineteenth epistle. Gold is described as 'a substance balanced in two natures, with a sound mixture, its soul being joined to its spirit, and its spirit joined to its body'. These qualities were strongly bound, and could not be separated, even by fire. The account moves to a consideration of humoral characteristics and issues of colour, texture and weight, also noting, more practically, qualities of ductility and malleability.[13] Other systems of classification can, of course, be found in the many works of reference produced across the Islamic world and medieval Europe. Their importance in the present context is the insights they bring into the ways in which medieval viewers approached commodities. Just as the concept of the 'period eye' can be employed to decode the production of visual culture, the study of commodities must be informed by the contemporary intellectual landscape.[14]

Lastly, the story of balsam can be viewed in the context of translation. This cannot be considered as a neutral process in which a text in one language is produced in an entirely equivalent form in a new language.[15] The practical problems of translating from Greek to Arabic, sometimes through the intermediary of Syriac, were discussed in Chapter 6, and similar points can be made about the transfer of Arabic texts into Latin. Furthermore, Dimitri Gutas has demonstrated that the patronage of translation in the Abbasid court must be viewed in the context of social and political factors. Thus, translation is not merely an academic exercise, but one which needs to be viewed in teleological terms; the broader purposes of the 'Translation Movement' also led to the privileging of some ancient texts for transmission into Arabic and the rejection of others, most notably Greek poetry and drama.[16] Beyond this world of textual history, however, is the question of whether balsam itself underwent changes as the result of translation into new socio-cultural environments at various stages during the centuries covered in this book.

The dissemination of Chinese porcelain across the Islamic world and medieval Europe was mentioned in Chapter 5, and provides a useful point of departure. These too were luxury commodities, circulated widely, particularly among wealthier elements of urban societies. Glazed porcelain and stoneware vessels were transformed in recipient societies, through their use in different social settings as well as the addition of metal fittings (sometimes when the ceramic body was broken) or even incrustation with precious and semi-precious stones. These hybrid creations can have a jarring aesthetic quality to modern eyes, and probably would have perplexed the potters who made them, but they illustrate a translation in which the Chinese prototypes take on a new set of meanings that are dependent upon the values and cultural practices of the Ottoman capital.[17] Such shifts in meaning did not require physical changes to the vessel itself, but could be achieved through the creation of a new utility. A striking example of this process is the practice of embedding decorated glazed bowls and platters into architectural contexts, as can be seen in regions such as Iran, Oman, East Africa and Syria (Fig. 9.1).[18] The same process occurs with the fixing of Islamic glazed wares to the walls of Italian churches.[19] New meanings could also be generated that related to the real or supposed material properties of imported goods. Chinese glazed wares were, for example, held to be alexipharmic, while the ceramic bodies were ground up for use in the treatment of toothache.[20]

Objects also had the potential to transform the identities of the recipients, as has been demonstrated by Finbarr Flood in his subtle analysis of the imposition of Islamic robes of investiture (sing. *khil'a*) on Indic rulers.[21] A similar point could be made about the gifting by Ottoman sultans of elaborate crowns, such as the one presented in 1605 to Stefan Bocskay (d. 1606), for his investiture as prince of Transylvania and Hungary. For all their magnificence, such crowns signalled the client status of the wearers, as did the wearing of a bow and quiver by John VIII Palaiologos (r. 1425–48). The bow and quiver were even captured on a bronze medal and drawings by Pisanello during the Byzantine emperor's attendance in 1438–9 at the Council of Ferrara-Florence, though their political connotations do not seem to have been understood by Italian audiences.[22] Balsam also operated in transactions between political dynasties, with Muslim sources of the Mamluk period making explicit reference to the reliance of Christian rulers on the largesse of the sultan (Chapters 3 and 5). The Davidic associations of anointing doubtless made it an attractive practice for the kings of early medieval Europe, though the decision to give balsam a central role introduced a problematic

Figure 9.1 Fifteenth- or sixteenth-century glazed dish set into a vault in the mosque of Nushabad, Iran. Photograph: Marcus Milwright.

dynamic with the Muslim authorities of Egypt. Willibald attests to the difficulty of exporting balsam from Egypt in the late eighth century, and from the late twelfth century, at least, the products of Matarea were under the control of the sultan. The creation of a 'celestial' oil had symbolic benefits for the French crown in positioning themselves among the royal houses of Europe, though it also had the practical advantage of reducing the ties with the Egyptian sultans.

It is in this ritual context that the translations of balsam are most apparent. After an initial rejection by the early Christian communities because of the association with secular Roman fragrances, balsam was embraced enthusiastically for a variety of liturgical applications. While this was partially justified through Old and New Testament references to anointing and incense, and perhaps even to the post-Biblical claims concerning the role of balsam in the anointing of the Jewish kings, the translation into a Christian setting produced *sui generis* meanings (Chapter 8). This occurred in the elaboration of the symbolic dimensions of balsam in the oil of consecration by medieval theologians. Other translations are less obvious, emerging from the study of acquired knowledge but also contingent upon external factors. An example is the European discourse around the employment of theriacs in the prevention of plague.

The balsam of Matarea was evidently a form of commodity in that it was exchanged in a variety of pre-modern networks. What makes the finest balsam 'oil' intriguing is that it is consciously positioned outside of the commercial realm – by sultanic restrictions over the supply and by the elevation of its 'spiritual' status as part of chrism/myron and royal anointing oils – and that the high esteem for the product is simultaneously expressed in monetary terms (worth its weight in gold). This ability of some rare commodities to be at one moment unique, and thus removed from practices of human exchange, and at other times reduced to a precise market value, has been noted in other historical and contemporary contexts.[23] What balsam offers is a wealth of source material about how organic commodities were distinguished from one another and the complex dynamics that determined the relative values given to them by the societies in which they circulated. The last specimen in Matarea has long since died, but the balsam trees still offer us crucial insights into the cultural processes underpinning the creation and dissemination of knowledge about the natural world.

Notes

1. See contributions in Arjun Appadurai, ed., *The Social Life of Things: Commodities in Cultural Exchange* (Cambridge: Cambridge University Press, 1986). See particularly the editor's introduction, 'Introduction: Commodities and the politics of value', pp. 3–63. More recent reflections on these issues appear in Wim van Binsbergen and Peter Geschiere, eds, *Commodification: Things, Agency and Identity (*The Social Life of Things *Revisited)* (Münster: Lit, 2005).
2. For example, see the arguments advanced in Helms, *Ulysses' Sail*.
3. On the construction of 'authenticity', see Brian Spooner, 'Weavers and dealers: The authenticity of an Oriental carpet', in Arjun Appadurai, ed., *The Social Life of Things: Commodities in Cultural Exchange* (Cambridge: Cambridge University Press, 1986), pp. 195–235.
4. For example, see R. B. Serjeant, 'Material for a history of Islamic textiles up to the Mongol conquest', *Ars Islamica* 9 (1942), pp. 54–92; 10 (1943), pp. 71–104; 11–12 (1946), pp. 98–145; 13–14 (1948), pp. 75–117; 15–16 (1951), pp. 29–85, 273–305; Lisa Golombek, 'The draped universe of Islam', in Priscilla Soucek, ed., *Content and Context of the Visual Arts of the Islamic World* (University Park, PA and London: Pennsylvania State University Press, 1988), pp. 25–38; Thomas Allsen, *Commodity and Exchange in the Mongol Empire: A Cultural History of Islamic Textiles*, Cambridge Studies in Islamic Civilization (Cambridge: Cambridge University Press, 1997).
5. Pegolotti, *Pratica della mercatura*, pp. 296, 363, 365; Ashtor, 'Levantine sugar industry'; Milwright, *Fortress of the Raven*, pp. 120–1, 158–64.
6. Andrew Ehrenkreutz, 'Extracts from the technical manual on the Ayyūbid mint in Cairo', *Bulletin of the School of Oriental and African Studies* 15.3 (1953), 423–47.
7. The episode from Jerusalem court records is translated in Dror Ze'evi, *An Ottoman Century: The District of Jerusalem in the 1600s*, SUNY Series in Medieval Middle East History (Albany, NY: State University of New York Press, 1996), pp. 155–6.
8. On the Islamic market law in theory and practice, see Ahmad Ghabin, *Ḥisba, Art and Craft in Islam*, Arabisch-Islamische Welt in Tradition und Moderne (Weisbaden: Harrassowitz, 2009). For a translated *ḥisba* manual, see al-Shayzari, *Book of the Market Inspector*.
9. Patrick Geary, 'Sacred commodities: The circulation of medieval relics', in Arjun Appadurai, ed., *The Social Life of Things: Commodities in Cultural Exchange* (Cambridge: Cambridge University Press, 1986), pp. 169–91. On the transport

of relics in the medieval Middle East, see De Smet, 'La translation'; Milwright, 'Reynald of Châtillon'.

10. Henry Maguire, *Icons of their Bodies: Saints and their Images in Byzantium* (Princeton, NJ: Princeton University Press, 1996), pp. 5–47.
11. For a summary of the Western publications on this issue and a review of the methods used by medieval Islamic scholars for measuring authenticity, see Wael Halleq, 'The authenticity of Prophetic ḥadîth: A pseudo-problem', *Studia Islamica* 89 (1999): 75–90.
12. Margaret Graves, *Arts of Allusion: Object, Ornament, and Architecture in Medieval Islam* (New York: Oxford University Press, 2018), pp. 46–50. Also Bernard Lewis, 'An epistle on the manual crafts', *Islamic Culture* 17 (1943): 141–51. Some of these criteria are employed later by Ibn Khaldun in his evaluation of the relative value of crafts. See Abu Zayd ʿAbd al-Rahman b. Muhammad ibn Khaldun *The Muqaddimah: An Introduction to History*, trans. Franz Rosenthal, Bollingen Series 43 (Princeton, NJ: Princeton University Press, 1958), II, pp. 286–7, 309–10, 316, 347–8, et passim.
13. Carmela Baffioni, ed. and trans., *Epistles of the Brethren of Purity. On the Natural Sciences. An Arabic Critical Edition and English Translation of Epistles 15–21* (Oxford and New York: Oxford University Press in association with the Institute of Ismaili Studies, 2013), pp. 318–19 (Arabic), p. 261 (English). For other metals, see pp. 263–7.
14. This notion of the 'period eye' is developed by Michael Baxandall in books such as *Painting and Experience in Fifteenth-century Italy: A Primer in the Social History of Pictorial Style* (Oxford and New York: Oxford University Press, 1972).
15. For a survey of these perspectives, see Anthony Pym, *Exploring Translation Theories* (London and New York: Routledge, 2014).
16. Dimitri Gutas, *Greek Thought, Arabic Culture*.
17. Regina Krahl, *Chinese Ceramics in the Topkapı Saray Museum*, ed. John Ayers (London: Sotheby's, 1986), I, pp. 42, 52, 133–5; Marcus Milwright, 'Prologues and epilogues in Islamic ceramics: Clays, repairs and secondary use', *Medieval Ceramics* 25 (2001): 77–80.
18. Milwright, 'Prologues and epilogues', p. 80.
19. For example, see Graziella Berti and Liana Tongiorgi, *I Bacini ceramici medievali della chiese di Pisa*, Quaderni di cultura materiale 3 (Rome: L'Erma di Bretschneider, 1981); John Carswell, 'Pottery and tiles on Mount Athos', *Ars Orientalis* 6 (1966): 77–90 (see particularly 79–80, figs 1 and 2).
20. Milwright, 'Pottery in written sources', p. 514.

21. Finbarr Flood, *Objects of Translation: Material Culture and Medieval Hindu-Muslim Encounter* (Princeton, NJ: Princeton University Press, 2009). See particularly chapter 2 ('Cultural cross-dressing'), pp. 61–87.
22. On the drawings and medals by Pisanello, see Raby, *Venice, Dürer and the Oriental Mode*, p. 2, n. 4, 5; Campbell and Chong, eds, *Bellini and the East*, pp. 66, 87, 89, fig. 26.
23. Cf. Michael Rowlands, 'Value and cultural transmission of things', in Wim van Binsbergen and Peter Geschiere, eds, *Commodification: Things, Agency and Identity (*The Social Life of Things *Revisited)* (Münster: Lit, 2005), pp. 267–81. On p. 267 he observes that some classes of object 'resist exchange and acquire value through cultural transmission rather than transaction'.

Glossary

Anointing (also inoiling): The applying of a liquid, usually some form of oil, to the body of a person as part of a religious or royal ritual.

Bashām (Arabic): A plant that grew on the Arabian Peninsula and the Horn of Africa that was similar to the balsam plants of Matarea. This may be identified as 'balm of Mecca'.

Caliph (Arabic: *khalīfa*): A spiritual leader of the Muslim community. This role was established after the death of the Prophet Muhammad in 632.

Carpobalsamum (Latin): A fragrant liquid derived from the fruit of the balsam tree.

Catechumen: A convert to Christianity who has not yet received the sacrament of baptism.

Chrism: A holy oil used by Christian Churches, also known as myron (q. v.). This oil was associated with rituals, most importantly the chrismation (q. v.) that occurs with baptism.

Chrismation: The ceremony of anointing (q. v.) with chrism/myron (q. v.), associated with baptism. Can also be employed in the ceremony for apostates returning to the Christian faith.

Collyrium (Latin): An eyewash used for medicinal purposes.

Congius (Latin, plural *congii*): A Roman measurement of capacity, equivalent to one eighth of an amphora (= c. 3.6 litres).

Denarius (Latin, plural *denarii*): A Roman silver coin, in circulation from the late third century BCE until the rule of Gordian III (r. 238–44) when it was largely replaced by the Antoninianus.

Dīnār (Arabic): A gold coin used across the Islamic world.

Dirham (Arabic): A silver coin used across the Islamic world.

Dog days: A phase during the summer when the constellation of Orion is followed into the night sky by Sirius. It occurs between 3 July and 15 August, although the calculation of the precise number of days varies.

Duhn (Arabic): Oil.

Fiddān (Arabic): An area of land equivalent to 0.42 hectares.

Fiscus (Latin): The emperor's personal treasury.

Frankincense: Refers to fragrant resin gathered from different trees of the genus *Boswellia*.

Galene (Greek: *galíni*): A theriac (q. v.) developed by Andromachus in the first century CE, and repeated in many later texts.

Ḥadīth (Arabic): Sayings and actions attributed to the Prophet Muhammad and other members of the Muslim community in the early seventh century.

Ḥisba (Arabic): Islamic market law.

Humoral medicine: A branch of medicine that conceptualises health and illness in relation to the balance of four humours: blood, black bile, yellow bile and phlegm. Hippocrates (d. c. 370 BCE) is credited with an early codification of this system, and it was elaborated by later scholars, most notably Claudius Galen (d. c. 216 CE).

Jizya (Arabic): A poll tax or head tax levied in Islamic polities against members of other recognised religions.

Khalūq (Arabic): A perfumed oil, containing saffron, used in anointing ceremonies by selected Muslim dynasties.

Khazindār (Arabic): Chief Treasurer

Lachobalsamum (Latin): Ash made from burning the branches of balsam plants.

Leechbook: Derived from the Old English term for a book of medical preparations.

Liber Pontificalis (Latin): A book containing the biographies of the popes from the time of St Peter onwards.

Mamlūk (Arabic): A slave who was trained as a soldier to serve in the army of a Muslim ruler. *Mamlūk*s formed their own dynasty in Egypt and Greater Syria between 1250 and 1517.

Masjid (Arabic): A mosque. A Congregational Mosque is known in Arabic as a *masjid al-jāmiʿ*, while a local mosque would be known simply as a *masjid*.

Mithqāl (Arabic): A measurement of weight equivalent to 4.25 g.

Mithridatium (Latin): A complex antidote associated with Mithradates VI Eupator, king of Pontos (r. 120–63 BCE). Different recipes are given for this antidote.

Muṣallā (Arabic): An open-air place of Muslim prayer.

Myron (Greek; Arabic: *mīrūn*): A term used for chrism (q. v.) in the eastern Churches.

Oleo-resin: A resin (q. v.) with a high proportion of volatile elements. It differs from a normal resin in that it does not solidify soon after extraction from the tree.

Opobalsamum (Latin): The finest liquid derived from the sap of the balsam plant.

Patrimonium (Latin): Property under the private ownership of a Roman emperor.

Pharmacopoeia (Latin): A reference work listing medicines and providing information about their applications and effects.

Raṭl (Arabic): A measurement of weight. In Egypt one *raṭl* is the equivalent of 144–50 *dirham*s, or about 449 g.

Resin: A water-soluble substance gathered from plants, particularly trees. Resins are complex compounds comprising terpenoids or flavonoids with volatile or non-volatile elements.

Sāqiya (Arabic; English, sakia): A simple water-lifting device, usually employing animal power.

Sextarius (Latin, plural *sextarii*): A Roman measurement of capacity, equivalent to one sixth of a congius (q. v.) (= c. 546 ml).

Simple: A single plant-, animal- or mineral-based product that could be employed for medical treatments. The most influential collection of information about simples was produced in the first century CE by Pedanois Dioscorides.

Stacte: The liquid form of myrrh, regarded as the most precious crop extracted from the myrrh tree.

Suffragan bishop: A bishop who assists a diocesan bishop.

Synaxarion (Greek): A hagiographic compilation.

Terra sigillata (Latin): Literally 'stamped earth', referring to medicinal clays that were gathered from sites around the Mediterranean and Middle East. The finest such clay was gathered from the island of Lemnos (*terra lemnia*).

Theriac: An antidote to plant and animal poisons. Recipes for famous theriacs, such as *Mithridatium* (q. v.), often contained numerous ingredients.

Ṭibb al-nabawī (Arabic): Literally 'prophetic medicine', referring to medical works that draw their information from *ḥadīth* (q. v.).

Treacle (French, *triacle*): A corruption of theriac (q. v.). Used to describe the complex antidotes that were produced in medieval and early modern Europe and the Middle East.

Waqiyya (Arabic): One twelfth of a *raṭl* (q. v.). If measured according to the Egyptian *raṭl*, this is equivalent to about 37 g.

Xerocollyrium (Latin): A dry form of collyrium (q. v.).

Xylobalsamum (Latin): A liquid made by boiling the branches of the balsam plant.

Ẓori (Hebrew): A plant-based balm, associated in the Old Testament with the region of Gilead.

Bibliography

'Abbasi, 'Ali Bey (Domingo Badía y Leblich). *Travels of Ali Bey: In Morocco, Tripoli, Cyprus, Egypt, Arabia, Syria, and Turkey between the Years 1803 and 1807*, 2 vols (London: Longman, Hurst, Rees, Orme and Brown, 1816. Reprinted Farnborough: Gregg, 1970).

Abdul-Ghani, A.-S. and R. Amin. 'Effect of aqueous extract of *Commiphora opobalsamum* on blood pressure and heart rate in rats', *Journal of Ethnopharmacology* 57 (1997): 219–22.

Abu al-Faraj, Gregorius (Bar Hebraeus), *Nomocanon Gregori Barhebraei*, ed. Paul Bedjan (Paris and Leipzig: Harrassowitz, 1898).

Abu al-Faraj, Gregorius (Bar Hebraeus). *The Abridged Version of* 'The Book of Simple Drugs' *of Ahmad ibn Muhammad al-Ghâfiqî by Gregorius Abu'l-Farag (Barhebraeus). Fasc. II: Leter BÂ' and GÎM*, ed. and trans. Max Meyerhof and G. Sobhy, The Egyptian University Faculty of Medicine Publications 4 (Cairo: Government Press, 1937).

Abu Lughod, Janet. *Before European Hegemony: The World System A.D. 1250–1350* (New York and Oxford: Oxford University Press, 1989).

Abu al-Makarim Sa'dallah ibn Jirjis ibn Mas'ud ('Abu Salih the Armenian'). *The Churches and Monasteries of Egypt, and Some Neighbouring Countries, Attributed to Abû Ṣâliḥ, the Armenian*, trans. Basil Evetts with notes by Alfred Butler, Anecdota Oxoniensia (Oxford: Oxford University Press, 1894–5).

Abu al-Makarim Sa'dallah ibn Jirjis ibn Mas'ud ('Abu Salih the Armenian'). *History of the Churches and Monasteries in Lower Egypt in thr* [sic] *13th Century*, trans. Mina al-Shamaa' and revised by Mrs Elizabeth (Cairo: Institute of Coptic Studies, 1992).

Adams, Robert. 'Anthropological perspectives on ancient trade', *Current Anthropology* 15 (1974): 239–58.

Adomnán (Arculf). *The Pilgrimage of Arculfus to the Holy Land (About the Year A.D. 670)*, trans. James MacPherson, Palestine Pilgrims Texts Society 3 (London: Palestine Exploration Society, 1889).

Aetius (Aetios) of Amida. *Libri medicinales [I–VIII]*, ed. Alexander Olivieri, 2 vols (Leipzig: B. G. Teubneri, 1935–50).

Aetius (Aetios) of Amida. *The Gynaecology and Obstetrics of the VIth Century, A.D. Translated from the Latin Edition of Cornarius, 1542 and Fully Annotated*, trans. and ed. James Ricci (Philadelphia and Toronto: The Blakiston Company, 1950).

Ahsan, Muhammad. *Social Life under the Abbasids 170–269A.H./786–902A.D.* (New York and London: Longmans, 1979).

Alexander of Tralles. *Oeuvres médicales d'Alexandre de Tralles. Le dernier auteur classique des grands médicins grecs de l'antiquité*, trans. Félix Brunet, Médicine et Thérapeutique byzantines (Paris: Librairie orientaliste Paul Geuthner, 1933–7).

Alhazmeh, Khalid. *Late Mamluk Patronage: Qanṣūh al-Ghūri's Waqf and his Foundations in Cairo*, unpublished doctoral thesis, Ohio State University, 1993.

'Ali ibn 'Isa al-Kahhal. *Chirurgia parua. Guidonis. Cyrurgia Albucasis cū cauterijs [et] alijs instrumentis. Tractatus de oculis Iesu Hali. Tractatus de oculis Canamusali* (Venice: Schott, 1500). Available online: https://wellcomelibrary.org/item/b129 54044#?c=0&m=0&s=0&cv=4&z=0.5646%2C0.2771%2C0.418%2C0.2626 (last consulted: 30 September 2019).

'Ali ibn 'Isa al-Kahhal. *Memorandum Book of a Tenth-century Oculist for the Use of Modern Ophthalomologists*, trans. and ed. Casey Wood (Chicago: University of Chicago Press, 1936).

Allen, James. 'Heliopolis', in Donald Redford, ed., *The Oxford Dictionary of Ancient Egypt* (Oxford and Cairo: Oxford University Press and American University in Cairo Press, 2001), II, pp. 88–9.

Allsen, Thomas. *Commodity and Exchange in the Mongol Empire: A Cultural History of Islamic Textiles*, Cambridge Studies in Islamic Civilization (Cambridge: Cambridge University Press, 1997).

Alpin (Alpinus), Prosper. *De balsamo dialogus. In quo verissima balsami plantae, opobalsami, carpobalsami, et xilobalsami cognitio plerisque* (Venice: Signum Leonis, 1591).

Alpin (Alpinus), Prosper. *Histoire du Baulme, ou il est prouvé qve novs avons vraye cognoissance de la plante qui produict le baulme, et par consequent de son fruict, et de son bois: contre l'opinion commune de plusieurs medecins et apoticaires anciens et modernes*, trans. André Colin (Lyon: I. Pillehotte, 1619).

Alpin (Alpinus), Prosper. *Histoire naturelle de l'Égypte par Prosper Alpin, 1581–1584*, trans. Raymond de Fenoyl and ed. Raymond de Fenoyl and Serge Sauneron, Collection des voyageurs occidentaux en Égypte 20, 4 vols in 2 (Cairo: Institut Français d'Archéologie du Caire, 1979).

Alpin (Alpinus), Prosper. *La médecine des Égyptiens*, trans. Raymond de Fenoyl, Collection des voyageurs occidentaux en Égypte 21, 2 vols (Cairo: Institut Français d'Archéologie du Caire, 1980).

Alpin (Alpinus), Prosper. *Plantes d'Égypte*, trans. Raymond de Fenoyl, Collection des Voyageurs occidentaux en Égypte 22 (Cairo: Institut Français d'Archéologie Orientale, 1980).

Amar, Zohar. 'Medicinal substances in Eretz-Israel in the times of the Bible, the Mishnah and the Talmud in the light of written sources', in Zohar Amar, *Illness and Healing in Ancient Times* (Haifa: The Reuben and Edith Hecht Museum, University of Haifa, 1996).

Ambroise. *The Crusade of Richard Lion-Heart*, trans. Merton Jerome Hubert with notes by John La Monte (New York: Columbia University Press, 1941).

Anawati, Georges. 'Le traité d'Averroes sur la thériaque et ses antécédents grecs et arabes', *Quaderni di Studi Arabi* 5–6 (1987–8): 26–48.

Anglicus, Bartholomaeus. *On the Properties of Things. John Trevisa's Translation of Bartholomaeus Anglicus* De proprietatibus rerum. *A Critical Text*, ed. Michael Seymour et al. (Oxford: Clarendon Press, 1975–88).

Anon. *A Medieval Herbal. A Facsimile of British Library Egerton ms. 747*, introduction by Minta Collins and list of plants by Sandra Raphael (London: British Library, 2003).

Anon. (Pseudo-Galen). *Kitâb al-Diryâq (Thériaque de Paris)*, with commentary by Marie Guesdon, Oleg Grabar, Françoise Michaeu, Anna Caiozzo and Jaclynne Kerner (Sansepolchro: Aboco Museum, 2008).

Ansary, A. R. *Qaryat al-Fau: A Portrait of the Pre-Islamic Civilisation in Saudi Arabia* (Riyadh and New York: University of Riyadh and St Martin's Press, 1992).

Appadurai, Arjun, ed. *The Social Life of Things: Commodities in Cultural Exchange* (Cambridge: Cambridge University Press, 1986).

Appadurai, Arjun, 'Introduction: Commodities and the politics of value', in Arjun Appadurai, ed. *The Social Life of Things: Commodities in Cultural Exchange* (Cambridge: Cambridge University Press, 1986), pp. 3–63.

Apuleius of Madaura. *The Metamorphoses, or Golden Ass*, trans. H. E. Butler, vol. 1 (Oxford: Clarendon Press, 1910).

Arora, R., V. Taneja, R. Sharma and S. Gupta. 'Anti-inflammatory studies on a crystalline steroid isolated from *Commiphora mukul*', *Indian Journal of Medical Research* 60 (1972): 929–31.

Ashtor, Eliyahu. *Histoire des prix et des salaires dans l'Orient médiéval*, École Pratique des Hautes Études – Vie Section. Monnaie. Prix. Conjoncture 8 (Paris: SEVPEN, 1969).

Ashtor, Eliyahu. 'Levantine sugar industry in the later Middle Ages: A case of technological decline', *Israel Oriental Studies* 7 (1977): 226–80. Reprinted in Abraham Udovitch, ed., *The Islamic Middle East, 700–1900: Studies in Economic and Social History* (Princeton, NJ: Princeton University Press, 1981), pp. 91–132.

Ashtor, Eliyahu. *Levant Trade in the Later Middle Ages* (Princeton, NJ: Princeton University Press, 1983).

Atasoy, Nurhan and Julian Raby. *Iznik. The Pottery of Ottoman Turkey* (London: Thames & Hudson, 1989).

Atchley, Edward. *A History of the Use of Incense in Divine Liturgy*, Alcuin Club Editions 13 (London: Alcuin Club, 1909).

Atiya, ʿAziz. *Egypt and Aragon: Embassies and Diplomatic Correspondence between 1300 and 1330 A.D.*, Abhandlungen für die Kunde des Morgenlandes 23.7 (Leipzig: F. A. Brockhaus, 1938).

Ayalon, David. *Gunpowder and Firearms in the Mamluk Kingdom* (London: Vallentine, Mitchell, 1956).

Babylonian Talmud: Kerithoth 6a. Judeo-Christian Research: https://juchre.org/talmud/kerithoth/kerithoth1.htm#6a (last consulted: 21 May 2018).

Babylonian Talmud: Berachot 43a. Sefaria.org: https://www.sefaria.org/Berakhot.43a?lang=bi (last consulted: 21 May 2018).

Babylonian Talmud: Shabbat 26a. Sefaria.org: https://www.sefaria.org/Shabbat.26a?lang=bi (last consulted: 21 May 2018).

Baer, Gabriel. *Egyptian Guilds in Modern Times*, Oriental Notes and Studies 8 (Jerusalem: The Israel Oriental Society, 1964).

Baffioni, Carmela, ed. and trans. *Epistles of the Brethren of Purity. On the Natural Sciences. An Arabic Critical Edition and English Translation of Epistles 15–21* (Oxford and New York: Oxford University Press in association with the Institute of Ismaili Studies, 2013).

Baghdadi, ʿAbd al-Latif al-. *The Eastern Key: Kitāb al-Ifādah wa'l-iʿtibār of ʿAbd al-Latīf al-Baghdādī*, trans. Kamal Zand Kamal, John Videan and Ivy Videan (London: Allen and Unwin, 1965).

Baghdadi, 'Abd al-Latif al-. *Kitāb al-ifāda wa'l-i'tibār*, ed. Ahmad Sabunu (Damascus: Dar Qutaiba, 1983).

Balfour-Paul, Jenny. *Indigo: Egyptian Mummies to Blue Jeans* (London: British Museum, 1998).

Baraz, Dan. 'Copto-Arabic collections of Western Marian legends: The reception of a Western text in the East', in Tito Orlandi and David Johnson, eds, *Acts of the Eighth International Congress of Coptic Studies, Washington, 12–15 August 1992* (Rome: C.I.M., 1993), II, pp. 23–32.

Baraz, Dan. 'The incarnated icon of Saidnaya goes West: A re-examination of the motif in the light of new manuscript evidence', *Le Muséon* 108 (1995): 181–91.

Bar Kepha, Moses. *Commentary on Myron*, trans. with introduction by Baby Varghese, Texts from Christian Late Antiquity 34 (Piscataway, NJ: Gorgias Press, 2014).

Bar Salibi, Dionysius. *Commentaries on Myron and Baptism*, ed. and trans. Baby Varghese, Moran 'Eth'o 29 (Kottayam: St Ephrem Ecumenical Research Institute, 2006).

Bass, George F. et al. *Serçe Limanı. Volume 2: The Glass of an Eleventh-Century Shipwreck* (College Station, TX: Texas A&M University Press, 2009).

Baxandall, Michael. *Painting and Experience in Fifteenth-century Italy: A Primer in the Social History of Pictorial Style* (Oxford and New York: Oxford University Press, 1972).

Beck, Curt and Larry Moray. 'Organic residues', in Donald Whitcomb and Janet Johnson, eds, *Quseir al-Qadim, 1978: Preliminary Report* (Princeton, NJ: American Research Center in Egypt, 1979), pp. 253–6.

Beckwith, Christopher. 'The introduction of Greek medicine into Tibet in the seventh and eighth centuries', *Journal of the American Oriental Society* 99.2 (1979): 297–313.

Beckwith, Christopher. 'Tibetan treacle: A note on theriac in Tibet', *The Tibetan Society Bulletin* 15 (June 1980): 49–51.

Behrens-Abouseif, Doris. 'The northeastern extension of Cairo under the Mamluks', *Annales Islamologiques* 17 (1981): 157–89.

Behrens-Abouseif, Doris. 'Gardens in Islamic Egypt', *Der Islam* 69 (1992): 302–12.

Behrens-Abouseif, Doris. *Practicing Diplomacy in the Mamluk Sultanate: Gifts and Material Culture in the Medieval Islamic World* (London: I. B. Tauris, 2014).

Belon du Mans, Pierre. *Observations du plusieurs singularitez et choses mémorables trouuées en Grece, Asie, Iudée, Égypte, Arabie et autres pays estranges* (Paris: G. Corrozet, 1553).

Belon du Mans, Pierre. *Voyage en Égypte*, trans. and ed. Serge Sauneron, Collection des Voyageurs occidentaux en Égypte 1 (Cairo: Institut Français d'Archéologie Orientale du Caire, 1970).

Benjamin, Walter. 'The work of art in the age of its technological reproducibility'. Third edition of the text translated in Howard Eiland and Michael Jennings, eds, *Walter Benjamin: Selected Writing, IV: 1938–1940* (Cambridge, MA: Harvard University Press, 2003), pp. 251–70. Reprinted in Donald Preziosi. *The Art of Art History: A Critical Anthology. New Edition*, Oxford History of Art (Oxford and New York: Oxford University Press, 2009), pp. 435–42.

Bernard, John, trans. *Guide-book to Palestine (circa A.D. 1350)*, Palestine Pilgrim Texts Society 6, no. 3 (London: Palestine Exploration Fund, 1894).

Berti, Graziella and Liana Tongiorgi. *I Bacini ceramici medievali della chiese di Pisa*, Quaderni di cultura materiale 3 (Rome: L'Erma di Bretschneider, 1981).

Biegman, Nicholaas. *Egypt: Moulids, Saints, Sufis* (The Hague and London: Gary Schwarz/SDU and Kegan Paul International Ltd, 1990).

Biruni, Muhammad ibn Ahmad al-. *Al-Biruni's Book of Pharmacy and Medicine*, ed. and trans. Hakim Said (Karachi: Hamdard Academy, 1973).

Blanc, Bernard, Sophie Denoix, Jean-Claude Garcin and R. Gordioni. 'À propos de la carte du Caire de Matheo Pagano', *Annales Islamologiques* 17 (1981): 203–86.

Bloch, Marc. *Feudal Society, II: Social Classes and Political Organization*, trans. L. A. Manyon (London: Taylor & Francis, 2005).

Bloom, Jonathan. *Paper before Print: The History and Impact of Paper in the Islamic World* (New Haven, CT and London: Yale University Press, 2001).

Boulos, Lutfi. *Flora of Egypt. Volume Two: Geraniaceae – Boraginaceae* (Cairo: Al Hadra Publishing, 2000).

Bouquet, Martin. *Recueil des historiens de Gaules et de la France*, vol. 5 (Paris: Les Libraires Associés, 1744).

Brand, Charles, ed. *Icon and Minaret: Sources of Byzantine and Islamic Civilization* (Englewood Cliffs, NJ: Prentice-Hall, 1969).

Brater, D. Craig and Walter J. Daly. 'Clinical pharmacology in the Middle Ages: Principles that presage the 21st century', *Clinical Pharmacology and Therapeutics* 67.5 (2000): 447–50.

Brejnik, Claire and Antoine, trans. and ed. *Voyage en Égypte de Christophe Harant de Polzic et Bezdruzic, 1598*, Collection des voyageurs occidentaux en Égypte 5 (Cairo: Institut Français d'Archéologie Orientale, 1972).

Brock, Arthur, trans. *Greek Medicine, Being Extracts Illustrative of Medical Writers from Hippocrates to Galen* (London and Toronto: J. M. Dent and Sons Ltd, 1929).

Brock, Sebastian. *The Holy Spirit in the Syrian Baptismal Tradition*, The Syrian Churches Series 9 (Poona: Anita Printers, 1979).

Bryan, Cyril, trans. *Ancient Egyptian Medicine: The Ebers Papyrus*, introduction by G. Eliot Smith (London: G. Bles, 1930. Reprinted Chicago: Ares Publishers, 1974).

Buckley, Ronald. *The Night Journey and Ascension in Islam: The Reception of Religious Narrative in Sunnī, Shīʿī and Western Culture*, Library of Middle Eastern History 36 (New York and London: I. B. Tauris, 2013).

Buckton, David, ed. *Byzantium: Treasures of Byzantine Art* (London: British Museum Press, 1994).

Budge, Ernest Wallis, trans. *Syrian Anatomy, Pathology and Therapeutics, or 'Book of Medicines'* (Oxford and New York: Oxford University Press, 1913).

Budge, Ernest Wallis, trans. *The Book of the Saints of the Ethiopian Church. A Translation of the Ethiopic* Synaxarium, *Made from Manuscripts Oriental 660 and 661 in the British Library*, 4 vols (Cambridge: Cambridge University Press, 1928).

Burchard of Mount Sion. *Travels in Palestine, A.D. 1280*, trans. Claude Conder and Aubrey Stewart, Palestine Pilgrim Texts Society 12 (London: Palestine Exploration Fund, 1896).

Burkill, Humphrey. *Useful Plants of West Tropical Africa*, vol. 1 (Richmond: Royal Botanic Gardens, Kew, 1985). Online entry: https://plants.jstor.org/stable/10.5555/al.ap.upwta.1_478 (last consulted: 22 May 2018).

Burnett, Charles. 'The coherence of the Arabic-Latin translation program in Toledo in the twelfth century', *Science in Context* 14.1/2 (2000): 249–88.

Burnett, Charles and Danielle Jacquart. *Constantine the African and ʿAlī ibn al-ʿAbbās al-Maǧūsī. The* Pantegni *and Related Texts*, Studies in Ancient Medicine 10 (Leiden and New York: Brill, 1994).

Burri, Carla and Nadine Sauneron, trans. *Bernardino Amico da Gallipoli, Aquilante Rocchetta, Henri Castela*, Collection des Voyageurs occidentaux en Égypte 11 (Cairo: Institut Français d'Archéologie Orientale, 1974).

Cameron, Malcolm. *Anglo-Saxon Medicine*, Cambridge Studies in Anglo-Saxon England 7 (Cambridge: Cambridge University Press, 1993).

Camille, Michael. *The Gothic Idol: Ideology and Image-making in Medieval Art* (Cambridge and New York: Cambridge University Press, 1989).

Campbell, Caroline and Alan Chong, eds. *Bellini and the East* (London and Boston:

Yale University Press for the National Gallery Company, London, and the Isabella Stewart Gardner Museum, 2005).

Canaan, Tawfiq. *Mohammaden Saints and Sanctuaries in Palestine*, Luzac's Oriental Religions Series 5 (London: Luzac and Co., 1927).

Cannuyer, Christian. 'Les Coptes, vingt siècles d'histoire chrétienne en Égypte', in Anon., *L'Art copte en Égypte: 2000 ans de christianisme* (Paris: Gallimard and Institut du Monde Arabe, 2000), pp. 26–33.

Carswell, John. 'Pottery and tiles on Mount Athos', Ars Orientalis 6 (1966): 77–90.

Carswell, John. *Blue and White: Chinese Porcelain around the World* (London: British Museum Press, 2000).

Carswell, John and Jean McClure Mudge. *Blue and White: Chinese Porcelain and its Impact on the Western World* (Chicago: University of Chicago Press, 1985).

Cartelle, Enrique, ed. *Constantini Liber de Coitu. El tratado de andrologiá de Constantino el Africano*, Estudio y edicion critica. Monografias de la Universidad de Santiago de Compostela 77 (Santiago de Compostela: Europa Artes Gráficas 1983).

Casson, Lionel, ed. and trans., *Periplus Maris Erythrae* (Princeton, NJ: Princeton University Press, 1989).

Castel, Ursula and Nadine Sauneron, trans., and Serge Sauneron, ed. *Voyages en Égypte pendant les années 1587–1588*, Collection des Voyageurs occidentaux en Égypte 6 (Cairo: Institut Français d'Archéologie Orientale, 1972).

Castelli, Pietro. *Opobalsamum examinatum, defensum, indicatum, absolutum, et laudatum* (Messina: Francisci, 1640).

Castelli, Pietro. *Opobalsamum triumphans* (Basle: Peter Perna, 1640).

Charas, Moyse. *The Royal Pharmacopoea Galenical and Chymical* (London: John Starkey and Moses Pitt, 1678).

Charrière, Ernest. *Négociations de la France dans le Levant* (Paris: Imprimerie Nationale, 1848–60).

Chazaud, A.-M. 'Inventaire et comptes de la succession d'Eudes, comte de Nevers (Acre, 1266)', *Mémoires de la Société Nationale des Antiquaires de France* 32, ser. 4, vol. 2 (1871): 164–206.

Ciggaar, Krijna. 'Manuscripts as intermediaries: The Crusader states and literary cross-fertilization', in Krijna Ciggaar, Adelbert Davids and Herman Teule, eds, *East and West in the Crusader States: Context – Contacts – Confrontations*, Orientalia Lovaniensia Analecta 75 (Leuven: Peeters, 1996), pp. 131–51.

Clark, John. 'Medieval enamelled glass from London', *Medieval Archaeology* 28 (1983): 152–6.

Classen, Constance, *The Color of Angels: Cosmography, Gender and the Aesthetic Imagination* (London and New York: Routledge, 1998).

Cockagne, Oswald, ed. and trans. *Leechdoms, Wortcunning, and Starcraft of Early England. Being a Collection, for the most Part never before printed, illustrating the History of Science in this Country before the Norman Conquest* (London: Longman, Green, Longman, Roberts and Green, 1864).

Collins, Minta. *Medieval Herbals: The Illustrative Traditions*, The British Library Studies in Medieval Culture (London, Toronto and Buffalo, NY: The British Library and University of Toronto Press, 2000).

Connolly, R. Hugh and Humphrey Codrington, ed. and trans. *Two Commentaries on the Jacobite Liturgy by George, Bishop of the Arabs and Moses Bār-Kēphā: Together with the Syriac Anaphora of St James and a Document entitled*, The Book of Life (London and Oxford: Williams & Norgate, 1913).

Conrad, Lawrence. '*Ṭāʿūn* and *wabāʾ*: Conceptions of plague and pestilence in early Islam', *Journal of the Economic and Social History of the Orient* 25.3 (1982), pp. 286–307.

Constantine the African. *Opera*, 2 vols (Basle: H. Petrus, 1536–9).

Coogan, Michael D., ed. *The New Oxford Annotated Bible*, third edition (Oxford: Oxford University Press, 2001).

Cotton, Hannah. 'Ein Gedi between the two revolts', *Scripta Classica Israelica* 20 (2001): 139–54.

Cotton, Hannah and Werner Eck. 'Ein Staatsmonopol und seine Folgen: Plinius, *Naturalis Historia* 12,123 und der Preis für Balsam', *Rheinisches Museum für Philologie* 140.2 (1997): 153–61.

Crone, Patricia. *Meccan Trade and the Rise of Islam* (Oxford: Basil Blackwell, 1987).

Cross, Frank and Elizabeth Livingstone, eds. *The Oxford Dictionary of the Christian Church*, third edition (Oxford: Oxford University Press, 1997).

Curtin, Philip. *Cross-Cultural Trade in World History*, Studies in Comparative World History (Cambridge: Cambridge University Press, 1984).

Cutler, Anthony. 'Gifts and gift exchange as aspects of Byzantine, Arab, and related economies', *Dumbarton Oaks Papers* 55 (2001): 247–78.

Daniel, Norman. *Islam and the West: The Making of an Image* (Edinburgh: Edinburgh University Press, 1960).

Dankoff, Robert. *An Ottoman Mentality: The World of Evliya Çelebi*, The Ottoman World and its Heritage (Leiden and Boston: Brill, 2004).

Da'ud al-Antaki. *Tadkhirat ulī al-albāb wa jāmiʿ lil-ʿajab al-ʿujāb*, ed. Muhammad al-Falaki, 3 vols in 1 (Cairo: Shakirat Maktaba wa Matbaʿa Mustafa al-Babi al-Halabi, 1952, reprinted 1982).

Davidson, Miles. *Columbus Then and Now: A Life Re-examined* (Norman, OK and London: University of Oklahoma Press, 1997).

Davillier, Jean-Charles. *Les origines de la porcelaine en Europe* (Paris: Librairie de l'Art, 1882).

Davis, Raymond, trans. *The Book of the Pontiffs (Liber Pontificalis): The Ancient Biographies of the First Ninety Roman Bishops to AD 715* (Liverpool: Liverpool University Press, 1983).

Degen, Rainer. 'Galen im Syrischen: Eine Übersicht über die syrische Überlieferung der Werke Galens', in Vivian Nutton, ed., *Galen: Problems and Prospects* (London: The Wellcome Institute for the History of Medicine, 1981), pp. 133–66.

Delaney, Paul. 'Constantinus Africanus' *De Coitu*: A translation', *The Chaucer Review* 4.1 (1969): 55–65.

Delatte, Louis, ed. *Textes latins et vieux français relatif aux Cyranides*, Bibliothèque de la Faculté de Philosophie et Lettres de l'Université de Liège, fasc. 93 (Paris: Société d'Édition des Belles Lettres, 1942).

De Maillet, Benoît. *Description de l'Égypte, contenant plusieurs remarques curieuses sur la géographie ancienne et moderne de ce païs, sur ces monumens anciens, sur les moeurs*, ed. Jean-Baptiste Le Mascrier (Paris: L. Genneau and J. Rollin, fils, 1735).

De Mondeville, Henri. *Die Chirurgie des Heinrich von Mondeville (Hermondaville) nach Berliner, Erfurter und Pariser Codices* (Book 1 of *Leben, Lehre und Leistungen des Heinrich von Mondeville [Hermondaville]. Ein Beitrag zur Geschichte der Anatomie und Chirurgie*), ed. Julius Pagel (Berlin: August Hirschwald, 1892).

De Rachewiltz, Igor. *Prester John and Europe's Discovery of East Asia* (Canberra: Australia National University Press, 1972).

De Smet, Daniel. 'La translation du *raʾs* al-Ḥusayn au Caire fatimide', in Urbain Vermeulen and Daniel de Smet, eds, *Egypt and Syria in the Fatimid, Ayyubid and Mamluk Eras* (Leuven: Peeters, 1998), pp. 29–44.

Di Varthema, Ludovico. *The Travels of Ludovico di Varthema in Egypt, Syria, Arabia Deserta and Arabia Felix, Persia, India, and Ethiopia, A.D. 1503 to 1508*, trans. John Jones and ed. George Badger, Works issued by the Hakluyt Society (London: Hakluyt Society, 1863).

Diderot, Denis and Jean d'Alembert, eds. *Encylopédie, ou dictionnaire raisonné des sciences, des arts, et des métiers*, 17 vols (Paris: Briasson et al., 1751–80).

Dimashqi, Shams al-Din Muhammad b. Abi Talib al-. *Kitāb al-nukhbat al-dahr fī 'ajā'ib al-barr wa'l-bahr*, ed. August Mehren (St Petersburg: Académie Impériale des Sciences, 1864. Reprinted Amsterdam: Meridian, 1964).

Diodorus of Sicily, *Library of History*, ed. and trans. Charles Oldfather, Charles Sherman, C. B. Welles, Russell Geer and F. R. Walton, Loeb Classical Library 279, 303, 340, 375, 377, 384, 389, 390, 399, 409, 422, 423, 12 vols (Cambridge, MA: Harvard University Press, 1933–67, reprinted 2014).

Dioscorides, Pedanios. *Pedanii Dioscurides Anazarbei* De Materia Medica. *Libre quinque*, ed. Max Wellman (Berlin: Weidmann, 1907).

Dioscorides, Pedanios. *The Greek Herbal of Dioscorides, Illustrated by a Byzantine, A.D. 512. Englished by John Goodyer, A.D. 1655*, ed. Robert Gunther (Oxford, 1933. Reprinted New York: Hafner Publication Company, 1959).

Dioscorides, Pedanios. *Pedanios Dioscorides of Anazarbus. De materia medica*, trans. Lily Beck, Altertumswissenschaftliche Texte und Studien 38 (Hildesheim, Zürich and New York: Olms – Weidmann, 2005).

Dols, Michael. *The Black Death in the Middle East* (Princeton, NJ: Princeton University Press, 1977).

Donceel-Voûte, Pauline. 'Traces of fragrance along the Dead Sea', *Res Orientales* 11: *Parfums d'Orient* (1998): 93–124.

Dönitz, Saskia. 'Alexander the Great in medieval Hebrew traditions', in David Zuwiyya, ed., *Companion to Alexander Literature in the Middle Ages* (Leiden and Boston: Brill, 2011), pp. 22–39.

Donner, Herbert. *The Mosaic Map of Madaba: An Introductory Guide* (Kampen: Kok Pharos Publishing House, 1992).

Doughty, Charles. *Travels in Arabia Deserta*, new edition in one volume (New York: Random House, 1937).

Duchesne, Louis, ed. *Le Liber Pontificalis: Texte, introduction et commentaire*, 2 vols (Paris: E. Thorin, 1886).

Ebbell, Bendix. *The Papyrus Ebers, the Greatest Egyptian Medical Document* (Copenhagen and London: Levin & Munksgaard, 1937).

Ehrenkreutz, Andrew. 'Extracts from the technical manual on the Ayyūbid mint in Cairo', *Bulletin of the School of Oriental and African Studies* 15.3 (1953): 423–47.

Einhard and Notker the Stammerer. *Two Lives of Charlemagne*, trans. Lewis Thorpe (London: Penguin Classics, 1986).

Eldredge, Laurence M., ed. *Benvenutus Grassus. The Wonderful Art of the Eye. A Critical Edition of the Middle English Translation of his 'De Probatissima Arte*

Oculorum', Medieval Texts and Studies 19 (East Lansing, MI: Michigan State University Press, 1996).

Eldredge, Laurence M. 'A thirteenth-century ophthalmologist, Benvenutus Grassus: His treatise and its survival', *Journal of the Royal Society of Medicine* 91 (1998): 47–52.

Evans, Helen and Brandie Ratliff, eds. *Byzantium and Islam: Age of Transition, 7th–9th Century* (New Haven, CT and London: Yale University Press and Metropolitan Museum of Art, 2012).

Fabbri, Christiane. 'Treating medieval plague: The wonderful virtues of theriac', *Early Science and Medicine* 12 (2007): 247–83.

Fabri, Felix. *Evagatorium in Terrae Sanctae, Arabiae et Egypti Peregrinationem*, ed. Konrad Hassler, 3 vols (Stuttgart: Societatis Litterariæ Stuttgardiensis, 1843–9).

Fabri, Felix. *Voyage en Égypte de Félix Fabri, 1483*, trans. Gisèle Hurseaux, Collection des voyageurs occidentaux en Égypte 14, 3 vols (Cairo: Institut Français d'Archéologie du Caire, 1975).

Faure, Paul. *Parfums et aromates de l'antiquité*, Nouvelles études historiques (Paris: Fayard, 1987).

Feliks, Jehuda. 'Balsam', *Encyclopaedia Judaica*, second edition (Detroit: Macmillan Reference USA, 2007), III, pp. 95–6.

Fleming, Ian. *Goldfinger* (London: Jonathan Cape, 1959. Reprinted St Albans: Triad/Panther Books, 1978).

Flood, Finbarr. *Objects of Translation: Material Culture and Medieval Hindu-Muslim Encounter* (Princeton, NJ: Princeton University Press, 2009).

Forsskål, Pehr with Carsten Niebuhr. *Flora Aegyptiaco-Arabica. Sive Descriptiones Plantarum quas per Aegyptum Inferiorem et Arabiam Felicem* (Hannover: Mölleri, 1775).

Freshfield, Edwin, trans. *Roman Law in the Later Roman Empire: Byzantine Guilds, Professional and Commercial. Ordinances of Leo VI, c. 895 from the Book of the Eparch* (Cambridge: Cambridge University Press, 1938).

Fretellus of Nazareth, Rorgo. *Fetellus (circa 1130 A.D.)*, trans. James MacPherson, Palestine Pilgrim Texts Society 5 (London: Palestine Exploration Society, 1892).

Furley, David and J. S. Wilkie, trans. and eds. *Galen on Respiration and the Arteries: An Edition with English Translation and Commentary of* De usu respirationis, An in arteriis natura sanguis contineatur, De usu pulsum, *and* De causis respirationis (Princeton, NJ and Guildford: Princeton University Press, 1984).

Gadalrab, Sherry. 'Medical healers in Ottoman Egypt, 1517–1805', *Medical History* 54.3 (2010): 365–86.

Galen, Claudius. *Claudius Galen, De theriaca ad pisonem: Testo Latino*, ed. and trans. Enrico Coturri and Michele Nardi, Biblioteca della 'Rivista di Storia della Scienze Mediche et Naturali' 8 (Florence: Olschki, 1959).

Garcin, Jean-Claude. 'The regime of the Circassian Mamlūks', in Carl Petry, ed., *The Cambridge History of Egypt, Volume I: Islamic Egypt, 640–1517* (Cambridge: Cambridge University Press, 2008), pp. 296–9.

Gately, Iain. *Tobacco: A Cultural History of how an Exotic Plant Seduced Civilization* (New York: Grove Press, 2003).

Gavignan, John, trans. *Christian Society and the Crusades. Sources in Translation Including the Capture of Damietta by Oliver of Paderborn*, ed. with introduction by Edward Peters (Philadelphia: University of Pennsylvania Press, 1971).

Geary, Patrick. 'Sacred commodities: The circulation of medieval relics', in Arjun Appadurai, ed., *The Social Life of Things: Commodities in Cultural Exchange* (Cambridge: Cambridge University Press, 1986), pp. 169–91.

Gerard, John. *The Herball, or Generall Historie of Plants* (London: Edmund Bollifant, 1597. Reprinted in The English Experience 660B, Amsterdam and Norwood, NJ: Walter J. Johnson Inc. and Theatrum Orbis Terrarum, 1974).

Ghabin, Ahmad. *Ḥisba, Art and Craft in Islam*, Arabisch-Islamische Welt in Tradition und Moderne (Weisbaden: Harrassowitz, 2009).

Gillett, Jan. *Burseracaeae*, Flora of East Africa (Rotterdam: Bulkema, 1991).

Ginzburg, Carlo. *Cheese and the Worms: The Cosmos of a Sixteenth-century Miller*, trans. John and Anne Tedeschi (London: Penguin Books, 1992).

Ginzberg, Louis. *The Legends of the Jews*, trans. Henrietta Szold, 7 vols (Philadelphia: Jewish Publication Society of America, 1909–38).

Gnoli, Tommaso. 'La production del balsamo nell'oasi di Engaddi (Israele). Su alcuni nuovi documenti dal deserto di giuda', in Alessandra Avanzini, ed., *Profumi d'Arabia: Atti del convegno* (Rome: 'L'erma' di Bretschneider, 1997), pp. 413–29.

Godefroy, Théodor. *Le ceremonial françois*, 2 vols (Paris: S. and G. Cramoisy, 1649).

Goitein, Shlomo. *A Mediterranean Society: The Jewish Communities of the Arab World as Portrayed in the Documents of the Cairo Geniza. Volume II: The Community* (Berkeley, CA and Los Angeles: University of California Press, 1971, reprinted 1999).

Goitein, Shlomo and Paula Sanders. *A Mediterranean Society: The Jewish Communities of the Arab World as Portrayed in the Documents of the Cairo Geniza. Volume VI: Cumulative Indices* (Berkeley, CA and Los Angeles: University of California Press, 1993, reprinted 1999).

Golombek, Lisa. 'The draped universe of Islam', in Priscilla Soucek, ed., *Content and Context of the Visual Arts of the Islamic World* (University Park, PA and London: Pennsylvania State University Press, 1988), pp. 25–38.

González, Antonius. *Voyage en Égypte du Père Antonius González, 1665–1666*, trans. and ed. Charles Libois, Collection des Voyageurs occidentaux en Égypte 19, 2 vols (Cairo: Institut Français d'Archéologie Orientale, 1972).

Grabar, André. *Ampoules de Terre Sainte (Monza-Bobbio)* (Paris: C. Klinksieck, 1958).

Graf, Georg, *Geschichte der christlichen arabischen Literatur*, 5 vols (Vatican: Bibliotheca Apostolica Vaticana, 1944–53).

Granet, François. 'La thériaque de Montpellier', *Revue d'Histoire de la Pharmacie* 229 (1976): 75–83.

Graves, Margaret. *Arts of Allusion: Object, Ornament, and Architecture in Medieval Islam* (New York: Oxford University Press, 2018).

Greenhill, Thomas. Νεκροκηδεια, *or the Art of Embalming, wherein is shewn the Right of Burial, the Funeral Ceremonies, and the several Ways of preserving dead Bodies in most Nations of the World. . .* (London: Printed by the author, 1705).

Gregory of Tours. *History of the Franks.* Reproduced in Medieval Sourcebook: http://www.christianiconography.info/gregoryHistoryFranks.htm (last consulted: 22 May 2018).

Griffin, J. P. 'Venetian treacle and the foundation of medicines regulation', *British Journal of Clinical Pharmacology* 58.3 (2004): 317–25.

Grisar, Hartmann and Moriz Dreger. *Die römische Kapelle Sancta Sanctorum und ihr Schatz. Meine Entdeckungen und Studien in der Palastkapelle der Mittelalterichen Päpste* (Freiburg im Breisgau: Herder, 1908).

Groom, Nigel. *Frankincense and Myrrh: A Study of the Arabian Incense Trade* (London: Longman, 1981).

Groom, Nigel. 'Trade, incense and perfume', in Ann Gunter, ed., *Caravan Kingdoms: Yemen and the Ancient Incense Route* (Washington, DC: Freer Gallery of Art and Arthur M. Sackler Gallery, 2005), pp. 104–13.

Guo, Li. *Commerce, Culture, and Community: The Arabic Documents of Quseir*, Islamic History and Civilization: Studies and Texts 52 (Leiden and Boston: Brill, 2004).

Gutas, Dimitri. *Greek Thought, Arabic Culture: The Graeco-Arabic Translation Movement in Baghdad and Early ʿAbbāsid Society (2nd–4th/8th–10th Centuries)* (London and New York: Routledge, 1998).

Hadas, Gideon. 'The balsam *afarsemon / apharsemon* and Ein Gedi during the Roman-Byzantine period', *Revue Biblique* 114.2 (2007): 161–73.

Haddad, Sami and Amin Khairallah. 'A forgotten chapter in the history of the circulation of the blood', *Annals of Surgery* 104.1 (1936): 1–8.

Haefeli-Till, Dominique, trans. *Der 'Liber de oculis' des Constantine Africanus: Ubersetzung und Kommentar*, Zürcher Medizingeschichtliche Abhandlungen, Neue Reihe 121 (Zurich: Juris Druck und Verlag 1977).

Halikowski, Stefan. 'Meanings behind myths: The multiple manifestations of the tree of the Virgin at Matarea', *Mediterranean Historical Review* 23.2 (2008): 101–28.

Hall, Joseph. *The Balm of Gilead, for the Distressed, both Moral and Divine: Most fit for these wofull Times* (London: Thomas Newcomb, 1650).

Halleq, Wael. 'The authenticity of Prophetic ḥadîth: A pseudo-problem', *Studia Islamica* 89 (1999): 75–90.

Hamdani, Abu Muhammad al-Hasan b. Ahmad ibn Yaʿqub al-. *al-Iklīl*. Published as Nabih Amin Faris, trans., *The Antiquities of South Arabia, being a Translation from the Arabic with linguistic, geographic, and historic Notes of the eighth Book of al-Hamdāni's al-Iklīl, reconstructed from al-Karmali's Edition and Ms in the Garrett Collection*, Princeton University Library, Princeton Oriental Texts 3 (Princeton, NJ: Princeton University Press, 1938).

Hamza, Hani. *The Northern Cemetery of Cairo* (Costa Mesa, CA: Mazda, 2001).

Harding, Catherine and Nancy Micklewright. 'Mamluks and Venetians: An intercultural perspective on fourteenth-century material culture in the Mediterranean', *Revue Art Canadienne/Canadian Art Review* 24.2 (1997): 47–66.

Harrison, Roland. *Healing Herbs of the Bible* (Leiden: Brill, 1966).

Hartmuth, Maximillian. 'Oral tradition and architectural history: A sixteenth-century Ottoman mosque in the Balkans in local memory, textual sources and material evidence', in Daniella Talmon-Heller and Katia Cytryn-Silverman, eds, *Material Evidence and Narrative Sources: Interdisciplinary Studies of the History of the Muslim Middle East*, Islamic History and Civilization, Studies and Texts 108 (Leiden and Boston: Brill, 2015), pp. 341–59.

Hasluck, Frederick. '*Terra Lemnia*', in Frederick Hasluck, *Christianity and Islam under the Sultans*, ed. Margaret Hasluck, 2 vols (Oxford: Oxford University Press, 1929).

Hawass, Zahi and Sahar Saleem. *Scanning the Pharaohs: CT Imaging of the New Kingdom Royal Mummies*, ed. Sue D'Auria (Cairo and New York: The American University in Cairo Press, 2016).

Heberden, William. *Antitheriaka: An Essay on Mithridatium and Theriaca* (London?: no publisher given, 1745).

Heberer, Michael. *Voyages en Égypte de Michael Heberer von Bretten, 1585–1586*, trans. Oleg Volkoff, Collection des Voyageurs Occidentaux en Égypte 18 (Cairo: Institut Français d'Archéologie Orientale, 1976).

Helms, Mary. *Ulysses' Sail: An Ethnographic Odyssey of Power, Knowledge and Geographical Distance* (Princeton, NJ: Princeton University Press, 1988).

Hepper, F. Nigel. 'An ancient expedition to transplant living trees: Exotic gardening by an Egyptian queen', *Journal of the Royal Horticultural Society* 92.10 (1967): 434–8.

Hepper, F. Nigel. 'Trees and shrubs yielding gums and resins in the ancient Near East', *Bulletin on Sumerian Agriculture* 3 (1987): 107–14.

Hepper, F. Nigel. 'Current research on the plant specimens from the Niebuhr and Forsskal Yemen expeditions, 1761–63', *Proceedings of the Seminar for Arabian Studies* 17 (1987): 81–90.

Hepper, F. Nigel and I. Friis. *The Plants of Pehr Forsskal's 'Flora Aegyptiaco-Arabica'. Collected on the Royal Danish Expedition to Egypt and the Yemen 1761–63* (Whitstable: Royal Botanical Gardens, Kew in association with the Botanical Museum, Copenhagen, 1994).

Hepper, F. Nigel and Joan Taylor. 'Date palms and opobalsam in the Madaba mosaic map', *Palestine Exploration Quarterly* 136.1 (2004): 35–44.

Herodotus, *Histories*, ed. and trans. Alfred Godley, Loeb Classical Library 117–20, 4 vols (Cambridge, MA: Harvard University Press, 1920, reprinted 2014).

Hertz, Bram. *Catalogue of the Collection of Assyrian, Babylonian, Egyptian, Greek, Etruscan, Roman, Indian, Peruvian, and Mexican Antiquities formed by B. Hertz* (London: 11 Great Marlsborough Street, 1851).

Heyd, Wilhelm. *Histoire du commerce du Levant au Moyen Âge*, trans., Furcy Reynaud, 2 vols (1885–6. Reprinted Leipzig: Harrassowitz, 1923).

Higgins, Iain, trans. with annotations. *The Book of John Mandeville, with Related Texts* (Indianapolis: Hackett, 2011).

Hildegard of Bingen, *Scivitas*, trans. Columba Hart and Jane Bishop. The Classics of Western Spirituality (New York: Paulist Press, 1985).

Hildegard of Bingen. *Hildegard von Bingen's* Physica: *The Complete English Translation of her Classic Work on Health and Healing*, trans. Priscilla Throop (Rochester, VT: Healing Arts Press, 1998).

Hill, Donald. *Islamic Science and Engineering*, Edinburgh Islamic Surveys (Edinburgh: Edinburgh University Press, 1993).

Hillenbrand, Carole. *Crusades, Islamic Perspectives* (Edinburgh: Edinburgh University Press, 1999).

Hirschberg, Julius. *The Ophthalmology of Aëtius of Amida*, translated with commentary by Richey Waugh, Hirschberg History of Ophthalmology. The Monographs 8 (Leipzig: Viet & Co., 2000).

Hirschfeld, Yizhar. 'The rose and the balsam: The garden as a source for perfume and medicine', in Michael Conan, ed., *Middle East Garden Traditions: Unity and Diversity. Questions, Methods and Resources in a Multicultural Perspective* (Washington, DC: Dumbarton Oaks Research Library and Collection, 2007), pp. 21–39.

Hoffman, Eva. 'The author portrait in thirteenth-century manuscripts', *Muqarnas* 10 (1993): 6–20.

Hoffman, Eva. 'The beginnings of the illustrated Arabic book: An intersection between art and scholarship', *Muqarnas* 17 (2000): 37–52.

Holt, Peter M. 'Ottoman Egypt (1517–1798): An account of Arabic historical sources', in Peter M. Holt, *Studies in the History of the Near East* (London: Frank Cass, 1973), pp. 151–60.

Hoyland, Robert. *Arabia and the Arabs: From the Bronze Age to the Coming of Islam* (London and New York: Routledge, 2001).

Hoyland, Robert and Sarah Waidler. 'Adomnán's *De Locis Sanctis* and the seventh-century Near East', *English Historical Review* 129.539 (2014): 787–807.

Humphreys, John, John Oleson and Andrew Sherwood, trans. and annotated. *Greek and Roman Technology: Annotated Translations of Greek and Latin Texts and Documents* (London and New York: Routledge, 1998).

Hunayn ibn Ishaq. *The Book of the Ten Treatises on the Eye Ascribed to Hunain ibn Is-Hâq (809–877 A.D.). The earliest existing systematic text-book on ophthalmology*, ed. and trans. Max Meyerhof (Cairo: The Government Press, 1928).

Hunayn, Jirjis, ed. *Kitāb mayāmir wa-ʿajāʾib al-sayyida al-ʿadhrāʾ Maryām* (Cairo: Matbaʿat al-Hilal, 1902).

Hunt, Tony, ed. *Anglo-Norman Medicine, Volume 1: Roger Frugard's* Chirurgia, *The Practica brevis of Platearius* (Woodbridge and Rochester, NY: D. S. Brewer, 1994).

Hunt, Tony, ed. *Anglo-Norman Medicine, Volume II: Shorter Treatises* (Cambridge and Rochester, NY: D. S. Brewer, 1997).

Ibn al-Baytar, Abu Muhammad ʿAbdallah b. Ahmad. *Kitāb al-jāmiʿ li-mufradāt al-adwīya wa'l-aghdīya*, 2 vols (Bulaq: El-Amiriya Press, 1291/1874).

Ibn al-Baytar, Abu Muhammad ʿAbdallah b. Ahmad. *Traité des simples*, trans. Lucien Leclerc in *Notices et Extraits des Manuscrits de la Bibliothèque Nationale* 23.1 (1876).

Ibn al-Hashsha', Ahmad b. Muhammad. *Glossaire sur la Mans'uri de Razès*, ed. Georges Colin and Henri-Paul Renaud, Collection de textes Arabes publiée par l'Institut des Haute-Études Marocaines 11 (Rabat: Institut des Haute-Études, 1941).

Ibn Hawqal, Muhammad Abu al-Qasim. *Viae et regna; descriptio ditionis moslemicae (Kitāb ṣūrat al-arḍ)*, ed. Michael de Goeje, Bibliotheca geographorum Arabicorum 2 (Leiden: Brill, 1873. Reprinted Brill, 1967 and 2014).

Ibn Iyas, Abu al-Barakat Muhammad b. Ahmad al-Hanafi. *Badā'iʿ al-zuhūr fī waqʾiʿ al-duhūr*. Published as Mohammad Mustafa, Moritz Sobernheim and Paul Kahle, eds, *Die Chronik des Ibn Ijas*, Bibliotheca Islamica 5, 5 vols (Wiesbaden: Franz Steiner Verlag, 1960–74).

Ibn al-Jazzar, Abu Jaʿfar b. Abi Khalid. *Ibn al-Jazzār on Sexual Diseases and Their Treatment. A Critical Edition of Zād al-musāfir wa-qūt al-ḥāḍir. Provisions for the Traveller and Nourishment for the Sedentary, Book 6*, trans. and ed. Gerrit Bos (The Sir Henry Wellcome Asian Series, London: Wellcome Institute, 1997).

Ibn Khaldun, Abu Zayd ʿAbd al-Rahman b. Muhammad. *The Muqaddimah: An Introduction to History*, trans. Franz Rosenthal, Bollingen Series 43, 3 vols (Princeton, NJ: Princeton University Press, 1958).

Ibn Khurdadhbih, Abu al-Qasim ʿUbayd Allah b. ʿAbdallah. *Kitāb al-masālik wa'l-mamālik*, eds Michael de Goeje and Qudamah ibn Jaʿfar, Bibliotheca geographorum Arabicorum 7 (Leiden: Brill, 1889. Reprinted Brill, 1967).

Ibn Qayyim al-Jawziyya, Muhammad b. Abi Bakr. *Medicine of the Prophet*, trans. Penelope Johnstone (Cambridge: Islamic Texts Society, 1998).

Ibn Ridwan, Abu Hasan ʿAli. *Kitāb al-kifāya fī'l-ṭibb*, ed. Salman Qataya (Baghdad: Maktabat al-Wataniyya, 1981).

Ibn Ridwan, Abu al-Hasan ʿAli. *Medieval Islamic Medicine: Ibn Ridwan's Treatise 'On the Prevention of Bodily Ills in Egypt'*, trans. with introduction by Michael Dols, Arabic text edited by Adil Gamal (Berkeley, CA and London: University of California Press, 1984).

Ibn Rushd, Abu al-Walid Muhammad b. Ahmad (Averroes). *Rasā'il Ibn Rushd al-ṭibbiyya* (Les traités médicaux d'Averroes), ed. Georges Anawati and Saʿid Zayed (Cairo: Centre de l'Édition de l'Héritage Culturel, 1987).

Ibn Rusta, Ahmad b. ʿUmar Abu ʿAli. In *Ibn Rusta's* Kitāb al-aʿlāq al-nafisa *and* Kitāb al-buldān *by al-Yaʿqūbī*, ed. Michael de Goeje, Bibliotheca geographorum Arabicorum 7 (Leiden: Brill, 1892. Reprinted Brill, 1967).

Ibn Sina, Abu ʿAli al-Husayn b. ʿAbd Allah (Avicenna). *Avicennae arabum medicorum principis, Canon medicinae*, trans. Gerard of Cremona with annotations by Giovanni Costeo, Joannes Mongio et al. (Venice: Apud Iuntas, 1608).

Ibn Sina, Abu ʿAli al-Husayn b. ʿAbd Allah (Avicenna). *Avicenne: Poème de la médicine*, ed. and trans. Henri Jahier and Abdelkader Nourredine (Paris: Société d'édition des belles lettres, 1956).

Ibn Sina, Abu ʿAli al-Husayn b. ʿAbd Allah (Avicenna). *The Canon of Medicine (al-Qānūn fī'l-ṭibb)*, vol. 1, ed. Laleh Bakhtiar and trans. Oskar Gruner and Mazhar Shah, Great Books of the Islamic World (Chicago: Kazi Publications, 1999).

Ibn Wahshiyya, Muhammad b. ʿAli. *Medieval Arabic Toxicology: The Book of Poisons of Ibn Wahshiya and its Relation to Early Indian and Greek Texts*, trans. and ed. Martin Levey, American Philosophical Society Transactions, New Series 56 viii (Philadelphia: American Philosophical Society, 1966).

Idrisi, Abu ʿAbd Allah al-. *Opus geographicum, sive 'Liber ad eorum delectationem qui terras peragrare studeant'* (*Kitāb nuzhat al-mushtāq fī dhikr al-amṣār wa'l-aqṭār wa'l-buldān wa'l-juzur wa'l-madā'in*), eds Enrico Cerulli, Alessio Bombaci and Umberto Rizzitano, published in 9 parts (Naples and Rome: Istituto Universitario Orientale, 1971–84).

Immerzeel, Mat. 'The renovation of the churches of Cairo on the Fatimid and early Ayyubid periods according to Abu al-Makarim's *Churches and Monasteries of Egypt*', *Eastern Christian Art* 9 (2012–13): 27–52.

Irwin, Robert. 'Gunpowder and firearms in the Mamluk sultanate reconsidered', in Michael Winter and Amelia Levanoni, eds, *The Mamluks in Egyptian and Syrian Politics and Society*, Medieval Mediterranean 51 (Leiden and Boston: Brill, 2004), pp. 117–39.

Irwin, Robert. *For Lust of Knowing: The Orientalists and their Enemies* (London: Penguin Books, 2007).

Ishbili, Umayya b. ʿAbd al-ʿAziz b. Abi al-Salt al-Dani al-. *Livre des simples*, ed. and trans. Barbara Graille, Bulletin d'Études Orientales: Supplément 50 (Damascus: Institut Français du Proche-Orient, 2003).

Istakhri, Abu Ishaq Ibrahim b. Muhammad al-Farisi al-. *Viae regnorum; descriptio ditionis Moslemicae* (*Masālik al-mamālik*), ed. Michael de Goeje, Bibliotheca geographorum Arabicorum 1 (Leiden: Brill, 1870. Reprinted Brill, 1967).

Jacquart, Danielle and Françoise Micheau. *La Médecine arabe et l'Occident médiéval*, Collection Islam-Occident 7 (Paris: Maisonneuve and Larose, 1990).

Jahier, Henri and Abdelkader Nourredine. '*Urguza fi't tibb – Cantica* (*Poème de la médicine*) d'Avicenne', *Bulletin de l'Association Guillaume Budé* 3 (1954): 95–7.

Jazari, Abu al-ʿIzz b. Ismaʿil b. al-Razaz al-. *The Book of Knowledge of Ingenious Mechanical Devices (Kitāb fī maʿrifat al-ḥiyal al-handasiyya)*, trans. Donald Hill (Dordrecht and Boston: D. Reidel, 1974).

Jean de Saint Amand. *Die Areolae des Johannes de Sancto Amando*, ed. Julius Pagel (Berlin: Georg Reimer, 1896).

Johnson, Edward, Gail Johnson and Melissa Johnson. 'The origin and history of embalming', in Robert Mayer, ed., *Embalming: History, Theory and Practice*, fifth edition with a foreword by John Reed (New York: McGraw Hill Medical, 2012), pp. 468–509.

Johnstone, Penelope. 'Galen in Arabic: The transformation of Galenic pharmacology', in Vivian Nutton, ed., *Galen: Problems and Prospects* (London: The Wellcome Institute for the History of Medicine, 1981), pp. 197–212.

Jones, Richard. 'Balm', *Anchor Bible Dictionary* (New York: Doubleday, 1992), I, pp. 573–4.

Josephus, Flavius, *The Jewish War*, ed. and trans. Henry St. John Thackeray, Loeb Classical Library 203, 210, 487, 3 vols (Cambridge, MA: Harvard University Press, 1923–56, reprinted 2014).

Josephus, Flavius, *Jewish Antiquities*, ed. and trans. Henry St. John Thackeray, Loeb Classical Library 242, 281, 326, 365, 410, 433, 456, 489, 490, 9 vols (Cambridge, MA: Harvard University Press, 1930–43, reprinted 2014).

Jullien, Michel-Marie P. M., *L'Arbre de la Vierge à Matarieh. Souvenirs du séjour de la Sainte Famille en Égypte*, fourth edition (Cairo: Imprimerie Nationale, 1904).

Kaimakis, Dimitri, ed. *Die Kyraniden*, Beiträge zur klassischen Philologie 76 (Meisenheim am Glan: Anton Hain, 1976).

Kamal, Hassan. *A Dictionary of Pharaonic Medicine* (Cairo: National Publication House, c. 1967).

Kantorowicz, Ernst. *The King's Two Bodies: A Study in Mediaeval Political Theology* (Princeton, NJ: Princeton University Press, 1957).

Kedar, Benjamin. 'Benvenutus Grapheus of Jerusalem, an oculist in the era of the Crusades', *Korot: The Israel Journal of the History of Medicine and Science* 11 (1995): 14*–41*.

Kennet, Derek. 'On the eve of Islam: Archaeological evidence from Eastern Arabia', *Antiquity* 79 (2005): 107–18.

Kindi, Abu Yusuf Yaʿqub b. Ishaq al-. *The Medical Formulary or Aqrabadhin of al-Kindi*, trans. and ed. Martin Levey (Madison, WI: University of Wisconsin Press, 1966).

King, Anya. 'The importance of imported aromatics in Arabic culture: Illustrations from pre-Islamic and early Islamic poetry', *Journal of Near Eastern Studies* 67.3 (2008): 175–89.

King, Geoffrey. 'Islam, iconoclasm and the declaration of doctrine', *Bulletin of the School of Oriental and African Studies* 48 (1985): 267–77.
King, Helen. 'Once upon a text: Hysteria from Hippocrates', in Sander Gilman, Helen King, Roy Porter, G. Rousseau and Elaine Showalter, *Hysteria beyond Freud* (Berkeley, CA: University of California Press, 1993), pp. 3–64.
Koller, J., U. Baumer, Y. Kaup and U. Weser. 'Herodotus' and Pliny's embalming materials identified on ancient Egyptian mummies', *Archaeometry* 47.3 (2005): 609–28.
Komaroff, Linda, ed. *Gifts of the Sultan: The Arts of Giving at the Islamic Courts* (Los Angeles: Los Angeles Museum of Art, 2011).
Kottek, Samuel. *Medicine and Hygiene in the Works of Flavius Josephus*, Studies in Ancient Medicine 9 (Leiden and Boston: Brill, 1994).
Krahl, Regina. *Chinese Ceramics in the Topkapı Saray Museum*, ed. John Ayers, 2 vols (London: Sotheby's, 1986).
Kritzeck, James. *Peter the Venerable and Islam*, Princeton Studies on the Near East (Princeton, NJ: Princeton University Press, 1964, reprinted 2016).
Kühn, Karl, ed. *Claudii Galeni opera omnia*, Medicorum graecorum opera quae exstant, 20 vols in 22 (Leipzig: Cnoblochius, 1821–33).
Kurlansky, Mark. *Salt: A World History* (New York: Walker and Co., 2002).
Kurz, Otto. 'Mamluk heraldry and the *interpretatio Christiana*', in *Studies in Memory of Gaston Wiet*, ed. Miriam Rosen-Ayalon (Jerusalem: Institute of Asian and African Studies, Hebrew University of Jerusalem, 1977), pp. 297–307.
Laing, Ellen. 'A report on the Western Asian glassware in the Far East', *Bulletin of the Asia Institute* New Series 5 (1991): 109–21.
Lane, Arthur. *Italian Porcelain* (London: Faber & Faber, 1954).
Lane, Arthur. 'The Gagnières-Fonthill vase: A Chinese porcelain of about 1300', *The Burlington Magazine* 103.697 (1961): 124–33.
Laufer, Berthold. *Sino-Iranica: Chinese Contributions to the History of Civilization in Ancient Iran*, Field Museum of Natural History Publication 201. Anthropological Series 15.3 (Chicago: Field Museum, 1919).
Laufer, Berthold. *Geophagy*, Field Museum of Natural History Publication 280. Anthropological Series 18.2 (Chicago: Field Museum, 1930).
Lefébure, Eugène. 'L'arbre sacré d'Héliopolis', *Sphinx: Revue critique* 5 (1902): 1–22, 65–88.
Leja, Meg. 'The sacred art: Medicine in the Carolingian Renaissance', *Viator* 47.2 (2016): 1–34.
Lemnius, Levinus, *An Herbal for the Bible; Containing a Plaine and Familiar Exposition*

of such Similitudes, Parables and Metaphors, both in the Olde Testament and the Newe, trans. Thomas Newton (London: Edmund Bollifant, 1587).

Leo Africanus, Johannes (born al-Hasan b. Muhammad al-Wazzan). *The History and Description of Africa and the Notable Things Therein Contained*, trans. John Pory with notes by Robert Brown, 3 vols (London: Hakluyt Society, 1896).

Lev, Ephraim. 'The contribution of the sixteenth-century Turkish physician Daud al-Antaki to the research of medical substances in use in the Levant (Bilad al-Sham)', *Turkiye Klinikleri Journal of Medical Ethics* 13 (2005): 74–80.

Levey, Martin. 'Medieval Arabic toxicology: The *Book on Poisons* of Ibn Waḥshīya and its relation to early Indian and Greek texts', *Transactions of the American Philosophical Society* 56.7 (1966): 1–130.

Levey, Martin. *Substitute Drugs in Early Arabic Medicine with Special Reference to the Texts of Masarjawaih, al-Razi, and Pythagoras*, Veröffentlichungen der Internationalen Gesellschaft für Geschichte der Pharmazie. Neue Folge 37 (Stuttgart: Wissenschaftliche Verlagsgesellschaft, 1971).

Levey, Martin. *Early Arabic Pharmacology* (Leiden: Brill, 1973).

Levine, Lee. 'The inscription in the "En Gedi synagogue"', in Lee Levine, ed., *Ancient Synagogues Revealed* (Jerusalem: Israel Exploration Society, 1981), pp. 140–5.

Lewis, Bernard. 'An epistle on the manual crafts', *Islamic Culture* 17 (1943): 141–51.

Lieber, Elinor. 'Galen in Hebrew: The transmission of Galen's works in the mediaeval Islamic world', in Vivian Nutton, ed., *Galen: Problems and Prospects* (London: The Wellcome Institute for the History of Medicine, 1981), pp. 167–86.

Lithgow, William. *The Rare Adventures and Painful Peregrinations of William Lithgow*, ed. Gilbert Phelps (London: Folio Society, 1974).

Lopez, Robert. 'Mohammed and Charlemagne: A revision', *Speculum* 18.1 (1943): 14–38.

Loret, Victor. 'Carnet de notes égyptologique. 2: L'arbre de la Vierge à Materiéh', *Sphinx: Revue critique* 6 (1903): 99–103.

Lorscher Arzneibuch (Staatsbibliothek Bamberg Ms. Med.1): http://digital.bib-bvb.de/view/bvbmets/viewer.0.6.4.jsp?folder_id=0&dvs=1560631547288-410&pid=4685473&locale=en&usePid1=true&usePid2=true# http://digital.bib-bvb.de/publish/lorscher-arzneibuch.html(last consulted: 15 June 2019).

Löw, Immanuel and Moses. *Die Flora der Juden*, 4 vols in 5 (Vienna and Leipzig: R. Löwit Verlag, 1924–34).

Lowick, Nicholas. 'The religious, the royal and the popular in the figural coinage of the Jazīra', in Julian Raby, ed., *The Art of Syria and the Jazīra, 1100–1250*,

Oxford Studies in Islamic Art 1 (Oxford: Oxford University Press, 1985), pp. 159–74.

Loynes, Robert. *Prepared for Eternity: A Study of Human Embalming Techniques in Ancient Egypt Using Computerised Tomography Scans of Mummies*, Archaeopress Egyptology 9 (Oxford: Archaeopress, 2015).

Luft, Diana. 'Uroscopy and urinary ailments in medieval Welsh medical texts', *Transactions of the Physicians of the Myddfai Society* 2018: https://www.ncbi.nlm.nih.gov/books/NBK540246/ (last consulted: 2 October 2019).

MacCauley, Leo and Anthony Stephenson. *The Works of Saint Cyril of Jerusalem*, Fathers of the Church. A New Translation 8, 2 vols (Washington, DC: The Catholic University of America Press, 1969–70).

MacGuckin de Slane, William. *Catalogue des manuscrits arabes de la Bibliothèque Nationale*, 3 parts (Paris: Imprimerie Nationale, 1883–95).

Mack, Rosamond. *Bazaar to Piazza: Islamic Trade and Italian Art, 1300–1600* (Berkeley, CA and London: University of California Press, 2002).

McKenzie, Judith. *The Architecture of Petra* (Oxford: Oxford University Press, 1990).

McVaugh, Michael. 'Theriac at Montpellier, 1285–1325 (with an edition of the "*Questiones de tyriaca*" of William of Brescia)', *Sudhoffs Archiv. Zeitschrift für Wissenschaftsgeschichte* 56.2 (1972): 113–44.

Maguire, Henry. *Icons of their Bodies: Saints and their Images in Byzantium* (Princeton, NJ: Princeton University Press, 1996).

Maimonides (Moses b. Maymun). *Moses Maimonides on the Causes of Symptoms*, ed. J. Liebowitz and Shlomo Marcus (Berkeley, CA and Los Angeles: University of California Press, 1974).

Maimonides (Moses b. Maymun). *Treatise on Poisons, Hemorrhoids and Cohabitation. Maimonides' Medical Writing*, trans. Fred Rosner (Haifa: Maimonides Research Institute, c. 1984).

Majno, Guido. *The Healing Hand: Man and Wound in Antiquity* (Cambridge, MA: Harvard University Press, 1975).

Mango, Marlia. 'Byzantine maritime trade with the East (4th–7th centuries)', *Aram* 8, 1–2 (1996): 139–63.

Mansi, Giovanni, Philippe Labbe, Gabriel Cossart et al., eds. *Sacrorum conciliorum nova, et amplissima collectio* (Venice: Antionium Zatta, 1759–98. Reprinted Paris: H. Welter, 1901–27).

Maqrizi, Taqi al-Din Ahmad b. ʿAli al-. *Kitāb al-mawāʿiẓ waʾl-iʿtibār fī dhikr al-khiṭaṭ waʾl-āthār*, 2 vols (Bulaq: El-Amariya Press, 1270–2/1853–5).

Maqrizi, Taqi al-Din Ahmad b. ʿAli al-. *Kitāb al-mawāʿiẓ waʾl-iʿtibār fī dhikr al-khiṭaṭ waʾl-āthār*, ed. Gaston Wiet, 5 vols (Cairo: Institut Français d'Archéologie Orientale du Caire, 1911–27).

Martinez, Dieter, Karlheinz Lohs and Jörg Janzen. *Weihrauch und Myrrh. Kulturgeschichte und wirtschaftliche Bedeutung. Botanik. Chemie. Medizin* (Stuttgart: Wissenschaftliche Verlaggesellschaft, 1989).

Martyr de Angleria, Petrus (Peter Martyr). *Opera: Legatio Babylonica de orbe novo decades octo opus epistolarum*, facsimile of edition of 1516 with an introduction by Erich Woldan (Graz: Akademische Druck, 1966).

Matthews, Victor. 'Perfumes and spices', *Anchor Bible Dictionary* (New York: Doubleday, 1992), V, pp. 226–8.

Maundrell, Henry. *The Journey of Henry Maundrell, from Aleppo to Jerusalem, A.D. 1697*, in Thomas Wright, ed., *Early Travels in Palestine* (London: Henry G. Bohn, 1848. Reprinted Mineola, NY: Dover Publications Inc., 2003).

Mauss, Marcel. *The Gift: The Form and Reason for Exchange in Archaic Societies*, trans. W. D. Halls with a foreword by Mary Douglas (New York and London: W. W. Norton, 1990).

Mayor, Adrienne. *The Poison King: The Life and Legends of Mithradates, Rome's Deadliest Enemy* (Princeton, NJ and Oxford: Princeton University Press, 2009).

Meinardus, Otto. *The Holy Family in Egypt* (Cairo: American University in Cairo Press, 1963, reprinted 1986).

Meinecke-Berg, Viktoria. 'Eine Stadtansicht des mamlukischen Kairo aus dem 16. Jahrhundert', *Mitteilungen des Deutschen Archäologischen Instituts, Abteilung Kairo* 32 (1976): 113–32.

Menevisoglou, Paulos. *Το Αγιον Μύρον εν τη ορθοδόξω ανατολικη εκκλησία* (The Holy Chrism in the Eastern Orthodox Church)', ed. Panayotis Christou, Analecta Vlatadon 14 (Thessaloniki: Patriarchal Institute for Patristic Studies, 1972).

Meyerhof, Max. 'Der Bazar der Drogen und Wohlgeruche in Kairo', *Sonderabdruck aus Archiv für Wirtschaftforschung im Orient* 3.4 (1918): 1–40, 185–218.

Meyerhof, Max. 'Alî at-Tabarî's "Paradise of Wisdom", one of the oldest Arabic compendiums of medicine', *Isis* 16.1 (1931): 6–54.

Micheau, Françoise. 'The medicinal value of the Book of Theriac', in *Kitab al-diryaq (Thériaque de Paris), édition en facsimilé du manuscrit arabe 2964 de la BnF* (Sansepolcro: Aboca Museum Edizioni, 2009), pp. 49–75.

Miller, J. Innes. *The Spice Trade of the Roman World, 29 B.C. to A.D. 641* (Oxford: Clarendon Press, 1969).

Milwright, Marcus. 'The cup of the *sāqī*: Origins of an emblem of the Mamluk *khāṣṣakiyya*', *Aram* 9–10 (1997–8): 241–56.

Milwright, Marcus. 'Pottery in written sources of the Ayyubid-Mamluk period (*c.*567–923/1171–1517)', *Bulletin of the School of Oriental and African Studies* 62.3 (1999): 504–18.

Milwright, Marcus. 'Balsam in the Mediaeval Mediterranean: A case study of information and commodity exchange', *Journal of Mediterranean Archaeology* 14.1 (2001): 3–23.

Milwright, Marcus. 'Prologues and epilogues in Islamic ceramics: Clays, repairs and secondary use', *Medieval Ceramics* 25 (2001): 72–83.

Milwright, Marcus. 'Reynald of Châtillon and Red Sea expedition of 1182–1183', in Maya Yazigi and Niall Christie, eds, *Noble Ideals and Bloody Realities: Warfare in the Middle Ages* (Leiden: Brill, 2006), pp. 230–55.

Milwright, Marcus. *Fortress of the Raven: Karak in the Middle Islamic Period (1100–1650)*, Islamic History and Civilization 72 (Leiden and Boston: Brill, 2008).

Milwright, Marcus. *An Introduction to Islamic Archaeology*, New Edinburgh Islamic Surveys (Edinburgh: Edinburgh University Press, 2010).

Mintz, Sidney. *Sweetness and Power: The Place of Sugar in Modern History* (New York: Viking, 1985).

Moldenke, Harold and Alma. *Plants of the Bible*, New Series in Plant Sciences 28 (Waltham, MA: Chronica Botanica, 1952).

Moore, Linda, Bryan Goodwin, Stacey Jones, G. Bruce Wisely, Cosette Serabjit-Singh, Timothy Willson, Jon Collins and Steven Kliewer. 'St John's Wort induces hepatic drug metabolism through activation of the Pregnane X receptor', *Proceedings of the National Academy of Sciences of the United States of America* 97.13 (2000): 7500–7502.

Morrisson, Cécile, ed. *Trade and Markets in Byzantium, Dumbarton Oaks Byzantine Symposia and Colloquia* (Washington, DC: Dumbarton Oaks Research Library and Collection, 2012).

Muhanna, Elias. 'The Sultan's new clothes: Ottoman-Mamluk gift exchange in the fifteenth century', *Muqarnas* 27 (2010): 189–207.

Münster, Sebastian. *Cosmographia*, 2 vols (Basel, 1628. Reprinted Antiqua-Verlag, Lindau 1984).

Muqaddasi (or al-Maqdisi), Muhammad ibn Ahmad Shams al-Din al-. *Descriptio imperii Moslemici* (*Aḥsan al-taqāsim fī maʿrifat al-aqālīm*), ed. Michael de Goeje, Bibliotheca geographorum Arabicorum 3 (Leiden: Brill, 1877, reprinted 1967).

Murdoch, John. *Album of Science: Antiquity and the Middle Ages*, Albums of Science (New York: Charles Scribner's Sons, 1984).

Nappi, Carla. 'Bolatu's pharmacy theriac in early Modern China', *Early Science and Medicine* 14.6 (1997): 737–64.

Nasir-i Khusraw, Abu Muʿin. *Nāṣer-e Khosraw's Book of Travels* (Safarnāma), trans. Wheeler Thackston, Persian Heritage Series 36 (New York: Persian Heritage Foundation, 1986).

Netzer, Ehud, *Nabatäische Architektur* (Munich: Von Zabern, 2003).

Nicodemus the Hagiorite. *Prologue to the Seventh Ecumenical Council*, in Nicodemus the Hagiorite and Agapius the Monk. *The Rudder (Pedalion) of the Metaphorical Ship of the One Holy Catholic and Apostolic Church of the Orthodox Christians, or All the Sacred and Divine Canons*, trans. Denver Cummings (Chicago: Orthodox Christian Educational Society, 1957).

Nicol, Donald. *The Last Centuries of Byzantium, 1261–1453*, second edition (Cambridge: Cambridge University Press, 1993).

Niebuhr, Carsten. *Voyage en Arabie et en d'autres pays*, 2 vols (Amsterdam: S. J. Baalde, 1776–80).

Niebuhr, Carsten. *Travels through Arabia and other Countries in the East*, trans. Robert Heron, 2 vols (Edinburgh: R. Morison and Son, 1792).

Nielsen, Harald. *Ancient Ophthalmological Agents: A Pharmacologico-historical Study of Collyria and the Seals for the Collyria during Roman Antiquity, as well as the Most Frequent Components of the Collyria*, Acta Historica Scientiarium Naturalium et Medicinalium 31 (Odense: Odense University Press, 1974).

Nutton, Vivian. 'The drug trade in Antiquity', *Journal of the Royal Society of Medicine* 78.2 (1985): 138–45.

Oates, Titus. *A Balm presented to these Nations, England and Ireland, to cure the Wounds of the bleeding Protestants, and open the Eyes of the deluded Papists, that are ignorant of the Truth* (n. p.: printed for J. G., c. 1680).

O'Sullivan, Shaun. 'Coptic conversion and the Islamization of Egypt', *Mamluk Studies Review* 10.2 (2006): 65–79.

Oxford English Dictionary Online. https://www.oed.com (last consulted: 6 October 2019).

Palerne, Jean. *Voyage en Égypte de Jean Palerne, forésien, 1581*, Collection des Voyageurs occidentaux en Égypte 2 (Cairo: Institut Français d'Archéologie Orientale du Caire, 1971).

Palladius. *The Lausiac History of Palladius*, ed. Cuthbert Butler, 2 vols in 1 (Cambridge: Cambridge University Press, 1898–1904).

Pancaroğlu, Oya. 'Socializing medicine: Illustrations of the *Kitāb al-diryāq*', *Muqarnas* 18 (2001): 155–72.

Paré, Ambroise. *The Works of that Famous Chirurgion Ambrose Parey, translated out of Latine and compared with the French by Th. Johnson* (London: Th. Coates and R. Young, 1634).

Patrich, Joseph. 'Agricultural development in Antiquity: Improvements in the cultivation and production of balsam', in Jean-Baptiste Humbert, Jürgen Zangenberg, Katharina Galor, eds, *Qumran, the Site of the Dead Sea Scrolls: Archaeological Interpretations and Debates* (Leiden and Boston: Brill, 2006), pp. 241–8.

Patrich, Joseph and Benny Arubas. 'A juglet containing balsam oil (?) from a cave near Qumran', *Israel Exploration Journal* 39 (1989): 43–59.

Paul of Aegina. *The Seven Books of Paulus Aegineta*, trans. with commentary by Francis Adams (London: Sydenham Society, 1844–7).

Pausanias. *Description of Greece. Vol. IV: VIII:22–X*, trans. and ed. William Jones, Loeb Classical Library 297 (Cambridge, MA: Harvard University Press, 1935, reprinted 2014).

Pearce, Sarah. 'The Cleopatras and the Jews', *Transactions of the Royal Historical Society* 27 (2017): 29–64.

Pegolotti, Francesco Balducci. *Pratica della mercatura*, ed. Allan Evans (Cambridge, MA: Harvard University Press, 1936).

Perlmann, Moshe. 'Notes on anti-Christian propaganda in the Mamlūk empire', *Bulletin of the School of Oriental and African Studies* 10 (1942): 552–69.

Petersen, Andrew. 'The archaeology of Islam in Britain: Recognition and potential', *Antiquity* 82.318 (2008): 1080–92.

Petrovska, Biljana and Svetlana Cekovska. 'Extracts from the history and medical properties on garlic', *Pharmacognosy Review* 4.7 (2010): 106–10.

Petry, Carl. *Twilight of Majesty: The Reigns of the Mamlūk Sultans al-Ashrāf Qāytbāy and Qānṣūh al-Ghawrī in Egypt* (Seattle and London: University of Washington Press, 1993).

Petry, Carl. *Protectors or Praetorians? The Last Mamluk Sultans and Egypt's Waning as a Great Power* (New York: State University of New York Press, 1994).

Pfister, Arnold, ed. with introduction to the facsimile edition. De simplici medicina. *Kräuterbuch-Handschrift aus dem Letzen Viertel des 14. Jahrhunderts im Besitz der Basler Universitäts-Bibliothek Hugo Berchten* (Basel: Sanz AG, 1960).

Pingree, David, ed. *Picatrix: The Latin Version of Ghayat al-Hakim*, Studies of the Warburg Institute 39 (London: Warburg Institute, 1986).

Platearius, Matthaeus (attributed). *Le Livre des simples médicines d'après le manuscrit français 12322 de la Bibliothèque Nationale de Paris*, ed. Ghislaine Malandin (Paris: Éditions Ozalid et Textes Cardinaux, 1986).

Pliny the Elder, *Natural History*, ed. and trans. A. C. Andrews, D. E. Eichholz, William Jones and Harris Rackham, Loeb Classical Library 330, 352–3, 370–1, 392–4, 418–19, 10 vols (Cambridge, MA: Harvard University Press, 1938–62, reprinted 2014).

Pomet, Pierre. *Histoire générale des drogues* (Paris: Jean-Baptiste Loyson and Augustin Pillon, 1694).

Pomet, Pierre. *A Compleat History of Druggs: Written in French by Monsieur Pomet, Chief Druggist to the Present French King; to which is added what is further observable on the same subject, from Messrs. Lemery, and Tournefort, divided into three classes, vegetable, animal and mineral . . .*, trans. J. Browne (London: R. Bonwicke et al., 1712).

Popper, William. *The Cairo Nilometer: Studies in Ibn Taghrî Birdî's Chronicles of Egypt I*, University of California Publications in Semitic Philology 12 (Berkeley, CA and Los Angeles: University of California Press, 1951).

Pormann, Peter and Emilie Savage-Smith. *Medieval Islamic Medicine* (Washington, DC: Georgetown University Press, 2007).

Post, George. *Flora of Syria, Palestine and Sinai*, second edition revised by John Dinsmore, 2 vols (Beirut: American University in Beirut Press, 1932–3).

Potts, Dan. *The Arabian Gulf in Antiquity*, 2 vols (Oxford: Clarendon Press, 1990).

Prioreschi, Plinio. *Byzantine and Islamic Medicine*, History of Medicine 4 (Omaha, NE: Horatius Press, 2001, reprinted 2004).

Prioreschi, Plinio, R. P. Heaney and E. Brehm. 'A quantitative assessment of ancient therapeutics: Poppy and pain in the Hippocratic corpus', *Medical Hypotheses* 51 (1998): 325–51.

Pym, Anthony. *Exploring Translation Theories* (London and New York: Routledge, 2014).

Qaddumi, Ghada al-Hijjawi al-, trans. *Book of Gifts and Rarities: Kitāb al-Hadāya wa al-Tuḥaf*, Harvard Middle Eastern Monographs 29 (Cambridge, MA: Harvard University Press, 1996).

Qazwini, Zakariya b. Muhammad b. Mahmud al-. *Zakarija ben Muhammed ben Mahmud al-Cazwini's Kosmographie* (*Āthār al-bilād wa akhbār al-ʿibād*), ed. Ferdinand Wüstenfeld, 2 vols (Göttingen: Verlag der Dieterichschen Buchhandlung, 1848–9. Reprinted Wiesbaden: Martin Sändig, 1967).

Rabinowitz, Louis. 'Oils', *Encyclopaedia Judaica*, second edition (Detroit: Macmillan Reference USA, 2007), XV, pp. 395–6.

Raby, Julian. *Venice, Dürer and the Oriental Mode*, Hans Huth Memorial Studies 1 (London: Islamic Art Publications, 1982).

Raby, Julian. '*Terra Lemnia* and the potteries of the Golden Horn: An antique revival under Ottoman auspices', *Byzantinische Forschungen* 21 (1995): 305–42.

Raby, Julian. 'In vitro veritas: Glass pilgrim vessels from 7th-century Jerusalem', in Jeremy Johns, ed., *'Abd al-Malik's Jerusalem. II: Jerusalem and early Islam*, Oxford Studies in Islamic Art 9.2 (Oxford: Oxford University Press, 2000), pp. 113–90.

Rao, R., Z. Khan and A. Shah. 'Toxicity studies in mice of *Commiphora molmol* oleo-gum-resin', *Journal of Ethnopharmacology* 76 (2001): 151–4.

Raymond, André. *Cairo*, trans. Willard Wood (Cambridge, MA: Harvard University Press, 2000).

Reeds, Karen. *Botany in Medieval and Renaissance Universities* (New York and London: Garland Publishing, 1991).

Reichert, Victor, trans. *The Tahkemoni of Judah al-Ḥarizi* (Jerusalem: Raphael Haim Cohen's Ltd, 1965, reprinted 1973).

Rich, Vivian. *Cursing the Basil and Other Folklore of the Garden* (Victoria, BC: Horsdal and Schubart, 1998).

Richards, Donald, ed. *Islam and the Trade of Asia: A Colloquium*, Papers on Islamic History 2 (Oxford: Bruno Cassirer and University of Pennsylvania Press, 1970).

Ricordel, Joëlle. 'Le traité sur la thériaque d'Ibn Rushd', *Revue d'Histoire de la Pharmacie* 48.325 (2000): 81–90.

Ricordel, Joëlle. 'Ibn Djuldjul: "propos sur la thériaque"', *Revue d'Histoire de la Pharmacie* 48.325 (2000): 73–80.

Riddle, John. 'The introduction of eastern drugs in the early Middle Ages', *Archiv für Geschichte der Medizin und der Naturwissenschaft* 49 (1965): 185–98.

Riddle, John. *Dioscorides on Pharmacy and Medicine* (Austin, TX: University of Texas Press, 1985).

Riddle, John. 'The medicines of Greco-Roman Antiquity as a source for medicines today', in Bart Holland, ed., *Prospecting for Drugs in Ancient and Medieval European Texts: a Scientific Approach* (Amsterdam: Harwood Academic Publishers, 1996), pp. 7–17.

Rosenthal, Franz. *The Classical Heritage in Islam*, trans. Emile and Jenny Marmorstein (Berkeley, CA and Los Angeles: University of California Press, 1975).

Rowlands, Michael. 'Value and cultural transmission of things', in Wim van Binsbergen and Peter Geschiere, eds, *Commodification: Things, Agency and Identity (The Social Life of Things Revisited)* (Münster: Lit, 2005), pp. 267–81.

Rufinus. *The Herbal of Rufinus*, ed. Lynn Thorndike (Chicago: University of Chicago Press, 1946).

Sadek, Mahmoud. *The Arabic* Materia Medica *of Dioscorides* (St Jean-Chrysostome, Quebec: Éditions du Sphinx, 1985).

Safrai, Ze'ev. *The Economy of Roman Palestine* (London and New York: Routledge, 1994).

Salaman, Redcliffe, *The History and Social Influence of the Potato* (Cambridge: Cambridge University Press, 1949).

Saliba, George and Linda Komaroff. 'Illustrated books may be hazardous for your health: A new reading of the Arabic reception and rendition of the *Materia Medica* of Dioscorides', *Ars Orientalis* 35 (2008): 6–65.

Sandys, George. *A Relation of a Journey begun Anno Domini 1610. Four Books containing a Description of the Turkish Empire of Egypt and the Holy Land, and of the remote Parts of Italy, and Lands adioyning*, second edition (London: W. Barrett, 1615. Reprinted in facsimile [The English Experience 554] Amsterdam: Theatrum Orbis Terrarum, 1973).

Sanudo (Sanuto), Marino, the Younger. *I Diarii di Marino Sanuto*, ed. Rinaldo Fulin, 58 vols in 59 (Venice: F. Vinsentini, 1897–1903).

Sanudo (Sanuto), Marino. *Part XIV of Book III of Marino Sanuto's Secrets for True Crusaders to Help them Recover the Holy Land, Written in* A.D. *1321*, trans. Eustace Conder and Aubrey Stewart, Palestine Pilgrim Texts Society 12 (London: Palestine Exploration Fund, 1896).

Saqati, Muhammad b. Abi Muhammad al-. *Un manuel hispanique de hisba. Traité d'Abu 'Abd Allah Muhammad b. Abi Muhammad as-Sakati de Malaga sur la surveillance des corporations et la répression des fraudes en Espagne musulmane*, ed. and trans. Georges Colin and Evariste Lévi-Provencal, Institut des Hautes-Études Marocaines Publications 21 (Rabat: Institut des Hautes-Études Marocaines, 1931).

Sattar, Zohreh and Mehrdad Iranshahi. 'Phytochemistry and pharmacology of *Ferula persica* Boiss.: A review', *Iran Journal of Basic Medical Sciences* 20.1 (2017): 1–8.

Saucier, Catherine. 'The sweet sound of sanctity', *The Senses and Society* 5.1 (2010), pp. 10–27.

Savage-Smith, Emilie. 'Ibn al-Nafis's *Perfected Book on Ophthalmology* and his treatment of trachoma and its sequelae', *Journal of the History of Arabic Science* 4.1 (1980): 147–206.

Savary, Claude Étienne. *Letters on Egypt*, 2 vols (London: G. G. and J. Robinson, 1786).

Savary de Brûlons, Jacques. *Dictionnaire universel de commerce*, 3 vols (Paris: Jacques Estienne, 1723–30).

Sawirus (Severus) ibn al-Muqaffaʿ and continuators. *History of the Patriarchs of the Egyptian Church, Known as the History of the Holy Church*, eds Yassa ʿAbd al-Masih, O. H. E. Khs-Burmester, Aziz Atiya, Antoine Khater et al., Publications de la Société d'Archéologie Copte. Textes et Documents, 4 vols (Cairo: Société d'Archéologie Copte, 1943–76).

Schafer, Edward. *The Golden Peaches of Samarkand: A Study of T'ang Exotics* (Berkeley, CA: University of California Press, 1963).

Schiltberger, Johannes. *The Bondage and Travels of Johann Schiltberger*, trans. John Buchan Telfer with notes by Filip (Philip) Bruun, Works issued by the Hakluyt Society 58 (London: Hakluyt Society, 1879).

Schramm, Percy. *A History of the English Coronation*, trans. Leopold Wickham Legg (Oxford: Clarendon Press, 1937).

Schweinfurth, Georg. *Arabische Pflanzennamen aus Aegypten, Algerien und Jemen* (Berlin: Dietrich Reimer, 1912).

Seetzen, Ulrich. *Reisen durch Syrien, Palästina, Phoenicien, die Transjordan-Lander, Arabia Petrae und Unter-Aegypten*, 4 vols (Berlin: G. Reimer, 1854–9).

Serjeant, R. B. 'Material for a history of Islamic textiles up to the Mongol conquest', *Ars Islamica* 9 (1942), pp. 54–92; 10 (1943), pp. 71–104; 11–12 (1946), pp. 98–145; 13–14 (1948), pp. 75–117; 15–16 (1951), pp. 29–85, 273–305.

Seth (Sethis), Simeon. *Syntagma per elementorum ordinem, de alimentorum facultate* (Petrum Pernam: Basle 1561).

Shackelford, Jole. *A Philosophical Path for Paracelsian Medicine: The Ideas, Intellectual Context, and Influence of Petrus Severinus (1540/2–1602)* (Copenhagen: Museum Tusculanum Press and University of Copenhagen, 2004).

Shalem, Avinoam. *Islam Christianized: Islamic Portable Objects in Medieval Church Treasuries of the Latin West* (Frankfurt-am-Main: Peter Lang, 1996).

Shaw, Stanford. *The Financial and Administrative Organization and Development of Ottoman Egypt, 1517–1798* (Princeton, NJ: Princeton University Press, 1962).

Shayzari, ʿAbd al-Rahman b. Nasr al-. *The Book of the Market Inspector:* Nihāyat al-rutba fī ṭalab al-ḥisba (Utmost Authority in the Pursuit of Ḥisba), trans.

Ronald Buckley, Journal of Semitic Studies Supplement 9 (Oxford and New York: Oxford University Press, 1999).

Sherratt, Andrew and Susan. 'From luxuries to commodities: The nature of Mediterranean Bronze Age trading systems', in Noel Gale, ed., *Bronze Age Trade in the Mediterranean. Papers Presented at the Conference Held at Rewley House, Oxford, in December 1989*, Studies in Mediterranean Archaeology 90 (Jonsered: Paul Åströms Förlag, 1991), pp. 351–86.

Sigismund, Reinhold. *Die Aromata in ihrer Bedeutung für Religion* (Leipzig: C. F. Winter, 1884).

Silverberg, Robert. *The Realm of Prester John* (Garden City, NY: Doubleday, 1972).

Sitwell, Hervey. *The Crown Jewels and Other Regalia in the Tower of London*, ed. Clarence Winchester (London: Published by the Viscount Kemley at the Dropmore Press, 1953).

Southey, Robert, trans., *The Chronicle of the Cid, Translated from the Spanish by Robert Southey with an Introduction by U. S. Pritchett and Illustrations by René Ben Sussan* (Haarlem: Joh. Enschedé en Zonen for the Members of the Limited Editions Club, 1958). Original edition: Robert Southey, trans., *The Chronicle of the Cid* (London: Longman, Hurst, Rees and Orme, 1808).

Spallanzani, Marco. *Ceramiche orientali a Firenze nel Rinascimento* (Florence: Cassa di Risparmio di Firenze, 1978).

Spooner, Brian. 'Weavers and dealers: The authenticity of an Oriental carpet', in Arjun Appadurai, ed., *The Social Life of Things: Commodities in Cultural Exchange* (Cambridge: Cambridge University Press, 1986), pp. 195–235.

Stannard, Jerry. 'Dioscorides and Renaissance materia medica', *Analecta Medico-historica* 1 (1966): 1–21.

Stannard, Jerry. 'Medieval herbals and their development', *Clio Medica* 9 (1974): 23–33.

Stannard, Jerry. '". . . findet man in den apotecken": Notices concerning the available of medicamenta in medieval *Fachliteratur*', in Peter Dilg, ed., *Perspectiven der Pharmaziegeschichte: Festschrift für Rudolf Schmitz zum 65. Geburtstag* (Graz: Akademische Verlag, 1983), pp. 365–76.

Stern, Menahem. *Greek and Latin Authors on Jews and Judaism* (Jerusalem: Israel Academy of Sciences and Humanities, 1974).

Stieb, Ernst. 'Drug adulteration and its detection in the writings of Theophrastus, Dioscorides and Pliny', *Journal Mondial de Pharmacie* 2 (1958): 628–34.

Strabo, *Geography*, ed. and trans. Horace Leonard Jones, based on an unfinished version by John Sterrett, Loeb Classical Library 49–50, 182, 196, 211, 223, 241,

267, 8 vols (Cambridge, MA: Harvard University Press, 1917–32, reprinted 2014).

Strohmaier, Gotthard. 'Galen in Arabic: Prospects and projects', in Vivian Nutton, ed., *Galen: Problems and Prospects* (London: The Wellcome Institute for the History of Medicine, 1981), pp. 187–96.

Suriano, Francesco. *Treatise on the Holy Land*, trans. Theophilus Bellorini and Eugene Hoade (Jerusalem: Franciscan Press, 1949).

Tabari, 'Ali b. Sahl Rabban al-. *Firdausu'l-hikmat or Paradise of Wisdom*, ed. Muhammad Siddiqi (Berlin: Buch und Kunstdruckerei, 1928).

Tabbaa, Yasser. 'Monuments with a message: propagation of *jihad* under Nur al-Din (1146–1174)', in Vladimir Goss and Christine Bornstein, eds, *The Meeting of Two Worlds: Cultural Exchange between East and West during the Period of the Crusades* (Kalamazoo, MI: Medieval Institute Publications, 1986), pp. 223–40.

Tacitus, Cornelius, *The Histories, Books I–V*, ed. and trans. Clifford H. Moore, Loeb Classical Library 111, 249, 2 vols (Cambridge, MA: Harvard University Press, 1925–31, reprinted 2014).

Tanukhi, Abu 'Ali al-Muhassin al-. *The Table Talk of a Mesopotamian Judge*, trans. David Margoliouth, Oriental Translation Fund. New Series 28 (London: Royal Asiatic Society, 1922).

Tanukhi, Abu 'Ali al-Muhassin al-. *The Table Talk of a Mesopotamian Judge, Being the First Part of the Nishwār al-muhādarah*, vol. 1, ed. Abood Shalchy (Beirut: Dar Sadir, 1971).

Tariq, M., A. Ageel and M. al-Yahya. 'Anti-inflammatory activity of *Commiphora molmol*', *Agents and Actions* 17 (1986): 381–2.

Taylor, Christopher. *In the Vicinity of the Righteous: Ziyāra and the Veneration of Saints in Late Medieval Egypt*, Islamic History and Civilization, Studies and Texts 22 (Leiden and Boston: Brill, 1998).

Taylor, John and Daniel Antoine. *Ancient Lives, New Discoveries: Eight Mummies, Eight Stories* (London: The British Museum Press, 2014).

Temkin, Owsei. 'Byzantine medicine: Tradition and empiricism', *Dumbarton Oaks Papers* 16 (1962): 95–115.

Temkin, Owsei. *Galenism. Rise and Decline of a Medical Philosophy*, Cornell Publications in the History of Science (Ithaca, NY and London: Cornell University Press, 1973).

Theophrastus. *Enquiry into Plants, and Minor Works on Odours and Weather Signs*, ed. and trans. Arthur Hort, Loeb Classical Library 70, 79, 2 vols (Cambridge, MA: Harvard University Press, 1916–26, reprinted 2014).

Thompson, Stephen. 'The anointing of officials in ancient Egypt', *Journal of Near Eastern Studies* 53.1 (1994): 11–25.

Thorndike, Lynn. 'John of St Amand on the magnet', *Isis* 36.3/4 (1946): 156–7.

Tobler, Titus, Aubrey Stewart, Claude Conder and John Bernard, trans. *Anonymous Pilgrims I–VIII*, Palestine Pilgrims Texts Society 4 (London: Palestine Exploration Fund, 1894).

Tomber, Roberta. 'Quantitative approaches to the investigation of long-distance exchange', *Journal of Roman Archaeology* 6 (1993): 142–66.

Totelin, Laurence. 'Mithradates' antidote – a pharmacological ghost', *Early Science and Medicine* 9.1 (2004): 1–19.

Totelin, Laurence. 'The world in a pill: Local specialties and global remedies in the Graeco-Roman world', in Rebecca Kennedy and Molly Jones-Lewis, eds, *The Routledge Handbook of Identity and the Environment in the Classical and Medieval Worlds*, Routledge Handbooks (London and New York: Routledge, 2016), pp. 151–70.

Trease, George and William Evans. *Pharmacognosy*, tenth edition (London: Ballière Tindall, 1972).

Tritton, Arthur. *The Caliphs and Their Non-Muslim Subjects: A Critical Study of the Covenant of 'Umar*, Islam and the Muslim World 14 (London: Frank Cass, 1970).

Truitt, Elly. 'The virtues of balm in late Medieval literature', *Early Science and Medicine* 14 (2009): 711–36.

Tsafrir, Yoram. 'The maps used by Theodosius: On the pilgrim maps of the Holy Land and Jerusalem in the sixth century C.E.', *Dumbarton Oaks Papers* 40 (1986): 129–45.

Tyerman, Christopher. 'Marino Sanudo Torsello and the lost Crusade: Lobbying in the fourteenth century', *Transactions of the Royal Historical Society*, ser. 5, 32 (1982): 57–73.

Ullmann, Manfred. *Islamic Medicine*, Edinburgh Islamic Surveys 11 (Edinburgh: Edinburgh University Press, 1978, reprinted 1997).

'Umari, Shihab al-Din Abu al-'Abbas Ahmad Fadl Allah al-. *L'Égypte, la Syrie, le Ḥiğāz et le Yémen* (*Masālik al-abṣār fī mamālik al-amṣār*), ed. Ayman Sayyid, Textes arabes et études Islamiques 23 (Cairo: Institut Français d'Archéologie Orientale, 1985).

Van Binsbergen, Wim and Peter Geschiere, eds. *Commodification: Things, Agency, and Identities (*The Social Life of Things *revisited)* (Münster: Lit, 2005).

Van Gelder, Geert Jan. 'Four perfumes of Arabia: A translation of al-Suyūṭī's al-*Maqāma al-miskiyya*', *Res Orientales* 11: *Parfums d'Orient* (1998): 203–12.

Vansina, Jan. *Oral Tradition as History* (Madison, WI: University of Wisconsin Press, 1985).

Veit, Raphaela, 'Dā'ūd al-Anṭākī', *Encyclopaedia of Islam* 3 (Leiden: Brill, 2010).

Vesey-Fitzgerald, Desmond. 'Vegetation of the Red Sea Coast south of Jedda, Saudi Arabia', *Journal of Ecology* 43 (1955): 547–62.

Vesey-Fitzgerald, Desmond. 'Vegetation of the Red Sea Coast north of Jedda, Saudi Arabia', *Journal of Ecology* 45 (1957): 447–89.

Viaud, Gérard. *Magie et coutumes populaires chez les Coptes d'Égypte*, Le soleil dans le cœur (Saint-Vincent-sur-Jabron: Éditions Présence, 1978).

Villecourt, Louis. 'Un manuscrit arabe sur la Saint Chrême dans l'Église Copte', *Revue d'Histoire Ecclésiastique* 16–17 (1921): 501–14.

Villecourt, Louis. 'Un manuscrit arabe sur la saint chrême dans l'Église Copte II', *Revue d'Histoire Ecclésiastique* 18 (1922): 5–19.

Villecourt, Louis, trans. 'Le livre du chrême. Ms. Paris arabe 100', *Le Muséon: Revue des Études Orientales* 41 (1928): 49–80.

Virgil (publius Vergilius Maro). *The Eclogues and Georgics of Virgil*, new edition, trans. John McKail (London and New York: Longmans, Green and Co., 1915).

Virgil (publius Vergilius Maro). *Georgics*, trans. Peter Fallon with notes by Elaine Fantham, Oxford World's Classics (Oxford and New York: Oxford University Press, 2006).

Voigts, Linda. 'Anglo-Saxon plant remedies and the Anglo-Saxons', *Isis* 70 (1979): 250–68.

Vollesen, Kaj. 'Burseracaeae', in *Flora of Ethiopia 3: Pittosporaceae to Araliceae*, eds Inga Hedberg and Sue Edwards (Addis Ababa and Uppsala: Uppsala University, 1989), pp. 475–77.

Von Breydenbach, Bernhard. *Die Reise ins Heilige Land: Ein Reisebericht aus dem Jahre 1483*, ed. with introduction Elizabeth Geck (Wiesbaden: J. Pressler, 1977).

Von Harff, Arnold. *The Pilgrimage of Arnold von Harff, Knight from Cologne, through Italy, Syria, Egypt, Arabia, Nubia, Palestine, Turkey, France and Spain, which he Accomplished in the Years 1496 to 1499*, trans. and annotated by Malcolm Letts, Works issued by the Hakluyt Society, second series 94 (London: Hakluyt Society, 1946).

Von Karabacek, Joseph. *Arab Paper*, trans. Don Baker and Suzy Dittmar (London: Archetype and the Don Baker Memorial Fund, 2001).

Von Staden, Heinrich, ed. and trans., *Herophilus: The Art of Medicine in Early Alexandria* (Cambridge and New York: Cambridge University Press, 1989).

Von Sudheim, Ludolph. *Ludolph von Suchem's Description of the Holy Land and the Way thither in the Year* A.D. *1350*, trans. Aubrey Stewart, Palestine Pilgrim Texts Society 12 (London: Palestine Exploration Fund, 1895).

Vrebos, Jacques. 'Thoughts on a neglected French medieval surgeon: Henri de Mondeville (ca. 1260–1320)', *European Journal of Plastic Surgery* 34 (2011): 1–11.

Vuckovic, Brooke. *Heavenly Journeys, Earthly Concerns: the Legacy of the Mi'raj in the Formation of Islam*, Religion, History and Culture 5 (New York: Routledge, 2005).

Walker, Winifred. *All the Plants of the Bible* (London: Lutterworth Press, 1958).

Walley, Thomas. *Balm in Gilead to Heal Sion's Wounds, or, a treatise wherein there is a clear discovery of the most prevailing sickness in New England, both in the civil and ecclesiasticall state* (Cambridge, MA: Samuel Green and Marmaduke Johnson, 1669).

Wallis, Thomas. *Textbook of Pharmacognosy*, fourth edition (London: J. and A. Churchill, 1960).

Walsh, Christine. *The Cult of St Katherine of Alexandria in Early Medieval Europe* (Aldershot and Burlington, VT: Ashgate, 2007).

Walton, Izaak. *The Compleat Angler, 1653–1676*, ed. with introduction by Jonquil Bevan (Oxford: Clarendon Press, 1983).

Wansbrough, John. 'A Mamluk letter of 877/1473', *Bulletin of the School of Oriental and African Studies* 24 (1961): 200–13.

Wansbrough, John. 'A Mamluk commercial treaty concluded with the Republic of Florence in 894/1489', in Samuel Stern, ed., *Documents from Islamic Chanceries*, Oriental Studies: First Series 3 (Oxford: Bruno Cassirer, 1965), pp. 39–79.

Wansleben (Vansleb), Johann. *The Present State of Egypt: or, A New Relation of a Late Voyage into the Kingdom, Performed in the Years 1672 and 1673* (London: John Starkey, 1678. Reprinted Westmead: Gregg International Publishers, 1972).

Watson, Gilbert. *Theriac and Mithridatium: A Study in Therapeutics*, Publications of the Wellcome Historical Medical Library. New Series 9 (London: The Wellcome Historical Medical Library, 1966).

Watt, James and Anne Wardwell, eds, *When Silk Was Gold; Central Asian and Chinese Textiles* (New York: Metropolitan Museum of Art, 1997).

Watters, David. 'A Turlington balsam phial from Monserrat, West Indies: Genuine or counterfeit?', *Historical Archaeology* 15.1 (1981): 105–8.

Watterson, Barbara. *Coptic Egypt* (Edinburgh: Scottish Academic, 1988).

Webb, John, trans., 'A survey of Egypt and Syria, undertaken in the year 1422, by Sir Gilbert de Lannoy, Knt. translated from a manuscript in the Bodleian Library at Oxford, with an introductory dissertation, and notes of illustration and reference to the Crusades', *Archaeologia* 21 (1827): 281–444.

Weitzmann, Kurt. 'Greek sources of Islamic scientific illustration', in George Miles, ed., *Archaeologica Orientalia. In Memoriam Ernst Herzfeld* (Locust Valley, NY: J. J. Augustin, 1952), pp. 244–66.

Welch, Evelyn. *Art and Society in Italy, 1350–1500*, Oxford History of Art (Oxford: Oxford University Press, 1997).

White, Evelyn. *The Monasteries of Wadi'n Natrûn, Part III: The Architecture and Archaeology*, Publications of the Metropolitan Museum of Art Expeditions 8 (New York: Metropolitan Museum of Art, 1933).

Whitehouse, David. 'Chinese porcelain in medieval Europe,' *Medieval Archaeology* 16 (1972): 63–78.

Whitehouse, David. 'Chinese stoneware from Siraf: the earliest finds', in Norman Hammond, ed., *South Asian Archaeology: Papers from the First International Conference of South Asian Archaeologists Held in the University of Cambridge* (Park Ridge, NJ: Noyes, 1973), pp. 241–55.

Whitehouse, David. 'Islamic pottery and Christian Europe from the tenth to the fifteenth century. The thirteenth Gerald Dunning Memorial lecture', *Medieval Ceramics* 21 (1997): 3–12.

Wild, Antony. *Coffee: A Dark History* (London: Fourth Estate, 2004).

Wilkinson, John, ed. and trans., *Egreria's Travels in the Holy Land*, revised edition (Warminster: Aris & Phillips, 1981).

Wilkinson, John. *Jerusalem Pilgrims before the Crusades* (Warminster: Aris and Phillips, 2002).

Wilkinson, John with Joyce Hill and W. F. Ryan, trans., *Jerusalem Pilgrimage, 1099–1185* (London: Hakluyt Society, 1988).

Williams, Caroline. 'The cult of the 'Alid saints in the Fatimid monuments of Cairo. Part I: the mosque of al-Aqmar', *Muqarnas* 1 (1983): 37–52.

Winlock, H. E., *Materials Used at the Embalming of King Tūt-'Ankh-Amūn*, The Metropolitan Museum of Art Papers 10 (New York: Metropolitan Museum of Art, 1941. Reprinted New York: Arno Press, 1973).

Wither, George. *Opobalsamum Anglicanum – an English Balme, lately pressed out of a Shrub, . . .* (London: unknown publisher, 1646).

Wolff, Anne. *How Many Miles to Babylon? Travels and Adventures to Egypt and Beyond, from 1300 to 1640* (Liverpool: Liverpool University Press, 2003).

Wren, Richard. *Potter's New Cyclopaedia of Botanical Drugs and Preparations*, revised and rewritten by Elizabeth Williamson and Fred Evans (Saffron Walden: The C. W. Daniel Company Limited, 1988).

Yaʿqubi, Ahmad b. Abi Yaʿqub b. Jaʿfar al-. In *Ibn Rusta's* Kitāb al-aʿlāq al-nafīsa *and* Kitāb al-buldān *by al-Yaʿqūbī*, ed. Michael de Goeje, Bibliotheca geographorum Arabicorum 7 (Leiden: Brill, 1892. Reprinted Brill, 1967).

Yaqut ibn ʿAbd Allah al-Rumi al-Hamawi. *Jacut's geographische Wörterbuch* (*Kitāb al-muʿjam al-buldān*), ed. Ferdinand Wüstenfeld, 6 vols (Leipzig: Brockhaus, 1866–70).

Yoeli-Tlalim, Ronit. 'Revisiting "Galen in Tibet"', *Medical History* 56.3 (2012): 355–65.

Younghusband, G. and Cyril Davenport. *The Crown Jewels of England* (London: Cassell and Co., 1919).

Zanetti, Ugo. 'Matarieh, la Sainte Famille et les baumiers', *Analecta Bollandiana* 111 (1993): 21–68.

Zarins, Juris. 'Mesopotamia and frankincense, the early evidence', in Alessandra Avanzini, ed., *Profumi d'Arabia: Atti del convegno* (Rome: 'L'erma' di Bretschneider, 1997), pp. 251–72.

Zeʿevi, Dror. *An Ottoman Century: The District of Jerusalem in the 1600s*, SUNY Series in Medieval Middle East History (Albany, NY: State University of New York Press, 1996).

Ziadeh, Nicola. 'al-Antāqi and his *Tadhkira*', *Aram* 11–12 (1999–2000): 503–8.

Zohary, Michael. *Geobotanical Foundations of the Middle East*, Geobotanica Selecta 3, 2 vols (Stuttgart and Amsterdam: Gustav Fischer and Swets & Zeitlinger, 1973).

Index

Locations

Aachen, 156, 157
Abba Kama, monastery of, 99
Abyssinia (Habash) *see* Ethiopia
Aegean sea, 229
Alexandria, 68, 77, 78, 90, 158, 169, 249
Amalfi, 164
Americas, 2, 108, 262
Amiens, Musée de Picardie, 259, 260
Amsterdam, 225
Anatolia, 198
Arabia, 2, 9, 37, 54, 55, 56, 57, 58, 60, 61, 62, 63, 106, 107, 118, 120, 126, 137, 138, 141, 171, 191–2, 196, 215, 229, 275
Arabia Felix *see* Yemen
Aragon, kingdom of, 157, 158, 160
Ariha *see* Jericho
Ascalon, 96
Ashmun Tanah, 144
Asia, 23, 186
Atlantic ocean, 12
Augsburg, 168
Augustamnica, 91
'Ayn Shams *see* Matarea

Babylon (Iraq), 256
Baghdad, 155, 157, 163, 196
    House of Wisdom (*bayt al-ḥikma*), 196
Bamberg, 168
Barling, 168
Basta, 99
Bastiyya *see* Basta
Bela *see* Zoar
Bethlehem, 38, 58, 255
Bobbio, 165
Bukhara, 127
Busra (Bostra), 57

Caesarea, 72
Cairo, 1, 7, 26, 29, 32, 36, 43, 87, 93, 100, 101, 102, 126, 138, 147, 157, 158, 160, 165, 167, 168, 171, 214, 226, 229
    Abu Serga, 43
    'Askar, 93
    Bab al-Futuh, 93, 94
    Bab al-Nasr, 93, 99, 100, 101
    Babylon (Old Cairo), 32, 36, 37, 43, 91, 158
    Birkat al-Hajj, 93, 99
    College of Jesuits, 26
    Fustat, 93, 94
    Husayniyya, al-, 93, 94, 100, 101
    Khalij, canal of al-, 94, 100
    Nilometer, Rawda Island, 262
    Qahira, al-, 41, 42, 93, 94, 100
    Qata'i', al-, 93
    Raydaniyya, al-, 100
    Za'faran canal, 99
Canterbury, 168, 253, 261
Cape of Good Hope, 161
Cave of Letters, Judaean desert, 64
Central Asia, 12, 153
China, 76, 153, 156, 164, 222
Chios, 165
Cluny, 218
Constantinople *see* Istanbul
Cordoba, 197
Cyprus, 160

Damascus, 160, 214
Damietta, 36
Daqahliyya, 144
Dead Sea, 22, 23, 23, 53, 58, 62, 64, 65, 72, 76, 120

Deir al-Bahri, 53, 54, 245
Delft, 103
Dengadda *see* En-Gedi
Derby, 3
Djibouti, 138

East Africa, 14, 57, 279
Edinburgh, 225
Egypt, 1, 2, 3, 6, 8, 9, 25, 29, 35, 36, 38, 39, 40, 41, 44, 54, 57, 59, 60, 63, 73, 75, 76, 77, 78, 87–109, 118, 124, 126, 137, 138, 142, 153, 154, 157, 160, 161, 163, 164, 167, 168, 169, 182, 225, 242, 244, 245, 251, 252, 254, 262, 275, 281
'Ein Boqeq, 64, 65
'Ein Feshka, 64, 65
En-Gedi, 8, 9, 16, 37, 59, 61, 63, 64, 66, 67, 68, 70, 71–3, 75, 76, 77, 78, 118, 140, 143, 144, 153, 154, 163, 261, 274, 275
England, 164, 167, 223, 257, 258
Eritrea, 138
Ethiopia, 60, 88, 138, 155, 158
Europe, 3, 9, 11, 12, 44, 91, 106, 131, 154, 155, 163, 164, 165, 167, 168, 194, 210, 212, 223, 224, 225, 228, 230, 244, 251, 257, 258, 260, 261, 262, 273, 275, 276, 277, 278, 279, 280

Ferrara, 280
Florence, 159, 280
  Palazzo Vecchio, 159
Fonthill, 164
France, 25, 91, 160, 167, 260

Genoa, 169, 225
Ghumdan, palace of, 6
Gilead, 7, 58, 59, 182
Giza, pyramids of, 29
Gondeshapur (Jundaysabur), 196
Greater Syria *see* Syria

Haberstadt, 168
Hadramawt, 55
Hague, the, 225
Hattin, 158
Hebron (al-Khalil), 242
Heidenheim, 75
Helenopolis, 78
Heliopolis, 8, 26, 29, 33, 40, 87, 89–91, 102, 135
  Temple of the Sun, 33

Hiericus *see* Jericho
Hijaz, 57, 100, 106, 107, 118, 137, 142
Holy Land, 164, 280
Horn of Africa, 9, 54, 55, 56, 142
Hungary, 164, 280

Iberian Peninsula, 158
India *see* Indian Subcontinent
Indian Subcontinent, 14, 57, 156, 158
Indus, 215
Iran, 142, 153, 154, 198, 222, 223, 279
Iraq, 128, 196
Israel, 61, 77
Istanbul, 1, 23, 108, 128, 156, 157, 161, 162, 163, 225, 229, 246, 248, 257, 279
Italy, 108, 125, 159, 163, 165, 227

Jericho, 8, 9, 16, 36, 37, 41, 42, 61, 62, 63, 64, 65, 67, 68, 71, 75, 76, 77, 118, 141, 154, 256, 257, 261, 274, 275
Jerusalem, 36, 39, 60, 67, 68, 75, 157, 163, 216, 262, 276
  Aqsa mosque, 39
  Dome of the Rock, 262
  Herodian Temple, 68, 69
  Holy Sepulchre, church of, 157
  Israel Museum, 67
  Solomonic Temple, 11, 247, 256
  Temple Mount, 262
Jidda, 138
Jordan, 56, 57, 58, 123, 170
Jordan river, 73, 75
Jordan Valley, 37, 53, 58, 62
Judaea, 11, 23, 39, 60, 63, 68, 118, 120, 121, 273

Kayfa, 198
Khandaq, 91–5
Khirbat Qumran, 65
Khuzistan, 196

Leiden, 128
Lemnos, 162, 197, 227
Lombardy, 131
London, 3, 131, 168, 225
  British Library, 31, 131
  St Paul's cathedral, 168
  Westminster Abbey, 252
Lourdes, 26
Lower Egypt, 89, 91, 142

Madaba, Church of St George, 73, 127
Mada'in Salih, 57
Main, 55
Mardin, 198, 250
Marseilles, 164, 167
Masada, 16, 64, 67
Mashhad, Shrine of Imam Reza, 128, 129, 132
Matarea, 1, 2, 3, 6, 7, 8, 13, 15, 16, 25, 26–44, 53, 72, 73–4, 77, 87–109, 118, 119, 124, 126, 131, 135, 140, 141, 143, 144, 145, 154, 161, 168, 169, 170, 171, 182, 211, 262, 273, 274, 275, 277, 281
   Church of St George, 95
   Malaqa bi'l-Matariyya, al-, 101, 102
Matariyya see Matarea
Mecca, 33, 99, 118, 126, 138, 154, 165, 166, 214
   Ka'ba, 154
   Zamzam, well of, 33, 165, 166
Medina, 99
Mediterranean, 10, 58, 64, 72, 73, 74, 92, 108, 154, 161, 163, 164, 167, 169, 192, 210, 224, 275
Mercia, kingdom of, 257
Merseburg, 168
Mesopotamia, 87, 198, 222, 223
Middle East, 3, 9, 14, 23, 56, 108, 143, 154, 163, 164, 186, 187, 192, 194, 273, 275
Minat Surad, 99
Miniat Matar see Matarea
Monte Cassino, monastery of, 217
Montpellier, 11, 210, 225
Monza, 165, 166
Mosul, 213, 249
Mount Sion, 23
Myos Hormos, 57

Najd, 142
Nazareth, 38
New York, Morgan Library and Museum (Pierpont Morgan Library), 128
Nicaea, 251
Nile delta, 73, 89, 91
Nile river, 1, 89, 91, 108, 252
Nisibis, 87
Nitria, 78
Noli, 164
North Africa, 12, 164, 273
Nuremburg, 225

Oman, 138, 279
On see Heliopolis

Palestine, 7, 8, 9, 23, 37, 57, 60, 61, 67, 73, 75, 77, 118, 119, 120, 126, 138, 140, 142, 165, 191
Palmyra, 70
Paris, 77, 130, 134, 198, 219
   Bibliothèque Nationale, 77, 130, 198
Persia see Iran
Peru, 262
Petra, 57, 123, 170
Pisa, 164
Pontus, 192
Prague, 167
Punt, 53–5

Qalyub, 96
Qaryat al-Faw, 57
Qataban, 55
Qumran, 16, 66, 67, 140–1
Qus, 100
Quseir, 164

Raamah, 58
Ramtha, 72
Ravenna, 163, 245, 246
Red Sea, 57, 100, 164
Rheims, 259
Rome, 8, 69, 70, 74, 162, 163, 246, 251
   Arch of Titus, 69, 70
   Church of Santa Croce in Gerusalemme, 251
   Church of Sts Marcellinus and Peter, 246
   Vatican, Sancta Sanctorum, 143, 168

Saba, 55, 58
Salerno, 11, 31, 210, 217, 218, 219, 275
   Schola Medica Salernitana, 217, 230
Salisbury, 168
Samarqand, 127, 198
Saudi Arabia, 57, 138
Serçe Limanı, 165
Sharqiyya, 41
Sheba, land of see Yemen
Sicily, 158
Simjur, 198
Sinai, 1, 73, 242
   Monastery of St Catherine, Tomb of St Catherine, 242
Sodom, 23
Somalia, 138

South America, 171–2
South Asia, 161
Southeast Asia, 161, 164
Spain, 170, 257
Staffelsee, 168
Sublime Porte *see* Istanbul
Sudan, 138
Syria, 2, 41, 56, 57, 59, 62, 68, 71, 75, 94, 96, 100, 104, 153, 155, 160, 163, 198, 279
Syrian littoral *see* Syria
Syro-Palestine *see* Syria

Taʿizz, 137
Thebes, 53
Tibet, 223
Tihama, 142
Tlemcen, 158
Toledo, 218
Transylvania, 280
Tunisia, 211

Turkey, 128, 225
Tyre, 58, 75

Uday, 3

Valencia, 243
Venice, 2, 160, 162, 224, 229

Wadi ʿAraba, 62
Wadi al-Natrun, Monastery of St Macarius, 251
Wessex, 164
Western Europe *see* Europe
Wilten, 168

Yanbuʿ, 138
Yemen, 2, 3, 6, 57, 58, 60, 126, 138, 142

Zion, 261
Zoar, 72, 78
Zughar, 76

People, Groups and Dynasties

Aaron, 256, 257
ʿAbbas, vizier, 95–6
Abbasid caliphate, 156, 279
ʿAbd al-Malik ibn Marwan, caliph, 91–2
ʿAbd al-Rahman III, caliph, 197
Abdlawadid dynasty, 158
Absalom, 255
Abu al-Hasin ibn Bastiya, 97, 99
Abu al-Makarim, 95–6, 97, 98, 99, 144, 145, 146
Abu'l-ʿAbbas, elephant sent to Charlemagne, 156
Acquisti, Marsilio, 109
ʿAdil I al-, Ayyubid sultan (al-Malik al-ʿAdil Sayf al-Din Abu Bakr Ahmad ibn Najm al-Din Ayyub), 98
Adomnán of Iona, 75
Aetius of Amida, 189, 190, 216
Afdal, Shahinshah al-, 94
Africanus, Leo (al-Hasan b. Muhammad al-Wazzan), 33
Agnellus, 245
Agrippa, 68
Akhnaten, pharaoh, 90
Alcuin of York, 257
Alexander III of Macedon (Alexander the Great), 63
Alexander of Tralles, 189, 190, 191, 200
Alfonso IV, king of Aragon, 157, 158

Alfred the Great, king of Wessex, 163, 216, 257
ʿAli Bey ʿAbbasi *see* Badía y Leblich, Domingo
ʿAli ibn ʿIsa al-Kahhal, 213, 219, 230
Alpi, Najm al-Din, Artuqid *atabak*, 128, 198
Alpin (Alpinus), Prosper, 2, 16, 26, 124–6, 132, 133, 135, 140, 142, 143, 171, 172, 220, 226
Ambroise, 168
Amico da Gallipoli, Bernardino, 33–4, 35, 109
Amir bi-Akham Allah, al-, Fatimid caliph, 96, 97
Amoun of Nitria, 78
Anba Mikhaʾil, bishop of Basta, 99
Anba Yaʿqub, 91
Andromachus the Elder, 194, 222, 230
Anghiera, Pedro d' (Peter Martyr), 105–6, 107
Anglicus, Bartholomaeus, 219
Anicia, Juliana, Byzantine princess, 126
Antaki, Dawud al-, 214
Anthony the Great, saint, 78
Apuleius (Lucius Apuleius Madaurensis), 246
Archelaus, 65
Arculf, 75

Aristotle, 187
Aten (solar disc), 89
Augustus, emperor (Octavian), 63
Aurelian, emperor, 70
Averroes *see* Ibn Rushd
Avicenna *see* Ibn Sina
Ayyubid sultanate, 8, 93, 97, 146, 154, 262

Bacon, Francis, 22
Bacon, Roger, 167
Badía y Leblich, Domingo, 137–8
Badr al-Jamali, al-Juyushi, 93
Baghdadi, ʿAbd al-Latif al-, 10, 31, 98, 99, 124, 141–2, 144, 145, 146, 167, 171
Bar Kepha, Moses, 76, 250, 252
Bar Kokhba, Shimon, 71
Bar Salibi, Dionysius, 250
Barbara, saint, 157, 158
Barbarossa, Frederick, 153
Barhebraeus, Gregory (Jamal al-Din Abu al-Faraj Griguriyus), 141, 170, 247, 248
Barquq, al-Malik al-Zahir Sayf al-Din, Mamluk sultan, 161
Barsbay, al-Ashraf Sayf al-Din, Mamluk sultan, 100
Baybars al-Bunduqdari (Baybars I), Mamluk sultan, 100
Beckett, Thomas, 261
Belon, Pierre, 107, 171
Benedict XII, pope, 164
Bernard the Monk, 44
Bihnam al-Mawsili, 198
Biruni, Abu Rayhan al-, 124, 141, 142, 163, 211, 213
Bocskay, Stefan, 280
Bordeaux Pilgrim, 262
Budge, Ernest Wallis, 43
Bukhari, Muhammad al-, 277
Burchard of Mount Sion, 23, 29
Burton, Sir Richard, 166
Byzantine empire, 44, 155, 196

Celsus, Cornelius, 192, 193
Chahine, Youssef, 249
Charas, Moyse, 167, 172
Charlemagne (Charles the Great), 155, 156, 245, 257, 258
Charles I, king of England, 253
Charles V, king of France, 160
Christ, Jesus, 7, 29, 33, 39, 40, 41, 43, 58, 88, 99, 106, 241, 242, 245, 250, 256
Chrysologus, Peter, 245
Chrysostom, John, 251

Cleopatra VII, queen of Egypt, 2, 7, 37, 63, 77
Clovis I, king of the Franks, 259
Collins, Minta, 128
Columbus, Christopher, 24
Constantine the African, 217–18, 252
Cornaro, Catherine, queen of Cyprus, 160
Cosmas, saint, 215
Cotton, Hannah, 64
Cranmer, Thomas, 261
Cyril of Jerusalem, patriarch, 251
Cyrus the Great (Cyrus II of Persia), 256

Da Gama, Vasco, 161
Damascenus, Nicolaus (Nicolaus of Damascus), 211
Damian, saint, 215
Darius I the Great, 55
David, king, 255, 257, 258, 259
Davis, Theodore, 245
De Brûlons, Savary, 168
De Foligno, Gentile, 228
De Lannoy, Sir Gilbert, 29, 44, 157
De Maillet, Benoît, 109, 135, 137
De' Medici, Clarice (Clarice Orsini), 159
De' Medici, Lorenzo, 159
De Villefavin, Madame de, 165
Dimashqi, Shams al-Din al-Ansari al-, 103
Diodorus of Sicily (Diodorus Siculus), 62, 120, 244
Dioscorides, Pedanios, 9, 10, 77, 121, 123, 124, 126, 128, 129, 131, 138, 139, 141, 143, 144, 145, 163, 167, 169, 172, 173, 185, 186, 187, 188, 190, 197–200, 210, 211, 213, 214, 216, 217, 275
Di Varthema, Ludovico, 154
Donceel-Voûte, Pauline, 69
Donne, John, 4
Doughty, Charles, 229
Dragas, Helena, 257
Dusay, Neymerich, 158

Ecgfrith, king of Mercia, 257
Edward II, king of England, 260
Edward VII, king of the United Kingdom and emperor of India, 253
Edward the Confessor, 253
El Cid (Rodrigo Díaz de Vivar), 153, 243
Elias III, patriarch of Jerusalem, 163, 216, 219
Elizabeth I, queen of England, 228, 253, 254

Elizabeth II, queen of the United Kingdom, 253, 254
Eusebius of Caesarea, 72
Evliya Çelebi, 103
Ezekiel, prophet, 58, 59, 61

Fabri, Felix, 29, 36, 103, 104–5, 153, 167, 247
Fakhr al-Din ʿUthman, 158
Faraj ibn Barquq, al-Nasir, Mamluk sultan, 104
Fatimid caliphate, 93, 96, 146, 154, 157, 262
Ferdinand IV, king of Castile, 158
Fleming, Ian, 14
Flood, Finbarr Barry, 280
Forsskål, Pehr (Peter), 2–3, 137
Frederick I Barbarossa, 153
Frescobaldi, Leonardo, 25

Galen, Claudius, 71, 77, 129, 186, 188, 193, 195, 196, 200, 211, 213, 214, 215, 217, 220, 221, 230
George II, king of Great Britain and Ireland, 3
George III, king of Great Britain and Ireland, 247
George of the Arabs, 76, 250
Gerard, John, 132–4, 167
Gerard of Cremona, 11, 218
Ghafiqi, ʿAbd al-Rahman ibn ʿAbd Allah al-, 141, 169, 170, 200
Goldfinger, Auric, 13
González, Antonius, 108
Grassus (Grapheus), Benvenutus, 219
Greenhill, Thomas, 182, 243–4
Gregory of Tours, saint, 6, 252, 259
Gregory the Great (pope Gregory I), 246
Grisar, Hartmann, 143
Groom, Nigel, 55, 59
Gutas, Dimitri, 279

Hadrian I, pope, 252
Hamdani, Abu Muhammad al-Hasan b. Ahmad ibn Yaʿqub al-, 6
Hamdanid dynasty, 213
Harant, Christoph, 108, 167
Harizi, Judah al-, 6
Harun al-Rashid, Abbasid caliph, 155
Hasmonean dynasty, 62, 65, 154, 257
Hatshepsut, queen, 53–4
Heberden, William, 229
Helias see Elias III, patriarch of Jerusalem

Henry VIII, king of England, 228
Hero of Alexandria, 198
Herod the Great, 1–2, 7, 37, 39, 63
Herodian dynasty, 62, 65, 154, 257
Herodotus, 55, 90, 182, 244, 245
Herophilus, 190
Hertz, Bram, 190
Hildegard of Bingen, 219, 230, 245, 251
Hincmar, archbishop of Rheims, 259
Hippocrates, 188, 215, 217
Holy Family, 8, 29, 39, 41, 44, 87, 96, 275
Holy Spirit, 250
Hugeburc, 75
Hunayn ibn Ishaq al-Ibadi, 128, 171, 197, 198, 200, 214, 217, 219, 220, 230
Husayn ibn ʿAli, 96
Hyracanus, John, 63

Ibn Abi Ashʿath, 200, 214, 214
Ibn ʿAli, Muhammad, 226
Ibn Basil, Istifan, 128
Ibn al-Baytar, Diyaʾ al-Din Abu Muhammad, 106, 169, 170, 171, 200, 210, 211, 213, 214
Ibn Butlan, Abu al-Hasan al-Mukhtar, 230
Ibn al-Hashshaʾ, Ahmad b. Muhammad, 211
Ibn Hawqal, Muhammad Abu al-Qasim, 87–8, 93
Ibn ʿImran, Ishaq, 211, 214
Ibn Iyas, Abu al-Barakat Muhammad b. Ahmad al-Hanafi, 3, 7, 105, 106, 107, 167
Ibn al-Jazzar, Ahmad b. Jaʿfar Ibrahim, 171, 200, 213, 217
Ibn Juljul, Abu Dawud Sulayman ibn Hassan, 170, 197, 200, 221
Ibn Mahfuz, 159
Ibn Malti, Abu Salim, 198
Ibn Mansur, Mihran, 128, 197, 198
Ibn al-Muqaffaʿ, Sawirus (Severus), 94–5
Ibn al-Nadim, Abu al-Faraj Muhammad, 197
Ibn Ridwan, Abu al-Hassan ʿAli, 212, 213, 218
Ibn Rushd, Abu al-Walid Muhammad ibn Ahmad (Averroes), 221
Ibn Samajun, 167
Ibn Sarafyun (Ibn Serapion), Yahyaʾ, 195, 218
Ibn Sina, Abu ʿAli, 11, 212, 213, 218, 220, 221, 223, 228, 230

Ibn al-Wardi, Abu Hafs Zayn al-Din 'Umar ibn Muzaffar, 88
Idrisi, Abu 'Abd Allah Muhammad, 87, 88
Ikhshidid dynasty, 157
Ikhwan al-Safa', 278
Inal, Sayf al-Din, Mamluk sultan, 161
Innocent III, pope, 258
Ishbili, Ibn al-Ha'im al-, 211
Ishmaelites, 58
Isra'ili, Ya'qub b. Ishaq al-, 214
Istakhri, Abu Ishaq Ibrahim b. Muhammad al-Farisi, 87–8, 93

Jacob of Edessa, 76, 195, 250
Jacob of Serugh, 252
Jaime I, king of Aragon, 157, 158
Jaqmaq, Sayf al-Din, Mamluk sultan, 161
Jazari, Badi' al-Zaman Abu al-'Izz b. Isma'il ibn al-Razaz al-, 198
Jean of Saint Amand, 219
Jeremiah, prophet, 58, 59, 61, 214–15
Jerome, saint, 72
Jeshoiada, 256
Jesse of Bethlehem, 255
Jesuit Order, 109
Jing, Su, 222
Joash, 256
John V, Coptic patriarch, 94, 96
John VIII Palaiologus, 280
John XXII, pope, 261
John the Baptist, 251
Joseph of Arimathea, 39–40, 41, 43, 47
Josephus, Flavius, 7, 23, 36, 37, 44, 60, 61, 62, 63, 118, 120, 126, 256
Josiah, king, 63
Josias son of Joseph, 77
Jullien, P. M., 26–7, 33
Julius Caesar, 62
Justinian I, emperor, 245

Kara Arslan, Artuqid *atabak*, 198
Khusraw I Anushirvan, 196
Kiechel, Samuel, 108
Kindi, Abu Yusuf Ya'qub ibn Ishaq al-Sabbah, 213, 214
Komaroff, Linda, 199

Lambert of Maastricht, 241
Le Brun, Corneille, 103
Lemnius, Levinus, 241
Leo IV, pope, 257
Leo X, pope, 248
Levant Company, 22

Linnaeus, Carl, 2
Lister, Joseph, 184
Lothair I, Holy Roman Emperor, 258
Louis I the Great, king of Hungary, 164
Louis II, Holy Roman Emperor, 258
Louis IX, king of France, 25

Macarius, saint, 251
Mahmud Shah, sultan of Malwa, 158–9
Maimonides (Moses ben Maimon), 212, 214, 221
Majno, Guido, 182, 183
Majusi, 'Ali ibn al-'Abbas al-, 217
Mamluk sultanate, 2, 8, 25, 154, 262, 280
  Bahri Mamluk period, 103
  Circassian Mamluk period, 99, 103, 104
Ma'mun, caliph al-, 156, 157, 196
Mandeville, Sir John, 22, 23, 24, 35, 37, 172–3
Manuel II, emperor, 257
Maqrizi, Taqi al-Din Ahmad b. 'Ali al-, 88, 103
Mark, evangelist, 58, 249, 252
Mark Antony, 2, 37, 63, 70
Mark III, Coptic patriarch, 94–5
Mary, Virgin, 7, 29, 32, 33, 39, 40, 41, 43, 44, 77, 88, 95, 96, 98, 105, 108, 109, 250
Mary I, queen of England, 253
Masarjawayh, 171
Maundrell, Henry, 22–3
Mehmed II Fatih ('the Conqueror'), Ottoman sultan, 161, 162
Menas, saint, 242
Menevisoglu, Paulos, 248
Menocchio, 24
Merovingian dynasty, 91
Messinor, Ottoman governor, 107–108, 126
Meyerhof, Max, 139
Michael VII Doukas, emperor, 216
Michael of Malij, 43
Mithradates VI Eupator, 192, 193
Mnevis bull, 90
Mondeville, Henri de, 220
Montluc, Jean de, 162
Moses, prophet, 256, 257
Mu'ayyad Shaykh, Mamluk sultan, 101
Muhammad, Prophet, 39, 262, 277
Münster, Sebastian, 30, 101
Murad II, Ottoman sultan, 161
Muslim ibn al-Hajjaj, 277

Mutawakkil, Abu al-Fadl Ja'far ibn Muhammad al-Mu'tasim billah al-, Abbasid caliph, 197

Nabataean dynasty, 56, 57, 70
Nasir-i Khusraw, Abu Mu'in, 87, 88, 144
Nasir Muhammad ibn Qalawun, al-, Mamluk sultan, 100, 101, 157
Nasir Muhammad ibn Qaytbay al-, Mamluk sultan, 105
Natili, Abu 'Abdallah al-, 198
Nero, emperor, 194
Nicander of Colophon, 192
Nicodemus, 58
Nicodemus the Hagiorite, 252
Niebuhr, Carsten, 33, 137
Notker the Stammerer, 156
Nur al-Din ibn Zangi, 157

Offa, king of Mercia, 257
Oliver of Paderborn, 36
Oribasius, 189, 211, 219
Ottoman empire, 1, 107

Palerne, Jean, 35, 107, 108
Palladius of Galatia, 78
Paré, Ambroise, 243
Paris, Matthew, 260
Paul of Aegina, 171, 189, 191, 200, 211, 212, 214
Paul the Apostle, 256
Pausanias, 191
Pegolotti, Francesco Balducci, 168
Pepin I, king of France, 258
Peter Martyr *see* Anghiera, Pedro d'
Peter the Venerable, abbot of Cluny, 218
Philo of Byzantium (Philo Mechanicus), 198
Philoxemus of Mabbug, 251
Pisanello (Antonio di Puccio Pisano), 280
Pius V, pope, 262
Platearius, Matthaeus, 131–2, 217
Pliny the Elder, 9, 36, 56, 62, 63, 68, 69, 70, 71, 72, 73, 77, 120, 121, 124, 138, 139, 141, 143, 145, 162, 163, 191, 192, 193, 216, 245, 246, 257
Pomet, Pierre, 36, 125, 134, 136, 140, 146, 165, 167, 168
Priscianus, Theodoros, 200
Psellos, Michael, 216
Ptolemaic dynasty, 57, 90
Ptolemy of Alexandria, 218
Pythagoras, 171, 200

Qansawh al-Ghawri, Mamluk sultan, 101, 103, 107, 142, 161
Qaytbay, Abu al-Nasr Sayf al-Din al-Ashraf, Mamluk sultan, 101, 102, 105, 159
Qazwini, Zakariya b. Muhammad b. Mahmud al-, 88

Rabbi Judah the Prince, 71
Rantzow, Henry, 108
Rav Joseph, 72
Razi, Muhammad ibn Zakariya al-, 171, 186, 200, 211, 217, 218
Remi (Remigius), saint, 259
Richard I, king of England, 261
Riddle, John, 172, 184, 185
Rocchetta, Aquilante, 108
Roman empire, 60, 63, 246
Romanus II, emperor, 197
Royal College of Physicians, 229
Rufinus, 219
Rüstem Pasha, vizier, 162

Saewulf, 241
Salah al-Din, al-Nasir Salah al-Din Yusuf ibn Ayyub (Saladin), 97, 101, 153, 157, 158
Salaman, Redcliffe, 12
Saliba, George, 199
Salome, 41
Samuel, prophet, 245–5, 257, 258, 259
Sandys, George, 1, 2, 7, 26, 108
Sanudo (Sanuto) the Elder, Marino, 29
Sanudo (Sanuto) the Younger, Marino, 105
Saul, king, 254–5
Savary, Claude Étienne, 2
Schiltberger, Johannes, 168, 171
Schweinfurth, Georg, 106
Secundus of Non, 246
Seetzen, Ulrich, 24
Selim I, Ottoman sultan, 107
Senusret, pharaoh, 89
Sergius of Resh 'Ayna, 195
Seth (Sethis), Simeon, 169, 216, 221
Severinus, Petrus (Peder Sørenson), 5
Shayzari, 'Abd al-Rahman b. Nasr al-, 170
Sheba, Queen of, 7, 37, 60, 61, 118, 126, 247
Simon, patriarch, 41
Solomon, king, 7, 60, 61, 118, 247, 256
Squires, Peter, 253
Stieb, Ernst, 172
Strabo, 62, 73, 77, 90, 120
Suriano, Francesco, 31, 33, 105

Tabari, 'Ali ibn Sahl Rabban al-, 200, 221
Tacitus, Publius Cornelius, 23, 36, 68, 120, 121
T'ang dynasty, 153, 222
Tanukhi, Sahnun ibn Sa'id ibn Habib al-, 246
Tarasios, patriarch, 251
Taymi, al-, 213
Theodius II, emperor, 77, 78
Theophilus, patriarch, 77–8
Theophrastus, 5, 59, 61–2, 63, 73, 118, 119, 120, 121, 123, 138, 141, 145
Thompson, Stephen, 254
Timur-i Lang (Temür or Tamerlane), 104
Titus, Roman emperor, 23, 68, 69, 70
Trogus, Pompeius, 120
Trotula (Trota), 217, 219
Tulunid dynasty, 157
Tumanbay II, al-Ashraf, Mamluk sultan, 107
Turlington, Robert, 3
Tutankhamun, pharaoh, 245

'Umari, Shihab al-Din Abu al-'Abbas Ahmad Fadl Allah al-, 103, 155, 213, 247
Umayyad dynasty, 156, 196, 262
'Uthman ibn 'Affan, caliph, 161

Van Ghistele, De Joos, 102, 103

Vespasian, emperor, 68, 69, 77
Victoria, queen of the United Kingdom, 253
Viner, Sir Robert, 254
Virgil (Publius Vergilius Maro), 191
Vitruvius, Marcus Pollio, 184
Von Boldensele, Wilhelm, 35
Von Breydenbach, Bernhard, 105
Von Harff, Arnold, 100, 105
Von Sudheim, Ludolph, 33, 35, 36, 37–8, 146, 155
Von Wedel, Lupold, 108

Walton, Izaak, 4
Wansleben (Vansleb), Johann Michael, 33, 35, 109
Willibald, 75, 157, 281

Yaqut al-Hamawi, Shihab al-Din ibn 'Abd Allah al-Rumi, 88, 98, 99, 124
Yashbak min Mahdi, Mamluk amir, 101, 102, 103, 104

Zacharie of Sakha, 41–2, 43, 76
Zadok, High Priest, 256, 257
Zafir, Abu Mansur Isma'il al-, Fatimid caliph, 956
Zenobia, queen of Palmyra, 70
Zirid dynasty, 211
Zucchelo, Pignol, 168

Plant Species, Simple Medicines, Compound Medicines and Ritual Oils

Abraham's balm, 212
Acacia, 125, 191
Aleppo pine, 192
Almond (and almond oil), 121, 192, 246
Aloe (and aloe wood), 58, 156, 160, 244, 262
Ambergris, 156, 262
Ammoniac *see* Sal ammoniac
Amomum, 195
Aniseed, 195
Apple of Sodom (*Calotropis procera*), 22–5
Aquatic mint, 212
Asfoetida, 200, 217
Asphalt, 244
'Awshir see Apple of Sodom

Balanus, 246
Balm of Gilead, 3, 7, 58, 59, 61, 138, 182, 214, 247

Balm of Mecca *see Commiphora gileadensis*
Balsam of Peru, 136, 165, 172, 184
Balsam of the Philosophers (also Balsam of Wisdom, or Brick Oil), 5
Balsam of Tolu, 136, 184
Bashām see Commiphora gileadensis
Bdellium, 136, 184
Ben oil (made from seeds of seeds of *Moringa oleifera*), 170, 171
Benzoin, 160, 253
Bitter almond oil, 121
Bitumen, 244
Bosem, 7, 58, 59, 61, 138
Boswellia papyrifera, 55
Boswellia sacra see frankincense
Brazil wood, 169
Bryon, 246

INDEX | 335

Cadmin, 195
Calamus, 249
Camomile, 212
Camphor, 97, 170, 228
Cardamom, 246
Carob, 107
Carpobalsamum (fruit or grain of balsam), 155, 167, 171, 172, 191, 212, 220, 221, 226, 229, 248, 278
Cassia, 55, 256
Cedar oil (*kedros*), 214–15
Chrism, 42, 96–7, 155, 247–52, 258
Cinnamon, 55, 169, 215, 226, 241, 244, 253
Citron, 212
Civet, 253
Clove, 172, 249
Coconut, oil of, 211
Colophonium *see* rosin
Commiphora erythraea, 55
Commiphora gileadensis, 9, 55, 106, 118, 119, 137, 138, 139, 140, 141, 142, 143, 170, 171, 186–7, 229, 248, 274, 275
Commiphora mukul, 186
Commiphora myrrha see myrrh
Commiphora opobalsamum see Commiphora gileadensis
Crocus, 249
Cubeb (or tailed pepper; *Piper cubeba*), 172

Date palm, 76, 107
Deer marrow, 219
Dill, 215
Dog's fennel, 212

Estumka, 195

Fennel, 217
Ferula persica, 200
Fig, 107
Frankincense, 55, 56, 57, 58, 136, 164, 195, 215, 216, 241, 244, 247, 262

Galbanum, 246
Galene, 191, 194, 221, 222, 224, 228, 229
Gall, 200
Garlic, 185
Gilly-flower, 212
Ginger, 160, 164, 169
Great hygieia, 215
'Great Treacle' *see* treacle
Ground-pine, 170

Gum, 249
Gypsum, 244

Hadramawt myrrh, 138
Hedychroum, pastilles (troches) of, 194, 222
Hemlock (*Conium maculatum*), 194, 221
Henbane, 215
Henna (and henna oil), 121, 122, 125, 169
Hiera of Theodoretus, 195, 196, 215
Honey, 125, 170, 192, 193, 195, 216
Hypericum (St John's wort), 193

Indian nard *see* nard
Indigo, 12, 76
Iris, 189

Jasmine, 212, 253

Kāzī (screw pine), oil of, 211
Khalūq, 93, 262

Lachobalsamum (ash of balsam wood), 167
Ladanum (labdanum; Hebrew: *lot*), 53, 58, 136
Laurus malabathrum (*Cinnamon aromaticum* Nees), 195
Ledanon *see* ladanum
Lemon, 125
Leopard's bane, 122
Lily (and lily oil), 121, 169
Lily of the valley, 212
Lime (calcium oxide), 244
Linseed, 249
Lovage, 215

Mace, 171
Marjoram, 189, 192
Mastic, 169, 218
Mendesian unguent, 246
Metópion, 121, 169
Mithridatium, 11, 162, 191, 193, 194, 218, 225, 226, 228, 229
Mummia *see* pissasphalt
Musk, 156, 157, 160, 253, 262
Musk rose, 212
Myrobalan, 160
Myron *see* chrism
Myrtle (and oil of), 120, 142, 215
Myrrh (*Commiphora molmol*), 55, 56, 57, 58, 119, 136, 182, 189, 190, 191, 193, 211, 215, 241, 242, 244, 247, 249, 256, 274

Narcissus, 212
Nard (and oil of), 189, 190, 193, 195, 215, 218, 226, 246, 249
Nitre (potassium nitrate), 244
Natron (and 'scum' of), 190, 244
'Ntyw, 55
Nutmeg, 164, 248

Oil of catechumens, 155, 249, 252, 258
Oil of lily *see* lily
Oil of myrtle *see* myrtle
Olibanum *see* frankincense
Olive oil, 211, 248, 253, 262
Opium, 191, 194
Opobalsamum ('oil' of balsam; Arabic: *duhn al-balasān*), 2, 60, 62, 72, 75, 77, 97, 121–2, 123, 130, 133, 135, 139, 142, 146, 167, 171, 172, 190, 191, 193, 194, 195, 196, 213, 221, 226, 246, 278
Opoponax, 195
Orange flower, 253

Papyrus, 74, 91–2
Parsley, 215
Pepper (and peppercorns), 169, 170, 195, 200
Petroleum, 216, 244
Pissasphalt, 244
Pomegranate, 119
Privet, 125, 189
Pyracanthus, 121

Rape-turnip (*Brassica rapa*), 76
Ritíni see Balm of Gilead
Rock salt, 200
Rose (and oil of, and dried leaves of), 189, 195, 213, 249, 262
Rosin, 190, 205, 244
Rue, 119, 133

Saffron, 169, 189, 191, 215, 226, 244, 249, 262
Salamander, 193
Sal ammoniac, 216, 241
Salt, 244
Sandarac, 164
Sapponaria, root of, 249
Scapwort, 200

Sesame oil, 253
Shubrum (tithymalus; *Euphorbia pithyusa* L.), 170
Skink, dried flesh of, 159, 193
Soft-haired basil, 212
Southernwood, 212
Spikenard (and oil of), 172, 195, 215, 216
Spruce resin, 190
Spurge, 221
Stacte ('liquid myrrh'), 171, 195, 241, 246
Storax, 193, 195, 246
Styrax, 189, 191, 249
Sugar, 12, 169
Sweet basil, 212
Sweet marjoram, 212
Sycamore fig (*Ficus sycomoros*), 26

Tapuah Sdom see apple of Sodom
Terebinth (*Pistacia palaestina*), 59, 119, 125, 138, 169, 189, 226, 246
Terra lemnia, 162, 228
Theriac, 159, 162, 192, 194, 221, 222, 226, 228, 229, 230, 243
Thyme, 212
Tīn makhtūm, 226
Treacle, 224–9
Turlington's Balsam of Life, 3–4
Turpentine, 172, 193, 244

Venice Treacle, 224, 225, 229
Viper, dried flesh of, 193, 194

Wax, 170
White incense, 249
Wild grape, 190
Wine, 220
Wolf's gall, 195
Wormwood, 212

Xylobalsamum (wood of balsam, and oil made by boiling wood of balsam), 65, 69, 75, 77, 122, 146, 155, 168, 171, 191, 194, 195, 211, 220, 221, 229, 278

Zori see Balm of Gilead
Zuchum oil, 121
Zvwtyh, 72, 144

EU representative:
Easy Access System Europe
Mustamäe tee 50, 10621 Tallinn, Estonia
Gpsr.requests@easproject.com

www.ingramcontent.com/pod-product-compliance
Lightning Source LLC
Chambersburg PA
CBHW071827230426
43672CB00013B/2776